CHILD OF THE REVOLUTION

WOLFGANG LEONHARD

CHILD
OF THE
REVOLUTION

TRANSLATED BY
C. M. WOODHOUSE

HENRY REGNERY COMPANY
CHICAGO, ILLINOIS

First published in German under
the title of
Die Revolution Entlasst Ihre Kinder
by Kippenheuer & Witsch

First published in the United States in 1958
Henry Regnery Company
64 E. Jackson Blvd.
Chicago 4, Illinois

Second Printing

PRINTED IN THE UNITED STATES OF AMERICA
BY THE COLONIAL PRESS INC., CLINTON, MASS.

Contents

TRANSLATOR'S NOTE

This English translation of Wolfgang Leonhard's *Die Revolution entlässt ihre Kinder* (first published in German in 1955) has been abbreviated from the original by the omission of some passages likely to be of less interest to English than to German readers. The responsibility for the cuts is my own, but I have been helped in making them by the author's understanding co-operation. He has also more than once improved my English.

I wish to record my thanks to a number of experts who have read through the translation and helped me to avoid the grosser solecisms in transliteration and the translation of political jargon. They include especially Mr. Edward Crankshaw, Mrs. Jane Degras, and Mr. Leonard Schapiro. I am doubly indebted to all three: to Mr. Crankshaw additionally for the introduction, and to Mrs. Degras and Mr. Schapiro for reading the proofs.

C. M. W.

Introduction

HERE IS a book which floods some very dark places with light. It is the story of a gifted and highly intelligent young man, not a Russian, who was brought up in the Soviet Union and in the bosom of the Soviet Communist Party. At twenty-seven, in 1949, he broke away, sacrificing a most promising career as a privileged Party functionary in Ulbricht's East Germany. He took this courageous step not because he hungered for the flesh-pots of the West, or because he had become infected with bourgeois ideas, but, as he saw it, for Lenin's sake. And he made his escape from East Berlin, carrying his life in his hands, not to the bright lights of the Kurfuerstendamm but to the then dreary rigours of Tito's Yugoslavia, in those days hungry, cold, and dangerous.

It is this aspect of his story which makes his testimony unique: he writes not as a lapsed Communist, or a man turning against his God, or a refugee from the harshness of the Soviet system, but as a convinced Marxist who thought he was a better socialist than his Soviet fosterparents. These had reared him in unimaginable seclusion, cut off from all reality, with the ruling idea of fashioning him in their own image; readers of this book will see how nearly they succeeded

in this aim. And just as a very good way of grasping
the true nature and structure of a foreign language is
to listen attentively to a foreigner talking broken English, so an excellent way of understanding the Soviet
Communist mentality is to listen, no less attentively,
to Mr. Leonhard telling his experiences. It took him
some time to learn the language of the West at all,
and even now he is far from word perfect and thus gives
us invaluable insights into the idiom he has forsaken.
Further, he refuses all truck with wisdom after the
event, which seems to me admirable and refreshing.
How easy it would have been for him to put a distance
between himself and his long years in Russia, to write
of his Russian life in the light of knowledge lately
acquired, to slant his narrative at an angle designed
to appeal to Western sentiment, to smother the absorbing actuality of his early life in hindsight, all done with
mirrors. Instead, apologising for nothing, he has given
us an exact image of that life as he lived it, and a
recension of his blinkered thoughts as he thought them.

I don't know at all precisely what Leonhard's politics
are now. He has promised to tell us in a later book. But
it is clear that he remains certainly a Marxist and
probably a Leninist of sorts. He was certainly an ardent
and uncritical Leninist when he broke with Russia.
But he has learnt a great deal since then. It was soon
after he had burst through the Iron Curtain that I had
the privilege of meeting him in Belgrade; and he was
rather like one of those legendary young men who, we
are told, from time to time emerge from the jungle
emitting strange sounds, having spent their childhood
and adolescence in the exclusive company of wolves—
or bears. Communication was, to put it mildly, incomplete. He had broken with Stalin, but he still could not

face the bourgeois world in its starkness. Although his instinct and his reason had told him that there was something badly wrong with the Soviet system he was still very much of the opinion that his quarrel was with Stalin only—an opinion then shared by Marshal Tito, on whose mercy he had thrown himself. At that time (it was 1949), when Yugoslavia was being made to suffer bitterly for Tito's defiance of Stalin, Djilas was publishing articles to justify the Yugoslav heresy. And I remember arguing with Leonhard that if Djilas went on developing his ideas he would soon find himself in direct opposition not only to Stalin but also to Lenin and the whole concept of the dictatorship of the proletariat. This turned out to be an accurate prophecy, but Leonhard contested it hotly. Nevertheless, although communication was incomplete, he was the first believing Leninist with whom I found it possible to talk politics in a sensible and coherent way.

I am sure Leonhard will not mind this somewhat clinical approach to himself and his very human narrative. After all, his story is gripping and enthralling by any standards, but its first value is essentially clinical. It is the story of a slow awakening, unconscious, like all awakenings. We may wake up in the small hours to the noise of a motor car revving up in first gear: we say this was the noise that woke us up. But in fact there have been many preceding noises, the slamming of doors, shrieks of unaccountable laughter, boisterous farewells, futile attempts to start the engine before the ignition is switched on. . . . These noises have been going on for a long time, and all the time they have been dragging us from sleep, slowly nearer to the surface of consciousness, perhaps weaving the inane racket into a waking dream. The noise we first consciously hear, the engine at last starting, marks only the moment of return to perfect consciousness. This was the moment in Leonhard's life represented by the expulsion of Yugoslavia from the Cominform. This, he thinks, is what woke him up. But in fact, it is clear from his narrative, he had been waking up long before then.

As a child he was fast asleep. His mother was one of those foreigners, a German, who went to Moscow to work for Lenin's revolution and found themselves sent to Siberia by Stalin. We are all by now familiar with the mood in the Soviet Union during the great purge years of the middle thirties, when Leonhard was at school in Moscow. Many know a great deal more than Leonhard knew—either then, as a schoolboy, or later, when he made his escape. A few may even be a little irritated by Leonhard's conscientious and far from complete recapitulation of matters so familiar to them. I ask them to lay irritation aside. For what they are being told is not the history of the purges but what the purge years looked like to a youngster brought up in the seclusion of a Party school. We have not had this before. We see a consciousness already, in childhood, three-quarters paralysed by careful conditioning, so that this child could accept the sudden and unexplained disappearance of his mother, the impact of the purges on teachers and the parents of his school companions, and still not ask questions. After that, Leonhard had no other parent than the Soviet Communist Party, which treated him well.

From my own observation, I should say that Soviet conditioning reaches its peak of completeness at about this period, twelve to fifteen. Then, on the surface, it may appear to be perfect. But soon afterwards, except in the case of those chosen in advance for total dedication to the Party apparatus (a mere handful of the Party membership) the effects of the conditioning begin to wear off, until they fall away under pressure from the irresistible drive of human nature—that human nature which reformers refer to in tones of contempt and contumely, but which, developing, is in fact the sole and glorious asset of our race—though always lingering in odd corners of the mind. For the ordinary Russian, brought up in the Pioneers and the Komsomol, but not going on to full Party membership, is, I should say, rather less thoroughly conditioned than the average product of a British public school, for reasons which we need not go into here—and a great deal less thoroughly conditioned than the average American high school product. Leonhard was not a Russian, but a German, thus, perhaps, more malleable than most Russians; he was a foreigner, thus, perhaps, tending to try harder in the desired sense; he was an intellectual, thus easy prey for the practical men of action who now rule Russia in the name of Communism; and he was chosen and dedicated from his childhood. His conditioning was thus unusually complete. But in the end it failed—as in fact it fails with everyone; and in Leonhard's case the failure was acknowledged and proclaimed because he was a man of unusual integrity who was prepared to sacrifice his career and put his life at hazard for the sake of principle.

It was a big sacrifice. He had gone so far that at the age of twenty-three he was selected to return to East Berlin in the train of Ulbricht to build up a Communist régime in East Germany. And he was so far gone that he enjoyed it. Even so, he had been turning uneasily in his sleep for a long time past. He had, indeed, under the shock of a certain stimulus, almost awakened in the summer of 1941. So artificial and cloistered had been his existence until then, that he is still able to say in good faith that the German invasion immediately gave the Soviet people a sense of identity with their leadership. In fact, at the moment of which he speaks, whole units and formations of the Red Army were surrendering with relief, others, still fighting, were cursing the leadership which had exposed them unprepared, undeployed, inadequately led and insufficiently equipped, to Hitler's tanks and aircraft. The civilian population of White Russia and the Ukraine were welcoming the invaders with bread and salt and flowers. Moscow was on the edge of an explosion. Leonhard knew nothing of this because, as a Party protégé, he was cut off from all reality. But he too, now, was to have his first glimpse of that reality, and it nearly broke him. Pitched out of his privileged shelter, one among a million evacuees, he found himself in Kazakhstan, living the life of the ordinary Russian refugee, half-starved, hounded by the back-area police, and meeting, as in a nightmare, honest peasants who not only hated the government but were also ready to say so. A few more weeks of this, and Leonhard would have woken up in 1941 instead of 1948. But on the very edge of waking he was put to sleep again. The nightmare vanished when he was suddenly picked up to continue his political indoctrination on a higher plane, this time in the Comintern School, with young men and women from all over Europe. The disaffected masses, angry, humiliated, abased, and dying of hunger, were left far behind, and young Leonhard went back to the womb.

It is his picture of this school which, for me, is the

highlight of the book. Everything that leads up to it
combines to give a unique picture of the Soviet Union
seen from the point of view of the Communist élite
(not always a comfortable picture, as the millions of
Party members who were condemned by Stalin at one
time and another could testify; but a picture very
different fom that of the ordinary Russian). Everything that follows, including the inside story of the
remarkably haphazard way in which the so-called
German Democratic Republic was built up by a handful of Moscow agents, sustains the interest of the
earlier part. But the account of the Comintern School
stands by itself. To my knowledge it has never been
publicly described, and to read Leonhard's description
is to understand why. Here the children of revolutionaries from all over the world were admitted for
training as the Kremlin's agents on condition that
they renounced utterly and for ever their previous
identities. To arrive at the school they were passed
from hand to hand, from cell to cell, shedding more of
their identities at every stage, through an elaborate
and obsessionally secret one-way channel, for all the
world like one of the escape routes organised by the
resistance movements of Europe during the last war—
but leading the individual to prison not to freedom.
They arrived inside with new names and elaborate
cover stories. These were the shining hopes of the
young generation of Communist management; they
were the most trusted of Moscow's agents: yet they
were not trusted even among themselves, even inside
the concentric circle of moral—and physical—fortifica-
tions which cut them off utterly from the outside world.
They were forbidden under pain of the most dire punishment to communicate their real identities with each

other or to exchange a word about their past lives to their closest companions and associates. The system of communal confession in case of the least transgression, or suspected transgression, was carried to its logical and appalling conclusion. Here is the complete apparatus of 1984—but without the spirit of 1984; because, as Orwell would have known had he ever lived in Russia, the apparatus does not work.

I have dwelt on the deeper implications of this remarkable book because they seem to me supremely important, and they go very deep indeed. But I should like to finish by stressing the interest and excitement of the book as the narrative of an extraordinary life story and a marvellously absorbing picture of the Soviet scene.

EDWARD CRANKSHAW

Prologue

On 15th March, 1949, I was supposed to give a lecture at the S.E.D. Party Academy. The students on the course sat in the great lecture hall, waiting for their instructor, their note-books in front of them. They waited in vain.

"Where is Comrade Leonhard?"

They went to look for me in my room in the Party Academy. I was not there. The lecture was cancelled. Suspicion was already beginning to dawn on some of them, and the whisper went round: "Could Wolfgang have bolted?"

The woman who was Secretary of the Party Academy was sent to visit my Berlin apartment. No result there either. Eventually no further doubt was possible: "Wolfgang Leonhard has defected."

The news of my defection spread immediately, and great excitement reigned at the Party Academy. Up to that moment only a few senior S.E.D. officials had defected from the Soviet Zone, most of them former Social Democrats. This time the fugitive was a responsible figure who came from the Communist Party—even from Moscow. There was another thing, too. Hitherto all S.E.D. officials who defected had fled to the West, where the West Berlin press had published circumstantial accounts of every case. But after my disappearance even the western newspapers remained silent. No more was known in West Berlin than in the East.

Where had Leonhard got to? Could he possibly be in Yugoslavia?

This last guess was convassed only very surreptitiously. One week followed another. Nothing was to be heard of Instructor Leonhard.

Speculation went on.

Meanwhile, I was in Belgrade writing a radio broadcast and a pamphlet explaining the political reasons for my defection from the Soviet Zone.

I had left East Berlin on 12th March, and reached Belgrade after a dramatic journey on 25th March. Four weeks after my arrival, I read out in a studio of Belgrade Radio my declaration attacking the Cominform Resolution and defending the Yugoslav Communists, who had been turned adrift by Moscow in the summer of 1948 to take their own independent path towards Socialism.

After this statement of my position, which was broadcast in twelve languages over Belgrade Radio on the evening of 22nd April and published in all the Yugoslav newspapers the next day, it was impossible for the S.E.D. leadership to maintain silence any longer. Four days later, on 26th April, 1949, my expulsion from the Party was announced in *Neues Deutschland,* the central party organ.

At the Party Academy a feverish burst of activity ensued. Meeting followed meeting in quick succession. Every student on my course was put to the most searching scrutiny in a series of private interrogations. But even that was not considered enough, and shortly afterwards a directive was issued dispersing the class supervised by Wolfgang Leonhard at the Party Academy. All my students were distrib-

uted among the other faculties. The whole programme which I, as instructor, had drawn up for
their future activities was systematically frustrated.
For instance, where I had recommended that a particular student should be given the chance of working at a scientific institute after completing his studies in the Party Academy, that student could now
count with certainty on being sent out to the provinces for "practical party work." Heinz Abraham,
one of the instructors who had been trained in the
Soviet Union and a self-styled hard-core Bolshevik,
began giving lectures on the lessons to be drawn from
the "Leonhard case."

Meetings were summoned one after another, at
which everyone who had had any kind of close relation with me was required to practise self-criticism.
These occasions brought to light such curious incidents as that of an evening quiz at which I had
used the word *Cominform*—a word which suppos-
edly was only used by "war-mongers," the official
term being "Information Bureau of the Communist
and Workers' parties." Such happenings were now
explained, in discussions that went on for hours, as
"indications of an anti-party attitude." Every speaker
emphasised *ad nauseam* that it was solely through
lack of vigilance that I had not been unmasked in
time.

All this uproar was due to the fact that I had given
a few of the instructors and students at the Party
Academy some of the Yugoslav Communists' literature to read. How terrified the S.E.D. leadership
must have been of this material, to feel compelled to
taken such extraordinary measures!

The agitation in the S.E.D. leadership was under-

standable. No previous defection had involved an
official distinguished by ten years' residence in the
Soviet Union; one who had grown up and received
his education and political training there. This book
records my experiences during those ten years
(1935-45) and during my four years' subsequent activity as an official in the central *apparat* of the S.E.D.
leadership (1945-49). It tells of Soviet schools and
universities, of students and *Komsomols*; of the early
days of the war in Moscow and of life at Karaganda
in wartime; of the training of foreign officials at the
Comintern School and the National Free Germany
Committee; of the "Ulbricht Group" in May, 1945,
and the first steps of Soviet policy in post-war Germany; of the creation of an administrative system in
the Soviet Zone; and of the party which is to-day
the governmental party in that Zone, with the fate
of eighteen million people under its control.

My purpose in recording these things is by no
means solely to expose aspects of the Stalinist system which have hitherto been little known. It is also,
and more emphatically, to depict for the benefit of
the contemporary non-Soviet world how the new
generation of trained party officials in the eastern
bloc thinks and feels; how it forms its judgments;
where its critical faculty comes into play. It is therefore my deliberate intention to present every encounter and discussion, every event and experience, exactly as I saw it and reacted to it and felt it at the
time, and as it then impressed itself on my memory.
This seems to me the only way of enabling a western
reader to understand what the break with Stalinism
means for a man who has been brought up in it. Such
a decision is the outcome of a painful process ex-

tending over years—years taken up with doubts and recantations, and pangs of conscience and fabricated theories to set conscience at rest. But once this process has begun there is no going back. One moves irresistibly, if not without a severe inner conflict, towards that decisive line of demarcation beyond which there is freedom from Stalinist dogmatism.

CHAPTER ONE

At School in the Soviet Union

OUR LAST EVENING in Sweden had come: it was 18th
June, 1935. My mother and I were going through the
streets of Stockholm for the last time. A few of her
friends, German émigrés like ourselves, came with us
to the boat that was to take us to the Finnish port of
Turku. "Good luck for the trip to Moscow!" they
shouted after us as we parted.

I can hardly remember anything of the journey
through Finland. I was so full of excitement at the
prospect of the Soviet Union that all other impressions faded beside it.

The next day the train in which we sat grew emptier and emptier as it approached the border between
Finland and the Soviet Union. There was no one but
ourselves in the entire carriage when the guard came
to tell us that we should be at the border in a quarter of an hour. He gave the name of the place—something quite unpronounceable full of y's and u's and
i's. In those days it was the border station on the
Finnish side; to-day, since the enforced transfer of
Finnish territory, the place no doubt has a Russian
name.

The Journey to Moscow

We stood on the platform of the almost deserted
little station, feeling rather lost. A railway official

readily gave us the information we wanted. "There's a shuttle service running between the last station in Finland and the first in Russia. The train will be along in about half an hour. You'll get a direct connection from the Russian border station to Leningrad."

It was not my mother's first journey to Moscow: she had visited the Soviet Union before, in 1924. During the First World War she had belonged to the *Spartakusbund,* and in 1918 she joined the Communist Party. For a time she worked as press secretary to the Soviet trade delegation in Berlin, but in 1925 she left the German Communist Party (K.P.D.), later attaching herself to the "left-wing independents." After Hitler seized power she worked clandestinely in Berlin until the spring of 1935, when she moved to Sweden.

And what about myself? I was then a boy of thirteen and a half, delighted to have the chance of going to the Soviet Union. I had grown up in Berlin and attended the Karl Marx School; from the end of 1931 I had belonged to the Young Pioneers, the K.P.D.'s organisation for children; and in the autumn of 1933 my mother had sent me to Sweden. There I went to a modern boarding school in the country, and I could soon speak fluent Swedish.

When my mother rejoined me in the spring of 1935 we had to decide where to go next. The clandestine group in Berlin which my mother belonged to had dispersed, and its members had been arrested. The Gestapo had also been searching for my mother. It was clear she could not return to Germany, but permission to stay in Sweden was difficult to get. So while I stayed on at Viggbyholm, my mother kept up a busy correspondence to try and find us a new place to live.

One afternoon, while we were taking a walk in the wonderful country round Stockholm, I was at last let into my mother's plans.

"You're a big boy now," she began, "and I want to have a talk with you about our future."

I nodded and put on a serious expression, like any other thirteen-year-old treated like a grown-up.

"I don't want to reach any decision without your agreement. This is the position. We can't stay in Sweden because I can't get work here, but I've written from here to various friends and people I know. There are two possibilities before us. We could go to England, and you could go to an English school and grow up in England as long as the Nazis are in power in Germany. That would be one possibility."

"And the other?" I asked.

My mother hesitated a moment. "We could go to the Soviet Union."

"I'm for the Soviet Union," I said unhesitatingly.

Whether it was my answer or other factors that turned the scale, I don't know. In any case, our journey was decided on.

Little did we know then how far-reaching this decision was to prove for us! How could my mother guess that only a year and a half later she would be arrested by the N.K.V.D., to disappear for twelve years into Soviet concentration camps, and return to Berlin only in 1948? And I too could not have known then that I was to spend a whole decade in the Soviet Union; or that there lay before me years of training as an official in one of the leading Soviet political schools; or that the day would come for me to break completely with the system I had believed in from childhood. All this lay in the future. We could see only the present. And so, on that sunny day of the month of June, 1935, we stood waiting at the Finnish border station for the train that was to take us to the Soviet Union.

The little train ran into the station exactly on time. On the engine and the tender I saw the sign of the hammer and sickle—our own sign—which up till then I had only seen on banners carried in processions and demonstrations. I was very excited. A stoker looked out from the footplate of the locomotive and gave us a friendly wave.

"That's your train," said the railway official. "It'll take you to Beloostrov, the border station on the Soviet side."

We moved hardly faster than a horse and cart, but within a few minutes we had reached the frontier. A large block of granite could be seen from the window, with a Finnish frontier guard standing on one side of it and a Red Army soldier on the other—the first Red Army soldier I had ever seen. A Soviet star and the sign of the hammer and sickle were clearly visible on his cap, and he held a rifle with fixed bayonet close to his side.

Some men in uniform and civilian clothes approached us. These were the Soviet frontier officials. They opened our luggage in the station building and searched it thoroughly. They seemed to take little interest in clothes or food, but they made up for this by examining every book we possessed. Although we had practically nothing with us except Communist literature, they picked out every single

book, one after another, and even went through
some of them page by page.

At last the examination was finished. As soon as
we had climbed aboard the Leningrad train, the
signal went for starting. The train was fairly full,
but room was readily made for us. We were the only
foreigners. The passengers looked us over with curiosity. It was obvious they were talking about us,
though I could not understand a word. No one spoke
to us.

We had to wait a few hours in Leningrad, where
everything looked much poorer than in Stockholm.
The houses were not so well painted and the people
were far worse dressed. I saw many children barefoot.
This sight was so strange to me that it made something of an impression; but I quickly forgot it, since
it failed to fit in with my preconceived ideas.

That evening we took the night train to Moscow.
After all the exciting events of the day, I slept like a
log. When I woke up I was in Moscow, the city in
which I was to spend so many years, and which
was to be my second home.

The Karl Liebknecht School in Moscow

As we were neither visitors under the auspices of
Intourist nor members of a delegation, there was no
ceremony or official welcome on our arrival, and no
hotel rooms had been booked for us free of charge.
But we were met by some friends my mother had
made on her last visit. We drove across Moscow
from the station to No. 5 Granovsky Street, where an
acquaintance of hers had an apartment (though to
call it an apartment is an exaggeration, for it was

only a single room). Here plans were discussed for
our new life in Moscow.

My mother's first thought was for myself. "The
boy must go to school—but he doesn't know a word
of Russian."

"That doesn't matter," our friends told us. "There
are two schools in Moscow for foreign pupils, one
English and one German. Your boy's in luck too,
the German school is getting a fine new building on
1st September, at No. 12 Kropotkin Street."

"Then there are Germans here in Moscow?" I
asked in astonishment. My new friends smiled. "Of
course there are. There are several thousand Germans living in Moscow, and Austrian émigrés too,
including many of the *Schutzbund* who took part
in the rising against Dollfuss in 1934 and came to
Moscow after it failed. There's a German club here,
and a German daily paper called the *German
Centre News,* and a Foreign Workers' Publishing
House which puts out a lot of books in German."

Such was the beginning of our life in Moscow.
Finding somewhere to live was by no means easy. For
the first few days we stayed with one or other of my
mother's acquaintances, and then at last we discovered a furnished room. While my mother looked for
work, I had a great deal of free time, as the schools
were closed for the summer holidays. I explored the
city and tried to comprehend the state of affairs.

"Wouldn't you like to see the Metro?" I was asked
the day after our arrival. The Metro, Moscow's
underground railway, had been opened to passengers
just a few weeks before, on 15th May, and everyone
was exceedingly proud of this achievement.

It occupied so central a place in the public eye that almost everywhere I went I was asked if I had been on the Metro yet. At once followed the question how I had liked it, and then a lengthy disquisition generally developed on its merits. I only came across one heretic, who expressed the view that it would be nice if Moscow were one tenth as splendid above ground as it was underneath.

This observation was entirely justified, for the contrast was indeed fantastic. At that time it was quite difficult to find your way in Moscow; there was not a street plan to be had. My mother still had a street plan going back to 1924, but that was little use to us, for many streets had had their names changed in the interval, apart from which the whole appearance of the city had been changed by the erection of many new buildings and the demolition of old houses. We were all the more delighted when suddenly town plans of Moscow began to appear in all the book shops; but it was a disappointment to find that these town plans on sale in July 1935 were dated 1945.

We had no idea what to make of this. "What's the use of a town plan for 1945 when I want to find my way about Moscow in 1935?" my mother asked in amazement.

"Quite simple," was the answer. "The overall ten-year building plan for Moscow was published at the beginning of July, and town plans for 1945 are being printed now in order to popularise it. After all, everyone knows what Moscow looks like to-day. . . ."

We used to take both town plans with us on our

walks from then on—one showing what Moscow had looked like ten years before, and the other showing what it would look like ten years hence.

Our experience with the town plans was really typical of that period, for 1935 was a year of transition in the Soviet Union.

The revolution and the civil war and even the first Five-Year Plan now belonged to the past. The years of the purges and the mass arrests, the Hitler-Stalin pact and the Finnish war, still lay in the future. The last food ration cards had been abolished at the beginning of 1935 and it had been announced at an Extraordinary Congress of the Soviets that a more liberal and democratic constitution was to be drawn up.

"The worst is over now. Things are bound to get better. Even the political system will get more democratic—that's clear enough already from the proposal for a new constitution." This was the key-note of many discussions during that year.

A few of our acquaintances (no more than a few) were rather less optimistic. From the very first weeks after our arrival I kept hearing one particular name: Kirov. Sergei Kirov, a member of the Politburo, had been murdered in Leningrad a few months before we arrived there, and the murder had been followed by mass arrests. But in contrast to similar cases in the past, the victims of the purge this time were no longer ex-adherents of other parties or non-party people, but Bolshevik party officials. There was often a frightened undertone in conversations about Kirov. "What worries me so much about the Kirov case," said one of our circle, "is the dissolution of the Society of Old Bolsheviks. Until a few weeks ago to be called 'an Old Bolshevik' was a title of honour with us, and to belong to the Society was a mark of distinction. Then on 26th May, the Society was dissolved without any political explanation, and its premises were requisitioned."

Though still a boy of thirteen I was already keenly interested in politics, and I heard many such conversations and discussions, both optimistic and pessimistic; for in those days, before the great purge of 1936-38, it was still possible, now and then, to talk freely in the Soviet Union.

On 1st September, 1935, I was admitted to the German School in Moscow, named after Karl Liebknecht, the great Socialist leader. It was a fine, modern, four-story building, with large sunny classrooms, and it was one of seventy-two new school buildings that had been put up in Moscow in 1935. The outside looked like that of any modern school in western Europe. But on entering it I was amazed to see standing in one corner a huge statue of Stalin, with an inscription on the plinth: "There is no fortress that the Bolsheviks cannot storm—STALIN." In the main corridor of the school another unfamiliar slogan was to be seen, glaring in white letters on a red cloth: "Learn, learn, and again, learn!—LENIN."

I reported to the headmaster, Comrade Zhelasko, to complete the formalities for admission to the school. Admission was not a simple matter. The Soviet school system differs considerably from that in other countries. Compulsory education begins at eight. There is a uniform type of primary school in which all children have to go up through seven classes, while the eighth, ninth and tenth classes are attended by those who hope to proceed to a college or university.

The headmaster told me that by Soviet standards I belonged in the sixth class.

I went upstairs somewhat nervously. The teacher introduced me as a new boy and the school children gazed at me curiously and whispered to each other. I sat down in my place, still rather self-conscious. A newspaper was pinned to the wall near where I sat. I looked round and saw that all my fellow pupils wore the red Pioneer's scarf . . . No, not quite all: at the second look I saw a girl right in front of me without it, but she was the only one.

The teaching was in German, but based entirely on Soviet text-books. Most of the pupils were German émigrés who had come there by way of Sweden, like ourselves, or France or Czechoslovakia. The programme, however, conformed exactly to the ordinary Soviet pattern. All the books, including those used in mathematics and physics, were literal translations from Russian originals. Though I was struck at first by the superficial similarities to my previous schools, it only took me a few days to notice a big difference. Much more was required of us at the Karl Liebknecht school than at any which I had gone to previously. We were assigned a great deal of home-work and it required an effort to get through the course.

We had Russian lessons for an hour practically every day, with English as our second foreign language. Great importance was attached to mathematics and scientific subjects. Even here in the sixth class there were lessons in algebra, geometry and physics. In place of drawing there was a subject called *cherchenie* or "technical draughtsmanship." We studied ancient history and the geography of the "capitalist world" (which meant every country outside the Soviet Union), with the economic structure and political relations of the individual countries. In the literature periods we learned Russian and German literature simultaneously. Once a week we had "current affairs," which dealt principally with the political development and public institutions of the Soviet Union. This subject was later replaced by a course in "constitutional studies."

The supervision of our exercises was very strict in comparison with the modern schools which I had been at before. Every answer we gave, however trivial, was noted down twice over; in the teacher's mark book, and also in the *dnevnik* or diary, which every pupil kept and which had to be counter-signed once a week by our parents. There was a recapitulation and a sort of intermediate examination once a quarter, and at the end of the school year very detailed individual examinations took place in all subjects, often written as well as oral.

I Become a Soviet Pioneer

We were constantly being spurred on to learn more. Pupils who got a bad mark or an "admonition" —that is, a direct reprimand for indiscipline—had to "clarify their attitude" in front of the class. What this meant was that, after a short preparatory speech by the teacher, the pupil concerned was asked by the teacher himself or by the head of the class: "How did you come to get a bad mark?" If the pupil made any sort of attempt to talk himself out of it, he was sharply interrupted by the keener members of the class: "It's a disgrace to have got a bad mark, but it's even more contemptible to try to talk yourself out of it." This was the first step on the ladder of "criti-

cism and self-criticism," so generally familiar in the
Soviet Union.

After two weeks had passed, one of the schoolmis-
tresses came and asked me: "Wouldn't you like to
join the Young Pioneers?"

"Yes, of course, but it isn't necessary in my case.
I've been a member of the Young Pioneers in Berlin
since 1932."

"Membership in Berlin doesn't count here. You'll
have to join again."

"All right. Where should I report?"

"You can't just go and report here. If you're ready
to join, I'll put your name on the list, and then you'll
be admitted at a ceremony of the unit. The Pioneer
leader will recite an oath which you have to repeat,
and then you'll get your Pioneer scarf."

This ceremony took place shortly afterwards. The
whole Pioneer unit was lined up at attention in the
school hall. The new recruits were marched into the
centre of the hall. At the head of the unit stood the
standard bearer. Somebody gave a signal, drums rolled,
and the Pioneer leader began to recite the oath: "I
solemnly promise, as a Pioneer of the Soviet Union,
in the presence of my comrades . . ." We repeated
this and the rest of the oath, a few words at a time:
". . . . to fight faithfully and bravely for the interests of the working class, to safeguard the sacred
legacy of Lenin, to set a good example at all times,
and to fulfil all the tasks and duties of the Young
Pioneers."

After that the Pioneer scarf was put round our
necks and the Pioneer buckle was presented to us
with the same extreme solemnity. On the buckle there
was a torch and the words: *Bud' gotov! Vsegda votov!*

This was the Russian form of the Pioneers' slogan which I already knew: *Be prepared! Ever prepared!*

Both the scarf and the buckle had a symbolic significance. The three corners of the red scarf signified Party, *Komsomol* and Young Pioneers. On the buckle there were five logs of wood, representing the five continents, and three flames representing the Third International. (The last point was afterwards omitted from the official interpretation.)

We studied the biographies of Lenin and Stalin and the history of the Soviet Pioneers. We learned that the first Pioneer bands came into existence in 1922, and that in 1925 the *Pionerskaya Pravda* was first published as the Pioneers' newspaper. The Young Pioneers' Organisation included boys and girls from eleven to sixteen, and at that date in 1935 it numbered ten million members. The function of the Pioneers, we were told, consisted in sticking up for our school, strengthening discipline, supporting our teacher, and educating ourselves to our responsibility towards the Socialist fatherland.

In the past there had been dangerous deviations in the Pioneer organisation. A treacherous "leftist deviation" had fostered the idea of transferring the functions of the school authorities to the Pioneers; and we were told that this had been not only a very dangerous notion, but one actually directed against the Party. There had also been a "right-wing opportunist deviation" as well as a leftist one. This had been equally dangerous, because it had fostered the idea that the Pioneer organisation should be integrated into the controlling authority of the school, or in practice, liquidated. But both these dangerous deviations among the Pioneers had been overcome by the resolution of April, 1932, condemning rightist and leftist deviations in the Pioneer organisation.

We learned to form radically divergent judgments on developments and phenomena and situations which at first sight appeared similar. All depended on whether the context was capitalist or Soviet society. After quite a short time we began to deal with concrete examples. A rise in the price of food in capitalist countries was assessed as "fresh evidence of the intensified exploitation of the workers," but a rise in the price of food in the Soviet Union was an "important economic contribution to the construction of Socialism." Dilapidated housing in the West was noted down instantly as a "proof of the miserable standard of living of the workers," but dilapidated housing in Moscow was a "relic of the past." We learned to condemn or approve any event without hesitation by observing where it had taken place. This habit of thought so deeply impressed itself on us all, including myself, that for many years I at least was incapable of imagining any other way of thinking.

Children's Home No. 6

In the summer of 1936 an event took place which changed my life. I was living with my mother in a furnished room at No. 26 Gorky Street. The regular tenant, an engineer, had been given an assignment at Igarka, a small town in Northern Siberia which was to be rapidly developed and extended. He was now expected back, and we had to move out.

My mother spent several weeks trying to find another room, but without success. Many prospects vanished as soon as the landlords realised that we were German. Some also refused to take a fourteen-year-old boy. So my mother's main anxiety was to secure somewhere for me.

One day she came home in great delight. "I've found something splendid for you. They'll take you at Children's Home No. 6, the home where the Austrian *Schutzbund* children are. You'll be well off there."

My mother was not exaggerating. The Home was at No. 12 Kalashny Lane, in the centre of the town, between Arbat Square and the Nikitsky Gate. It was a large house, rather dark but almost sumptuous by Moscow standards, which had previously belonged to a rich Moscow merchant.

Children's Home No. 6 was the home of the *Schutzbund* children. After the failure of the revolution of February, 1934, in Austria, hundreds of men from the *Schutzbund* came to the Soviet Union, and also a great many children, including some whose parents had been killed in the fighting. August 8th, 1934, was the date on which the special train reached the Soviet frontier with the Austrian children, and it was celebrated as a festival every year in the Children's Home, with a series of receptions in honour of the occasion. All the Soviet papers had carried news of the arrival of the *Schutzbund* children. The Artek Pioneers' camp in the Crimea, which was the finest in the Soviet Union, had invited the children down there for their first summer. Then it was Moscow's turn, and here the splendid house at No. 12 Kalashny Lane was made available to the children as their permanent home. Besides the children of the Austrian Social Democrats and members of the *Schutzbund,* there were also a few children of German Communists there.

Despite its unassuming name, Children's Home No. 6 had nothing in common with the usual Children's Homes in the Soviet Union. The inmates were at first almost as highly privileged as members of a delegation on a conducted tour. Their clothes were made in special tailors' shops. Their feeding was in the charge of an Austrian cook. The Home had a motor coach of its own to take the children to the Karl Liebknecht School and bring them back again, and it was available for journeys of other kinds as well. The children's health was supervised by a special clinic under a German woman doctor, and their temperatures were taken each morning. Everywhere the *Schutzbund* children went they were rapturously received. Tickets for the *premières* of every opera, musical comedy and play were provided for them on such a lavish scale that they generally went unused.

The Warden was a German Communist called Beiss. His assistants were German or Austrian émigrés with a few Russian girls who spoke fluent German. The latter had been specially selected by the central committee of the *Komsomol*.

When I joined the Home on 26th September, 1936, it had already been going for two years. The constant receptions were now a thing of the past. The motor coach had been withdrawn and the children had to go on foot. The daily temperature-taking had ceased. The luxury feeding was gradually getting simpler, though it was still much better than Russian children enjoyed. There were still some invitations, but not so many as formerly. And the German Warden had been replaced by a Russian called Semyonov.

The children in the Home when I joined it were

between eight and sixteen years old. Those in the four
lowest classes were known by the Austrian name of
Gschroppen (juniors); those in the fifth and sixth
classes were called "intermediates"; and those in the
seventh, eighth and ninth classes were called "seniors." We were still a kind of shop window. Our talents were encouraged and developed. There was
special tuition for those who had musical gifts; and
a theatrical society existed for those interested in the
stage, under the direction of Weiland Rodd, a negro
who had emigrated to the Soviet Union, and had
played parts in *Circus* and other Soviet films. We
also had a literary society, which was quite often
visited by German writers who had settled in the Soviet Union. Foreign delegations were usually brought
to see us. Representatives of the Austrian and German sections of the Comintern frequently visited
us, and at our celebrations on May Day or on 7th
November or New Year's Day we often had Koplenig,
the Secretary-General of the Austrian Communist
Party, or Wilhelm Pieck as our guest. Apart from the
official holidays, we had others of our own. We kept
February 12th every year in memory of the rising of
the *Schutzbund,* and August 8th as the anniversary
of the arrival. On these holidays the "model pupils"
(a very elastic expression in our case) received valuable prizes, which were far superior to any given to
other children in the Soviet Union.

We were invited to all the major celebrations that
took place in Moscow in those days, and the whole
audience would greet us with applause as junior
guests of honour. One of our special treats was when
our "model pupils" were allowed to go on the maiden
journey on the Moscow-Volga canal.

The people in charge of us were exceptionally friendly. We could be certain that the slightest wish we expressed would be fulfilled if it lay within the bounds of the permissible. There was even a *soviet* in the Home, which we chose ourselves and which had a right to take part in deciding every question that arose. Our only permanent link with the outside world was the Library of Foreign Literature in Stoleshnikov Lane, about fifteen minutes' distance from our Home. It had been set up in a little church, which had been closed in the early years after the Revolution. There we found German, English, French, Spanish, and Italian books.

I went to the reading-room for a few hours almost every day with some of my friends. Apart from the classics of German literature, there were also many newer books: Thomas Mann, Heinrich Mann, Franz Werfel, Max Brod, Stefan Zweig, Jakob Wassermann, Arnold Zweig, Lion Feuchtwanger, Ernst Ludwig, and of course, all the expatriate authors who sympathised with the Soviet Union—Friedrich Wolf, Anna Seghers, Johannes R. Becher, Erich Weinert, Bodo Uhse, Fritz Erpenbeck, Willi Bredel.

This reading-room was practically a paradise to us, but it was not long before I learned its darker side too. When I picked up a book by Traven, I discovered to my utter astonishment that whole paragraphs had been made unreadable by means of a special Indian ink. All my efforts to read the deleted passages—for instance, by holding the page up to the light—were unsuccessful. The deletion was completely effective. Moreover, this kind of special censorship was practised not only on books but also on newspapers and journals; and fantastic as it seemed, I found it applied even to journals published by the K.P.D. or by fellow-travellers. The reading-room contained not only Soviet newspapers but also the *Rote Fahne,* which was still printed in Czechoslovakia, and the *Pariser Tageblatt* and the *Neue Weltbühne.* Even in these friendly publications passages were deleted if they carried news of events which had not been reported in the Soviet press.

We older children were by that time already interested in politics as well as literature. This was not surprising, since in the Soviet Union every aspect of life is involved in politics to an extent unparalleled in any other country on earth. There is hardly any question that is not regarded as political, and campaigns and conferences and demonstrations follow each other non-stop.

Westerners who try to picture life in the Soviet Union tend to feel pity for people who have to endure such a "politicalisation." This pity may be justified in the majority of cases, but it is not so universally, for many of the younger generation have a passionate interest in political problems. Most of us older children in the Children's Home—those between fourteen and seventeen—had no intention of waiting until political questions were dealt with at school or in the *Komsomol.* We were already devoting our spare time to Marxism-Leninism. As soon as we had finished our school work, we flung ourselves on any political literature we could get hold of, such as the works of Marx, Engels, Lenin and Stalin. No one compelled us to do this, and we were never once adjured to acquire a political education. It was our own free will and our personal interest that impelled us to it, and it soon became a matter of habit for us older children to spend our time discussing what we had read, on our long rambling walks through the streets of Moscow.

In the Home on Kalashny Lane we still had no inkling of things that had already begun to take place in the Soviet Union. But it is hard to live a secluded life in that country. There are no retreats to withdraw to, no places where one can subsist untouched by public events. And so it proved for us too.

My Mother's Arrest

When I went to Children's Home No. 6, my mother moved to a primitive little cubicle which hardly deserved the name of a room. It was in an old house near the Nikitsky Gate. Even to call it a cubicle was an exaggeration, for it was really no more than a bit of floor space marked off by a primitive wooden partition. But it was only after a great deal of difficulty that my mother had been able to find even this place to live in. I used to meet her once or twice a week, and we would walk about Moscow together. These were happy hours. Much as I enjoyed the Children's Home, it was still a great happiness every time I had a chance to see my mother and talk to her.

One rainy day at the end of October, 1936, a few weeks after my admission to the Children's Home, we were sauntering through the streets of the town. I was nibbling sweets which I had bought at my favourite shop, the *Vostochnye Sladosti* ("Oriental Confectionery") by the Nikitsky Gate.

"I've something very important to tell you, Mummy," I said.

"And what's that, my child?"

"You know, the worst thing of all at school is this technical drawing. We've got a perfectly frightful drawing to do by the day after to-morrow, and I simply can't get the thing right."

So my mother took the hint and promised to have the drawing done for me by the following day. Then I had to hurry off so as not to be late back at the Home. I turned round for one last look: my mother stood there with her handbag and my roll of drawings under her arm, lovingly waving back to me.

The next day I was waiting at our rendezvous at the agreed time. My mother was not there. I waited. Ten minutes passed . . . a quarter of an hour . . . half an hour. Still my mother did not come.

I decided to go and find her at home, in her little wooden cubicle; I thought perhaps she was ill. I was uneasy as I rang the front door bell. One of the occupants opened the door and gave me a peculiar look, but let me in. I ran down the corridor and stopped in amazement in front of the primitive wooden partition. The door was locked, and on the outside I found two seals—one on the partition and one on the door. I could not make head or tail of it. Then the door of the next room opened, and a voice asked me. "What do you want?"

"I want to see my mother, who lives here."

"Your mother's not here any more."

"Where is she then?"

"She's gone."

"But how? . . . why? Hasn't she left anything behind?"

"No, she left nothing behind. She had to go in a hurry. Probably she's gone on an assignment: she'll soon be back. Go home and don't worry."

I went home, full of doubts and uneasiness. I had been long enough in Russia to know what an "assignment" was—a sudden order from some official department to go and do a particular job somewhere else. But who could have given my mother an assignment? Where had she gone? When would she come back?

At the Children's Home these uneasy thoughts soon subsided. I comforted myself with the idea that she had probably been "assigned" to give language lessons, perhaps to Army officers, and was not allowed to write. I got on with my technical drawing.

One week passed after another. I went again several times to my mother's apartment, but each time there was nothing to do but gaze disconsolately at the sealed door. The occupants of the next room were friendly at first, but soon they changed.

"Why do you keep on coming here?" one of them asked me severely, almost angrily. "We've told you already, your mother's on an assignment. As soon as she comes back, she'll let you know. It's no good your running around here all the time."

After that I did not go again. In the meantime I had met some of my mother's friends, who also told me that my mother was on an assignment, but no one seemed to know exactly where she was.

"I've heard she may be in Tiflis," said one of them.

"But then why doesn't she write to me?"

"There are some assignments where you're not allowed to write," was the answer. I understood that, as I had often heard the same thing before; so I gave up asking.

Soon afterwards other things began to happen, which were to tear me away from the peaceful life

of the Children's Home. In January, 1937, began the
trial of the so-called conspirators of the "Anti-Soviet
Trotskyite Centre," including Pyatakov, Radek,
Sokolnikov and Serebryakov. All of them were leading figures who had hitherto been held up to us as
models of what a Bolshevik should be. The *German
Centre News*—which had hitherto followed *Pravda*
in publishing almost nothing but reports of successes
of socialist construction and photographs of new
factories or model *kolkhozes*—was now full of denunciations of "Trotskyite spies" and "traitors to the
country" and "capitalist reactionaries." This was
not the first of the treason trials, but it was the first
of which I became fully aware.

Our tuition in current affairs was immediately
adapted to the new requirements, and devoted exclusively to the trial. We learned that the men we had
previously known as loyal party leaders had in reality
been spies, agents and deviationists. They had conducted secret negotiations with Hitlerite Germany
and Japan with the object of surrendering the
Ukraine to Germany and the Soviet Far East to Japan,
as well as re-establishing capitalism in the Soviet
Union. The accused had been saboteurs, spies and
public enemies for many years, even decades, we
were told. They had succeeded in deluding their
comrades while carrying out their ostensible roles
as loyal officials, but they had in reality been sabotag-
ing production plans, organising outbreaks of fire
and explosions, promoting deviationism, causing railway accidents, and bringing about the death of workers and peasants by deliberately spreading germs in
ration stores and medical clinics. At the same time
they had been forming terrorist groups, with the ob-

ject of murdering the head of the Party and the Soviet Government.

The trial came to an end on 30th January, 1937. Pyatakov, Serebryakov and others of the accused were condemned to death, Sokolnikov and Radek to ten years' imprisonment. The newspapers carried pictures of meetings at factories and collective farms, with every hand raised in approval of the verdict of the court. There were great demonstrations carrying slogans like: "Shoot the Fascist mad dogs!" and "The enemies of the people must be wiped off the face of the earth!"

We were not yet capable of fully assessing the significance of this trial. Our life was still one of happy seclusion. We had still no suspicion of the mass arrests of this period; we went to school as usual, and read our books and talked. The only thing we had begun to notice was that there was much mention of "vigilance," of "enemies and agents" and of their criminal activities, whenever we had tuition in current affairs or at school assemblies or in the Home.

The great wave of arrests had started as far back as the autumn of 1936, but it was not until the late spring of 1937, when it was impossible to conceal things from us any longer, that we began to notice for ourselves what was happening in the country. For the arrests did not halt even at the doors of the Karl Liebknecht School. One after another, from March 1937 onwards, our teachers were arrested. The first to disappear was Gerschinski, a German Communist who taught German. He had been to the Karl Marx School in Berlin-Neukölln as a boy, and had been in the Soviet Union since 1933. Next went Luschen, our history and geography master, who was also a graduate of the Karl Marx School. Finally our mathematics and chemistry master, Kaufmann, was also arrested.

It was not only in our class that this happened, but throughout the school. The few teachers who were left were completely exhausted, as they had to take over all the teaching hours of those who had been arrested. And they had fear to contend with as well as exhaustion, for each of them knew that it might be his own turn next day. They thus lost all sense of security and we could not fail to notice what a strain it was for them to get through their lessons.

Sometimes their fears would play them gruesome tricks. Once when we were having tuition in current affairs, our teacher was quite carried away with enthusiasm about the democratic character of the constitution and the moral and political unity of the Soviet people. He wanted to close his exposition with the familiar Stalinist slogan: "But as for those who seek to harm our country, they will get a stinging rebuff which will make them think twice in future before they stick their hogs' snouts into our Soviet paradise." As luck would have it, he made a slip at this point and resoundingly declaimed at us: ". . . which will make them think twice before they stick their Soviet snouts into our hogs' paradise."

Some of the class burst out laughing at this, but I and others sat thunderstruck. What next? What would happen now?

A few seconds later our teacher noticed his blunder, and went white as chalk and trembled in every limb. We could not help noticing how feebly he brought the lesson to an end, and we were all dreadfully sorry for him. We knew that this was the end of him, because he would have to report his lapse to the Party himself. A few days later he disappeared. We never saw him again, and nothing more was heard of him.

Even our examinations took place under the shadow of the arrests. We were sitting in class one morning in June to do our written examination in German. We were a little excited, as was natural at examination time. When our teacher came into the room he began by going through the roll call, and then he told us the subject for the examination: "I shall now read you a passage out of a book by the anti-fascist author Georg Born, and you will then reproduce its contents in your own words. You have three hours for it, so you can take your time."

With these words he opened his satchel to get out the book by Born, when suddenly a whisper ran round some of the benches.

"What's the matter?"

One pupil stood up. "Comrade teacher, my father told me that Georg Born was arrested a few days ago as an enemy of the people."

Our teacher went pale as ashes. With trembling hands he replaced the book in his satchel, fumbled in it and examined several other books, and quickly put them away again. Finally he picked out a book by Kisch, who was living in Mexico at that time. He could be fairly sure that Kisch was not going to be unmasked as an enemy of the people.

By this time our teacher had somewhat calmed down and got a grip on himself. "I should like to offer you my apologies for the grave mistake I made. It goes without saying that we are not going to pay any attention to a book by an enemy of the people, who is now undergoing his well-merited punishment. I shall read you instead a descriptive passage by Egon Erwin Kisch, and you will then reproduce it in your own words."

He read the passage out to us with a slight tremor still in his voice. He was far more nervous than we were, although it was we who had to do the examination.

It was while the examinations were on, in June, 1937, that the purges reached their climax. At the beginning of June, in common with the whole Soviet population, we were shocked by an extraordinary piece of news. Professor Pletnev, one of the most celebrated names in Soviet medicine, was accused of criminal assault on a Soviet citizen called Mrs. B. As sexual cases were never reported in the Soviet press, the general astonishment was all the more marked: the circumstances of the assault were described, and there were even references to the fact that the professor had bitten the woman several times in the breast. The result of this assault, according to *Pravda*, was that she would be an invalid for life.

There immediately followed the usual series of resolutions from medical institutes of every kind condemning the "sexual sadist" Pletnev. A public trial was announced and eagerly awaited, and a new slogan came into circulation for the occasion, which was to be read in the papers and heard at public meetings every day: "The Soviet Security Service is growing stronger, larger, and more powerful! Spies and deviationists and murderers beware! The Soviet Security Service has yet to show its full might!"

A few days later, on 11th June, 1937, it was announced that an alleged conspiracy had been un-

covered, under the leadership of the then Chief of
the General Staff, Marshal Tukhachevsky, along
with seven other Red Army Generals. The names were
those of men who occupied the top posts in
the Army's high command, or of party members of
long standing and senior state and party officials. But
they were accused of being spies in the service of
a foreign power. They had carried out acts of sabotage in the army, in order to weaken it and bring about
its defeat and the restoration of power in the U.S.S.R.
to the great landowners and capitalists.

In the last few months we had reached a state of
mind where almost nothing surprised us, thanks to
the trials and the perpetual threats and denunciations
directed at "mortal enemies," "agents," "enemies
of the people and the Party," "spies," "swindlers,"
"traitors," and "deviationists." But the announcement
of the discovery of the "Tukhachevsky conspiracy"
eclipsed everything that had gone before.

Five out of the six pages of *Pravda* on 12th June,
1937, were devoted exclusively to this subject. It
was the only time in the history of the Soviet press
that every page of the paper carried banner headlines:

SPIES, DESPICABLE HIRELINGS OF FASCISM,
TRAITORS TO THEIR COUNTRY—
SHOOT THEM!

This was in huge letters on the first page; and on
the second page the banner headline read:

SPIES, MUTINEERS, TRAITORS TO THEIR
COUNTRY AND THE RED ARMY—
SHOOT THEM!

The headline on the third page read:

SPIES SOUGHT TO BREAK UP OUR COUN-
TRY AND RE-ESTABLISH POWER OF LAND-
OWNERS AND CAPITALISTS IN U.S.S.R.—
SHOOT THEM!

On the fourth page was:

SPIES CARRIED OUT SABOTAGE TO UNDER-
MINE MIGHT OF RED ARMY—
SHOOT THEM!

And on the fifth:

SPIES WORKED FOR DEFEAT OF RED ARMY—
SHOOT THEM!

The leading article carried the title: "The firing
squad for spies, for espionage and treason to our country!" and ended with the same words which were
now appearing everywhere: "The Soviet Security
Service has yet to show its full might!"

The whole issue was full of resolutions cursing
and vilifying the alleged traitors and demanding their
immediate execution. However, these spontaneous
popular demands were already out of date, because
there was a brief paragraph announcing that Tukhachevsky and his fellow defendants had already been
condemned to be shot, and, in fact, had been executed the night before.

Although these happenings did not directly affect
us in the Children's Home, there was nevertheless a
reaction to them. On the evening of the day on which
Tukhachevsky was condemned to be shot, one of
my fellow pupils—a boy of thirteen or fourteen, but

not yet among the seniors—came up to me, pale in the face.

"What on earth am I to do? I've done something quite dreadful."

"What have you done?"

"In the examination we had to do an essay on the Red Army, and I gave Tukhachevsky a big write-up."

"In your essay?"

"Yes, but worse still—I actually ended my essay with the words: 'Under the leadership of Stalin and Tukhachevsky the Red Army was victorious in the civil war and remains invincible to-day!' What on earth will happen now?"

Luckily nothing at all happened to him, but there were many anxious faces about even in the Children's Home, especially among the grown-ups. It seemed almost a deliverance when we were assembled one evening and given the unexpected good news that we were going to Gurzuf in the Crimea for our summer holidays.

That same evening I had an experience which at the time I did not understand at all. One of the officers at the Home came up to me, gazed gravely at me and squeezed my hand in a warm grip, but said nothing at all. I was mystified: what could be the matter with him?

A week went by in preparations for the journey. On the last day before we left, the same officer came up to me again, but this time he was quite cheerful. "Everything's all right again," he said, giving me a slap on the shoulder.

"But what was wrong, then?"

He answered hesitantly: "There was something,

but it's been cleared up. Now—chin up and pack your things—we're off to the Crimea!"

The authorities of the Home had hired some splendid buildings in the picturesquely situated spa of Gurzuf on the Black Sea, and there we spent a wonderful time. The events of the past months seemed no more than a bad dream in the lovely countryside of the Crimea, under the palm trees and in the cool sea. We believed, or we hoped, that everything would come right again, and that when we got back to Moscow we should find things just as good as they had been a few months before.

Three weeks after our holiday in the Crimea began, I fell ill. I was put to bed in the sick room under the care of our German woman doctor, who always looked after us devotedly. When I was getting better, she came to me one day in bed and said: "Here's some mail for you!"

I read the postcard excitedly. It had been addressed to the Children's Home, and it was from my mother! The address for reply was given as L. P. Shor, Chibyu, Komi A.S.S.R., and underneath was the note: "K.R.T.D. 5 years."

At last I knew what had happened. It hit me like a blow—my mother had been arrested! I knew that L.P. was the abbreviation for *Lagerpunkt* (camp site) and K.R.T.D. was the Russian abbreviation for *Kontr-revoliutsionnaya Trotskistskaya deyatelnost* ("counter-revolutionary Trotskyite activity").

I understood now why the room had been sealed, why the neighbours had been suspicious, why people had talked about my mother being on some kind of "assignment" in order not to frighten me. The horror of the situation was brought sharply home to me; my mother had been under arrest for the last ten months and was now somewhere in the most appalling conditions of the Arctic Circle, while I was living in the most highly privileged Children's Home in the Soviet Union and enjoying myself under the palm trees of the Crimea.

After this it was only with the greatest reluctance that I took part in excursions to Simferopol or Livadia or Yalta, or visits to the castles, or rambles in the beautiful hill country. The image of my mother was constantly before my eyes, and I wondered desparingly what had become of her.

I told nobody anything about the postcard, or about my mother's arrest and exile, but I was sure that the Warden of the Home and his assistants knew about it. Then I remembered that assistant's peculiar behavior just before our departure. Could it be that this had something to do with my mother's arrest? I tried to talk to him about it again, but he motioned me away. It was not until a year later that I learned the explanation of his behaviour. Not only my mother, but the parents of eight or ten other inmates had been arrested at the same time. Then came a directive that all the children whose parents had been arrested by the N.K.V.D. were to be taken away from our Home and transferred to an N.K.V.D. Children's Home. That was the day the assistant had come up to me to shake my hand for the last time, without of course telling me anything about it. A few days later the order had been countermanded. We were to stay in the Home, and that was why he had approached me so cheerfully the second time, to tell me that everything was all right.

I do not know to this day whom we had to thank

for our rescue. Was it on the intervention of the Comintern that the order had been countermanded? However it may have been, we were saved from the terrible fate of going to one of the many N.K.V.D. Children's Homes which were run at that time for the children of those who had been arrested. It is true that we were separated from our parents for many years, but we were spared the worst. And now we had only one thing left to cling to—our Children's Home, which was now not only our home, but our family and our shield.

But what would happen if our Home were broken up?

The Day of Decision: A Russian School

After six weeks' holiday in the Crimea, we returned to Moscow in the second half of August. The very next day the Warden assembled the seniors in his room for a special talk.

"Comrades, you have all finished the 7th class, and we must now have a serious discussion about your future. All of you know Russian well by now, and I should like you to consider whether it would not be better for you to leave the Karl Liebknecht School and go to Russian schools. Naturally, there is no compulsion about this. We can talk it over again in a few days' time."

Some of us decided in favour of the Russian schools on the spot. I myself and some others hesitated. I knew Russian pretty well by then, but still not so well as German. If it had only been a question of the language, I would rather have stayed at the German school. But it was quite clear to me, even though Semyonov had not said so, that his prosposal was actuated by political motives. Probably the others had the same idea, for when we met again in the Warden's room two days later, all had decided in favour of Russian schools.

Twelve seniors, including myself, made the move on 1st September, 1937. We were distributed among various schools, while the juniors and the intermediates stayed at the Karl Liebknecht School for the time being. I went to Moscow School No. 93, in a side street near Arbat Square. Like many schools in Moscow, it was a fine modern building, and the equipment was just as magnificent as I was used to. The pupils and staff made us at home in the friendliest spirit of true comradeship. They helped us at first when we failed to understand the more difficult things in Russian, and there was never a trace of hostility in their attitude towards us.

Although we knew Russian fairly well by this time, it was not easy at first to follow the lessons. The top three classes in the Soviet school were primarily intended for those who were going to continue their studies at a college. In the 8th, 9th and 10th classes the curriculum was much compressed, and a very great deal was expected of pupils in their last three years. I am convinced to this day that at least as much is learned in Soviet schools as in most West European and American schools—probably more—though of course much of it is presented from a biased point of view. Admittedly we learned neither Latin nor Greek, only one foreign language being taught, but in other subjects (particularly in the scientific field) the requirements were very stiff.

In most subjects there was direct continuity between the previous seven years' study and the 8th class, but in a few cases there were wholesale changes. Mathematics was now divided into three subjects—algebra, geometry and trigonometry. Physics and chemistry were carried a stage farther; and the geography periods were devoted to a fairly detailed exposition of the economic geography of the U.S.S.R. In biology we covered human anatomy and physiology. In history we went over the historical evolution, of the constituent peoples of the U.S.S.R., starting not with early Russian history but with Urartu, a state which had existed from the 9th to the 6th century B.C. in the area at present occupied by Soviet Armenia. During the school year 1937-38 our lessons gave emphasis for the first time to Ivan the Terrible, whose historical treatment underwent an important change. Much to many people's surprise, he suddenly began to be praised as a progressive ruler who had united Russia. Apparently he had been misrepresented by reactionary historians: the nickname "Terrible" was entirely unjust. His progressive achievements in centralising the state and purging Russia of traitors were underlined at great length, with special reference to the *Oprichnina* (Life Guards), who used to wear a badge consisting of a dog's muzzle and a broom——the dog's muzzle to smell out traitors, and the broom to sweep them from the country.

The 8th class included neither constitutional nor social studies, nor any other political subject. Instead we had twice a week a period called *voennoe delo* or "military science." In this period we were trained in parade ground drill, civil defence, and air-raid precautions. Technical drawing (*cherchenie*) was still a particular headache for me, and it grew more difficult every week. The importance of this subject was much emphasised, clearly because it was assumed that most of the graduates of the 10-year course at school were eventually going to a technical college, as was in fact the case.

The tendency to direct our education towards the colleges was unmistakable, and gave rise to a number of interesting practices. For instance, from the 8th class upwards we were occasionally invited to "open-house days" at colleges of many different kinds. On these days the normal life of the college was interrupted and professors and lecturers, with their assistants and representatives of the students, made themselves available to welcome interested pupils from the 10-year schools and explain to them what went on in the college. This gave good publicity to the institute concerned, and at the same time helped young pupils to decide their future career. I went several times to these open-house days at the colleges, and had already made up my mind which to go on to later.

One result of our transfer to Russian schools was that many of us began to speak Russian even among ourselves. This was the first step towards our complete sovietisation and russification, which became more and more marked after 1937. The second step came at the beginning of 1938: the Karl Liebknecht School was closed. The arrest of the teaching staff —including the headmaster, Zhelasko, and his successor, a woman called Kramer—made it impossible to carry on the management of the school. So all the rest of the Austrian and German children were transferred to Russian schools.

Our Home became steadily more like the Russian

Homes. We still had visits from representatives of the Austrian and German sections of the Comintern, and we listened to lectures on the struggle against Fascism in Germany and Austria or on events in Spain; but Soviet lecturers too became increasingly frequent, the object being to familiarise us more with political questions in the Soviet Union.

We learned to treat every question in a political light, or "from the standpoint of principle" as it was usually expressed. It became a matter of habit to justify everything done by the Soviet Union, however extraordinary it might be, even in cases where the action was intrinsically contradictory to Socialist ideas.

At first many of the children in our Home went on writing letters to their parents or relatives in Austria, but as time went on the links grew weaker. We thought less and less of Germany or Austria, and more and more of the Soviet Union. When we had meetings in the Home, at first we always referred to the Soviet Union as our "second home," but eventually the word "second" was left out and we gradually came to feel that the Soviet Union was our only real home. Austria and Germany were now very seldom mentioned in our conversations. Memory was fading. We were turning into young Soviet citizens; still Germans or Austrians by nationality, but already belonging to the Soviet Union in thought and emotion.

Between 1934 and 1938, our Children's Home had taken on quite a new look. By this time it was not really a "Children's Home" at all. The juniors had imperceptibly become intermediates and the intermediates had become seniors, while the original seniors hardly fitted into a Children's Home any longer.

We had dances on Saturdays and Sundays now, and a visitor would hardly have taken the dancing couples for inmates of a Children's Home.

Only a little while before, the authorities had had to intervene in furious battles between children hurling tins of tooth powder at each other. Now they were faced with new problems, born of the experience which many of their pupils were beginning to have of the enchantments of love. But we had picked on a bad time to enjoy these happiest years of our youth!

The Great Purge seen from a Children's Home

Still there was no end to the arrests. Indeed, they had grown more frequent since our return from the Crimea at the end of August, 1937; and in the autumn of that year, everything that had so far happened was eclipsed.

I no longer found it extraordinary when I visited a friend to find the door sealed, or another family installed since my last visit in a room that belonged to someone under arrest. Only a few years before, the idea of being under arrest had meant something exceptional and terrible. Now it was a commonplace. Almost every day on my short journey to school, I used to see the familiar green lorry carrying away those who had been arrested.

More and more often now we used to hear of the arrests of leading Comintern officials, who had previously been held up to us as examples for our imitation. It was not only the teachers at the Karl Liebknecht School who vanished overnight. There were the editorial staff of the *German Centre News* and the staff of the Foreign Workers' Club as well. We heard constantly of new arrests in the "Home for

Émigrés" and among the *Schutzbündler*. We could see the constant fear in which our schoolmasters and the staff at the Home and the Comintern lecturers who visited us were living all the time.

The "survivors," which was the name those who had not yet been arrested gave themselves, reacted in different ways. Most of them suffered from a permanent fear-psychosis. They ran about the place like hunted deer, concentrating all their energy on doing the right thing to escape arrest. But what was the right thing?

"The most important thing to-day is, so far as possible, to say nothing whatever, and above all of course to avoid any kind of political expression, even if it be strictly in accordance with the party line," some people said. "Silence, silence, and again silence— that is the need of the hour."

Others argued: "There's nothing more dangerous to-day than to go about saying nothing at all. That only rouses suspicions that you are harbouring secret thoughts and may actually be a public enemy. The present situation is one in which it is specially important to be active and to speak your mind openly, in the same sense as *Pravda,* on every subject."

"You can't tell who's going to be arrested as a public enemy to-morrow, so the best thing is to avoid everybody and isolate yourself entirely": that was one view. The other view was: "Now is the time to see as many people as possible. It's no use behaving as in the past, pretending not to have noticed the great purge going on at all. Nothing could be more dangerous than to shut yourself up in a cell."

"The important thing to-day is to purge your books," said one school of thought. "Any book that is open to even the slightest possibility of a suspicion of deviating from the party line should be thrown into the stove at once."

"As long as the purge is on," said the opposite school, "there's nothing more dangerous than to put even the smallest scrap of paper into the stove. Other tenants will notice it at once, and infer that you've been burning documents. Then you will automatically be suspected of being a spy. Better a dozen anti-party books in the bookcase than a single bit of charred paper in the stove."

But in the last analysis all discussion was in vain. Those who went about as quiet as mice got arrested just as much as those who never missed any possible (or impossible) opportunity of enthusiastically quoting the leading articles of *Pravda* at the top of their voices. People who went straight back to their garrets after work, and never stirred out again, still fell victims of the N.K.V.D.; so did those who made principle of noticing nothing unusual and behaving precisely as before. Those who were over-cautious and burned half their libraries (including authorised books) were no likelier to escape arrest than those who refused even to make up their stoves for fear of being suspected of having documents they wanted to burn. There was simply no such thing as a formula by which innocent people could make their innocence look convincing.

By this time it was common knowledge even in our Children's Home that ninety-nine per cent of those arrested had never done anything against the Soviet state, and therefore with the best will in the world could not confess anything at their interrogations. But generally the N.K.V.D. succeeded, so I was told, in finding out something intrinsically innocent (such as a postcard from abroad, or a visit to the *Café National* while a foreign diplomat was also sitting there, several tables away), and with a certain imagination this kind of harmless incident could then be built up into participation in a conspiracy against Stalin.

The question the "survivors" used to discuss was this: Should one persist in refusing to admit to imaginary crimes or to sigh confessions, or should one help the examining magistrate to build up his story and then sign it, in order at least to show goodwill?

Among my friends opinions on this point were divided. One argument ran thus: "I have never done anything at all against the Soviet state, and if I am arrested I have no intention of confessing to any kind of crime that I haven't committed. I will not admit anything or sign anything."

The contrary opinion went like this: "Arrests have nothing whatever to do with guilt or innocence. A refusal to admit anything helps nobody. On the contrary, you just get a severer punishment and no one is any the better for it. I'm going to start thinking out the most plausible possible story now, so as to make it simple for the N.K.V.D. if I am arrested, and thus perhaps get a comparatively light sentence."

A few days later I came across one of my most intelligent acquaintances, who had shortly before met a man—naturally he gave no name—who had been arrested by the N.K.V.D. and later released again.

"I believe I have found the solution," said my friend. "The thing to do is think out some perfectly idiotic story for the interrogation, which can be accepted by the examining magistrate as a confession, but is really so stupid that the first scrutiny will be enough to show it up as impossible."

"What sort of story, for instance?"

"I haven't thought up a story for myself yet: I'm still turning it over in my mind. But I've heard a good example from one of my friends, about a chemist who confessed at his interrogation that he had sold an important chemical formula to the Nazi Secret Service. Of course he was asked at once what the formula was. He wrote down the formula H_2SO_4. His confession was accepted."

"I can't believe it!"

"But you see, many of the trained N.K.V.D. officials have been arrested themselves by this time, and you often find uneducated peasants sitting as examining magistrates, and stories like that could well be true of them. There have been even crazier cases: do you know the story about the Leningrad dockyards?"

"No," I said.

"Somebody confessed to being a member of a dangerous conspiracy against the Navy. He said that he and his friends had a plan to throw stones into the harbor at Kronstadt, to sabotage the fleet and the naval installations."

"Well, and what happened?"

"He got eight years. If he hadn't confessed, he would probably have been sentenced to ten or twelve years. Besides, he's sure to be one of the first to be released when the whole case is reviewed, as he hopes it will be."

It was a fantastic, inconceivable situation. Generally when people live under a dictatorship and go in for activities against it, they do their best under interrogation to avoid admitting anything and to refute everything they can in order to escape with a lighter sentence. But here we were witnessing responsible men, who had never done anything against the system, solemnly and anxiously debating what they could confess after their arrest!

The wildest rumours sprang up, as they always do at such times. "Yezhov is going to be replaced soon," people whispered hopefully; and in October the rumour was current that on 7th November, 1937, the twentieth anniversary of the October revolution, there would be a great amnesty and everyone would be released again.

The 7th November came. There was an amnesty, but unfortunately only for a few hundred criminals who had nothing whatever to do with the great purge. Soon, too, the rumours about the replacement of the dreaded Commissar for State Security petered out. Yezhov stayed at his post, and was in even higher favour than before.

The most persistent rumour concerned Marshal Blücher, who was then Commander-in-Chief of the Far Eastern Special Military District. There had been an earlier story about Blücher that in the 1920's he had made several visits to China and collaborated with Sun Yat-sen, then the leader of the Chinese revolution. When the rank of Marshal was introduced he was one of the first five to hold it, and he enjoyed a quite exceptional status as Commander-in-Chief of the Far Eastern Special Military District. In June, 1937, he was one of the tribunal that condemned Marshal Tukhachevsky to death; and after that, so the whisper went now, he had returned at once to

the Far East. Soon afterwards the first rumours began
to circulate.

"Marshal Blücher's keeping out of it," whispered
one of my friends to me delightedly. "There's no
purge going on in the Far Eastern Military District."

"No arrests at all?"

"Not quite that, of course, but only routine arrests,
not what we're going through here."

"But how can he do it?"

"Why shouldn't he? He has complete authority
and he just doesn't let it happen. Ah, if only one
could get to Vladivostok!" His eyes lit up at the
thought. "But I'm afraid it would get to be known,
and then one would be arrested for sure just before
starting out."

The rumour soon developed into a new and more
elaborate version: "A few days ago the N.K.V.D. decided to arrest Marshal Blücher for insubordination.
A whole train-load of the N.K.V.D. set out on the
job, but as soon as they crossed the boundary of the
Far Eastern District, the train was surrounded by
Marshal Blücher's special units. They even say artillery was used! The N.K.V.D. troops had to give
in, and they were arrested; now they're sitting in
gaol at Vladivostok! A desperate character, Marshal
Blücher!"

At that time I assumed these rumours to be nothing
but wishful thinking and to-day I am convinced of
it. It was the last ray of hope in a hopeless situation.
But even these rumours gradually dried up, for soon
afterwards the word went round that Marshal
Blücher had been arrested. It was as if the earth had
swallowed him up. His name was never mentioned
again in the Soviet press or at any meetings.

The arrests went on without interruption. People became more and more indifferent. They looked upon their fate as a natural calamity, which nothing could avert. More than that, there were actually jokes going round in this grim period, perhaps because everything seemed so inevitable anyway.

The most popular was the "4 a.m." joke, an allusion to the time of day when most of the arrests took place. At four o'clock in the morning there was a knock on the door of a Moscow house, which was occupied by five families. All of them leapt out of bed but none of them dared to open the door. They stood and waited, trembling, at their bedroom doors. The knocking grew louder. Finally one of the tenants, Abram Abramovich, took his courage in both hands and opened the front door. He was heard whispering for a few moments with a man standing outside. Then he came back to his terrified fellow tenants with a bright smile on his face: "Nothing to worry about, comrades—the house is on fire, that's all!"

First Doubts

Meanwhile, I was no longer the only one in the Home whose mother had been arrested. By this time several other pupils had learned, through letters or postcards, of the arrest of their own parents. Little by little tongues were loosened, and we confessed to each other that our mothers or our fathers, or even in some cases both parents, were now in custody.

Curiously enough, we all reacted in the same way. Each of us knew from the first that his mother or father was innocent of the charges. But our Soviet indoctrination had progressed so far that we did not base our judgment on the fate of individuals, even when those individuals were our own parents and we well knew them to be innocent. Not one of the ten or so of us whose parents had been arrested allowed this cruel personal blow to lead us directly into opposition against the system. We instinctively recoiled from the thought that what was happening in the mass arrests of these years was in diametrical opposition to our Socialist ideals. We still went on trying to convince ourselves that what was happening was no more than an exaggeration of measures which were in themselves both necessary and justified.

One evening, when we were sitting together in the Home as usual, the discussion was opened by a young girl whose father had been arrested by the N.K.V.D. and sentenced to ten years' deportation.

"I think the best way to explain what is happening is through a concrete example," she said. "Let us suppose that one of us has an apple, which is of great value to him, because it is the only one he possesses. In this apple there is a rotten spot, which may even be poisonous. If he wants to save the apple, there is no alternative but to cut out this spot, in order to preserve the rest of it. In the process of cutting it out, he may be compelled, in order not to risk being poisoned, to remove not only the rotten spot, but also some other parts of the apple, so that only the really healthy parts remain. Perhaps this is what is really happening in our great purge."

Another of our company confirmed this opinion: "Certainly, there is no doubt that spies, agents and deviationists do exist in the Soviet Union. Possibly the authorities are aware only that they exist, not where they are to be found, or what they are up to. In order to be on the safe side, and to preserve the

Soviet state, it is inevitable, for good or ill, that innocent people should be arrested as well as guilty. This
is certainly very unpleasant for the individuals, but
looked at from the standpoint of principle, it is justified, considering that what is at stake is to preserve
the only Socialist state in the world."

"In the last analysis, what is going on is a historical
process," said a third. "I have just been reading
a number of books about the French Revolution, and
especially about the Jacobin dictatorship. In this
period, too, there were trials and executions which
were possibly wrong, if you judge them from the point
of view of legalistic formality. But nevertheless they
did contribute to the victory of the Revolution."

But at this point there was an objection. "That's
a very dangerous example you've brought up there.
Wasn't the effect of the Jacobin dictatorship, with
its trials and its revolutionary terrorism, to narrow its
own foundations and consequently—in the last analysis—to contribute willy-nilly to the victory of the
counter-revolution?"

The discussion continued pro and con. We were
really on the brink of discovering the historical explanation of the purge. The seniors in the Children's
Home were to be seen at that time with their heads
bent over every kind of book that dealt with the Jacobin dictatorship. We studied it so minutely that we
had already given ourselves the title of the "1793
Club" as a joke.

In the evenings two or three of us used to go for
walks along the banks of the Moskva river, engaged
in lively discussion about the problems of the French
Revolution, but our discussions never got us any
farther forward. People in the West find it difficult

to understand how helpless we felt. We had nothing
to go on but the reports of the trials. We never heard a
single voice expressing a contrary point of view, or
making a critical remark of any kind. We had no
newspapers, with the exception of *Pravda,* no books
with the exception of those which conformed to the
party line, and were therefore authorised. We had
no opportunity to listen to foreign broadcasts. We
had no idea that all the leading newspapers abroad
were commenting on the trials and the mass arrests,
or that many books had been written about them and
that the most diverse theories were being evolved to
account for them. In all our speculations and discussions, we had nobody to rely on but ourselves.
Besides, even in our own small circle we did not
discuss everything openly. However unwillingly, we
were compelled to adopt a language of hints and
metaphors, a language of allegory.

What we were always trying to do was to find a
justification for the purges, in order to maintain our
ideals and our belief in the Soviet Union as the first
Socialist country. It is possible, we told ourselves,
that there are definite reasons which we do not know
about, but which are certainly cogent, for carrying
out these trials and mass arrests. It may even be that
the accused are not spies at all, from the subjective
point of view, and yet that objectively considered
they constitute an obstacle to the development of
Socialism. Was it not Marx himself who spoke of
force as the midwife at the birth of a new society?
Was it not possible that many of those arrested were
in fact spies; and that as there was no positive evidence, all the ministries and all the official agencies
had to be purged; and was not the real question in the

last analysis that of ensuring the survival of the first Socialist state in the world? To many of us, these events had the appearance of historical necessity —perhaps serving purposes which were unknown to us, but which were so important that they could not be sacrificed by those in positions of the highest authority.

It was about this time that I happened to come across an excellent book by the American Communist, John Reed, called *Ten Days That Shook The World*. John Reed was describing the days of the Revolution in November, 1917, which he had himself lived through in Petrograd. I was astonished to find that in this book Stalin was never so much as mentioned, while those who were now being described at the trials as spies and agents were presented by John Reed as the leading figures of the Revolution. I then set about comparing the newspapers again with the accounts of the trials. No, I thought, this could not be true! It was quite simply impossible, that the same Communists who had led the October Revolution, who had been at the head of the party since the year 1917, and who had led the Russian workers to victory over the White Guards and the foreign intervention, who had played leading roles in the task of constructing Socialism—it was impossible that they could now turn out to have been Imperialist agents and foreign spies for twenty years.

The longer the arrests went on, the more critical my thoughts became. I spent the evenings pondering over what was happening and seeking some kind of an answer. The purges had had the effect of making me look at much of what was going on with a more sceptical eye. They had somewhat shaken my faith

and diminished my enthusiasm, but they had not yet
brought my inner self to the point of a rupture with
the system. These were my first serious doubts, but
my breach with Stalinism had to wait more than another ten years before it came about.

Arrests at the Children's Home

One fine spring day in March, 1938, a small group
of us were so deep in conversation after lunch that
we were the last to leave the dining-hall. Just as we
were crossing the front hall, the big front door opened
and two men in civilian clothes came in and walked
slowly up the steps.

My next-door neighbour whispered to me: "N.K.
V.D. men!" There was no need for him to tell me.

Meanwhile one of the staff, the Austrian, Karl
Zehetner, came out of the lecture room into the front
hall with another inmate. They had also noticed the
two men.

"Well, Karl, look out, they've come for you!" the
boy joked.

"You shouldn't joke about such things, you know
very well that in the Soviet Union innocent people
are never arrested," said Zehetner, trying to speak
firmly.

The N.K.V.D. men came up to him.

"We are looking for Karl Zehetner," they said
sharply in Russian.

"I am he," whispered Zehetner.

"You are under arrest. We are representatives of
the N.K.V.D."

Karl Zehetner said nothing more. Without even
looking round, he followed the two men to the front

door. Outside we heard the engine of a car as it moved off.

Only a few months before, an event like this would have let loose a flood of discussion and agitation, talk and speculation. By now, in the spring of 1938, it was accepted almost with indifference. We did not even have an explanation of Zehetner's arrest from the Warden. There was simply no further mention of him. The only result of his arrest was that most of the members of the staff were more careful than they had been hitherto.

A few days later, a sharp dispute broke out in the seniors' dormitory between the two oldest boys—both at this time about seventeen years old.

"Have you heard R . . . has been arrested?— he's the one we often saw in the Foreign Workers' Club," said a senior as he came into the dormitory.

One of the two oldest boys thereupon jumped up, went into the classroom and came back with his note-book.

"What are you up to?" the seventeen-year-old Rolf Geissler shouted at him (he was the son of a Communist from Penig in Saxony).

"You'll soon see," the other replied. He picked up his pen and carefully deleted the name and address of the arrested man R . . . from his note-book, so that it was impossible to read it. He examined the page carefully, but he was still not content, so he took a razor blade and cut out the whole page.

"One must be careful," he said apologetically.

Rolf Geissler laughed contemptuously. "Anyone would take you for a shopkeeper, you miserable coward. To think you call yourself a Communist! I've nothing but contempt for your sort of panic-stricken *petit bourgeois*. You'll never be a fighter!"

"It's got nothing to do with panic, it's just necessary to be cautious and vigilant."

A heated quarrel then broke out between Rolf Geissler and the other boy. Finally the latter shouted: "Just you wait, my friend Rolf, we shall see which of us two is the first to be arrested—you or I!"

After this conversation—a somewhat unusual one for the dormitory of the Children's Home—we went to sleep. Early the following morning, about 4 o'clock, we were woken up by a loud knocking on the door. Two men in civilian clothes came into the dormitory, just as if they were in their own house. Behind them we saw the face of our night sister distorted with fear.

"Is Rolf Geissler here?" shouted one of the two in a loud voice.

"Yes, here I am," Rolf answered. He was still half asleep and spoke in German, but he repeated what he had said in Russian when he saw the two men.

"You are under arrest. We are representatives of the N.K.V.D." This was the second time I had heard the same formula, which was always used in the process of arrest. "Where are your things?"

Rolf Geissler pointed to the little box standing beside his bed.

"Have you any weapons?"

"But my dear comrade, this is a Children's Home!" interrupted the night sister.

"We're not asking you." The question was put to Geissler again. "Have you any weapons?"

"No."

"Good, then pack your things. Any written material you have should be put here on the table."

By this time we were all wide awake. At the last phrase we remembered with horror that the evening before we had made up a party game—we were after all still half children—in which one of us who had a talent for designing had made some dies out of linoleum, with imaginary designs of postage stamps and coins on them. By means of these we had produced a dozen or so counters and some imitation money. Now Rolf Geissler put them on the table, and every one of us had the same thought: the N.K.V.D. men would never believe that this was only a party game— they were bound to assume that they had discovered clues to a secret organisation.

That was exactly what happened. As soon as Rolf put the imitation dies and the money on the table, the two N.K.V.D. men cast a significant look at them. By this time Rolf had dressed and packed a change of clothing in his little case.

"Before you go, you must sign every piece of paper with writing on it." One after another Geissler signed all his letters, exercise-books, note-books and sketches. Then came the turn of the little counters.

One of us tried to explain: "Comrade, that is . . ."

"We didn't ask you—no one here need speak!"

A few minutes later the whole process was ended. Rolf Geissler was taken away. Once more, as the front door of the house was opened, we heard the engine of the car outside.

Nothing more was ever heard of Rolf Geissler.

At the time when these arrests in the Children's Home took place the whole country was again in a

ferment over a major trial. This time the victims were
the so-called "anti-Soviet bloc of right-wing Trotskyites." The importance of the accused and the
crimes attributed to them were much greater than in
the preceding trials.

Chief among the accused was the celebrated party
theoretician, Nikolai Bukharin, who had been a member of the Central Committee and the *politburo* since
1917. He was also the editor-in-chief of *Izvestiya,* and
had been for many years a member of the Executive
Committee of the Communist International. With
him was the veteran Bolshevik Rykov, who had been
People's Commissar for Internal Affairs in the first
Soviet Government of November, 1917, and since
Lenin's death the Chairman of the Council of People's Commissars of the Soviet Union. With Stalin's
rise to power, Rykov had been gradually pushed into
the background, and had finally been downgraded
to the post of People's Commissar for Posts and
Telegraphs. Then, on 27th September, 1936, he had
been removed even from this post without explanation, and since that time nothing more had been
heard of him.

The prosecutor, Vyshinsky, not only called the
accused (as usual) a band of spies and criminals,
but also an "accursed generation of vipers" and a
"putrefying heap of human scum." Bukharin, the
principle accused, whom Lenin had once called
"the favourite son of the Party," was now described
by Vyshinsky as a "loathsome hybrid of fox and
swine." Vyshinsky's speech demanded that the accused should be shot like mad dogs.

There followed the now familiar mass meetings, at
which "attitudes" were taken on the trials. Every day

there were more and more resolutions demanding immediate execution, in language full of familiar clichés. The press carried photographs of these gatherings, in which it could be seen that every hand was raised in token of agreement.

On 15th March, 1938, judgment was officially announced. The former State and Party leaders, Bukharin, Rykov, Yagoda, Krestinsky, Rozengolts, Chernov and Grinko, together with two doctors, Levin and Kazakov, and a few other accused, were condemned to death. The former President of the Ukrainian Government, Rakovsky, and Professor Pletnev were condemned to twenty years' imprisonment each.

On the following day two hours of our normal lessons were cancelled, so that we could study the trial and the verdict. Our teacher laid down for us the basic principles of discussion, sticking naturally enough to the report of the trial and the leading article on the subject which had appeared in *Pravda*. She then required us to formulate our "attitude," as was customary everywhere at that time.

The outcome of this discussion had clearly been settled in advance. One after another, with a punctilious respect for the official terminology, a number of pupils expressed their horror against the criminals and traitors and their gratitude towards the Security Service and the Supreme Court for having relieved the Soviet people of these scum.

"Has anyone anything to add?" asked the teacher.

"Yes," declared one of the pupils at the back, "I should like to say that I am not in complete agreement with everything that has been said."

The class was struck dumb with dismay. Everyone turned to look at the speaker, who seemed to have sealed his fate with his words. Is he mad? was the thought of most of his companions.

The most anxious person present was of course the teacher, who had been made responsible for everything that took place during the period. At first she wanted to stop the pupil from speaking, and then suddenly she abandoned the attempt. No doubt she had realised in a flash of illumination that if she prevented the pupil from speaking, she might render herself guilty of hushing something up, and consequently of being objectively guilty of abetting a pupil who was a public enemy.

By this time the pupil had begun to speak: "I have carefully followed the trial from beginning to end, and in my opinion it was just to condemn to death these public enemies, these saboteurs and spies; but I must honestly confess that I am quite unable to understand why three of the accused were not sentenced to death, but only to fifteen or twenty years' imprisonment. Pletnev, Rakovsky and Bessonov ought also to have been shot."

The pupil who uttered these words had proved himself to be generally a highly intelligent boy, and he was one of the best in the class. He spoke with a tone of ringing conviction, from his heart; he really believed in the trials!

The teacher breathed again. Her pupil had, it was true, expressed dissent, but he had done so in a way that was relatively safe. She took control of the discussion again, and corrected her over-enthusiastic pupil: "Comrade Vyshinsky has expressly drawn attention to the point that the criminals were not all responsible in equal degree, and that the degree of punishment had to be determined individually in each case. It is certainly not our place to criticise the decision of the Supreme Court of the U.S.S.R., which reached its verdict after mature reflection. But one thing can certainly be said: the fact that a clear distinction has been made between those who were principally guilty, and those who were less so, is yet one more example of the impartiality of justice in the Soviet Union."

The Shock of the Hitler-Stalin Pact

The arrests did not come to an end with the trial of the "right-wing Trotskyite bloc," which was the last and greatest of the three trials in the years of purges from 1936 to 1938. In the autumn of 1938 the wave of arrests reached another exceptionally high peak, which lasted several weeks. After that, towards the end of 1938, a brief announcement appeared in *Pravda* that Yezhov had been relieved of his duties as Minister of the Interior, and that Beria had been appointed in his place.

The horrible affair was over. There was hardly a single official department which had not seen its entire personnel arrested at least once, or more often. Millions of human beings, including hundreds of thousands of technical specialists with years of laborious training behind them, were now in camps in Siberia, Kazakhstan or the Far East.

Among the veteran Bolsheviks who had fought in the civil war the number of victims was exceptionally large. Practically all of Lenin's colleagues had been arrested. Of the seven members of the *politburo* in Lenin's time, Tomsky had committed suicide in an N.K.V.D. prison at the end of 1936, when the purge was beginning; Zinoviev, Kamenev and Rykov were shot in the course of the purge; and soon afterwards, in the summer of 1940, Trotsky was murdered in Mexico by N.K.V.D. agents. Only Stalin survived the purge. Bukharin and Pyatakov, who had been described by Lenin in his testament on the 25th December, 1922, as the "shrewdest heads among the younger generation," were shot by the N.K.V.D. Of the twenty-one members of the Central Committee of the Communist Party in 1917, sixteen disappeared during the purges, having presumably been shot; three had already died natural deaths; and only two survived —Stalin and Alexandra Kollontai.

On 7th November, 1937, when the purge had reached its climax, the 20th anniversary of the victorious October Revolution and the creation of the first Soviet Government was celebrated. Of the fifteen members of this first Soviet Government, nine People's Commissars had by this time been arrested by the N.K.V.D.; Trotsky was already in exile; four had died before the purge; and only a single member of the first Soviet Government of November, 1917, survived the purge—Stalin.

Not less numerous were the victims among the high command of the Red Army. Out of five Marshals of the Soviet Union, three—Tukhachevsky, Blücher and Yegorov—fell victims to the purge. The same fate overtook the most celebrated Soviet Generals of the day. Garmanik, who was chief of the Political Administration of the Red Army and Deputy People's Commissar for Defence, committed suicide.

Moreover, the purges were by no means limited to leading personalities. The casualties in the individual Republics of the Soviet Union, and in the local State and Party organs, and in particular among ordinary Party members, were even more severe. With negligible exceptions all the old Bolsheviks, and especially those who had spent their youth fighting against the Tsar and had already spent many years in exile, were now either in prison or in camps. It was the most frightful campaign of liquidation that had ever taken place anywhere in the world.

Foreign Communists living in the Soviet Union were attacked with special severity. In the course of a few months more officials of the Comintern *apparat* were arrested than under all the capitalist régimes put together for the past twenty years. A mere list of the names would fill several pages.

At the turn of the year 1938-39 the bloody purge came to an end, just as suddenly and abruptly as it had begun two years before. To-day I find it astonishing to recall how quickly people in Moscow, including myself, were able to wipe out the whole of this horror from their memory. I suppose we had simply lived through too much during those horrible months: our feelings were numbed.

Only a few weeks after the removal of Yezhov it was quite exceptional to hear the arrests spoken about at all. All the rumours and "prescriptions" disappeared just as quickly as they had sprung up two years earlier. Only occasionally in conversation did brief reminiscences occur of the *Yezhovshchina*, as the purge was called in Moscow. It was as if one were talking of events which belonged to ancient history.

We seniors spent the summer of 1939 at Yeysk on the Sea of Azov, as guests of a large Military Academy. Yeysk was a garrison town, where civilians were rarely to be seen. Everywhere there were men in uniform with letters on their caps, reading "V.M.A.U. imeni STALINA." This mysterious abbreviation stood for the Russian equivalent of Naval Air War College. It must have been an exceptionally big school, for the entire town seemed to consist of officers and naval airmen of the V.M.A.U. We had been allotted a single fine building some distance from the town. It was not right on the sea, but the V.M.A.U. had put a bus at our disposal to take us to the sea every day and bring us back in the evening.

After the gruesome years of the purge these holidays were particularly wonderful. We were enjoying our first real rest, though it is true that even here we were not entirely out of touch with our ordinary life. During our holiday we were preparing ourselves for our entry into the *Komsomol,* which was soon to come. Every other afternoon we had a session with our political director, Igor Speransky, for political tuition. Our studies centered as a matter of course on the *Short History of the Communist Party of the Soviet Union.* This book had been published in the autumn of 1938, and naturally I had already read it through carefully. While on holiday we worked through it for the second time. (Later on I had to do it again by myself, three times.)

In the middle of August we were invited to a ceremony in the great Palace of Culture of the V.M.A.U. The lecture on international affairs was devoted to the usual bitter attack on Fascism and Hitlerite Germany, and the speaker did not miss the opportunity of adding: "Comrades, men and women, we have here in this hall some of our foreign guests, the children of the German and Austrian anti-

Fascists who took part in the struggle against the hideous dictatorship of Hitler." Every head was then turned towards us, and after that we became well-known all over the town of Yeysk, and had a wonderful time. Our hosts visited us frequently to ask whether everything was to our liking. We found as much attention paid to us as in the early days in the Children's Home.

Three days later, our political director, Igor Speransky, was summoned into town at midday. "Just go and have your swim," he said. "I shall be back in the evening—I've been summoned into town."

"What's up, then?"

"I've no idea, but it can hardly be anything important." We went off happy and contented, to have our bathe. We had hardly got back, half an hour later, when suddenly our political director burst in in a state of great excitement.

"Here's something really important," he shouted breathlessly. "I've got hold of a proof copy of to-morrow morning's paper in Yeysk."

"What's the news?" we all asked in chorus.

"We've just signed a non-aggression pact with Germany!"

We stared at him open-mouthed. This was the last thing we could conceivably have expected. We had naturally been following the press closely, and we had assumed confidently that in spite of all difficulties in the negotiations, a treaty would soon be concluded with England and France against the Fascist aggressors.

Our political director read out to us in solemn, official tones the announcement of the pact between the Soviet Union and Hitlerite Germany. From the first few sentences we still assumed that the substance of the treaty was no more than an obligation on each side to refrain from aggression. But then our political director read out the later articles of the treaty, and we listened dumbfounded to the words: "The Governments of the two contracting parties will in future maintain contact in continuing consultation with a view to keeping each other informed on questions touching their common interests. Neither of the two contracting parties will enter into association with any other group of powers formed directly or indirectly against the interests of the other party."

This was not simply a non-aggression pact; this was a complete reversal of the whole foreign policy of the Soviet Union. What could be the meaning of "keeping each other informed" about interests in common with Hitler's Government? Or not joining any group of powers formed against the interests of Hitler? It could mean only one thing—the complete abandonment of the struggle against Fascist aggression in all its forms!

We were thunderstruck. We sat there bewildered and silent. Finally Egon Dirnbacher, the youngest among us, said sadly: "Ah, what a pity, now we shall certainly never be allowed to see Charlie Chaplin in *The Great Dictator!*"

Young Egon had certainly understood the situation correctly. For in fact, as we were to see in a few days, the conclusion of the pact had an immediate effect on the internal political situation. But for the present it was impossible to go on with the discussion, since nobody, not even our political director, could offer any elucidation of the pact.

"To-morrow morning there are certain to be detailed comments in the press," he said to calm our excitement. "Besides, to-morrow I am going to visit the party headquarters in Yeysk. After that I shall be able to give you more detailed information, and to-morrow evening we shall be able to talk the whole thing over more fully."

But this was never to come about.

The Home is Closed

The following morning, the first day after the conclusion of the pact, we were awakened very early by our political director: "I've just had a telegram from Moscow. We're to go back at once."

"To-day?" we asked.

"Yes, I've just gone into it. We can get to Rostov in a couple of hours, and be on our way back to Moscow."

Troubled speculations absorbed us in the train on the way to Moscow. What could be the significance of this sudden reversal of policy? What would be the effect on our personal lives of the conclusion of the pact between the Soviet Union and Hitler's Germany? We anxiously awaited our arrival in Moscow and the expected elucidation. We had not long to wait.

At the station we were met by some of the inmates of the Children's Home, who had spent their holidays at other resorts and had got back sooner than ourselves.

"The Home has been closed!" they shouted at us.

It was the most shattering piece of news I could possibly have heard. The Home was everything in the world for us: it was where we lived, it was our life, our shield, our friend; and now it was gone for ever. We were standing suddenly on the brink of a void, and life henceforth was impossible to picture.

"What will become of us now?"

"We've no more idea than you. Everything is going to be decided this afternoon."

With heavy hearts we went from the station to our Home at No. 12 Kalashny Lane. The scene there was like the aftermath of a battle. Furniture removers, house painters and plumbers were running about doing the house up and packing things away. All our possessions had been put together in a single room. Some of the pupils had already packed their things and were standing ready to move, but they had no idea where to. Others were running round the house, which for so many years had been our home, in a state of bewilderment and despair.

Some meetings had been held, but no one seemed to know what was to become of us. In reply to our questions, the teachers shrugged their shoulders helplessly and said: "We have no more idea than you have. The headmaster has gone to a conference."

After his return there was a shout of: "All of you into the big hall—the meeting's just going to begin!"

In contrast to all our previous meetings, this one could hardly be described as formal. We sat on boxes or sacks or leaned against the walls. As usual, the proceedings began with a political introduction. Our headmaster explained the pact to us, drawing attention particularly to the fact that the Western Powers had refused to negotiate on a basis of equality. Their intention had been to make use of the Soviet Union to fight for the interests of the western imperialist powers, but the great Stalin had seen through their game. The immediate conclusion of a pact with Germany had provided the conditions necessary for the Soviet Union to continue to live in peace and build up its power. He then went on to speak of our Home: "In the context of the new requirements of foreign policy, we too shall have to do some reorganisation."

By the phrase "some reorganisation" we were to understand the immediate closing of our Home. The new lines of policy were then announced by the headmaster in brief, cold and unemotional tones. Clearly no more trouble was to be taken to make the transition to the new situation easier for us to bear. Instinctively I had the impression that we had already been written off.

"All pupils of the Home who have not yet finished the 7th class will be transferred this afternoon to the Russian 'Spartak' Children's Home. The seniors will be able to go into a factory, where their accommodation will also be taken care of. Those who want to finish their ten-year course at school will be transferred with the juniors to the Russian Children's Home, where they will have to conform to the same regulations as all the other pupils in the Russian Home."

Within half an hour the whole thing was decided. The very same afternoon forty pupils joined the "Spartak" Children's Home.

From the outside the difference between the two homes did not seem so very great. True, the building was smaller, but it was still a very fine one. We shivered as we entered our new Home. We were greeted on our entry with a cry of: "Everyone into the hall at once!" It did not sound very friendly! We stood disconsolately in the hall, until a large, severe-looking, black-haired man came in, and shouted out crossly: "Get into line!" This was not the tone of voice we were accustomed to in our own Home, but reluctantly we obeyed.

Orders now began to shower down on us like a rain of blows: "No one is allowed to leave the Home without permission of one of the masters. All exercises will be done under the supervision of one of the masters. Everyone must conform to the established rules of the Home. Seniors have no right to expect special treatment. Smoking is strictly forbidden, even in the courtyard outside the Home. Anyone who smokes would be well advised to own up at once and give up his cigarettes. Anyone who does not can expect to be severely punished later on."

Most of us were between seventeen and nineteen years old, and some of us, including myself, had packets of cigarettes in their pockets. In our previous Home there had been no veto on smoking for the seniors.

The headmaster repeated threateningly: "For the last time, I call upon you to give up your cigarettes voluntarily. Anyone who does not do so can expect to be severely punished later."

One of us made a start and we all reluctantly followed his example one by one. We were then shown where we were to sleep. We were horrified when we saw the dormitory, with its primitive beds standing packed together in rows. The difference from our previous Home was appalling. A heretical thought passed through my mind: "There will certainly be no foreign delegations visiting us here!"

After that came the evening meal. It needs no saying that it was uneatable. But what depressed me most was not so much the change in our material conditions as the encroachment on my personal liberty, in being compelled to submit myself to strict regulations, and even to have to get special permission to go for a walk. Many of our younger friends were near to tears.

"It isn't nice here!" they cried. "Everything's so different from the Home we were in." I could never have imagined the difference between our own Home and a Russian Children's Home would be so great.

The date was the last week of August, 1939. It was five years since the establishment of Children's Home No. 6, the Home for the children of the members of the Austrian *Schutzbund* and the German émigrés, where I had spent three years. During the whole of that time we had got to know the Soviet Union from the point of view of young people growing up in privileged homes, with no daily worries and a life far above the average of the rest of the Soviet population. It is true that we had lived through the terrible years of the purge, but even so with nothing like the same intensity as people who spent their lives in other institutions and organisations.

Now our exceptional position had suddenly come to an end. The conclusion of a non-aggression pact with Hitlerite Germany and the closing of our Home had transformed us overnight into ordinary young citizens of the Soviet Union. It seemed barely credible that it was only two weeks since we had been travelling to the sea in a special bus provided by the Military Academy, to be treated as honoured guests at a party given by hundreds of officers.

It may be that Western readers will find this experience easy to understand if they remember that in the Soviet Union—and consequently also in this book—political events occupy an exceptionally important position, and personal experiences are generally relegated to the background. But how could it be otherwise in a country where political events are so directly involved in one's personal life? At the age of fourteen I had already experienced the beginning of the gigantic wave of arrests, which separated me from my mother; by the time I was fifteen there had followed the arrest of my teachers and masters, the trials, the savage attacks on personalities who had been held up to us only a few months before as examples to model ourselves on. At the age of sixteen I had witnessed the arrest of a pupil in the dormitory of our Children's Home, and at the age of seventeen and a half I had been made to realise that the fate of our Children's Home was at the mercy of a political arrangement made with a foreign power.

CHAPTER TWO

Life as a Soviet Student

"IF YOU CAN FIND a chance of a job, or of continuing your studies within five days, then there will be no objection to your release from the Home. If not, then you must stay here and submit to the conditions of the Home, just like everybody else," the headmaster of the Spartak Home explained to me in severe tones.

My decision had already been taken: I would not remain in the cheerless conditions of the Russian Spartak Children's Home at any price. I simply had to get out of the place, which had come to seem like a strait-jacket to me. So I was already in search of a school which would take students who had finished the 9th class, and provide me with a scholarship and accommodation.

My Escape: The Training Course

"Unfortunately, we cannot take anyone else—we've already had to turn down some of those who were expecting to come in August, because the course is already full up." This was the answer I got at the Moscow Teachers' Institute, which was established in an old building in the neighbourhood of the Kirovskaya Underground Station.

I showed my certificate of outstanding merit.

"Perhaps we can make one exception—come and see us again the day after to-morrow."

The "day after to-morrow" was the last of the five days' grace that my headmaster had given me.

On my way back from the Teachers' Institute I passed the Home in Kalashny Lane where I had once been so happy. By this time it had already been occupied by Russian children, but as it had been impossible to disperse our pupils quickly enough, the remainder of the Austrian and German children were allowed to retain two rooms for the time being. I was told that it would be possible for me to stay there for the time being if the Teachers' Institute could not provide me with anywhere to sleep at once.

The fifth day of my reprieve dawned. In trepidation I entered the building of the Teachers' Institute.

"We have been reconsidering your case. We shall be able to take you after all."

Overjoyed, I was beginning to congratulate myself and to feel as if I had already escaped from the Spartak Home and become a student of the Teachers' Institute; but I had congratulated myself too soon.

"It will be at least a week before the formalities are completed and we are able to send you an official notification of your admission here."

Another week—it was impossible for me to wait so long! The headmaster would never allow it. I simply had to have something in my pocket. A paper of some kind immediately—that was the only thing that could save me!

"Perhaps you would like to join the training course? In that case, we could take you at once, but you would lose a year."

It was all one to me at that moment: anything to get out of the Russian Home! I had no idea at all what was the purpose of this training course, but as soon as I heard them say they could take me on it at once, I had no hesitation. A few minutes later the certificate I so eagerly desired was in my hands: "This is to certify that Comrade W. Leonhard is a student on the training course of the Moscow Teachers' Institute for Foreign Languages."

Bursting with joy, I left the Teachers' Institute, and half an hour later I was back in the Spartak Home. Soon afterwards I was standing in front of the headmaster, who tried to look friendly and even congratulated me. I made my farewells to my German and Austrian friends who had been with me in Children's Home No. 6. We had lived together for so many years, and now they were to be absorbed into the Spartak Children's Home. They too wished me all good luck as the headmaster had, but there was more warmth and sincerity in their words than in his.

So, in September, 1939, began my life as a student on the training course of the Moscow Teachers' Institute for Foreign Languages.

One-year training courses for the academies were at that time fairly common in the Soviet Union. Their object was to train up a future generation for each particular academy, and to familiarise future students with their special subjects before they entered the academy. At the end of the year there was to be an examination, which was identical with the matriculation examination for the academy. As I was now a pupil on the training course I could assume with confidence that one year later, that is to say in September, 1940, I would be accepted in the Moscow Teachers' Institute for Foreign Languages, which was known as "M.U.I.I.Ya."

Instruction did not take place at the Institute, but

in the afternoons and evenings in rooms of a school in the centre of Moscow. Although my new companions were something like university students, the work of the training course was in many respects more like that of a school. There was a fixed curriculum of instruction, just as in a school, with classes and home-work to be done. There was a system of marks and many examinations to be passed, as is usual in all Soviet schools. More than half of the periods of instruction were devoted to the English language. As subsidiary subjects, which were nevertheless compulsory, we had Russian, Russian riterature and Russian history. I was delighted to have to do no more mathematics, physics, chemistry or technical drawing, and to be able to concentrate on the subjects which interested me.

Progress in the training course was very methodical, but also extremely slow. For the first three or four months we devoted ourselves exclusively to phonetics, since great emphasis was laid on the importance of pronunciation. All dictation was written in the international phonetic script. A great deal of time was devoted to the pronunciation of phonetic symbols, which we had to practise in front of mirrors in order to learn the correct position of the tongue and palate. It was not until the second six months that we got on to the English alphabet and written English at all.

This method of instruction may well seem extremely tedious by West European standards, but it had the advantage that when we got to our first English text, most of us already had an unusually good pronunciation; and this was really the only way of giving instruction in a foreign language in a country where one could hardly ever listen to an English broadcast, or see English or American films, or even read more than a few English or American books—quite apart from the fact that we naturally never had the opportunity of talking with English or American visitors. We were taught by a system which was at least suited to the Soviet way of life. I was particularly interested in the method of instruction in history, which had changed in many respects since the conclusion of the non-aggression pact with Germany.

Only a year earlier, for instance, the victory of Alexander Nevsky over the Teutonic Knights in the battle of Lake Peipus in April, 1242, had been habitually described as the most important event in Russian history. To-day, since the conclusion of the pact with Germany, this battle did not rate even a mention in a parenthesis. In its place particular emphasis was laid on the historical significance of Peter the Great's foreign policy, especially his supporting the creation of the Prussian state in the year 1701, which laid the foundation stone of the close collaboration between Prussian Germany and Russia, which to-day, etc., etc. . . . Then followed the familiar presentation of the historic significance of the pact between the Soviet Union and Germany.

The conclusion of the pact was also followed by noticeable changes in many other contexts. In the Library of Foreign Literature quantities of Nazi newspapers now took the place of the "émigré" newspapers. Numerous anti-Fascist novels by German expatriates had been removed from the library. The word "Fascism" ceased entirely to appear in the Soviet press; it was as if no such thing as Fascism had ever existed.

Changes in domestic policy appeared immediately after the conclusion of the pact. On the evening of the 23rd August, 1939, the well-known anti-Fascist Soviet film *Professor Mamlock* (from a play by Friedrich Wolf) and the film *The Oppenheim Family* (from a novel by Lion Feuchtwanger) were taken off at all the cinemas in the Soviet Union where they were appearing. All plays with anti-Fascist themes disappeared from the theatres the same night, including one called *The Sailors of Cattaro*, although this was a play about a naval mutiny in the year 1918, directed against the Austro-Hungarian monarchy. No doubt the theatrical censorship had come to the conclusion that in these affairs it was impossible to be too careful.

After the outbreak of the Second World War, with Hitler's attack on Poland on 1st September, the official explanation was that the war was simply an imperialist war on both sides, in which the Soviet Union had succeeded in remaining neutral thanks to the inspired genius of its foreign policy.

A few days later the first patriotic joke became current:

"Have you heard about our great new advance in aircraft production?"

"No, what is it?"

"Yesterday in Western Europe, twelve British and eight German aircraft were shot down in air battles."

"But what has that got to do with our aircraft production?"

"Why, it's obvious—we're twenty aeroplanes up."

On 17th September, 1939, when the Poles had

already been almost completely overrun by Hitler's armies, the entry of Soviet troops into Poland was announced. Thereupon mass meetings were held everywhere, including our own Institute of course, at which the measures taken by the Soviet Government were elucidated. The official justification for the entry of Soviet troops into Poland was based on the necessity of "protecting the lives and property of our cousins in the Western Ukraine and the western part of Belorussia." Yet only a few weeks before, the Soviet Union had proclaimed itself ready to protect and defend the Poles against attack by Hitler.

The campaign in Poland was soon over, and it was announced on 28th September that in addition to the non-aggression pact with Germany a treaty of friendship and an agreement about the new frontiers between the two countries, in what had previously been Polish territory, were to be concluded. Even after the conclusion of the treaty of friendship, the official party line stuck to its contention that the war was an imperialistic war on both sides.

We had long since learned, however, to pay careful attention to even the smallest indications in the newspapers and on the radio, so we could hardly fail to notice that in both cases the German war *communiqués* were invariably published in the first place, while the corresponding *communiqués* from England and France always took second place, and *Pravda* always gave more space to extracts from Hitler's speeches than to extracts from Churchill's. So it was not difficult for us to draw the conclusion that the trend of our official propaganda was substantially more favourable to Hitlerite Germany than to the western powers.

Good Resolutions in the Komsomol

The latest developments in foreign policy had increased the doubts I felt about many aspects of Soviet life, but they had not yet destroyed my fundamental confidence. So there is no inconsistency in the fact that it was at this time that I made particular efforts to join the Communist youth organisation of the Soviet Union. I sincerely wanted to become a good member of the *Komsomol*. I had already read much about members of the *Komsomol*—about their heroic deeds in the revolution and the Civil War and in the first Five Year Plan—and I had been particularly impressed by Nikolai Ostrovsky's book called *How the Steel was Tempered,* which had influenced so many young Soviet citizens, guiding them when they were in doubt and giving them new confidence, new strength and new energy.

The *Komsomol* was about to celebrate the twenty-first anniversary of its foundation. It was on 29th November, 1918, that the first All-Russian Congress of Working and Peasant Youth had proclaimed its solidarity with the Communist Party and adopted the name of the "Communist League of Youth." It was from this title in Russian that the abbreviation *Komsomol* eventually came.

The years of the Civil War were the heroic age of the *Komsomol*, and they were also a period of immense expansion. The number of members increased from 22,000 at the date of its foundation in November, 1918, to 400,000 at the beginning of 1920. At that time the *Komsomol* was not subjected to any politically unified control, requiring all its members to follow a party line laid down from above. Rather, it was a vigorous revolutionary organisation of young people, in which there were still many currents of opposition.

For instance, in 1920-21 an opposition movement broke out in the Ukrainian *Komsomol*, with the idea of founding an independent youth organisation for the Ukraine. This represented a trend in the same direction as the so-called *Borotbisti*, a group within the Bolshevik Party of the Ukraine, which was at that time fairly strong. The *Borotbisti* favoured a Socialist development of the Ukraine on its own, independently of Moscow.

Still more interesting was the trend represented in the *Komsomol* by the so-called "Young Syndicalists," who inclined towards the Workers' Opposition of Shlyapnikov. Their opposition was directed against the progressive centralisation of the economy and the apparatus of Government, and against the appointment by the State of directors to control nationalised enterprises: they demanded autonomy for the workers. The control of nationalised enterprises on this plan was to be exercised by elected councils of workers, their activity being co-ordinated at a higher level by elected councils of producers. This idea was not unlike the system of Workers' Councils introduced twenty-five years later in Yugoslavia after the breach with Moscow. In 1939, when I joined the *Komsomol*, these exciting trends of opposition and the disagreements between them were naturally characterised as dangerous deviations which it was the *Komsomol's* duty to destroy. To-day, they are no longer so much as mentioned.

After the death of Lenin in January, 1924, the organisation had grown rapidly in numbers. In October, 1924, the number of members was 700,000 and in

May, 1928, it had reached 2,000,000 but by this time its revolutionary ardour had waned. Independent movements and tendencies and ideas were crushed from above, and dependence on the Party was re-imposed, especially after Stalin's declaration that "the League is an instrument of the Party and a tool for doing the Party's work."

The *Komsomol* appeared to take on a vigorous new lease of life in 1928, when the first Five Year Plan got going. Just as in the Civil War, the members of the *Komsomol* vied with each other in enthusiasm, energy and versatility. Ten thousand of them took part in the building of the gigantic industrial instal-lations at Stalingrad and on the Dnieper, in the Urals and in Siberia. In the Far East there grew up a com-plete town built entirely by members of the *Komsomol* and named Komsomolsk in their honour. In the middle of the 1930's when the *Komsomol* num-bered about 4,000,000 members, there came a turning-point, as in so many other fields.

The programme, which had been both in form and content a reflection of the revolutionary times of Lenin, was replaced by a new one. Old ideas of the revolution, of internationalism and the struggle of the oppressed classes in every country, were pushed into the background. More and more their places were taken by ideas like "Soviet patriotism," "national consciousness" and "vigilance." Social origins, on which hitherto much emphasis had been laid, now played no significant part in enrolment into the *Komsomol*. What was decisive now was loyalty to the system. The educational functions of the *Komsomol* were now raised to a position of exceptional impor-tance: political education, sport and military train-

ing, as well as literary study, musical performances
and dances. The new slogan of "the happy life of
Soviet Youth" soon began to lose its appropriateness,
however, for not long afterwards came the great
purges of 1936 to 1938, which had a disastrous effect
even in the *Komsomol*.

Even Kosarev, the League's veteran Secretary-general, was not spared. Alexander Kosarev, who was now
thirty-five years old, had joined the *Komsomol* in 1918
immediately after its foundation. At the age of sixteen
he had taken part in the defence of Petrograd as a
member of the *Komsomol* and had then been through
the whole of the Civil War at the front. After his
return he was first elected Secretary of the Baumann
district of Moscow; in 1926 he became Secretary
of the Moscow Organisation; and since March, 1929,
he had been at the head of the whole *Komsomol* organisation as Secretary-general. Shortly before the end of
the purge the deadly hand of Yezhov's secret police
fell upon him. Kosarev and his closest associates in
the leadership of the *Komsomol* were accused of
being "double-crossers and moral degenerates." They
were public enemies. They had been attempting
to undermine the work of the *Komsomol*.

When I joined the *Komsomol* in the autumn of
1939 it already had nine million members, and the
purge lay far back in the past. My political preparation for enrolment in the *Komsomol* had lasted more
than a year. I had studied the programme and the
statutes; I had read the more important writings of
Lenin and Stalin; and naturally I had worked my way
through the *Short History of the Communist Party
of the Soviet Union*.

By this time I felt myself ripe for enrolment, so

I wrote an application to the appropriate section of the *Komsomol* in the usual form, setting out my wish to join the *Komsomol* and my political qualifications for doing so. A few days later, I was sitting in a bare room surrounded by Russian members of the *Komsomol*, who were looking me over attentively.

Now, we have here an application for enrolment from Comrade Leonhard, whose case we will deal with next," said the secretary. He read out my application. Silence reigned and I felt almost as if I were taking an examination. "As usual, it would probably be best if Comrade Leonhard would now give us a brief account of his life. Will comrades please listen carefully and then put questions?"

In this solemn, official atmosphere, I then had to tell the story of my life—a somewhat unusual one for Russian members of the *Komsomol*. A year or two earlier, at the time of the purges, I should certainly not have been admitted. No member of the *Komsomol* would have had the courage to support the application of a young man who had passed his childhood in Germany and whose mother had been arrested by the N.K.V.D. But now, in the autumn of 1939, the situation was entirely different. I was able to complete the story of my life without interruption.

"Are there any questions for Comrade Leonhard?" asked the secretary.

"What sort of social work have you done up till now?"

"I was on the staff of the wall-newspaper for a year at school, and for two years I was a member of the editorial board of the wall-newspaper at the Children's Home."

"What about your studies?"

"I had distinction in the sixth class and in the ninth class in the school year 1935-36. In the seventh and eighth classes, I got good marks in most subjects." My lower marks in 1937-38 were not held against me. It must have been the same with the others too: in the years of the purges, standards generally dropped.

"Have you been through the *Short History of the Communist Party of the Soviet Union?*"

"Yes," I replied. "I am prepared to answer questions on that." But no questions were asked. Clearly they had little appetite for going into the subject, of which they had already had more than enough. Instead, there followed the usual questions about the *Komsomol*.

"What are the most important duties of a member of the *Komsomol?*"

My reply faithfully followed the statutes: "The most important duties of every member of the *Komsomol* are as follows: to study the works of Marx, Engels, Lenin and Stalin; to improve his political knowledge continually; to encourage Marxist-Leninist studies among the broad masses of young people; to carry out the resolutions of the Bolshevik Party and the *Komsomol;* to take an active part in the political life of the country; to adopt a correct Socialist attitude towards labour; to protect the Socialist heritage and to oppose anything that threatens the stability of the Socialist state; to acquire scientific and technical knowledge and to take part in cultural life; to develop his physical fitness, to take part in sport and always be ready to give everything in his power, and if necessary his life, for the defence of the Socialist Fatherland; to take an active part in the work of the *Komsomol* organisation; to attend meet-

ings of the *Komsomol* regularly; to carry out the tasks
of the organisation quickly and precisely without
hesitation, and to pursue everything he undertakes
unfailingly to the end."

"Who is entitled to be enrolled in the *Komsomol?*"
was the next question.

"The *Komsomol* is open to young people aged between fifteen and twenty-six, who have familiarised
themselves with the statutes and programme of the
league, who have been active in one of its organisations, and who comply with all the rules of the
league and pay their subscriptions regularly."

"What is the organisational principle on which
the *Komsomol* rests?"

"The *Komsomol* rests on the principle of democratic centralism. This means that its controlling
organs are elected, the lower being subordinate to
the higher; the minority must conform to the majority and the agents of the *Komsomol* are responsible to
their organisations."

"Good! That's enough," said the secretary. "Are
there any other questions?"

There was a moment's silence.

"If there are no more questions to be put, then we
come to the voting. Will everyone in our group who
is in favour of Leonhard being enrolled in the *Komsomol* please raise his hand?"

Everyone present raised his or her hand; but even
this did not complete my admission to the *Komsomol.*

"Our proposal now goes to the Regional Committee of the *Komsomol.* You will receive notification
from there, and you will report to the Regional Committee at a time to be fixed."

About two weeks later I was summoned to the Regional Committee of the *Komsomol*. The Regional Secretary put a few questions and spoke about the honour implied in entry into the *Komsomol*, about the confidence that was thus being shown towards me, and about my duty to justify this confidence. Gravely, almost solemnly, he presented me with a little dark grey book bearing the inscription, "V.L. K.S.M." In replying that I would justify this confidence with all my might, I found myself again using the prescribed formula, but I uttered it with emotion and with sincere conviction.

A Western reader may possibly find this peculiar. My mother had been arrested, I had witnessed the arrest of my teachers and friends, and it goes without saying that I had long since realised that reality in the Soviet Union was completely different from the picture presented in *Pravda*. But somehow I dissociated these things, and even my personal impressions and experiences, from my fundamental political conviction. It was almost as if there were two separate levels—one of everyday events and experiences, which I found myself often criticising; the other that of the great party line which at this time, despite many hesitations, I still regarded as correct, from the standpoint of general principle.

I suppose that very many members of the *Komsomol* adopted a similar dissociation. For many of them this way of thinking was typical. Of course, there were (and still are) young people who joined the *Komsomol* without feeling any deep conviction. This fact soon became apparent to me, for from now onwards I regularly took part in league meetings and sessions and soon learned to recognise many different types among the members. In my own mind, they could be divided into four groups.

There were first the enthusiasts—young people bursting with activity and initiative who devoted themselves to the *Komsomol* with energy, devotion and self-sacrifice, but were not inclined to think very much about political problems, and seemed hardly even to notice the political contradictions or the abrupt changes of the party line. For them, the *Komsomol* offered the only outlet for their youthful vigour, but I often had the impression that another movement or organisation which offered the same opportunities would have been just as attractive to them.

Then there was another type of *Komsomol* member, to which I belonged myself at that time. Members of this type joined the organisation from political conviction and found themselves principally attracted by questions of the organisation's programme and political discussions. They were also active, though not to the same extent as the enthusiasts. They certainly saw many of the contradictions, and from time to time had serious scruples, but they pursued long and devious and often highly complicated lines of thought to justify everything to themselves.

The third type, comprising those whom I called "careerists," were to be found principally among the sons and daughters of officials of the Party, state, and economic organisations. They wanted to make something of their lives and often said so quite frankly. They saw in the *Komsomol* nothing but a springboard to enable them to advance their careers more quickly.

Finally, to my astonishment, I came upon a type which I could only describe as the "take-it-for-granted" type of *Komsomol* member. These were young people who had manifestly given no thought whatever to their enrolment in the *Komsomol*. They had simply joined it because that was what everybody else did, because their boy friends or girl friends were in the *Komsomol*, because it was the thing to do. I found this type mostly among the girls in the *Komsomol*, but they were by no means the only ones.

Altogether, I was a member of the Soviet *Komsomol* for six years. It was only after a considerable time, when I had made friends with a number of my colleagues sufficiently closely to be able to speak openly to them about my heretical ideas, that I realised to my great astonishment that I was not alone. I gradually found myself closer and closer to a few "opposition" members of the *Komsomol*. Here, unfortunately, I must avoid any more precise identification, in order not to endanger those concerned. One of my friends in the *Komsomol* confessed in a conversation I had with him to being an anarchist. My other friends in the opposition were Marxists and Leninists, but as they took the doctrines of Marx and Lenin seriously, they were on many points in opposition to the existing system, and especially to the omnipotence of the N.K.V.D. and the purge of the old-guard Bolsheviks. Once a girl in the *Komsomol* read me a poem which had been circulated in manuscript among such circles; it was a revolutionary ode to freedom. Later I heard of a novel written by an opposition member of the *Komsomol*, which others had copied out by hand and were circulating among those of their comrades who were completely reliable. The title of this novel was *Gulliver's Travels in the Land Where Walls Have Ears*.

The Shock of the Finnish War

In October, 1939, we read in *Pravda* that Finland
had rejected an offer by the Soviet Union to con-
clude a mutual assistance pact. We were told that
the Soviet Union had requested Finland to agree to
an adjustment of the frontier in the neighbourhood
of Leningrad to a depth of thirty kilometres, and had
been prepared to return to make territorial concessions to Finland five times as extensive.

At the time I found the Finnish attitude inexplicable. Like any other ordinary Soviet citizen I had no
other sources of information. I knew nothing of the
debates in the Finnish Parliament, and practically
nothing of the attitude adopted in Western Europe
and America towards the questiion. In particular, I
had absolutely no inkling of the fears felt by the Finnish population that the pact would prove to be the
beginning of the end of Finnish sovereignty—fears
which were to be justified only a few months later
by the examples of Estonia, Lithuania and Latvia.

The tone adopted by *Pravda* towards Finland was
now becoming daily more hostile. In the second half
of October, references to the Finnish Government
ceased altogether and were replaced by phrases like
"the Finnish ringleaders, adventurers, gamblers." The
names of influential Finnish personalities were always
accompanied by abusive epithets.

On 29th November, the powder-barrel exploded:
Soviet troops crossed the Finnish frontier. It was officially announced that Finnish troops had committed
a series of provocative encroachments across the
Soviet frontier, but this was not taken very seriously,
even by those who were generally unqualified supporters of the régime. Whenever in conversation with

them one used the official formulæ about the Finnish aggression, the usual reply took the form of the familiar wink which was later to become so much a part of my experience.

A few days after the beginning of the Russo-Finnish war an announcement was made with a great flourish of the capture of the first town in Finland, Terioki, and of the establishment of a Finnish People's Government under the presidency of Kuusinen. This newly established Government had launched an appeal to the Finnish people and had even awarded honours to the unit which was to be the first to march into Helsinki.

After the first rapid advance and the capture of Terioki, the Soviet troops were held up on the Mannerheim Line. There were many reports of heavy losses and the so-called "minor action" of the Leningrad Military District changed into a full-scale war. This was something inconceivable to us. The great, glorious, invincible Soviet Army, which had always been paraded in our eyes as the most powerful in the world, was now in a state of war against little Finland whose population numbered only three and a half million.

Even more extraordinary than the weeks of deadlock on the front was all the confusion in the transport and rationing system. From the very first days of the war there had been hours of delay and even complete stoppages of passenger trains. A few days after the war broke out there were already queues to be seen in front of the bread shops in Moscow. Many kinds of provisions were never delivered at all.

People in Moscow began to ask at that time what would happen when the Soviet Union was driven to fight a really serious war against a great power, if even a localised conflict with a minor country was accompanied by such disorganisation? Public anxiety found expression in a little rhyme, which went the rounds in Moscow in whispers at that time:

> "There's nothing on now,
> And there's nothing to be had.
> What shall we have
> When there's really something on?"

Three weeks had already passed since the outbreak of war. At first it was commonly said that the war would certainly be over by Stalin's birthday. But Stalin's birthday on 21st December went by, and still the war was not at an end. The months of winter passed. Every day we read on the front page of *Pravda*, towards the bottom of the left-hand column, the *communiqué* of the Leningrad Military District. It consisted exclusively of accounts of the capture of strongly defended points: names of towns were never mentioned, since none were being captured.

Although the war was unpopular, I believed like many of my friends that in the end it would be fought to a successful conclusion. After all, the new Finnish People's Government had now been established for some time and the members of the official Finnish Government had been so frequently described as murderers, bandits and Fascists, that we could hardly believe the Soviet Union would in the end conduct negotiations with this same Government. All the greater was our surprise, then, when suddenly on 12th March, 1940, a peace treaty was signed in Finland. By this treaty the Soviet Union obtained the Karelian

Peninsula and the town of Vyborg, and at certain other points the frontier was adjusted to the advantage of the Soviet Union. Finally, the Soviet Union obtained a lease of the Hangö Peninsula. But all these results fell far short of our expectations at the beginning of the war.

The fact was that the Soviet Government had signed a peace treaty with the same Finnish leaders whom *Pravda* a few weeks before had been describing as adventurers and gamblers. Everywhere mass meetings were held, at which the termination of the war was represented as an indication of the peaceful policy of the Soviet Union and of its leader, Stalin. As usual, it was announced at the end of every meeting that the speaker would answer questions—and for once there were questions.

"I do not understand, Comrade speaker," I heard one student ask. "There has been a Finnish People's Government in existence for several months, but it is not mentioned at all in the treaty. What has happened to the People's Government?"

The speaker was somewhat embarrassed. "That is a question which I cannot answer on the spot. There is no mention of it in the official *communiqué*. There can be no doubt, however, that our Soviet Government will take the necessary steps in this matter."

From one of my friends who worked in a factory, I learned that the same question had been put there too. The lecturer, a man of working-class origin, dealt with the question quite simply: "Well, for Christ's sake, the People's Government—what in God's name ever became of that? Nobody told us anything about it at our agitation briefing!"

As these questions had evidently come up at many

meetings, a few days later an article was published in *Pravda* stating that as a result of the Soviet-Finnish Treaty, a new situation had been created and the People's Government had been dissolved. With this incidental paragraph, the fate of the Finnish People's Government was settled. The war was at an end, and thereafter, for reasons which are easily understood, it was very seldom mentioned again, for the Soviet-Finnish War of 1939-40 had been one of the greatest political and military miscalculations of the Soviet Union.

While the war was still going on, I had had several conversations with a few of my friends with whom I had been in the habit of cautiously exchanging ideas even during the time of the purges. Each of them had a different explanation to account for the failure of Soviet arms: "The Red Army was clearly not ready for the campaign." "The military strength of Finland had been seriously underestimated." "The political expectations linked with the establishment of the People's Government were not justified by events." "The Soviet Army had been decimated and crippled by the great purge and the mass arrests of generals and senior and middle-grade officers." To this day, I still believe that the last argument contains the real reasons for the failure of the Soviet campaign in Finland in 1939-40.

Many years later, when I had reached the West, I was astonished to hear the opinion expressed that the Soviet Union had deliberately conducted the war in Finland so feebly in order to mislead foreign countries and to create an impression of military weakness among them. In my view, this opinion is completely mistaken. It had seldom been so much in the Soviet Union's real interests to appear strong as it was at just that time, so soon after the outbreak of the war in Europe and while the U.S.S.R. was partner to a treaty with Hitlerite Germany. It was of greater consequence to her at that time than at any other to be considered a strong, great power, in order to be accepted by Hitlerite Germany as an equal partner, and to strengthen her position as the one great power not involved in the World War and therefore well placed to be courted by the rest and gain concessions from them.

A clear indication that the Finnish war disclosed a real and not a fictitious weakness of the Red Army is to be found in the fact that the great reorganisation of that army began just a few weeks after the war ended. There was no compunction then even about recalling arrested officers from the concentration camps to entrust them with new commands. At the beginning of May, 1940, Voroshilov, the veteran People's Commissar for Defence, was replaced by Marshal Timoshenko.

Shortly after that personal ranks were introduced for the highest positions of command in the Red Army and Navy; and at the beginning of July punishments for desertion or wilful dereliction of duty were drastically increased. The practice of saluting was strictly enforced, and new regulations governing charges and arrests were brought in. Finally, in the autumn of 1940, the disciplinary regulations which had been enforced since 1925 were replaced by new and severer regulations in which special emphasis was laid on unconditional obedience to superior orders, and failure to comply with an order was designated as a crime.

The great reorganisation of the Red Army was not the only event that marked the period between the spring and autumn of 1940. This was also the time when the emphasis on friendship with Hitlerite Germany was most marked.

Moscow During the Hitler-Stalin Pact

Our great surprise over the non-aggression pact of 23rd August, 1939, and the friendship pact of 28th September, had died down. People in the Soviet Union, including myself, were now used to the new facts of the situation. It had become something virtually to be taken for granted that there were no more anti-Fascist films or anti-Fascist books; we were constantly reminded with increasing pride that the genius of the Soviet Union's peaceful policies had kept us out of the conflict; and it was frequently hinted more or less openly that the war between the Western Powers on the one hand and Hitlerite Germany and Italy on the other hand could only be a source of profit to the Soviet Union.

From the beginning of 1940 there was a buzz of rumours to the effect that relations with Germany were going to become even closer. There was even talk from time to time about the possibility of a military alliance between Germany and the Soviet Union, and there were many people in Moscow at the time who believed in the possibility. In the middle of February, 1940, the conclusion of a new economic agreement between Hitlerite Germany and the U.S.S.R. was enthusiastically welcomed. There were innumerable articles about the imperialist plans of England and France for world domination, and ex-

tracts from Hitler's speeches were frequently reproduced.

The emphasis on the responsibility of England and
France for the war became increasingly marked in
the Soviet press. "The war caused by the conspiracy
of the French and British imperialists to maintain
their predominance has now lasted six months,"
wrote *Pravda* at the beginning of March, 1940, "but
the Anglo-French imperialists have so far achieved no
success with their plans for a new division of the
world. To get out of their impasse they are constantly
planning new adventures with the object of turning
the present imperialist war into a new World War."
This new line was hammered home at innumerable
meetings of the Soviet population.

At the beginning of April, *Pravda* published long
extracts from the so-called "White Book" of Hitler's
Foreign Office, with corroborative comments. Even
Hitler's attack on Denmark and Norway was justified.

It was now beyond all possibility of doubt that the
official line no longer rested on absolute neutrality.
The tendency to side more and more closely with
Hitlerite Germany became clearer every day. Generally speaking, the policy of absolute neutrality in
the first weeks after the peace had been popular, but
the new turn of events which succeeded it caused
doubts in many people's minds. In one of the Moscow
academies a student had even dared to give open expression to the misgivings which were now widespread. This happened after a lecture about the Marxist-Leninist theory of justified and unjustified wars.
The lecturer had been expounding the distinction

between just and unjust wars: a just war could never be a war of conquest, but only a war of liberation, either to protect a people against external attack or against attempts to keep them under subjection. Examples were the liberation of a people from the enslavement of capitalism, or of colonies from the yoke of imperialism. Unjust wars, on the contrary, were wars of aggression and conquest in which the object was to overrun foreign countries and enslave foreign peoples. He analysed all the various well-known wars of history, and ended his lecture by pointing out that it was the duty of Marxist-Leninists to analyse every particular war and then to formulate their attitude towards the war in question.

As always, the lecturer had expressed his willingness at the end of the lecture to answer questions from the students. One student then expressed himself as follows: "Comrade lecturer, a few days ago we heard of the beginning of military operations by Germany against Denmark and Norway, which according to *Pravda* were necessary. How should these military operations be designated? Can they be called a just war? In that case, is the war unjustified on the part of the Norwegians and Danes?"

A breathless hush fell on the lecture hall.

The question was exceedingly unwelcome to the lecturer. He extricated himself by explaining that these questions could not be handled in so formal and theoretical a fashion, but must be examined in the light of their wider context and "the balance of reciprocal influences." To apply terms like "just" and "unjust" in the present case was an inaccurate and unscientific way of looking at the question,

which could not therefore be answered in the form
in which it was put.

Although we students, like other strata of the population no doubt, were very uneasy about the correctness of the party line, I observed to my astonishment
on the other hand that the new line towards Hitler's
Germany was not without effect on the formation
of public opinion in general. One morning when I
was passing a newspaper kiosk, I heard two men,
neither of them particularly well-dressed, talking
about the war in Western Europe.

"This Hitler's a pretty good chap, putting Europe
to rights," said one of them.

"He's certainly giving them a good thrashing, those
Anglo-French imperialists and warmongers," agreed
the other.

Another time I was asked, "Did those Nazi concentration camps we used to hear so much about a
little while ago really exist, or were they perhaps just
propaganda inventions by the Anglo-French imperialists?"

At this date I was spending relatively little time
in German émigré circles. I had only a single opportunity of a talk with the Communist poet Erich
Weinert, who later became President of the National
Committee for Free Germany. His daughter, Marianne, had been a friend of mine since childhood,
and I used to visit her sometimes in the New Writers'
Club in the Lavrushinsky Alley. When Erich
Weinert came into the room, I asked him what attitude a German anti-Fascist ought to take nowadays
towards the whole situation. Erich Weinert, whom
I found personally very sympathetic, replied by speak-

ing of the completely altered situation, and about changed requirements and new perspectives which were entirely different from what we had previously supposed. "The Non-aggression and Friendship Pact of September, 1939," he said, "is perhaps only the beginning, in which case we have certainly to reckon with the possibility of an even more far-reaching collaboration with Germany."

This was a point of view which I heard frequently expressed in the first half of 1940. There was much talk at that time of the possibility of a military alliance with Hitlerite Germany, and some people even went so far as to talk of the possibility of joint military action against the western imperialists.

When Hitler's attack on Belgium, Holland and France began on 10th May, 1940, the battles in France were followed with great interest by the population of Moscow. There were long queues waiting patiently at the newspaper kiosks for the morning papers or the *Vechernaya Moskva*, which was the only Moscow evening paper. Most people read the newspapers without giving voice to any comments. Comment was a practice which had gone out of fashion completely in the years of the purge.

A representative of Soviet Intelligence told me at that time that Hitler's attack on France had led to a swing of opinion in Intelligence circles in Moscow. "So long as the war was confined to Poland and Scandinavia, most of us were neutral; some even sympathised a bit with Hitler. The attack on France has completely changed all that. A noticeable antipathy to Hitler is gradually emerging. It is not so much out of sympathy for England as from a feeling for the tragedy of France, in particular. Many Intelligence

people feel themselves spiritually linked with France."
I had noticed a similar change among the students,
too, but I am not sure whether the same swing of
opinion was yet to be noticed at this time among
other sections of the population.

On 15th June, 1940, the Moscow morning papers
carried the news of the capture of Paris by the German Army. I had just bought a newspaper and was
going by tram towards Taganka Square. Beside me
was sitting an older man, obviously a peasant, who had
presumably come on a visit to Moscow.

"Now, young man, what's the news about the war
in France?"

"German troops have entered Paris," I told him.

He clapped his hands with pleasure. "Hitler's certainly shown those French!"

None of the other passengers in the tram who heard
him had a word to say against it, but a few minutes
later I was back again at a newspaper kiosk. There
I saw a young boy of Jewish appearance, perhaps
fourteen years old, open the newspaper and read the
news of the capture of Paris with visible emotion.
"Paris is taken!" he cried sadly, and tears came to
his eyes. Then he ran home, no doubt to tell his parents the unhappy news. So diverse were the reactions
of people in Moscow at that time.

The end of the campaign in France and the beginning of the air battles over Great Britain did not attract so much attention, however, because in the
meantime the whole country was taken by surprise,
unexpectedly as always, by domestic political events
which now occupied the foreground for weeks and
months on end.

On 26th June, 1940, an appeal by the Central

Committee of the Soviet Trade Unions was published on the front page of *Pravda*, proposing that working time in all factories should be increased from seven to eight hours and from six to eight hours for clerical workers. Even the working day of young people between sixteen and eighteen, who had hitherto worked only six hours, was now to be extended to eight hours. Instead of the six-day week which had hitherto been used, the Trade Unions were also proposing to adopt the seven-day week as elsewhere. (Until now, unlike every other country in Europe, the week in the Soviet Union had consisted of five working days and one free day; even the names of the days of the week had been abolished and they were known as Day 1, Day 2 and so on.)

The proposal of the Trade Union leaders was not limited merely to a lengthening of the working day and the working week. They also intended to abolish freedom of choice in the place of work. The exact text was as follows: "The Central Committee of the Soviet Trade Unions considers that workers and employees in national, party and communal enterprises should not be allowed to leave their place of work, nor to change from one factory or office to another without permission." Naturally, it was clear that these proposals by the Trade Unions would soon be followed by a decree of the Government, which was duly published the very next morning. There then followed the organised campaign of unanimous welcome for the proposal.

All the measures proposed by the Trade Unions— the extension of the working day to eight hours, the change to a seven-day week and the ban on changing places of employment—were included in the decree of the Presidium of the Supreme Soviet. In paragraph 5, the resolutions forbidding workers to leave their place of work were formulated as follows: "Workers and employees who leave their state, co-operative, or communal factories or enterprises without permission will be prosecuted, and on conviction by the People's Court will be sentenced to terms of imprisonment from two to four months." Not only were the workers threatened with sentences of imprisonment; so too were the factory directors if they failed to exercise sufficiently strict control.

Although, strictly speaking, we were not immediately affected by this law, naturally a meeting of the students on the training course was held as soon as it was published. The law of 26th June had to be regarded as a directive for increased activity in studies on our part as well, we were told. Naturally, we too welcomed it unanimously. Not long afterwards, the law was made even more severe. An order by the People's Commissariat for Justice, dated 22nd July, 1940, decreed that twenty minutes' lateness at work was to be regarded as punishable absence. The punishment was to be disciplinary educational work at one's place of work for up to six months, subject to a reduction of pay by 25 per cent.

The "20-minute law" had devastating effects. I heard about what was going on from former pupils at our Home who were now working in factories—and it was appalling. Transport facilities in most areas were so bad that there were many cases of workers being twenty minutes late through no fault of their own, but no excuses were accepted. The factory directors were in a panic of terror themselves. The number of those prosecuted or condemned to disciplinary educational work reached astronomical figures. In spite of the grim seriousness of the situation, there was soon a joke circulating in Moscow about the law:

"Have you heard—the Bolshoi Theatre has been burnt to the ground?"

"How did that happen? Couldn't the fire brigade stop it?"

"No. The fire brigade is in prison."

"In prison?"

"Yes, they came twenty minutes late, so instead of being allowed to put out the fire, they were sent to prison for disciplinary educational work."

The wave of arrests and sentences on the basis of the new Labour Law soon reached such a scale that the courts could no longer keep up with their work. So a special dispensation of the Presidium laid it down on 10th August, 1940, that all cases involving offences against the labour legislation could be tried by People's Courts without empanelling assessors. These events came to occupy so central a position in the life of every inhabitant of the Soviet Union that others were hardly noticed at all. The collapse of France, the air battles over England, the occupation of the Baltic States by Soviet forces and their conversion into Republics of the U.S.S.R., the annexation of Bessarabia and the northern part of Bukovina to the Soviet Union—all paled into significance in comparison with the struggle against so-called skirkers, idlers and disruptive elements.

Outside this context only one event has remained in my memory—the death of Trotsky.

On 24th August, every Soviet newspaper carried in a conspicuous position a short notice of Trotsky's death. It was stated that, according to reports in American newspapers, an attempt on Trotsky's life had been made by one of his own entourage. His skull had been fractured and he had died in a sanatorium in Mexico.

The announcement was restricted to these few lines in every newspaper in the Soviet Union, except *Pravda*, the central organ of the Party, which continued to abuse Lenin's colleague even after his death in a longer article under the title of "death of an International Spy." The article was full of abuse and distortions of history. "Trotsky had been an agent of foreign Intelligence Services and an international spy since 1921," said the article in so many words. Referring to the former chairman of the Petrograd Soviet in 1917 and the founder of the Red Army, *Pravda* ended with the words: "This contemptible creature's life ended as it deserved. He has gone to the grave bearing the mark of Cain as an international spy and murderer."

The same evening, as I was going for a walk, I met a former member of the *Schutzbund* who was now working in a Soviet factory. Inevitably we started talking about Trotsky's death.

"Can it really have been one of his entourage?" he said, and went on to express the very same thought which had occurred to me while I was reading the announcement; but of course neither of us had any inkling of the real course of events that had led up to Trotsky's death. We continued our walk a little way. On the advertising pillars, large notices were just being put up announcing a popular festival which was to take place in the Park of Culture.

"Do you know what some of the workers in the

factory are saying? They say that this festival has been announced now just because of Trotsky's death."

I did not reply. In spite of the end of the purges, it was still too dangerous to talk about Trotsky. I thought it interesting, however, that in August 1940, thirteen years after Trotsky's expulsion from the party and eleven years after he had been exiled from the Soviet Union, there were still a few workers who did not believe the official version of Trotsky's death and considered Stalin capable of celebrating the death of the revolutionary by a popular festival.

At the Academy for Foreign Languages

In the summer of 1940, the training course for the Institute came to an end. The final examinations were soon over. A few days later, full of anxiety, I was waiting in the rooms of the reception commission of the Moscow Educational Academy at No. 38 Metrostroevska. It was a large, old, three-story building about half-way between the underground stations of the Palace of Soviets and the Park of Culture. Fellow students told me that an earlier academy had been housed in this building too, and that Gogol and other Russian poets had studied there.

"So you have been through the preparatory course for the Teachers' Institute. Why didn't you go straight on to study there?" I was asked.

"I had a special feeling for your academy."

The reception official laughed. "Well, we'll soon see what the meaning of that is. Are you ready to do our entrance examination?"

"Yes, certainly. When shall I do it?"

"Not so fast! First of all, please fill in this questionnaire and bring it back to-morrow, and then we'll see."

It was a very detailed questionnaire. Naturally, there was a series of questions about my parents, and in the appropriate space for my mother I wrote the reply which was so common at that time: "Arrested by agents of the N.K.V.D." This was the official formula which one had to use to indicate arrests in answer to a questionnaire. Before I handed it in, I inquired from one of my friends among the students: "What happens if I put down about my mother's arrest? Will it damage my prospects? Are there any special regulations?"

He laughed dryly. "As if you were the only one to come out with that! It's all in the day's work now! If the examining commission were going to be sticky about that sort of thing, one might as well close all the academies."

Another student gave me much the same information. "In 1937 and for part of 1938, all applications in which the parents were put down as arrested used to be marked with a cross. It was said that the examinations were particularly strict in these cases, but they soon gave that up, because it was making it obvious to the examiners how widespread the wave of arrests had become."

My two friends were right. In reading my questionnaire, the chairman of the reception commission passed without comment over the part where the arrest of my mother was put down.

"You can do your entrance examination in about two weeks. Till then, we'll give you a card so that you can eat here. There'll be nothing to prevent your being admitted to the students' hostel as soon as you have passed the examination."

I went off delighted, and spent the next two weeks, as so often before, working in preparation for the examination. In the middle of August I received a short note: "This is to certify that Comrade Leonhard is enrolled in the preliminary course of the Moscow State Educational Academy for Foreign Langauges." A few days later my admission to the students' hostel was also arranged.

On 1st September, 1940, when the freshmen joined the Academy for the first time, each of us was put down for one of three faculties—German, English or French. I chose the English faculty. All the faculties together attended lectures in education, psychology, the history of education, Marxism-Leninism, and military training. Besides these general subjects, we had lectures on English history, English literature, phonetics, and English grammar and philology. These lectures were naturally attended only by the students of the appropriate term in our English faculty. As soon as we had decided on our particular faculty, we received a detailed lecture programme. Attendance at all lectures was compulsory, and it was carefully checked.

I was astonished at the sumptuous manner in which the Academy was equipped. Besides the large lecture halls and an exceptionally fine library, there were also "studies" or small rooms allotted to each of the particular subjects which were studied at the Academy: psychology, education, phonetics, history, and literary history. In these studies, one could find the most important specialised literature on that particular field and here, too, the Dean of the faculty in question or one of his colleagues was to be found always ready to be consulted.

But the pride of the Academy was the Marr Study which was devoted exclusively to the Soviet philologist, Nikolai Yakovlevich Marr. Marr's writings were held up to us at that time as the most important published work on philology, and in the study bearing his name was to be found a statue of him larger than life. His philological theories were then practically as inviolable as the writings of Stalin. They were presented to us as a theory founded on Marxism-Leninism, which had given the death blow to bourgeois conceptions of philology. In contrast to bourgeois ideas, it was explained that Marr treated language as a part of the "super-structure," arguing that its evolution could be understood only in association with the evolution of society. Human beings had produced their language in the course of their work and in particular social conditions, and language changed continually with the changes in the conditions governing the social structure of their life. None of us would have dared at that time even to dream of the idea that the great unassailable Marr would ten years later be attacked by Stalin in terms as unequivocal as those in which we were now taught to praise him.

At this date there were about 2,500 young Soviet students at the Moscow Academy for Foreign Languages—2,440 girls and 60 men. Of all the Academies in the whole Soviet Union, it could point to the largest percentage of women students. This was the reason why it was jokingly known in student circles in Moscow as the "Institute of the Virtuous Maidens," but it was known not only for its virtuous maidens, but also for its foreign students—the sons and daughters of émigrés and functionaries of the

Comintern or of Soviet diplomats who had been many years abroad.

Before long I had found good friends not only among the Russian students but also among the foreign ones. Among them was a Pole who had fought in the International Brigade in Spain. There were also a young American girl, a Korean girl, and a Soviet girl who had spent many years in Harbin because her parents were working in the management of the Manchurian Railway. I was also able to enjoy a happy reunion with many of the former students of the German Karl Leibknecht School.

In spite of these unusual features, our Academy was a typical Soviet Academy. As in all other Academies, our studies included what was called social work—the distinctive feature of which was the *Komsomol* or Party meeting (a number of students being already Party members). *Komsomol* meetings in the Academy were not very different from any others, and were generally conducted perfunctorily and without enthusiasm. Almost the only questions discussed were practical ones, such as how so-and-so was getting on with his studies; whether he was doing well in "socialist competition," and so on. Political questions were practically never dealt with except when national holidays came round; for instance, immediately before the 1st of May, the anniversary of the Revolution on 7th November, or Red Army Day on 23rd February. Even then, we had to listen to the usual standard lecture, which was given automatically on these days at every institution and factory, so that the one privilege members of the *Komsomol* had from the political point of view was that of hearing the same lecture twice. Even less

active were the so-called "mass organisations," to
which naturally every member of the *Komsomol* also
belonged.

Then there was the *Osoaviakhim* (the Society for
the Promotion of Defence against Air Attack and
Chemical Warfare), whose task was to train para-
chutists at special "aero clubs" and to organise
courses in rifle shooting and in defense against air
and chemical warfare. In practice, however, our
role in this society was limited to the duty of paying
our subscriptions and attending lectures on air-raid
defense three or four times a year.

Another organisation of which very little was heard
in our Academy, as in other institutions, was the
M.O.P.R. (known in English as the "International
Class-War Prisoners' Aid"), upon which many
émigrés were dependent. All that happened was that
meetings of the M.O.P.R. were convened on 18th
March, the day of the Paris Commune, which had
been chosen as the day of the M.O.P.R. On 18th
March, 1941, Wilhelm Pieck spoke to us and gave
a review of the international situation.

The third mass organisation which I belonged to,
like all other members of the *Komsomol* at our Academy, was the "League of Militant Atheists." This
organisation, too, had long since completely lost
all significance. On the one hand, a new policy towards the Church was already beginning to emerge
at the end of the 1930's, which became all the more
pronounced during the war. On the other hand, this
organisation was in practice superfluous so far as
students and members of the *Komsomol* were concerned. We had grown up without any religious instruction and we remained completely unmoved by

these questions, to which we gave no thought whatever. I, at least, never met a single person of my own generation in my circle of acquaintance during the ten years I lived in the Soviet Union who was not an atheist. In the spring of 1942, by which time I was no longer living in Moscow, we received a brief, curt communication without any explanation: "The League of Militant Atheists is dissolved."

The decision to dissolve the League was not published in the press. From the spring of 1942 onwards the League was simply not mentioned again. True to the Soviet practice of projecting the course of present policy back into the past and altering the interpretation of history accordingly, the authorities took a further step, too. There was no longer any mention of the fact, even in the new edition of the Soviet Encyclopædia, that such an organisation as the League of Militant Atheists ever had existed.

Ever since the great purge came to an end at the beginning of 1939, I had lived in the conviction that the terrible denunciations and the iniquities of police spies were over. I regarded them as an inseparable part of the period of the purge, but soon I was to learn that I was wrong. I had made friends with a girl student whom I do not intend to describe more precisely because she is still living in the East today. She was one of the few people to whom I could speak openly. During our long walks in the Park of Culture, or along the Moskva River, we used to talk about all the things that interest young people in every country; and sometimes even about the things that oppressed us in the Soviet Union, which we both felt a passionate need to discuss. One day, when I met her in the corridor of the Academy she whispered to me: "Volodya (this was the name by which I was known in the Soviet Union), I must talk to you this evening alone about something very serious."

I waited anxiously for the evening. The first thing she did was to exact a promise from me: "Promise me that in no circumstances will you ever tell anyone what I'm going to say to you now."

I promised, and I have never broken the promise.

"Promise me, too, that you will never show by your behaviour that you know my secret."

When I had given her this promise too, she went on haltingly: "For the last few days I have been working for the N.K.V.D. I was sent for and made to sign a paper stating that I was ready to give all the information I was asked for, and never to tell anyone about my activities. Now I have to write regular reports about certain students. I have been given a new name for this work, and I have to sign it under my reports."

"What have you got to report on? Derogatory remarks about the Party?"

"Not only that. There wouldn't be much to write about if it were only that. I have to report on everything I am told by the people assigned to me—everything that has anything to do with politics, however indirectly."

"And am I on your list?"

"No: not so far, but I'm sure that I shall be questioned about you too. I've been told that this is only the beginning, and later on further names will be added. I don't know if I shall be able to manage to leave out things you say to me. I don't believe I shall, and that's why I beg you from this day onwards never to have a political conversation with me again."

I looked her in the eyes. She was very sad—sad that

she could no longer speak openly with me, which had hitherto been such a relief for her as well as for me; but above all, it seemed to weigh on her heart that now she had to work for the N.K.V.D. I could see it all clearly, but after what she had told me I knew she had no other choice. To have refused would have put her under suspicion herself, and probably led to her arrest.

That she had told me of her recruitment and even described it in detail—detail which I have avoided reproducing in order to give no clue to the N.K. V.D.—was probably the greatest proof of friendship that I have ever received in my whole life. Deeply impressed as I was by this, I was nevertheless equally horrified by what she had told me. She was certainly not the only one. There must have been other students, both boys and girls, who were sending in running commentaries in writing on all the conversations which they heard in the Academy and the Students' Hostel to the N.K.V.D.

How many could there be of them? I went over in my mind all the men and women students whom I knew. Which of them would be reporting to the N.K.V.D.? I could not believe it possible of any of my acquaintances, but could I be so sure? Would I ever have guessed that this particular girl had to write reports for the N.K.V.D.? What guarantee could there be that the other students whom I knew were not compelled to do the same thing? Would they have the courage to tell me, and thus give away something which they had strictly bound themselves to keep secret? An uneasy feeling came over me. Every single political statement, however trivial, was perhaps being taken down in writing and sent in a weekly

report to the N.K.V.D. I was myself not opposed to
the system, but did I not occasionally say something
which did not exactly correspond to the party line?
From that day on, I resolved to be even more cautious
than before about keeping to the party line in any
political conversation, and to get away from political
subjects as quickly as possible and confine myself
to neutral topics.

2nd October, 1940: the Great Blow

Four weeks after I had joined the Academy, we
were suddenly informed on the morning of 3rd October, 1940, without any warning, of an abrupt
change affecting the life of the whole student body.
Someone who happened to be out on the streets early
in the morning had brought a newspaper with him,
and was knocking at the doors with the cry: "Our
scholarships have been abolished."

"The fool's gone off his head!" said the boy who
shared my room, but he dressed in a hurry nevertheless.

I did the same. As we came out into the corridor,
we found the early riser already surrounded by a group
of students. He had *Pravda* in his hands, and was reading a decree of the Council of People's Commissars
of the U.S.S.R. introducing compulsory fees for
students in the higher classes and academies of the
U.S.S.R.

"Having regard to the improvement in the
material well-being of the workers," he began reading;
and this kind of preamble made us fear the worst.
There then followed the introduction of school fees
for the three top classes in the secondary schools.
Next came a blow which affected us:

"The following will be the level of payment for students at the Academies of the U.S.S.R.:

"(a) At Academies in Moscow, Leningrad and the capitals of constituent Republics—400 roubles *per annum*.
"(b) At Academies in other towns—300 roubles *per annum*.
"(c) At Academies of Music, the Arts and Theatre—500 roubles *per annum*.

"Fees will be paid to the appropriate institution in two equal annual payments on the 1st September and 1st February. N.B.: payment must be made for the first half of the school year, 1940-41, not later than 1st November this year."

Long faces were to be seen everywhere, not only because of the introduction of students' fees, but more particularly because of the fact that the first installment had to be paid by 1st November.

"We've still got twenty-seven days," said someone; but it sounded hopeless.

We still thought that perhaps part of our scholarships could be diverted to pay the students' fees, but then the next blow fell: the same decree simultaneously abolished our monthly scholarship allowances. In future, scholarships were to be given only to exceptional students.

As usual, meetings were held to justify the alterations in the regulations for the allotment of scholarships, as the official formula had it, and the introduction of fees for schools and students. At our Academy this meeting went according to plan. When the speaker had finished, the customary ap-

plause followed. We were then asked whether anything remained to be cleared up or anyone wished to
ask questions or express his opinions. No one took
advantage of the opportunity.

One student told me a few days later that at the
Moscow Academy the Deputy Minister for Education had spoken on the new law. After his address a
student had put the question, in front of the whole
meeting, how the new law was to be reconciled with
Article 121 of the Constitution of the U.S.S.R. It
was a delicate question, for in fact Article 121 of the
Constitution of the U.S.S.R. expressly laid it down
that education should be free in all educational institutions of the U.S.S.R., including academies. The
Deputy People's Commissar had explained that the
justification for this measure was included in the law,
and the appropriate paragraph of the constitution
would be amended accordingly to conform with the
new law. This was duly done. It was not the first time
that laws had been enacted in the Soviet Union
which were in conflict with the constitution.

But what worried the students after this date was
not whether the law was contrary to the constitution,
but what they were to do now. As the introduction
of students' fees came simultaneously with the abolition of scholarships, it was practically impossible
for many of the children of workers or kolkhoz peasants to continue their studies. I myself saw many
tear-stained faces at that time, and we had to say good-
bye for good to many of our fellow students. I was
particularly saddened by the separation from a small
red-headed student who came from a poor peasant
family. He had devoted himself doggedly to his
studies and looked forward to his future activity as a

schoolteacher in the higher grades. But he was not
the only one. More and more students whose parents
belonged to the poorer classes were leaving the academy. In fact, there soon remained only the sons and
daughters of the privileged classes, such as officers
and other people in positions of responsibility.

Few of the foreign students and none of the Russians who had been brought up in Children's Homes
belonged to the privileged classes. We assumed at
once that we, too, should have to give up our studies,
but a few days later the Russian students who had
been at Children's Homes were given means of support to ensure their further studies. Meanwhile we
foreign students had run to the M.O.P.R. one after
another, as it had so often helped us before. We soon
learned to our great relief that we were not going to
be left in the lurch. The M.O.P.R. promised not
only to pay our annual fee of 400 roubles, but also to
guarantee the monthly sum needed for our mainte-
nance.

When I look back on these events to-day, it is not
only the unhappy parting from so many friends at
the Academy that I remember. I also have a clear
impression that this law represented a new step in
the evolution of the Stalinist system. Appointment
to practically all important positions in the Soviet
Union depended on graduation from an academy.
Until 2nd October, 1940, it was possible in practice
for any gifted and industrious child of a working
class or peasant family, irrespective of their parents'
financial situation, to have ten years at school and
then go on to the Academy. After that, every kind
of possibility was open to them—a fact which was
constantly emphasised by Soviet propaganda. But

from 2nd October, 1940, onwards, as a general rule
the only young people who could rise to the higher
positions were those whose parents had already held
high office. The wheel had come full circle: the
bureaucratic ruling class which had arisen since
the end of the 1920's and had consolidated and
strengthened its power in the purges of 1936 to 1938,
thanks to the liquidation of the old guard, was now
beginning in 1940 to shut itself off from outsiders
and was thus taking the first step towards making its
privileges and functions hereditary.

Fresh Questioning of the German Émigrés

At the end of 1940, almost a year and a half after
the conclusion of the Non-aggression Pact with
Germany, and a few weeks after Molotov's visit to
Berlin, people in Moscow suddenly remembered the
German émigrés again. After the closing of our
Children's Home, we had met only occasionally and
by chance. Most of us were working in factories,
though a few were still in Russian Children's Homes
and others had gone to study at various academies.
Many had married Russian girls and had now become
completely Russianised.

I was all the more surprised to receive an invitation to a meeting at the Central Committee of the
M.O.P.R. towards the end of November, 1940, a few
weeks after Molotov had left Berlin. I was very
pleased, hoping that this was going to be an opportunity to see my former friends again. I went to the
M.O.P.R. building, where the meeting was to take
place at eight o'clock in the evening, in a state of
great excitement. It was an uproarious reunion, for in
fact I found there many of my earlier friends from

Children's Home No. 6 as well as other young Austrians and Germans, the sons and daughters of German émigrés who were living with their parents. Almost all of them were members of the *Komsomol* and all spoke fluent Russian: many of them, indeed, knew Russian better than German. However, we had little time for greetings and chatting and reminiscences before we were summoned into the great hall. The official proceedings began with a speech by an Austrian official of the Comintern:

"Comrades, we have called you together in order to renew contact with you. This is not going to be just one isolated meeting: from now on we shall meet every Monday evening for political instruction. All of you present this evening will be assigned to specific groups for seminars. You will be required not only to come here every Monday evening to hear the lecture, but also to read the literature which you will be given, and to take part in the seminars. In particular, I should like to draw your attention to the fact that this instruction will be confined to a limited circle and for reasons which you will understand it must not be generally talked about."

We had all been long enough in the Soviet Union to respect this directive, and we told our Russian friends nothing about it. It was clear that great importance was attached to the instruction. For instance, anyone who was on the Monday evening shift at a factory was released from work; this was clearly on orders from higher authority, without the managers at their places of work even knowing why the instruction was given.

I, too, told my Russian student friends nothing about our special instruction, but naturally I gave a good deal of thought to it. The very fact that after a year and a half German and Austrian Party members were meeting again in Moscow seemed to me an indication that possibly things were not so rosy as was officially represented at that time in our relations with Hitler's Germany.

There was not the slightest inkling to be found in the Soviet press of a deterioration of relations, however. Every report in the foreign press which might do the least damage to our relations with Germany was immediately and emphatically denied. Great importance was attached to Molotov's journey to Berlin, and there were many comments on it. Later on, in the middle of November, *Pravda* published a picture of a session in the negotiations, at which Molotov and Hitler were to be seen together.

In the early days of our Monday evening instruction at the Central Committee of the M.O.P.R. there was no mention of any kind of theme which touched on the current international situation or the relations between the Soviet Union and Hitlerite Germany. Apart from the compulsory study of the *Short History of the Communist Party of the Soviet Union* which I now went through for the third time at this school, we discussed certain fundamental principles of Marxism-Leninism and listened to lectures on the history of the German Workers' Movement. On our second evening of instruction, I listened to a lecture by an official whom at that time I knew only by name: Walter Ulbricht. He dealt with the 1918 Revolution in detail, but said nothing at all about current questions arising from the struggle against Fascism. Another time we listened to a discussion of the character of the World War. It was still argued at the end of 1940, on the basis of the official distinction between justified and unjustified war, that the present war was an unjust Imperialist war on both sides—the German and Italian side as well as the British and French side.

In the spring of 1941, I detected a slight modification of this line for the first time. Walter Ulbricht spoke in one of his lectures of the possibility that the character of the war might change while it was actually going on, as had frequently happened in history before. There was a breathless hush in the room, because this remark was one which was never to be found in Soviet newspapers at that time.

"This fact," Ulbricht explained, "is particularly important in connection with the attack by Germany and Italy on Yugoslavia and Greece. There are certain factors to be noted, especially in the case of Yugoslavia, which point to the possibility that one might speak in some respects of a justified defensive war on the part of these two peoples against foreign attack."

Although Ulbricht expressed himself extremely cautiously and avoided even in this context the use of the word ("Fascism" which was forbidden throughout the whole period of the German-Soviet Non-aggression Pact), the indication which he had given was nevertheless clear enough to me.

A few weeks went by, during which no more delicate themes were touched on. On Monday evening, 16th June, 1941, we assembled as usual in the house of the Central Committee of the M.O.P.R. for our instruction. Walter Ulbricht was the speaker again. At the end of his lecture, which lasted about an hour and a half, there followed the usual announcement that questions could be put. There followed a series of questions based on Ulbricht's lecture, which so far as I remember had no direct connection with the current situation. Then the course of the discussion gradually led up to the present time, and one of those present put the question: "Comrade Ulbricht, foreign newspapers are carrying more and more frequent reports of the danger of a German attack on the Soviet Union. It is true that these reports are categorically and explicitly denied in the Soviet press, but would it perhaps be possible to hear something in more detail on the subject?"

However, Ulbricht did not go into this question. He simply repeated briefly the official denial, and ended with the words: "These are nothing but rumours spread with the intention of provoking trouble. There will be no war."

Six days later Hitler attacked the Soviet Union.

CHAPTER THREE

The Beginning
of the War in Moscow

AT THE BEGINNING of June, 1941, our end-of-year examinations began. Lights could be seen burning till late in the night in practically every room of the students' hostel. All our conversations were centred on the examinations. We soaked ourselves so deeply in phonetics, Latin, education, English history and literature, Marxism-Leninism, and other subjects that for weeks on end what was going on in the political world touched only the fringe of our consciousness. But even in these weeks of strenuous study we were not entirely unaffected by outside events.

One day I was talking at the Academy to a girl student, when she looked round anxiously to make sure nobody was near. "The Red Army soldiers in units on the Soviet-Finnish frontier have been made to remove their divisional numbers from their uniforms. That always happens when there is a danger of fighting breaking out."

I was sceptical. "On the Soviet-Finnish frontier? But Finland has only just lost a war against the Soviet Union. They couldn't attack the Soviet Union now."

"Could it be with Germany? The news is absolutely definite. A friend of mine has a brother who is an officer there, but you mustn't say a word about it to anyone else."

I thought it over anxiously. Could there really be a danger of war? I was certainly not the only one in the Soviet Union to have such thoughts at that time. However, a few days later our doubts and anxiety were put at rest. On the 8th June the front page of *Pravda* carried an announcement about relations between the Soviet Union and Finland. Although the Finns had failed to fulfil satisfactorily their commercial agreement with the Soviet Union, nevertheless, on Stalin's initiative, the Soviet Union was going to deliver a further 20,000 tons of grain in the immediate future to Finland, over and above the quantities of goods already delivered.

Like many other people in the Soviet Union, I found myself much reassured by this announcement. People in Moscow were telling each other that if there were even the slightest danger of an attack on the Soviet Union from Finland in the foreseeable future, then certainly we should not be sending them 20,000 tons of grain.

A Comforting Démenti from Tass

A few days later, on the road to Dzerzhinsky Underground Station, I noticed building work going on in the cellars of some of the houses. At the time I attached no significance to this, but when I was taking a longer walk through Moscow the following day I saw similar work going on at many points. Naturally I was not the only person who had noticed this, and again the rumours began to circulate through the town.

"Have you noticed they are making air-raid shelters?"

"Nonsense!—they're storerooms."

"No, I am sure it's for civil defence."

"Rubbish! They are making storerooms for winter potatoes."

So the rumours conflicted with each other through the first half of June in Moscow—some disturbing, some reassuring. The announcement about the 20,000 tons of grain had silenced rumours about Finland, but a few people, especially those who owned radio sets and could listen to foreign broadcasts, continued to express anxiety about Hitlerite Germany.

"In England they're saying Hitler's going to start a war against the U.S.S.R.," one of them told me. "But obviously that's only British propaganda. They want to sow mistrust between us and Germany," he added hastily, for the Pact still stood above any possible criticism.

Most people with whom I talked in Moscow at that time were of the same opinion, and even the few who were anxious finally had their fears set at rest on 14th June, 1941; for on this day every newspaper of the Soviet Union published in a prominent position an announcement that all rumours about a deterioration of relations between Germany and the U.S.S.R. were pure fantasy. (This was eight days before the beginning of the war.) The announcement emphasised that the Soviet Union adhered to the Soviet-German Non-aggression Pact in conformity with her peaceful policy, "and intends to continue to adhere to it; consequently all rumours to the effect that the Soviet Union is preparing for a war against Germany are baseless inventions by provocateurs."

What followed next must have been unique in the whole history of diplomacy. The Soviet announcement was not limited to reiterating our continued adherence to the Non-aggression Pact, but went on to controvert on its own initiative all rumours about German preparations for war. This paragraph naturally attracted the greatest attention in the Soviet Union. It read as follows: "The Soviet Union's information is that Germany adheres to the provisions of the Soviet-German Non-aggression Pact just as firmly as the Soviet Union. Opinion in Soviet circles rejects as without foundation all rumours about German intentions of breaking the Pact and initiating an attack against the U.S.S.R. The regrouping of German troops released since the operations in the Balkans, which has recently been taking place in the Eastern and North-Eastern sectors of Germany, can be assumed to be based on reasons which have no connection whatever with Soviet-German relations."

On this particular morning, the 14th June, the entrance hall of our student hostel was filled to overflowing with students in spite of the examinations. They were all pressing round a copy of *Pravda* which was pinned up in its usual place on the wall. The atmosphere was one of cheerfulness and almost of relief. Everyone was delighted to find that the disturbing predictions had proved groundless. Our talk was turning already to holiday plans.

"The last papers are on the 22nd June, and after that we'll be off for our holidays!"

I, too, was delighted, although I had no definite plans. One thing was now quite clear in any case:

there was nothing more to fear. Only the examinations to get through, and then a good rest!

"Molotov will Speak"

On the morning of 22nd June many students in our hostel were up early. Some had set their alarm clocks for five or six o'clock in order to have a last hour or two before the examination for revision of this or that subject. The Polish student with whom I shared a room, Benek Girshovich, and I were not among them. He had adopted my own theory that it was much more important to come to the examination room after a good night's sleep, so we had decided to sleep till nine o'clock. But it was not to be. From early in the morning we heard an excited running to and fro in the corridor.

"Damned idiots! Why can't they let one have a good night's sleep before the examination?" said Benek, half asleep I agreed, adding a hearty curse in Russian. However, the noise outside grew worse and worse. It was impossible to think of sleeping any longer. We had hardly got up when there was a hammering on our door.

"Molotov is going to speak! It was announced half an hour ago and it's being repeated over and over again!" shouted a student excitedly through the door. "It's going to be a very important announcement!"

"What time?"

"About twelve," the answer echoed through from the corridor.

We looked at the clock. It was just nine, so we had plenty of time. We tried to concentrate on our

examination paper, but it was impossible. Never had
the time seemed to go by so slowly; and then at last
the announcement began.

"This is Moscow calling! You will now hear a
speech from the Deputy Chairman of the Council
of People's Commissars of the U.S.S.R. and Foreign
Commissar of the U.S.S.R., Vyacheslav Mikhailo-
vich Molotov."

There was a second's pause and then we heard
Molotov's voice.

"Citizens, men and women of the Soviet Union!"
he began in grave and somewhat solemn tones. "This
morning, at four o'clock, German troops attacked
our territory, without presenting any kind of demands
on the Soviet Union and without a declaration of war.
They have crossed our frontiers at many points and
bombed Zhitomir, Kiev, Sevastopol, Kaunas and several other towns. Hostile attacks from the air and by
artillery fire have also been carried out from Rumanian and Finnish territory. This treacherous, out-
rageous attack on our country is without precedent
in the history of civilised states. The attack on our
country has taken place in spite of the existence of
a Non-aggression Pact between the U.S.S.R and Germany, and in spite of the Soviet Government's scrupulous fulfilment of the conditions of that treaty. The
attack on our country has taken place in spite of the
fact that the German Government has never presented
any demands upon the U.S.S.R. during the whole
period of the Pact. The entire responsibility for this
predatory onslaught on the Soviet Union therefore
falls clearly and unequivocally on the German Fascist rulers."

We could not help wincing at hearing the word "Fascist" again on Moscow radio for the first time in nearly two years.

Molotov's speech, which was the shortest I had ever heard in the Soviet Union, was brought to an end with an appeal to the Soviet population: "The Government appeals to all of you, men and women, citizens of the Soviet Union, as never before to close your ranks around our glorious Bolshevik Party, our Government of the Soviet Union, and our leader, Comrade Stalin. Our cause in just, our enemy will be beaten! Victory will be ours!"

Before we had consciously taken it all in, Molotov had finished speaking. His words still echoed in our ears: "Our cause is just, our enemy will be beaten! Victory will be ours!"

We sat dumbfounded. This was the last thing in the world we had expected, and it was simply impossible to grasp. Benek and I left our room; we could not stay by ourselves for a minute longer. In the next room a few students were talking and we sat down with them. They too were in a subdued and anxious mood. The radio was playing Soviet marching songs and battle songs, which were hardly appropriate to our feelings. Various opinions were expressed, hesitantly and thoughtfully.

"This will be the end of Hitlerite Fascism!"

"Now Hitler will be made to pay for all he's grabbed in Europe!"

"Our troops are sure to march straight into Poland!"

One student was more sceptical: "It's going to be a hard struggle. It's perfectly possible Hitler will march straight into the Western Ukraine and Western Belorussia. His offensive may possibly not even be stopped until he's actually on the frontiers of the Soviet Union. After all, the aggressor always has the advantage."

This opinion was repudiated by everybody else present. It had continually been rubbed into us since 1936 that the intervention of 1918-19 would never be repeated. At every meeting we were told again and again that if the Soviet Union were attacked, the Red Army would advance and smash the aggressor on his own soil. This idea had become so much part of our flesh and blood that we no longer even contemplated the possibility of a war on Soviet territory.

At this point one of the students raised the question which was being put at every gathering of the Soviet people, wherever they were, on 22nd June, 1941: "What will England do?"

Opinion was divided: "We and England will surely fight Hitler together now!" said one girl confidently, although this thought was a new one to us after two years of the Pact.

Another of the students, remembering Hess's flight, was sceptical: "Surely the war between Germany and England so far has been nothing but a put-up show? Now they'll join forces and march against the Soviet Union." Someone immediately contradicted him. The majority of our little group of students took the view, on this morning of 22nd June, that we would now be forming a common front with England against Hitler.

Then one of the girls brought us back to earth with an impulsive cry: "Our examinations!"

As we came out of the student hostel, the sight which confronted us was like an agitated ant heap.

The whole of Moscow was in the streets and all the shops were full to overflowing. Everybody seemed to be in a hurry to buy something or other, no doubt because they remembered that the first thing that war meant in Russia was hunger. We, as politically conscious members of the *Komsomol,* looked on this hoarding with contempt. The salesman at a cigarette kiosk looked at me in astonishment when I asked only for a single packet: everyone else was buying them by the dozen.

At our Academy the atmosphere was noticeably calmer. One or two *Komsomol* officials were going round exhorting us all to go calmly on with our studies, and to control any tendency to panic. We replied, somewhat hurt, that "we knew that already."

At the entrance to the examination room, a number of students were standing about waiting to be called in. This was enough to bring the atmosphere of examination home to us again, but it was soon all over. A few days earlier, I should have rushed enthusiastically out of the examination room to join my fellow students in celebrating and making plans for the summer holidays; but this time nothing like that was in my mind. I had only one thought: "What news of the war?"

There was no news. The war had begun at four o'clock in the morning. It was now four in the afternoon. Twelve hours had passed, and the radio had made no further announcement about the course of hostilities. Loudspeakers had been put up all over the town so that Molotov's speech and the marching songs could be heard everywhere. Now and then a commentary was transmitted, with an appeal to join the struggle against Fascism. I wandered about Mos-

cow like most other people that day. As I was crossing
the square in front of the Theatre, the loudspeakers
announced: "The Fascist barbarians . . ."

Suddenly I heard beside me a somewhat ironic
English voice saying: "So now they've become anti-
Fascists, too!" I moved away quickly, well knowing
how dangerous it could be to be found in the neighbourhood of foreigners, even if they were now to become our allies.

As Moscow Radio still announced nothing about
the first day of hostilities, the most diverse rumours
began to circulate in the town.

"The aggressors have been thrown back from the
frontiers!"

"The Germans have landed airborne divisions near
Kiev!"

"The Red Army is pushing back the Germans—
they're already on Polish territory!"

But over everything still hung the question: "What
will England do?" The news in the evening brought
us the answer. Moscow Radio began its news bulletin
with excerpts from Churchill's speech about the
common struggle against Hitler. We breathed again.
A wave of optimism came over the students' hostel
—and probably over the entire Soviet Union.

The First Days of the War

The morning papers carried new slogans in banner headlines:

"The entire Soviet people is resolute and united as
never before!"

"Under the leadership of the mighty Stalin, the
Soviet people will smash the perfidious enemy!"

"In the name of Stalin, we have conquered before:

in the name of Stalin, we shall conquer again!"

By the next day anti-Fascist films were on show again for the first time in two years. In front of the larger cinemas were to be seen gigantic advertisements of *Professor Mamlock* and *The Oppenheim Family*. The newspapers carried their first reports of resistance movements in the countries occupied by Hitlerite Germany.

At last the first communiqué was published. Optimistic rumours about the first few days of fighting proved to be untrue. The truth turned out to be what none but a very few had expected: the war was being fought on Soviet soil. It was put vaguely in the *communiqué*, to the effect that German troops had succeeded in penetrating ten to fifteen kilometers at certain places.

Simultaneously with the new slogans and the first *communiqué* from the front came the official formula defining the war as "the great patriotic war of the Soviet people." Momentarily I was taken aback. It was true that in recent years I had lived through a complete reversal of Soviet propaganda, as it gradually eliminated all ideas of revolutionary internationalism, and gave clearer and clearer emphasis to Soviet patriotism; and I had been aware of this change and had even given some thought to it, so that the new phrase did not entirely take me by surprise. But I had expected that at least the war would be conducted as an anti-Fascist war of liberation, with a clear-cut emphasis on the common goal which we shared with all the other people under Nazi oppression. The designation of "patriotic war," on the contrary, limited it exclusively to the Soviet Union and even, strictly speaking, to Russia. Obviously a parallel was to be established with the war against Napoleon in 1812-13, and perhaps the emphasis on the concept of patriotism was from the point of view of the Soviet leaders the most effective method of winning over the great mass of the population to support the war. However, in the early days, like almost everyone else in the Soviet Union, I had other things to think about than political formulæ.

The state of war had been proclaimed in the three Baltic Republics, in Belorussia, in the Karelo-Finnish and Moldavian Republics, in the whole of the Ukraine and the thirteen regions of Russia, including Moscow and Leningrad. In these regions, the military authorities were empowered to take any necessary steps for defence, including the mobilisation of the entire civilian population. A special decree was issued calling up the classes of 1905 to 1918 for military service, not only in the Western Military Districts of the country, but also at Archangel, in the Urals, in Siberia, on the Volga and in the Caucasus. Then followed very far-reaching measures for the defence of Moscow and the Moscow district in air raids. All houses had to be blacked out and air-raid shelters prepared for use. All theatres, cinemas, clubs, parks, restaurants, cafés and shops had to be closed at 10:45 p.m. (hitherto many food shops in Moscow had stayed open till midnight). Finally, all rights of leave were suspended for the duration of the war: leave was to be replaced by monetary compensation. Directors of factories and departmental heads were given the right to order overtime work, which was to be compensated by payment at the rate of time-and-a-half.

On the evening of the 23rd, there was a meeting of

members of the *Komsomol* in our Academy, as every-where else, on the occasion of the outbreak of war. We sat in the great hall of our Academy, packed tight. There was an expectant silence. The prevailing atmosphere was like that described in *Komsomol* books about the period of the Revolution and the Civil War.

"The time has come for the *Komsomols* to be put to the proof," we were told. We knew it, and indeed practically all of us welcomed the chance to prove ourselves.

"From this morning, members of the *Komsomol* in this Academy are to go to work on the new underground railway line," we were informed by our branch. "It has to be got ready as a matter or urgency as an additional air-raid shelter for the people of Moscow."

One or two members of the *Komsomol* then spoke in turn. The word *verolomny* (perfidious) was much used. There was constant emphasis on the fact that Hitler's Germany had committed aggression against the Soviet Union in spite of the Non-aggression Pact. One could sense the resentment at this perfidious attack and the determination to beat down the aggressor. This feeling was just as genuine among those who had taken a critical or even hostile attitude towards the régime; it was shared even by those whose parents were at that moment prisoners in Stalin's forced labour camps. Hitler had now achieved what Stalin had never been able to do completely, either by propaganda or by terror. On that day in the year 1941, most people in the Soviet Union really came to look on the Government in the Kremlin as the true representative of their interests.

Standing beside me was a girl student with whom I had more than once had conversations hinting at opposition to the régime. "This time it is *really* different!" she whispered to me.

At the close of the meeting, one or two of the students struck up the "International," and it echoed through the hall. We went back to our hostel in an excited frame of mind. We had slept only a few hours when the sirens began to sound. (It was the night of the 23rd-24th June.) Then the radio began to give out in a long-drawn-out chant those three incessantly repeated words which we were to hear so often from then on: *"Grazhdane! Vozdushnaya trevoga!"* (Citizens! Air raid warning!).

That night was the first time we had heard it, and some minutes passed before the meaning of the words penetrated my consciousness. I leapt out of bed, quite drowsy with sleep. My Polish companion, who had fought in the Spanish Civil War, grumbled: "Damn it all! I'd got completely out of the habit —it's more than two years now since we used to hear that sort of thing in Barcelona."

We slung on our gas masks and went to the air-raid shelter. It was simply an ordinary cellar, for no preparations at all had been made yet. At first everything was quiet, and then we could hear the drone of engines in the distance and anti-aircraft fire. It was all terribly new and frightening for us. As always, there were a few among us who boasted of their military experience, and claimed to be able to recognise the type of aircraft from the sound of the engines. I was sceptical, however, for the only types they mentioned were those which we had learnt about in our military studies.

The only one who could give a plausible explanation for everything was my room-mate, the Pole, who had fought in the Spanish Civil War. His prestige rose minute by minute, though it lasted only until the following morning, when unfortunately for him the morning newspapers announced that it had been nothing but a practice alarm. The air-raid precautions in the capital were being tried out, and certainly it was high time. It was impossible to conceal the fact that practically no preparations at all had been made in this field. It was clear that even the top leaders of the Party and Government had not reckoned on a war in June 1941. Everything now had to be overhauled: the organisation of air defenses; the training of A.R.P. and medical services; the conversion of cellars into air-raid shelters; and anti-aircraft defences, black-out and camouflage.

Shortly after the outbreak of war, it was announced that all radio sets were to be withdrawn. Everyone who owned a set was instructed to hand it in within forty-eight hours to the nearest post office, against a receipt. Long queues of people formed outside the post offices and had to wait patiently to hand in their sets. The receipt stated that at the end of the war the set would be given back again. Few people believed that; most of them had reconciled themselves in advance to the fact that they would never see their sets again. They were just piled up in the courtyards at the post offices, and left in the open.

At the same time, it was decreed that loudspeakers in all communal apartments, institutions and factories were to be left switched on. There was no inconsistency here. In the year 1941, just as to-day, radio sets were available only to a limited section of the population, but in every institution, communal apartment, students' hostel, workers' club or other public place, small black loudspeakers looking like electric fans were installed, and these transmitted only the programmes of the nearest radio station. This was, at that date, the commonest way of listening to the radio in the Soviet Union.

The withdrawal of all radio sets now made it possible to provide all Soviet citizens with the same information and the same programmes, since the radio stations were normally limited to exact repetitions of the broadcasts from Moscow radio. To fill up the programme there was simply a short local transmission. In this way the influence of a single central propaganda service was exerted over the entire population. No doubt the Soviet leadership regarded this as more necessary now than ever before, and the very first days of the war saw their propaganda achieve its most extraordinary feats.

It was amazing how quickly the complete transformation of Soviet propaganda had its effect on national feeling about Soviet patriotism and the idea of a patriotic war; and how quickly the ideas of Party, and of Socialism and Communism, disappeared from the propagandist's vocabulary. This change was not, however, as was frequently assumed, merely a piece of tactical opportunism. It was a logical development of the ideological changes which had taken place in the last few years before the war. Whereas up to about 1935 all articles or songs which had hinted at the possibility of an attack on the Soviet Union or a future war still spoke of a revolutionary or class war, these ideas had already receded into the background some time before the war broke out. There was more and more talk of Soviet patriotism, even though the earlier ideas did not completely disappear all at once. Now with the outbreak of war, the same development was carried a step farther. In the whole of Soviet propaganda there was practically no mention of anything except "our Fatherland," "our home," "Russian soil" and "patriotism." This new line was popularised not only by the press and the radio, but particularly through the visual influence of posters.

From the very beginning of the war Soviet propaganda gave the greatest possible prominence to German desertions. We began to hear about them at meetings of the German émigrés only a few days after war broke out. When we met in the building of the Central Committee of M.O.P.R., the tension was unexampled. Everyone knew that the German émigrés would no longer be having their usual evening's instruction. The Chief Instructor confined himself to the announcement: "Comrade Ulbricht will address you."

Ulbricht made a short speech. He spoke of the crimes of Fascism, of the gravity of the situation, of the need to strain every nerve for victory over Fascism. "We are living through the early days of war, but already I have an encouraging announcement to make to you. As early as 22nd June, the first German soldier deserted to the Soviet side!"

Ulbricht's announcement was received with terrific applause. We listened anxiously to the rest of his announcement. "This soldier was stationed in Rumania on the River Pruth. On the night of 21st-22nd June, he heard the order issued to his unit to attack the Soviet Union. He left his unit at once and swam by night across the Pruth, to join the Red Army and to tell us that a few hours later the Nazi attack on the Soviet Union was about to begin."

My next-door neighbour whispered to me: "If a soldier deserts to the Soviet side before the war has begun, what will it be like when it has really got going?"

A few days later this German soldier was well known throughout the Soviet Union. His action was mentioned in one of the first Soviet war *communiqués* and *Pravda* published his picture and his statement. "I have long been against the Hitlerite system," declared Alfred Liskov. "As soon as I learned that the attack was imminent, I took my decision to go over to the Red Army. Even on the very day before the attack on the Soviet Union, no one really believed that such treachery was possible. It is easy to imagine how the German people will react to this crazy adventure."

Two days later, it was announced that a Ju.88 had landed at Kiev. All four occupants of the aircraft— Sergeant Hans Hermann from Breslau; the observer, Hans Kratz from Frankfurt; Corporal Appel from Brunn; and the radio operator, Wilhelm Schmidt from Regensburg—had agreed together to land at a Soviet aerodrome. In a statement which was published in every Soviet newspaper, they announced that they had been flying together for more than a year and had taken part in raids on London, Portsmouth, Plymouth and other English towns. "We often asked ourselves the question, Why is Hitler fighting against the whole world?—why is he bringing death and destruction to all the people of Europe? Now that Hitler has declared war on Russia we have decided to act. On 25th June, we dropped our bombs in the River Dnieper and landed at Kiev."

The very next day the crew of another German aircraft deserted to the Soviet troops. These reports about German deserters gave rise to a wave of confidence. Among German émigrés serious illusions prevailed in the early days of the war. I later learned that Soviet circles also cherished high hopes of influencing the advancing German troops by propaganda. At the *Iskra Revoliutsii* press in Filipovski Street as many as twelve different leaflets a day in German were sent to press in the first weeks of the war, but they must certainly have been very ineffective, and generally caused nothing but laughter among the advancing troops of the German *Wehrmacht*.

The high hopes of the early days of the war were soon to prove groundless. Deserters became rarer and rarer with the rapid advance of the German armies. There was a reduction of propaganda directed at the German *Wehrmacht,* and military questions now came to occupy the foreground. For the civilian population of Moscow this meant principally the completion of air-raid precautions and civil defence.

The German Advance

From the White Sea to the Black Sea the Germans advanced along the whole front with ever-increasing rapidity. Soviet *communiqués* from the front were kept exceptionally vague in these first weeks of the war. Generally, reference was made only to points of the compass and to the areas in which the fighting was taking place. There were no maps accurately showing the front line. The directions and areas indicated showed us how fast the advance of the German armies was proceeding, but there were no comments on this advance.

Only two weeks after the outbreak of war, German troops were already in occupation of Lithuania, almost the whole of Latvia and Estonia, and a large part of Belorussia and Western Ukraine. The advance had been more rapid than even the most pessimistic guesses on 22nd June. Disquieting rumours were rife in Moscow. One of the girl students told us in a whisper: "The Germans are saying that Stalin's son has deserted to them. They say he's given a broadcast on the radio for them, full of exact details about conversations he'd had with his father. He's called on everyone openly to fight against Stalin's dictatorship!"

She naturally hastened to denounce this rumour, but it gave us food for thought for a long time, not because we let ourselves be influenced by it—of course we were all for a victory of the Soviet Union —but because we were afraid that a rumour of this kind might have a dangerous effect on people who were politically uneducated.

We were not the only ones to feel this anxiety. On 7th July a special decree of the Presidium of the Supreme Soviet of the U.S.S.R. was issued in the following terms: "It has been decided that for the duration of the war, anyone guilty of spreading false rumours and thus causing unrest among the population, shall on conviction by court martial be punished by a term of imprisonment from two to five years, except in cases where the crime requires severer punishment."

During these weeks we were so completely pre-occupied by the war that our earlier attitudes of criticism and opposition on particular questions quite receded into the background. The struggle against Fascism had first priority for all of us. It seemed as if no doubts existed any more. No one thought any more of those tragic trials and mass arrests which had taken place a few years earlier in the Soviet Union. Of all the students and members of the *Komsomol* known personally to me, the great majority sincerely longed for a victory of the Soviet Union over Hitler, though they also linked with it at the same time a hope that life in the Soviet Union after the war would be freer and less restricted than before. We had been far too thoroughly educated in the spirit of the system and indoctrinated with Stalinist ideas to reject the system in principle, as such. What we wanted was nothing more than to be able to live a freer and less restricted life, and to enjoy more intellectual contact with the outside world, within the system which at this stage was the only one that I, at least, could conceive.

A few days later I became aware how far we were from the fulfilment even of this modest desire. I had been invited one afternoon to visit Willi Fink, the Austrian Comintern official, in the Hotel Lux. With me was Hans Hanslichek, a young Austrian who had formerly been a pupil at the Children's Home No. 6 and had now been working for some time as a skilled worker in the Stalin Motor Works at Moscow. Being a member of the Comintern, Willi Fink had the privilege of regularly reading the foreign press, including Nazi newspapers. While we were sitting together over tea, we talked about the latest air raids on Moscow. Willi Fink had been reading the *Völkischer Beobachter* and he told us that the Nazi press had contained reports of tremendous fires in Moscow. We laughed, for the few air raids had certainly not produced any such conflagrations. Hans particularly enjoyed the joke, and said: "I must tell that to my colleagues at the factory; they'll laugh their heads off at such nonsense!"

After that the conversation turned to other subjects, but Willi Fink seemed uneasy, and as we parted he remarked: "Just one thing I'd like to mention—better not say anything about the news in the Nazi press of fires in Moscow, if you don't mind."

We understood. We knew that even officials of the Comintern had no right to pass on even a single paragraph of what they had read in the foreign press. It left me with a disagreeable feeling to think that one could not even talk about items which did no harm at all—items, indeed, which helped the Soviet Union.

I learned that evening that a Volga-German student had been arrested in the next room of our hostel. Shortly after that, I met two girls from Berlin called Gerda and Käthe, who were the daughters of the Communist writer, Albert Hottop. They were in tears. Their father—who had emigrated to the Soviet Union and survived right through the purges and was the author of *Fischkutter HF13.*—had been arrested by the N.K.V.D.

Two weeks later I went to the Udarnik Cinema with two girl students. In the lobby we saw something which even a few months before would have been quite inconceivable—a display of pictures from British and American films, with short captions and photographs of the stars. The walls of the lobby of the Udarnik Cinema were completely covered with them. We were pleasantly surprised, and made the most of this breach in our isolation, slight as it was. Having grown up and been educated in the Soviet Union, we were accustomed to notice the slightest change at once and often to attach far-reaching political implications to it; so we studied the pictures from Western films with great interest.

"It really is nice to see pictures like that for once," said one of the two girls. I nodded in agreement and said: "Perhaps these stills from films are only the beginning." We realised then that we had both had the same thought, and we began cautiously to speak a little more openly.

"It's lucky for us that we're not going along with Hitler any more, but fighting the war against him with England—and perhaps later with America too!" she said hopefully to me in a low voice. "Once Hitler's beaten, perhaps things will be different for us here too!"

"I hope so, too . . . after the war . . ." I could not say any more. The other girl, who had been looking round anxiously from our first words, whispered to us in conspiratorial tones: "Sh! Sh! Please stop! Don't say any more!"

Again I was struck by the sense of conflict in our position. We certainly wanted the Soviet Union to defeat Hitler, and we were equally certainly not against the system, but why on earth shouldn't three Moscow students, all members of the *Komsomol,* talk about the possibility that after Hitler was beaten things would be a little freer?

The following day, which was 14th August, *Pravda* announced: "A few days ago, our troops withdrew from Smolensk."

A few days ago—that meant that the German troops

were already beyond Smolensk and on their way to Moscow!

Departure from Moscow

The new term at our Academy began on the 1st September, 1941. By this time, however, many of us, including some of the girls, had been recruited into the Army or Civil Defence. The rest of us were supposed to be putting even more effort than before into our studies while the war was on, but it was not so easy to concentrate on English philology and comparative linguistic studies while German troops were encircling Leningrad and simultaneously advancing on Moscow. However, I did my best to work seriously.

On the evening of 14th September, a militiaman came to the door of the students' room. This did not disturb me, for it was only the N.K.V.D. that carried out political arrests. I did feel a little uneasy, however, when he took a paper out of his pocket and looked at me severely.

"Are you Comrade Leonhard, studying at the Moscow State Educational Academy for Foreign Languages?"

There was no use denying it.

"You are requested to come to the militia post to-morrow afternoon at four o'clock. Please sign this paper."

The scene at the militia post might almost have been a gipsy camp. Between 100 and 150 people were crushed together in the ante-room, and to judge by their faces, many of them had already been waiting for hours. Most of them were German émigrés and some of them were accompanied by their wives and children. I soon discovered many I knew.

One after another the families were summoned to the chief of the militia post. As new ones were continually pushing into the ante-room, however, the number hardly seemed to get less. The whisper went round that all Germans were going to be deported for the duration of the war to Kzyl-orda. It was to happen in the next few days; and there were to be no exceptions.

"Are members of the *Komsomol* to go, too?" I asked.

"Everyone," I was told, "even those who have become members of the Russian Communist Party since they came here. The only exceptions are a few members of the Comintern."

There was much puzzled questioning: "Where is this place, Kzyl-orda?"

"In the Kazakh Union Republic."

"Yes, but where is the Kazakh Union Republic?"

Proud of our recently acquired knowledge of geography, we younger ones explained: "Kazakhstan is the second largest Union Republic in the Soviet Union and stretches from the Volga in the west to the Chinese borders in the east; from Siberia in the north to the Kirgiz and Uzbek Union Republics in the south."

"Yes, but what's it like in Kzyl-orda?"

Here our expert knowledge failed. "All I know is that Kzyl-orda is among the four or five biggest towns in Kazakhstan. Kzyl-orda is a Kazakh word. It means the Red Horde."

The name was not calculated to set the anxieties of our older comrades at rest.

After about two hours my name was called. The chief official sat behind a mountain of files with two assistants busy around him. They were frankly overwhelmed by the task of coping with this gigantic and unexpected transfer of population. In spite of that, the senior official was not actually unfriendly as he quickly put a few questions.

"How long have you been living in the Soviet Union?"

"Since 1935. I was in the Home for Children of the *Schutzbund* from 1936 and since 1940 I have been a student."

"Where are you studying?"

"At the Moscow State Educational Academy for Foreign Languages."

"You will probably have to interrupt your studies now. We have had instructions to remove all Germans living in Moscow to Kzyl-orda for the duration of the war. It is simply a necessary precaution while the war is on. At the end of the war, you will be able to come back to Moscow."

While he was speaking his assistant had taken my identity card from me. When I received it back, I saw a large red stamp mark on the document saying: "The holder of this card is entitled to reside only in the Kzyl-orda District of the Kazakh Soviet Republic."

Our deportation to Kzyl-orda was the sole subject of conversation among the German émigrés for days. Rumours quickly sprang up that the Comintern (that is to say, the German Communist delegation in Moscow) was preparing a list of comrades whose presence in Moscow was absolutely imperative. I made up my mind to try my luck in this direction. At the time I knew only three Comintern officials reasonably well. These were Hans Mahle, who worked on Moscow Radio as an editor; the Austrian Youth repre-

sentative, Willi Fink; and Lea Lichter, a woman in
the Comintern who had been a member of the first
joint clandestine group of Communists and Catholics in West Germany under Hitler, and was now
working in Moscow in the German Youth organisation.

I succeeded in finding Lea. "You're lucky," she
said. "You're going to be needed on Moscow Radio,
so you're on the list of comrades who will be able to
stay here. The list has been signed to-day, and you'll
hear about it shortly from the militia post."

A few days later I duly received a certificate and
set out for the militia post again, this time full of
pleasurable excitement. The chief official did not
seem to share my enthusiasm. However, he gave my
identity card to his assistant with instructions to
provide me with a new one, omitting the deportation
order. While this was going on, he explained to me:
"Of course, I shall have a new document prepared
for you at once which will give you the right to stay
in Moscow even while the war's on; but if I were in
your place, I should not be inclined to claim this
right. It could happen that you may have to leave
Moscow a few weeks later under far more difficult
conditions. So my advice to you would be to take
this new document and go just the same, on an
entirely voluntary basis, with the same convoy
for which you were originally intended. Then, when
the convoy reached Kzyl-orda, you would be able
to show your papers to the transport officer, and be
allowed to choose a place for work or study to suit
yourself."

This proposal was somewhat unexpected, but it

seemed to me convincing. Meanwhile he had been looking through my papers.

"So you're studying at the Moscow Academy for Foreign Languages?" he said. "Isn't that going to be evacuated too?"

"Yes, I've heard that it is to go to Alma Ata in Kazakhstan."

"Well, look, that fits excellently. You can travel to Kzyl-orda and from there go on to Alma Ata."

I let myself be convinced. Before I had got back to the students' hostel, I had taken my decision. I now had an identity card exempting me from the compulsory deportation, but I was free to go of my own accord. I would go on from Kzyl-orda to wherever my Academy had got to in the meantime. Nobody would prevent me from doing so, because I no longer belonged to the category of "compulsory deportees." The future lay clear and bright before me, and on this September day of the year 1941 I had complete confidence in it. Little did I know what bitter disappointments I should experience only a few weeks later.

In a few days we received word that we were to start early on 28th September. There was much excited running to and fro, as a large number of students from the Academy were to take part in the move. Yet another parting lay before us.

CHAPTER FOUR

Deportation to Karaganda

ON 28th September, 1941, the good station at Moscow, with its barbed wire and sentries, was like a hive of bees. Every ten or fifteen minutes new lorries drove up with their loads of Germans, all of whom were to be deported. Even in the worst days of the war, while the *Wehrmacht* was advancing on Moscow and every railway-wagon and lorry was urgently needed, there was still no limit to the number of trucks and trains and staff available for this task. Uniformed men were going to and fro all the time along the goods train shouting: "What are you standing around here for? Get into the train!"

We went along the train in the hope of still finding an empty space somewhere, but the people who were already sitting squashed together in the trucks shouted out at us: "No more room!" Then the uniformed men turned up again: "Why aren't you in the train?"

"It's impossible, Comrade officer. The trucks are all full to overflowing." The men in uniform were unimpressed.

"We'll soon see to that!"

Not a **hand** was raised in resistance by the crushed mass of Germans. With no more than a groan or two, we and several other new arrivals were pushed aboard in less than half an hour. It was impossible

154

even to sit. We could only stand and wait to see what
would happen next.

Journey into the Unknown

There were about fifty people in our little goods
wagon, representing every age and profession and
social class: from the unskilled worker to the profession who had made a name for himself in the field
of television; from an old man of nearly eighty to a
thirteen-year-old child. With the exception of a few
German émigrés, none of them had ever been in Germany. Most of them had never even learnt German
and were as completely Russian as anyone else in
Moscow. Two or three of our travelling companions
were domestic servants, who came originally from
the Volga Republic and had been in Moscow since
childhood.

I gradually began to understand why all these people suddenly had to be shipped off to Kzyl-orda just
for being Germans. In January, 1939, a census had
taken place in the Soviet Union, in which people
had to indicate not only their national status but their
national origin. In giving this, one could use one's
own discretion whether to follow family tradition or
a personal sense of belonging to a particular culture.
Many Soviet citizens, without giving much thought
to the question, had simply written *"Nemets"* or
"Nemka" (German). Little did they know that this
was one day to determine their fate. To-day, without
knowing even a word of German, they sat here classed
as Germans, on their way to an unknown destiny.

I quickly attached myself to those who were real
Germans. These included officials of the German
Communist Party who had fought in Spain in the

International Brigade and emigrated to the Soviet Union in 1939, only to find themselves now treated as enemy aliens. There was the wife of the Communist writer, Albert Hottop, with her two daughters, Käthe and Gerda; and there was Irmgard Sickert, the daughter of the German Communist, Alfred Sickert, who had fought in the International Brigade and been interned in Switzerland during the war. She had come to the Soviet Union in 1934, and like myself later studied at the Academy for Foreign Languages.

Slowly we journeyed across the plains of Russia. We had to stop often for long stretches of time. There was no hurry. The first towns that we passed were Ryazhsk and Morshansk, south-east of Moscow, which made a relatively peaceful impression on us. But that was soon to change. On the sixth day of our journey, we arrived at Penza, about 350 miles south-east of Moscow. Here there were thousands of people sitting and lying about all over the place—in the station, on the steps, on the streets and squares. They were refugees and evacuees from the western areas of Russia.

Late in the evening the journey went on, in the direction of Syzran and Kuibyshev. When we had passed Kuibyshev and were moving eastwards, the train suddenly halted between stations and remained where it was for several hours. We had to get out, and as I was walking along the train, I suddenly noticed on one of the trucks the inscription "Chelyabinsk."

"Chelyabinsk? That's surely not on the line to Kzyl-orda!"

We asked the officials accompanying us. "Are we definitely going to Kzyl-orda?"

A man in uniform nodded, though somewhat uncertainly.

"Then what's the meaning of this inscription: 'Chelyabinsk'?"

"I don't know—can't say," was the answer given in a tone of voice which was only too familiar to me after six years' residence in the Soviet Union.

During the night we had travelled in a northeasterly direction and we were now in Buguruslan in Bashkiria, so it was not to be Kzyl-orda!

On the seventeenth day there was suddenly a fresh stir of excitement all along our train. "We're in Kazakhstan!" somebody shouted, and in a flash the cry was taken up all the way down the eighty trucks of the train. At a little station we saw Kazakh signs among the inscriptions in Russian. Out came the maps again. We were indeed between the West Siberian town of Kurgan and Kazakh town of Petropavlovsk.

That evening we arrived in the first big town of the Kazakh Republic, though the name Petropavlovsk is Russian in origin. Someone remembered that Petropavlovsk had once been a meeting place of the caravans coming from Bokhara and Tashkent, which off-loaded their wares there for onward transport into Russia; but at this moment our own interest was concentrated on the present.

We saw Kazakhs here for the first time. Almost all of them had pitch-black hair, dark eyes shaped like those of the Mongols in pictures, and a yellow-brown skin. What particularly struck us was their peculiar walk and the shortness of their legs in relation to the upper parts of their bodies.

From Petropavlovsk we turned in a southerly direction. As the railway line only reached Balakhash, our journey must come to an end somewhere between Petropavlovsk and the Balakhash lake. At five o'clock in the morning of the twenty-second day of our journey, the train came to a stop. The sentries ran puffing up and down the train. All the doors were pulled open.

"We've arrived; you can all get down!"

We jumped down. There was not a house or a road or a tree or a bush to be seen. All round us was nothing but the steppe. We questioned the soldiers guarding us. There was no reply. It was not till an hour later that we learned that we were in the neighbourhood of a small town called Ossokarovka, about seventy-five miles north of Karaganda. So that must be the goal of our journey.

Villages Without a Name

We stood perplexed in front of our goods train. By this time our luggage had been unloaded. It was gradually getting lighter, and we could now distinguish in the distance the outline of Ossokarovka. Soon some peasant carts approached. A few of them were pulled by horses, but the majority by oxen and camels. I could hardly believe my eyes when I saw the camels pulling them.

The officer in charge of our convoy ran up and down in a state of excitement. A few minutes later our own sentry arrived with a list.

"Close up on me, all of you. I'll tell you how you're going to be divided up. You're all being distributed among the surrounding villages." Then he began to read out the list. But what could it mean? I heard not a single name of a village. Only: "Settlement No. 5, Settlement No. 12, Settlement No. 24," and so on.

It seemed there were no villages here, only settlements without names, settlements which simply had numbers.

Then I heard my name: "Leonhard, Settlement No. 5."

Soon the roll call was finished. Again I had the same disagreeable feeling as when we set out, but this time it was more for the fate of my friends and fellow travellers than for myself, since I, after all, still held an identity card without the notorious deportation stamp on it.

Cautiously I took my identity card out of my case: it was now the only link with freedom that I still had. Right at the beginning of the journey I had had a talk with the officer responsible for the transport, and he assured me that everything would come out right. Now I wanted to remind him of this.

"Comrade transport officer, as you know, I haven't got the deportation stamp, and I've only come with the convoy at the suggestion of the Chief of the Militia in my Moscow District. He categorically assured me I had the right to travel on freely from here by myself. I should like now to have my things so that I can go on to Alma Ata."

Never in my life, I thought to myself, had my fate depended so entirely on the answer of one man, but I was sure of my case. And then something incomprehensible happened.

"All that's nothing to me—I've nothing to do with all that! If what you say is true, then you'll be able to clear up your affairs when you get there. But for the present, in any case, you must go on to the settlement where you've been allocated."

"Comrade officer, you can see my personal identity

card here. It was newly issued in Moscow on 21st
September, 1941, and it contains no limitations of
any kind."

He laughed contemptuously: "Well, I suppose
they simply forgot to give you the stamp in Moscow.
We can soon put that right here. After all, it's down
in your document that you're a German."

There was no sense in saying any more. So I gave
way and decided to try my luck again when we had
reached Settlement No. 5. But I no longer had much
hope.

By this time our cases had been loaded on to the
camel-carts and ox-carts. The women and invalids
were also put in the carts. The rest of us followed
silently beside the vehicles. It was a melancholy
picture—a long trail of exhausted human beings,
straggling over the countryside after twenty-two days
in over-crowded goods wagons, now sent to live in
a place which ten years before had been a place of
exile for *kulaks*. Even the men driving the carts
were silent. They appeared to take no notice of us.

"How far is it to Settlement No. 5?"

"Ah, not so far, my boy! Might be about fifteen
miles. We shall be there by the evening—perhaps
even before the afternoon's over."

We asked more questions, and our driver said something about a collective farm.

"Collective farm? I thought it was exiled *kulaks*
who lived here?"

He replied in the slow way that Russian peasants
have: "Yes, we were *kulaks*, but now we are a kind
of collective farm."

"What do you mean, a kind of collective farm?"

The driver who had once been a *kulak* himself began to explain that in 1930 and 1931, the *kulaks* who had been expropriated and deported from the Ukraine and Central Russia had been settled in this area. He spoke just as indifferently and unconcernedly as if he were talking about things which had happened many centuries ago in some far distant part of the earth.

"There was nothing at all here in those days. There were just some pegs stuck in the ground with little notices on them saying: Settlement No. 5, No. 6, and so on. The peasants were brought here and told that now they had to look after themselves. So then they dug themselves holes in the ground. A great many died of cold and hunger in the early years. Well, after that they gradually built themselves clay huts, and then things were better."

"What happened then?"

"Oh, nothing else. After that we got the order to form a collective farm."

"Who did the order come from? The local Soviet?"

The driver shook his head. "There's no local Soviet here," he said.

I couldn't help smiling. The peasant seemed not to be quite right in the head; he had no idea what he was saying. There were local Soviets everywhere in the Soviet Union . . . But before the evening was out, I was to discover that he was right all the same.

We jogged along beside the ox-carts. After twenty-two days' travelling in a goods wagon, it was unpleasant to have to march across the steppe for even one full day, but the anxiety about what was awaiting us was for me worse even than exhaustion. Late in the afternoon we saw something in the distance, which looked like human habitations. We could soon see that the little huts were not built either of stone or wood, but of some brown substance. There were no windows to be seen: each of these little houses had simply a single opening which, as we were later to learn, was merely stopped up in the winter.

When we arrived, we were told that we would have to report to the *nachalnik* (chief). As we had a long time to wait, we wandered about and engaged in conversation with the natives. Practically all of them were Russians, though a few were Ukrainians or Tatars; none were Kazakhs. A few peasants came up to us. "Ah, there you are?" they said. "We've been waiting for you for a long time. We thought from the beginning you Germans would be sent here too."

In vain a few of us, including myself, tried to explain to them that we were anti-Fascists and enemies of Hitler. The peasants laughed: "Germans are always Germans!"

There was an astounding frankness about everything. It was my first experience in the Soviet Union of people who expressed their opinions so freely and bluntly. It was soon quite clear to us that many of the deported *kulaks* were still openly hostile to the régime. No one took our explanations seriously. They obviously took us for adherents of Hitler.

"Well, how far has your Hitler got? What d'you think? Will he get as far as this and liberate us?"

I went hot and cold all over. I had never heard anything like this in the Soviet Union. We tried again to explain our situation to these peasants but they laughed good-humouredly and waved aside our protests, saying: "Just you stay here a few years, then you'll see!"

In the evening we called on the *nachalnik*. He

lived in the only large building in the settlement. We sat on the ground and waited patiently until we were called in, one after another in quick succession. Every one received a paper on which was indicated the name of the peasant family to which he had to report. The peasants were compelled to take in the new arrivals. If there was the slightest difficulty, the Commandant was to be informed at once; but there were no difficulties. The peasants took in the new arrivals without demur. It was quite clear to them on whose orders everything was being done and who was responsible for assigning the billets.

I held my unstamped identity card firmly in my hand, knowing that here in this room with the *nachalnik* was my last chance. At last I was called in.

"Comrade *nachalnik*," I said, "I should like to draw your attention at once to the fact that I do not belong to this convoy. I have simply travelled with it at the suggestion of the Chief of the Moscow Militia. Here is my identity card issued in Moscow. You see for yourself that it does not contain the deportation stamp. I should like to go on from here to Alma Ata at once—to-morrow morning, or at the latest the day after. That is where my Academy is, therefore I would be glad if you would not include me in this settlement."

He seemed to be only half interested. "Well, all right," he said, "in that case, we can strike your name out of the list. There are too many here already." In my wildest hopes I had never expected so simple and rapid a solution. I left his office overjoyed.

Up till now all my thoughts had been concentrated on one idea: to avoid staying in this *kulak* settlement at any price—only to get away from here. But now that the opportunity was mine, I began to think of the difficulties of the undertaking. I must first get away from here, and then travel several thousand miles to Alma Ata. I should be asked continually for identity cards and documents. It was true that I had no deportation stamp on my document, but the word "German" was clear and unmistakable. And then there was another thing: I had hardly any money left. When I set out from Moscow, I had a few hundred roubles with me, and for a student at that time that was a lot of money; but in my present position, it was a perfectly derisory sum.

However, in spite of everything, I did not let myself get downhearted. I had absolutely made up my mind on this expedition. I was nineteen and a half years old and in good health: I spoke Russian fluently and I was filled with an optimism which might almost be called light-hearted.

Next I went in search of a purchaser for my few spare bits of clothing. The only things I had to offer were an overcoat and a pair of trousers. After a good deal of bargaining I reached an agreement with a Tartar peasant woman. I did not get much, and a quarter of the sum had to be paid to a peasant for taking me with him to the railway station at Ossokarovka. My heart beat fast as I went up to the booking office to buy a ticket to Karaganda. The clerk simply looked for a moment at my identity card and without hesitation gave me a ticket. Four hours later I was in Karaganda.

Arrival in Karaganda

Could it really be Karaganda—a town of a quarter

of a million inhabitants, the newest centre of industry to be built under the first Five Year Plan? The station was a dirty little wooden building not much bigger than the small station at Ossokarovka. Leaving the station building, I saw a dirty, crooked, half-plastered street of small, dilapidated houses. Everything was dark grey from coal dust. It was difficult to breathe.

Thoroughly depressed, I went slowly up the street. True, I had seen poverty before now in Moscow, and during my residence in the Soviet Union I had come to know a whole series of medium-sized industrial towns, but never yet had I encountered anything so completely wretched. I could not help recollecting the picture that Jack London gave of the improvised settlements of the gold diggers at the time of the gold rush, but even this comparison was inadequate.

Only a few minutes after I had left the station, I saw my first *zemlyanki*—holes in the ground covered over with cardboard or wood and a layer of earth about two feet thick, with a few poles to support the roof. People lived in them. It was an appalling sight, but I comforted myself with the thought that these were only relics from the past, inevitable in an industrial town which had developed so quickly, and impossible with the best will to eliminate to-day while the war was on.

But the more I looked at the town, the less encouraging my prospects seemed to be. There was no Academy, no technical institution; there were nothing but *zemlyanki*, dilapidated wooden houses and here and there more or less presentable office buildings, several stories high. Never had I been so forcibly struck by a contrast in the Soviet scene as I was by the difference between the wretched huts of the inhabitants and the tall office buildings of plastered stone, which looked by comparison so splendid in these surroundings.

At that moment I noticed a new bus, which made a deep impression on me amid the general squalor. I ran to catch it.

"Where are you going?"

"To the new town," was the answer, as the signal was given to start.

After half an hour's journey, I saw a blaze of light in the far distance. As we came closer my astonishment knew no bounds. We were travelling on a good asphalt surface, past a splendid park, and I saw modern houses of four or five stories, brilliantly lit up.

Cautiously I asked the conductor: "Excuse me, could you give me some advice whether I can spend the night here—and if so, where?"

He laughed. "At the hotel, of course."

"At the hotel?" I looked at him somewhat discouraged. After everything I had been through in the last few weeks, the word "hotel" sounded to me like something out of a fairy story.

"Of course there's a hotel here, and if you have a permit they'll take you in at once."

I was even more astonished as I entered the hotel. It was very comfortably furnished: carpets, flowers, well-dressed people going about without a care in the world. I went hesitantly up to the reception desk.

"Have you got a permit?"

"Yes, here it is."

"Good, then you can have a bed."

It seemed almost incredible, after the ordeal of the last four weeks, to be able to sleep in a real bed in a real hotel! But even better was to follow. A few minutes later I discovered that dinner could be had in the dining-room of the hotel. I was shown into a restaurant, which at that time seemed to me the height of elegance, with a little orchestra and an elaborate menu. Everything was like the best days of peace time. The contrast with the old town of Karaganda and the mud huts of the deported *kulaks* was simply beyond belief.

The next morning I took my first walk through the new town. My first impression was not disappointed. The whole town consisted of fine, modern four-story houses with electric light and running water. The name "new town" was admittedly somewhat exaggerated. It was not a town at all, but a great collection of new buildings which pointed to the future development of a town. The walk from one end to the other took about fifteen minutes.

In the middle of the town was a square, on which stood the largest building. This housed the District Committee of the Party. On my first walk, I found in the neighbourhood of this building a modern cinema, the headquarters of the N.K.V.D. and the offices of the District and Town Soviet of Karaganda—the last, however, in a noticeably smaller building. The rest of the buildings seemed to be residential. Suddenly I found myself standing in front of an extensive modern two-story building on which I saw a tablet bearing an inscription of three words: "Karaganda Educational Institute." In great delight, I rushed inside and soon found the secretary's office.

At the Educational Institute

It was obvious at first glance that the privileged

days of the Moscow Academy for Foreign Languages were finally over. Instead of living two or three in a room as before, the students with whom I continued my academic career were herded together twenty to a room. There were no cupboards. We had to stow our things in a trunk or a parcel under the bed.

Our studies were based on the official history books prepared for educational institutes and used throughout the entire Soviet Union. The students were mostly the sons and daughters of *kulaks* banished to the Karaganda District in 1930 and 1931, but twelve years had passed since the collectivisation, and now that the *kulaks* had long since been displaced as the principal public enemies by the Trotskyites, they had been given permission for study. I made a number of friends among the students in my first days there.

Most of them had been exiled to this area as small children with their parents at the beginning of the 1930's. They had lived through terrible experiences in their childhood. From conversation with them, I learned how they had been expelled from house and home with their parents and deported into this wilderness. In the early years, they had been exposed to cold and hunger without protection, until their parents had built mud huts. On top of all this, they had had much mental suffering to put up with in the early years. At the beginning of the 1930's, it was not an easy fate to grow up as the child of an exiled *kulak*.

In one of our franker hours of conversation, a fellow student told me about life in the early years of their exile. "Party officials would often ride on horseback into the settlements while they were being built. It wasn't so bad when they just bellowed at us or insulted and abused us, but sometimes they came with whips and anyone who was in the way got a taste of them—they would even lash out at children at play! After that we learned to be careful. Whenever any one we didn't know arrived here from the town, we shut ourselves up at home."

He told me this without any bitterness, rather as if he were talking about a storm which had passed over long ago. "You must understand," he went on by way of explanation, "that this was in the hey-day of the struggle over collectivisation, and many of the junior officials let themselves be carried away, but it was condemned by the Party later on. You can't avoid that sort of thing happening in a gigantic up-heaval like the collectivisation."

Most of my fellow students used to go home at the week-ends. That is to say, they used to go to one of the settlements which lay in the inner or outer en-virons of Karaganda. When they came back, they often spoke indignantly about their parents. "They still don't understand anything at all!" I often heard them say. "I've tried so often to explain to them why collectivisation is justified, but the old people just never will understand it!"

These sons and daughters of the *kulaks* who had been exiled here as small children had in fact be-come Stalinists with the passage of time. Of course it may be that some of them were only putting on a pre-tence of devotion to the Stalinist system, but most of my fellow-students may well have had the same attitude of mind as many of my young friends in Moscow and I myself, whose parents had been arrested during the purges of 1936-38. The fate of one's own family might admittedly be tragic and certainly unjustified we thought; but on an objective assessment one had to support the Soviet Union, and from that point of view all measures were justifiable. In our Institute, there were not only Kazakh students and the sons and daughters of deported *kulaks,* but also children of senior Party and State officials; for instance, the son of the public prosecutor and the daughter of the secretary of the women's department of our Institute. Both of them showed themselves highly conscious of the position held by their parents. In particular, the senior teacher of general history had a great deal to put up with from them.

"Why are they both so hostile to the teacher?" I once asked one of the students.

"The teacher pretty well counts as a deportee," he whispered to me in reply.

"A deportee?"

"He's not exactly a real deportee, but he's a Finn. During the Soviet-Finnish War of 1939-40, many Finns were transferred here from the Leningrad District. That's how he came to Karaganda, and now he obviously has to be on his guard."

A few days later I was able to see for myself that life was indeed not easy for the Finnish teacher. After every lecture, it was the teacher's job to list the literature relating to the subject in question, and the relevant references had to be carefully divided into two groups: the classics of Marxism-Leninism on the one hand and the source literature on the other. The teacher had been doing this as usual on one occasion, but he had perhaps not made the distinction between the two groups sufficiently clear. In the course of listing some of the required literature, he

mentioned a work of Plekhanov. Suddenly he was
interrupted by the son of the public prosecutor.

"Does this text of Plekhanov belong to the category
of classics of Marxism-Leninism, or the category of
source literature?"

He put it in the form of a question, but the point
of the question and the aggressive tone in which it
was put made all of us start. The teacher went red
in the face for a few seconds and then recovered
himself with amazing rapidity: "Obviously, the text
of Plekhanov belongs to the category of source literature. I should like to take advantage of this opportunity to emphasise explicitly that the category of
classics of Marxism-Leninism comprises exclusively
the works of Marx, Engels, Lenin and above all, first
and foremost, the works of Comrade Stalin. The
reason for citing a text of Plekhanov in connection
with this lecture is simply that a number of his writings are useful and correct. This fact has been expressly made clear by Stalin in his great speech of
6th November, 1941."

We all sighed with relief. The teacher had got
himself out of the jam with great skill. There was
nothing left even for the over-enthusiastic son of the
public prosecutor to do except to nod his head in
agreement, since the teacher had cleverly concluded his reply with a quotation from Stalin. But
how many such situations must he not already have
had to get out of, and how many more still lay before
him? It was certainly not an easy life being a deported teacher.

A Meeting with Ulbricht in Karaganda

All unsuspecting I came out of the lecture hall

one morning to find the Director's secretary coming to meet me in a state of excitement.

"There has just been a summons from the Militia! You are to go there at once!"

"To the Militia?" As I went to Mikhailovka, where the militia had its headquarters, I was somewhat uneasy but conscious of having done nothing wrong.

"You are to report to the Chief of the Militia in person."

The Chief of the Militia was a Kazakh. He had a threatening and angry look.

"Are you the German, Leonhard?" he growled. "If so, you have twenty-four hours' notice to get out of Karaganda!"

I was dumbfounded. Had not my immigration permit been arranged with the agreement of the District Committee? Could it be that the deportation orders issued in September, 1941, for Moscow and other major towns in the western part of the Soviet Union, had now been extended to all towns in the Soviet Union?

"Where am I to go then if I have to leave Karaganda? Am I allowed to travel to Alma Ata?"

"It's all one to me where you go. Every town is banned to Germans. You can choose anywhere you like to reside in the district of Karaganda with the exception of the town itself. Why don't you go to the settlements at Ossokarovka? There are lots of Germans there already anyway."

"Comrade *nachalnik*, I have been a member of the *Komsomol* for many years and my registration has been approved."

The Militia Chief's face became even angrier. "I know that," he said, "but I have already told you that the deportation order applies to all Germans. If you are still in Karaganda in twenty-four hours' time, you will have contravened orders and the responsibility will be yours. Is that clear?"

It was evident that the matter was now irrevocably settled: within the next twenty-four hours—which by now had become only twenty-three—I had to leave Karaganda, and the little educational institute, and all my new-found friends and fellow pupils. In utter despair, I wandered through the new town.

Without any particular object in view, I went into the *Univermag,* the only shop. At the counter stood a well-built man in fur boots reaching above his knees, a fur cap and a heavy fur-lined coat. He might almost have been a Polar explorer. Then I heard his voice, and it sounded to me somehow familiar. As I came nearer I noticed that this peculiar sort of Polar explorer spoke Russian with a German accent. At that moment I recognised him: it was Hans Mahle, an official whom I had got to know in Moscow on the training course in November, 1940. He had often spoken on Moscow Radio since the war broke out. I rushed up to him: "Hans, this is wonderful! How do you come to be here?"

He too was delighted, but he answered my question evasively. "We're on our way through here with a number of other comrades, and we shall only be staying a few days in this area. Well, and what about you? Tell me how you're getting on."

"I went with the deportation train on the 28th September. We reached Ossokarovka, seventy-five miles north of Karaganda, in the middle of October. We were all billeted among the *kolkhozes* in the neighbourhood, but I had no stamp on my pass, so I came on here. I am studying at the Educational Institute."

"So, anyway, everything's all right with you?"

"Unfortunately not, Hans. Something frightful has happened, just to-day. I was called to the militia and told that I must leave Karaganda within twenty-four hours. Now I have simply no idea what to do."

"Well, in that case, we've arrived just at the right moment. The best thing is for you to come along at once. I'll introduce you to Comrade Ulbricht and the others."

Ulbricht in Karaganda? What could Ulbricht be up to in Karaganda in December, 1941? Naturally, I did not try to ask—I had been long enough in the Soviet Union to know that one never puts questions about Party matters. One waits to be told.

A few minutes later we reached the hotel—the one and only hotel, in which I too had passed my first few days in Karaganda. In front of the building stood five or six people, also dressed like Hans Mahle.

I knew none of them personally at that time, and Ulbricht only by sight from the time when he had lectured to us during our training in Moscow from the autumn of 1940 to June, 1941. Hans Mahle led me up to Ulbricht, who shook hands casually and muttered something which might perhaps have been, "How do you do?" just as if it was the most natural thing in the world that German émigrés should meet each other in Karaganda in December, 1941. After that I was introduced to a woman party member called Lotte Kühne. This was the first time I had heard her name, and it was not until four years later that I learned she was Ulbricht's wife.

We stood waiting in front of the hotel, while two

American jeeps drove up. It was obvious that the
officials were going to leave in a few minutes. They
put a few questions about the émigrés who had been
deported to this area. I told them as briefly as possible
in telegraphic phrases about the comrades I knew and
their unhappy fate, but the officials listened without
much interest and put no questions. The fate of their
forcibly deported German comrades seemed to be a
matter of comparative indifference to these senior
officials of the German Communist Party headquarters. From this I concluded that they had not come
here on the émigrés' account.

"And are you living in Karaganda?"

"Yes, up till to-day. I've been studying here in the
history faculty of the Educational Institute, but to-
day I was given strict orders to leave Karaganda
within twenty-four hours."

Ulbricht merely made a gesture with his hand.
"That will be put right. We shall be having discussions in the next few days with all our comrades at the
District Committee of the Party, and you'll be invited
there too."

By this time the jeeps were ready to leave, and the
officials climbed into them. At midday I was summoned to the District Committee. The member in
charge of the Agitation and Propaganda (*Agitprop*)
department was beaming and said; "Everything's all
right. You can stay on in Karaganda, and don't worry.
There's to be a conference here at the District Committee of all the German émigrés in the Karaganda
District, within the next few days. As you're already
living here in the town as a student, you will be able
to stay here, but all that will be discussed at the conference."

"Can I ask when the conference will take place?"

"It's supposed to be on 22nd December, as soon as Comrade Ulbricht and the others are back from their visit to the prisoner-of-war camp."

This was the first I had heard of a prisoner-of-war camp: so that was why Ulbricht and the other officials had come here! I had had no idea that there was a prisoner-of-war camp in the neighbourhood of Karaganda at all. Even later on, during the ten months I lived in Karaganda, I learned nothing more about the prisoner-of-war camp—neither where it was nor how many prisoners were in it.

This little episode is by no means unique. It frequently happens in the Soviet Union that people living in a particular town for years on end have no suspicion of the existence of institutions which are to be found either in the very same town or in its immediate neighbourhood, to say nothing of the existence of camps or prisons.

The Conference of Émigrés

The German émigrés' conference began on 22nd December, 1941, in the building of the Karaganda District Committee of the Communist Party. There was a great deal of chatter and happy scenes of reunion. I met a man from my goods-wagon who had fought in the Spanish Civil War, and also my friend Irmgard Sickert and the two daughters of the German writer Albert Hottop, who had been arrested soon after the outbreak of war, as well as other émigrés who had been on the same train and were now all living in the Ossokarovka district. There was also another reunion for me—with my friends from those happy days in the Children's Home No. 6, whom I had not seen again for so many years. They had been here even longer than myself, having travelled with the first convoy from Moscow.

One by one, up to fifty German émigrés assembled in the front hall of the District Committee building, and we were then invited into the meeting hall. It was a curious spectacle. The splendidly decorated meeting hall, which was normally attended only by well-dressed Russian and Kazakh officials, was now for the first time in the history of the Party in Karaganda filled exclusively with Germans. It was terrible to see how much these German émigrés had changed. Even their few weeks' stay in Karaganda had left on them its marks of suffering, deprivation and misery. It did not matter so much for us younger ones, but the older comrades had suffered a great deal from the compulsory evacuation and the lack of food and the terrible living conditions.

An unsuspecting observer would never have supposed that these were Germans. By this time it had got very cold in the Karaganda District, and the thermometer already registered forty degrees centigrade below zero. It was impossible to tell the émigrés from Russian exiles. They were wearing the unlikeliest articles of clothing, one on top of another, and they had obviously put on everything they possessed. Little did we know that only a few weeks later it was to become even colder.

By this time several officials of the Agitation and Propaganda Department of the District Committee had entered the meeting hall with Walter Ulbricht. The conference was opened. An official of the Karaganda District Committee explained in Russian by way of introduction that the District Committee of the Party had invited the German émigrés (who were referred to as "our political émigrés comrades") to a meeting to discuss a number of political and other questions. He was delighted that Comrade Ulbricht was present, and with that he called upon him to deliver his political address.

Self-possessed and quite at ease, Walter Ulbricht mounted the platform, just as if nothing unusual had happened in the last few months. I could not help thinking of the last time I had heard him in June, 1941, in Moscow at the course I was then on. Less than six months had passed since then, but what a lot had happened in that time! German forces had seized Estonia, Latvia, Lithuania and Belorussia, and overrun the greater part of the Ukraine. Millions upon millions of people had been evacuated; the whole population of the Volga German Republic and every other German had been compulsorily deported; and now, six months after the outbreak of war, German émigrés were meeting in Karaganda!

Walter Ulbricht had nothing much new to say in his speech. He confined himself mainly to a repetition of what could be read every day in the Soviet press. Faithful to the theory current at the time, he explained how the severe economic situation in Germany, the lack of raw materials and in particular of fuel, would soon compel Hitlerite Germany to retreat. He told us about the growing movement of resistance in the subjugated countries and the spread of discontent in Germany itself. Finally, Ulbricht drew attention to the fact that since Japan's attack on Pearl Harbour and the entry of the U.S.A. into the war against the Axis Powers, the balance of forces had been fundamentally altered to Hitler's detriment

—but this too was something which we already knew from the Soviet press.

It was only in the last part of his speech that he told us something that was not so well known. He spoke of the work which had begun in the last few weeks in the prisoner-of-war camps. Ulbricht explained that this work would be built up in the future, with the object of converting prisoners-of-war into anti-Fascists. Then he drew a manuscript out of his pocket and raised his voice to a shout: "Here is the proclamation of 158 German prisoners-of-war!" Then he read passages out of it. He described it as an important document, indicating a new direction, and he commented on the proclamation clause by clause.

When Ulbricht finished his speech there followed the usual applause, but one could see that many of the émigrés had not entirely followed what he had been saying. They were tired, weak and hungry, and many of them were not so receptive to political ideas as under normal conditions.

Next it was announced that, after we had had lunch together, there would be a further discussion, at which a number of practical questions about the émigrés' life in the Karaganda District would be dealt with. We were then invited to a large and excellent lunch. A table had been laid for a meal that made a striking contrast with our usual starvation diet. How quickly the atmosphere changed! Even before the meal was finished, the terrible experiences of the last few weeks—the cold, hunger and misery —seemed to have been almost completely forgotten.

Then we waited anxiously for the second discussion, which we hoped was going to lead to a change in our life at Karaganda. Walter Ulbricht and two officials of the Agitation and Propaganda Department, who were personally very friendly but did not have much influence (as I had already learned), together with the District Secretary of the M.O.P.R., began to talk to us about practical problems of our daily life. An official of the District Committee began by briefly referring to the general situation, including the indescribable sufferings of the Soviet people, the great difficulties of the time and the need to make sacrifices and to put up with even the most trying conditions patiently and unflinchingly. Although the difficulties were very great and resources extremely limited, he announced that the District Committee would do everything possible in these trying times to mitigate any unnecessary hardship among the German political émigrés. It was particularly satisfactory that a permanent link had been formed between the political émigrés and the District Committee of the M.O.P.R., which would certainly do everything possible to help them.

Then one comrade after another was called upon to give his present address and place of work, to state his wishes, and to report briefly on his difficulties. It was only then that I realised how lucky I had been. My comrades' reports were appalling. They were humiliated by the authorities of the *kolkhozes* and the brigade leaders; they were abused and ridiculed for being Germans; offensive words were shouted at them, and often they were actually attacked. In many cases they were deliberately given inferior rations. When they tried to complain and demand the proper application of rationing regulations, they were told: "That doesn't apply to you Germans—you should be glad to have anything to eat at all." Many of the German émigrés had been assigned to the worst accommodation available in the villages—houses with gaps and holes in the ceilings and walls, leaving them with no protection from the icy wind known at the *buran*. They described these things unemotionally and factually, without hatred or bitterness. The disciplined behaviour of the émigrés and their quiet acceptance of their fate were astounding. Even what they asked for was extremely modest; most of them only sought some redress of the worst injustices, which could be removed by a telephone conversation or a short note from the District Committee. In one or two cases there were requests for clothing or roofing material, or for soap or food. With the possible exception of a few who were engaged on special work, our rations at that time consisted only of 400 grammes of damp bread a day—and this weighed only 200-300 grammes when dried out. There was nothing else at all—no fat, no sugar, no meat. Whereas the inhabitants had long-established connections in the country and friends and relatives, we German émigrés had come to an entirely new locality and found ourselves in a position of quite exceptional difficulty.

In spite of the general difficulties of the situation, it would have been possible to meet the requests completely for those whose need was greatest—the old and sick and the veterans of the Spanish Civil War. Every one of us knew just as well as the officials that in this part of the Karaganda District, as everywhere else in the Soviet Union, there were "reserved" shops, "reserved" restaurants and "reserved" distributors, limited to a particular circle of people. Everyone knew too that even in times of difficulty such as these for the rest of the Soviet population, every kind of food was to be found in abundance in the "reserved" restaurants and shops. Given the authority, it would certainly have been possible for the M.O.P.R. to divert something from them in order to provide at least a little alleviation of the existence of their comrades, who had belonged to the Workers' movement for decades and had risked their lives in Spain. But the "reserved" shops were not so much as mentioned. They were passed over as if they did not even exist. Since this was a subject about which one did not talk, not a word was said about it on the part of the émigrés, and it was not raised on the official side.

The minor material needs and appeals for help by German comrades were dismissed as they arose, with the remark that the M.O.P.R. would do what it could for cases of exceptional hardship. Everyone knew that this was the end of the matter, for it was clear that an organisation so feeble on its own account as the M.O.P.R. had no food or clothing available at a time like this. The longer the discussion dragged on, the more obvious it became that nothing was really going to change for the émigrés. No doubt this was not the fault of the two district officials, who would personally have been glad to help us, but evidently the matter was out of their hands, for their power too was limited.

My turn to speak came last, perhaps because I was the youngest. I expressed my wishes in two sentences—to continue my studies in the Educational Institute and to be allowed to live in Karaganda. My wishes were granted. "That shall be done. In the next few days, you will get your certificate from the militia and you can go on studying in the Educational Institute."

After a few closing words, the meeting of the
émigrés was at an end. It was clear to all of them that
they would have to spend a long time yet in the Karaganda District and that so far as the present situation of the German émigrés present was concerned,
it was not a matter of local shortcomings, but of the
official line. Only a few of the worst excesses would
be avoided in the future. The high hopes which many
had cherished at the beginning of the meeting were
dissipated; however, we had all lived long enough in
the Soviet Union to have learned not to complain,
but to adjust ourselves to everything and to look on
the bright side of even the most difficult and disagreeable situations. Thus some of us told ourselves that
we had now "made contact with the Party" and
that we should certainly be invited to more such
meetings.

This however was not the case. The conference
in December was the only meeting to be held for
the deported émigrés in the Karaganda District. I
have never seen anything more of any of the participants at that émigrés conference in Karaganda in
December, 1941, with the exception of Irmgard
Sickert, who returned to Germany in 1947 and subsequently worked on the East German Radio and later
in the Foreign Ministry of the Soviet Zone Government. It is perfectly possible, and indeed even probable, that many of our comrades who had served the
Party for years and decades are still in the Karaganda
District, unless they have died in the meantime of
their sufferings and deprivations.

In the Soviet Zone of Occupation of Germany after
1945, there was never any official mention of the
forcible deportation of the German émigrés in the

Soviet Union. The sole exception was a report in *Neues Deutschland*, the central organ of the S.E.D. on 12th December, 1952, about the death of the German artist, Heinrich Vogeler: "He died in 1942 in Kazakhstan, where he had been evacuated as a precautionary measure from Moscow." Anyone who went through the forcible evacuation and lived in the Karaganda District knows only too well what is the real meaning of such a "precautionary measure."

My Life in the New Town

The end of the conference was the beginning of what became my normal life in Karaganda. The conference had been a good start. Although nothing appeared about it in the press, not even the local newspaper called the *Socialist Karaganda*, nevertheless all the Party officials in Karaganda and also the instructors at the Educational Institute knew about it. For me the result was a perceptible relief. On the day after the émigrés' conference, I was asked by the Director, the Party Secretary and some of the teachers how I liked the Institute and whether I was satisfied with the lectures, or whether I had any suggestions to make. Immediately afterwards, without any hindrance, I was admitted to the local *Komsomol* organisation. At the Institute I was appointed to be the responsible secretary of the M.O.P.R., and at one of the periodical celebrations, I was even elected to the Presidium of the Institute.

After that I was soon over the worst. I was invited to various functions and politely welcomed; and I had what was then, for a German, the great good fortune not to be treated as an enemy alien. My case was indeed exceptional. In other towns and villages, there had been no such conference of the émigrés, and many Germans were subjected to severe sufferings, mental as well as physical, in these wartime conditions. It was little help to them to explain that they were German Communists who had fought against the Nazis even in the days of the Weimar Republic, and had carried on the struggle at the risk of their lives, either clandestinely or in the Spanish Civil War. In spite of this, they were often abused for being German, and treated with contempt: they were held responsible for what Hitler was doing, even though they had spent their whole lives in resisting the Nazis.

One day I received an invitation to come to a lecture given to a restricted circle at the District Committee of the Party the following Sunday morning at ten o'clock. This was something entirely new for me. I had often noticed in conversation with Russian Party members that some of them seemed to know more than they could have learned from the newspapers and leaflets, but it was never clear to me how they obtained this knowledge. Now I imagined that I had penetrated the secret, because what happened in Karaganda no doubt also happened in other towns.

Besides the usual official gatherings which took place in Karaganda as well as everywhere else in the Soviet Union, and in which nothing was said that had not already appeared in the newspapers, every Sunday morning at the District Committee there were lectures of a more interesting and instructive character given to selected audiences. Written in-

vitations to each of these functions were sent out
and had to be shown at the entrance where strict
control was exercised.

As a rule about eighty of the more important and
politically educated officials in the town took part.
The lectures were on a consistently high level. There
were no trivial commonplaces, and often international
problems were dealt with, as far afield as South America. I was very glad to attend. I was interested in politics, and it was a privilege to be invited there to hear
things which remained concealed from others.
Hitherto, apart from a short educational course in the
spring of 1941, I had belonged to the great mass of
the population who only knew what was published
in *Pravda*: now I was beginning to learn a little more.
Later on it became clear to me that this was only the
first step towards higher things.

Looking back in retrospect on much of what happened in the Soviet Union, it seems to me that this
gradual division between those who knew nothing,
those who knew more, and those who knew a great
deal, with the corresponding careful gradation of the
doses in which information was given to the population, was an important and distinctive feature of the
Stalinist system. Thanks to these gradations, being
well informed gave one a feeling of "belonging." This
feeling is inseparably linked with the hierarchical
structure of Soviet society, and no doubt contributes
to the cohesion of particular groups of officials—all
the more so because in the Soviet Union the whole of
the press and radio are under a central direction and
control, and the great mass of the population learns
very little indeed; in fact, only as much as the leadership of the Party and State wishes it to learn.

At that time, I did not think much about such topics. I listened with interest to our instructors, but only occasionally found myself speculating where they themselves could have learned what they told us, which was not to be found in newspapers or periodicals. But it was not till a year later that I learned the answer.

Hubert in Wonderland

As I was wandering through the streets one spring morning in 1942, I suddenly saw a young man dressed in rags and tatters coming towards me. I could hardly believe my eyes. Could it be the boy we knew as "Hubert in Wonderland"?

The story of Hubert Lhoste begins in 1934, when he was still a small boy. He was the son of a miner's family in the Saar district, and never in his wildest dreams would he have suspected what the next few years were to bring him. In January, 1935, the population of the Saar district was to decide its future in a plebiscite. The choice lay between unification with Hitler's Germany and a continuance of the status quo, that is to say as a mandated territory under the League of Nations. At that time *Pravda* had sent one of the most celebrated Soviet journalists, Michael Koltsov, to the Saar district, where he was sending daily reports to his newspaper. One day Michael Koltsov had the idea of adopting a small boy belonging to a miner's family in the Saar district. His name was Hubert Lhoste.

People soon learned about the adoption in the Soviet Union. The newspapers carried pictures of the little boy, and described in detail the conditions he was living in. When the plebiscite was over, Michael

Koltsov, the *Pravda* correspondent, travelled back to the Soviet Union accompanied by his new charge. On his arrival a triumphant reception awaited the little worker's child from the Saarland. He could hardly get away from the huge banquets and celebrations. All the newspapers published his picture, together with long articles about him. Wherever he went, his appearance at once became known. He was passed on from one party to another, always sitting at the principal table, where sometimes it was impossible to see him for the quantities of flowers. He was not so badly off at home either, living as he did with so powerful a protector as Michael Koltsov, who at that time enjoyed not only position and prestige, but also a considerable influence. Michael Koltsov had been a member of the Party since 1918, and on the staff of *Pravda* since 1920. He had spent a long time as member of the People's Commissariat for Foreign Affairs, and since 1934 he had been a member of the Editorial Committee of *Pravda,* besides being editor of the satirical newspaper, *Crocodile.* It was easy enough for him to provide the miner's son, Hubert Lhoste, with an agreeable life; and naturally the little thirteen-year-old boy enjoyed himself immensely.

This proved to be no more than the beginning of his career, for by now everything that happened to him in the Soviet Union was carefully recorded, including the pæans of praise and expressions of enthusiasm which he delivered generously in return. His experiences and his enthusiastic statements about the Soviet Union were eventually collected and appeared as a book under the title of *Hubert in Wonderland.*

This book had a rapid sale, and made Hubert even more popular. He was invited to the Kremlin and received by Marshal Budenny and Marshal Tukhachevsky. Children's cinemas and theatres and schools were called after him. Pictures of the little red-haired, chubby-faced, freckled Hubert, larger than life, were even carried in processions and demonstrations. He must really have felt as if he were in Wonderland.

Hubert's happy existence was to come to a sudden end, however. His great patron, Michael Koltsov, was suddenly arrested as a public enemy, and this was the beginning of Hubert's descent into obscurity. The pictures disappeared; the children's theatres had their names changed; the book called *Hubert in Wonderland* was removed from all the bookshops and libraries; and Hubert, who by this time had reached the age of fourteen, had no idea what he was to do next. He had got so used to his life as a little popular hero that it must naturally have been twice as difficult for him to adapt himself again to the life of an ordinary young man. Thanks to the intercession of some of his friends who had not yet been arrested, he finally joined Children's Home No. 6.

That was how he became a pupil at our Home. He gradually adjusted himself to his new life and made friends with some of us, including myself. After a year or two, he had got used to being no longer *"Hubert in Wonderland,"* but just ordinary Hubert Lhoste. But no sooner had he adjusted himself to our life at the Children's Home than a new blow fell on him, in August, 1939. On the conclusion of the pact with Hitlerite Germany, the Children's Home was dispersed. This was a shock for all of us, but most of all for Hubert: for him it was yet one more setback just after he had adapted himself to the new situation.

All this happened in August, 1939. And now we were in the spring of 1942. I had not seen him for two and a half years, and I had no idea what had become of him. There he was now standing before me, half-starved and dressed in rags and tatters, looking like a little tramp. Although my own appearance at that time was probably not much better, I was appalled to see my celebrated friend Hubert before me in such a state.

Automatically he spoke to me in Russian. "You needn't speak Russian," I said, "you can speak to me in German."

He smiled, but it was a melancholy smile. "I've got out of the habit. It is so long since I spoke to anyone in German."

He thereupon reverted to Russian again to tell me his story. Like every other German, he had been summoned to the Militia in the autumn of 1941 and deported to the Karaganda District in the first convoy. When it came to the turn of our convoy, the Germans had been settled in large groups, but the arrangements for the first convoy had been less well managed. Hubert found himself sent to an outlying village of the Karaganda District all by himself, and he was placed in a *kolkhoz* the very next day after his arrival.

"What are you doing in the *kolkhoz*?"

"I look after the cattle."

I studied the dirty, ragged figure in front of me, and listened to him cursing in Russian. There was nothing to remind me of the Hubert in Wonderland that had once been, except the lively eyes and the freckles.

He was no more resentful of his fate than I was of my own. For us it was something to be taken for granted, almost self-evident, that in the Soviet Union one could fall from the highest peaks into the depths just as one could sometimes go in the reverse direction.

I wanted to talk to him at greater length, but unfortunately it was impossible. Hubert suddenly clutched his head and exclaimed: "For heaven's sake! I can't go on talking like this for so long! I was sent here to buy something, and I must not be absent from the *kolkhoz* for more than a few hours. If I don't get back in good time, it may be very unpleasant."

I understood. We parted. Rather sadly, I gazed after my friend from Children's Home No. 6—once the hero of the Soviet Pioneers and now a ragged cow-herd; once an honoured guest in the Kremlin and now living in terror of the officer in charge of a petty *kolkhoz* in Northern Kazakhstan. I made many sub-sequent attempts to get in contact with him again, but it was in vain. The celebrated Hubert in Won-derland had vanished, never to reappear.

The Secret Telegram

At the end of June, 1942, I was summoned to the District Committee of the M.O.P.R.

"We have a new position to fill," I was told. "It is for an M.O.P.R. Instructor in the Karaganda District, and he will be specially concerned with political émigrés. It has been proposed that you should be appointed."

I hesitated to reply, and my silence was clearly misinterpreted by the M.O.P.R. secretary. She imagined that I must have doubts.

"You would of course discuss everything with me here in your capacity as an instructor, and you would represent me on any journey you might make. The pay amounts to 500 roubles a month and we would try to find somewhere for you to live."

At last I began to understand what was being offered to me. I agreed joyfully. The next day, I received an official notice: "The District Committee of the Party has confirmed your appointment, and a place has been found for you to live."

The secretary then gave me a list of fifty-eight German émigrés. The list gave in each case the age, place of birth, and address of their place of work. "Your task will be to maintain a regular correspondence with these German émigrés. You must keep yourself informed of anything they need and make proposals as to how we can help them. If they ever need documents, you must prepare them and submit them to me for signature. Apart from correspondence by post, I would suggest that you should make a tour through the Karaganda District as early as possible to visit our comrades on the spot. At the same time, you must also look after the M.O.P.R. organisations in each particular place. When we have food, soap or clothing material available, you will be responsible for their distribution to the German émigrés on your list, and also for taking care of cases of special need in order of priority."

One brilliant summer morning, some three weeks after my appointment as an M.O.P.R. Instructor, I went all unsuspecting to my place of work. Hardly had I arrived when the M.O.P.R. secretary handed me a telegram saying, "Here—this is for you."

I read: "Comrade Leonhard is to come at once Ufa. Signed Vilkov."

Ufa? I knew that Ufa, the capital of the Bashkir Autonomous Soviet Republic, lay about eighteen hundred miles west of Karaganda, so that I had another long journey in front of me. Ufa? This was the town where the Comintern authorities and the leaders of the German Communist Party were established.

A few minutes later the telephone rang for the M.O.P.R. secretary. The conversation was short. "You are to report at once to the cadre section of the District Committee."

Once more, as in November, 1941, I went to inquire at the District Committee. This time I was directed to a Party Secretary of the cadre section.

"My name is Wolfgang Leonhard. I have just been told to come here."

She examined me with a quick glance. "We have had a telegram from Ufa. You are to go there at once," said the Party secretary in a severe voice. "You will report first to the Central Committee of the M.O.P.R. there. You will then be given further directions. It would be as well to get there as quickly as possible. You will collect your ticket and rations here tomorrow morning."

That was all. She had not a word to say as to why I had to go to Ufa or who this mysterious Vilkov was. I knew, of course, that these were things about which one did not ask questions.

To-day, I realise that those few days marked a decisive turning point in my life. I was now to get to know the Soviet Union from an entirely new standpoint. This was the period in which I was admitted to the official class, but at the time the significance of what was happening was not clear to me. It was only later that I began to realise that I was now released from all the burdensome difficulties and adversities which I had experienced before. No more sleepless nights at railway stations. No more struggling to find a niche. No more trotting round offices. No more starvation. But at the same time, I was to learn that the life of an official had also its shady side. It meant being permanently watched and watching oneself, and by comparison my previous life as an ordinary citizen of the Soviet Union seemed almost to bear the stamp of freedom.

The train left Karaganda in the late evening. Once more it crossed the Kazakh Desert, which I was now to see for the last time. We travelled northwards to Petropavlovsk, and from there westwards to Ufa. It was the same track that I had travelled over in 1941, under guard as a deportee. But now the train was going in the opposite direction. To me the change of direction was more than a matter of geography. The train was going to Ufa and in Ufa was the Comintern.

CHAPTER FIVE

At the Comintern School

THE COMINTERN had been evacuated from Moscow to Ufa in the autumn of 1941. Ufa was the capital of the Autonomous Bashkir Republic, about seven hundred and fifty miles from Moscow. It was not one of the more important evacuation towns. Government offices and diplomatic missions had taken refuge in Kuibyshev on the Volga. Novosibirsk and Chelyabinsk had taken in the majority of the evacuated industries of Western Russia, and became for the duration of the war among the most important industrial centres. The most valuable scientific records, pictures and works of art from the museums were removed to Tomsk at the outbreak of war. Alma Ata and Tashkent became the wartime centres of evacuated artists and scientists. Ufa, on the other hand, lay rather on the periphery. That was perhaps the reason why the Comintern moved there.

Political work in the prisoner-of-war camps played an important role at that time. From the end of 1941 onwards there were frequent conferences with those of the prisoners-of-war who were willing—in most cases from genuine conviction but sometimes also for reasons of opportunism—to sign appeals and proclamations against Hitler. Many of the émigrés who had been deported as unreliable aliens as recently as

the autumn of 1941 were now called in again for
political work.

All this was still unknown to me when I arrived
in Ufa in July, 1942. The town presented much the
same picture as other towns in the Soviet Union during the war: overcrowded stations, exhausted population, starving and impoverished refugees . . .

Ufa, the Comintern Town

In my inner coat pocket, secured by a safety-pin
against any risk of falling out, was the little piece
of paper on which everything now depended. On this
paper was the address of the Central Committee of
the M.O.P.R., the authority to which I had now to
turn.

After about half an hour's search, I found the
building with a notice outside: "Central Committee
of the M.O.P.R." The secretary examined me with
a suspicious look. After a year's residence in
Kazakhstan, my appearance cannot have been one
to inspire much confidence.

"I come from Karaganda, and I've been told to
come here. I am to report to the Comrade President."

Half an hour later, I was received by the President
of the Central Committee of the M.O.P.R. In front of
him on his desk lay a number of papers—no doubt
my personal documents and details. The President
looked from me to the documents lying on the table
before him and from them back to me. They contained, I knew, full and accurate information about
me. Nevertheless, I had to answer the usual questions
about my name, place of birth, date of birth, date of
entry into the Soviet Union, studies, and my membership of the *Komsomol*.

Then his face took on a serious look, and I began to feel that at last we were coming to the point.

"Comrade Leonhard, you have been summoned here by the Comintern. This is merely a reception point."

He took a piece of paper and on it he wrote a name and address. He handed it to me and I read: "No. 7 Lenin Street, Vilkov."

"The Comintern is established in what used to be the Pioneers' House. If you can't find it right away, you can ask for the Pioneers' House, which anyone in Ufa can show you."

He got up. Our discussion was at an end, and I set out immediately, feeling extremely nervous. I had no idea at all who Vilkov was, but clearly he must be very influential to be able, in spite of all the obstacles in the way, to fetch back deported German émigrés from Kazakhstan so quickly.

I was still thinking these things over when I reached the house I had been told to find. It was a relatively large building for Ufa, in the rather elaborate style typical of the Pioneer Palaces that were put up in the Soviet Union at the beginning of the 1930's. In front of the house was a small garden. The entrance was flanked by huge columns. The great doors were covered with metal, but there was no notice at the entrance and nothing to indicate that this was the building which housed the headquarters of the Comintern.

Nervously I entered. In the lobby I found an old friend from Children's Home No. 6—Ernst Apelt, the son of a German Communist Party official. I rushed up to him.

"Tell me who this Vilkov really is?"

He stared at me in amazement. "My dear fellow, don't you know? He's the Comintern's chief of cadres."

"Yes, but what's it mean, my suddenly being summoned to Ufa? Are we going to be put into special units of the army, or what can it be?"

"The army? No, I don't think it's that. Probably you'll be put into a school. There's a whole lot of them here. Perhaps you'll go straight into the Comintern School—that would be the best."

Suddenly, in a loud voice he broke into the Austrian dialect: "Well, now, come along! They're waiting for you!"

I would have liked to have learned more from young Apelt, but he left me at this point. When I reported to Vilkov's secretary, the first thing she asked me was whether I wanted anything to eat. I was astounded: nobody had asked me that sort of question for more than a year. Without waiting for my answer, she gave me a little card. On the ground floor I found myself standing in astonishment at the entrance to a splendid dining-room. Hardly had I sat down when a waitress came and took my card and brought me soup, white bread, lavish helpings of beef, and finally a sweet. It was the first meal of so many courses that I had had since the beginning of the war. When I had finished I leant back in my chair with a feeling of optimism such as I had not felt for a long time.

The waitress came along again: "Do you want anything more to eat?" I was completely speechless. In the middle of the war, after such a magnificent meal——!

The cashier gave me a second ticket on the spot

and asked with a smile: "Are you from Kazakhstan too?"

When I had finished, I went to the secretary's room and a few minutes later I was received by Vilkov, a big man with a grave demeanour. We had only a brief conversation. Then came the usual series of questions, to which I rattled off the answers. I knew well enough in any case that he already had full information about me, and he too knew that I knew he knew everything. Then he went on in a low, firm voice: "We have been thinking of giving you the opportunity to study at the Comintern School. A number of our comrades will be going there in the next few days. We think the best thing would be for you to report daily to the secretary: she will then give you further instructions. In the meantime, you will stay in Ufa for a few days. The secretary will make the necessary arrangements."

The Comintern School! I could hardly take it in. It was not till afterwards that it occurred to me that Vilkov had not even told me where it was. However, I was not much disturbed then at the thought that I had been told no more than the barest minimum. Subsequently, I realized that this was not simply a personal peculiarity of Vilkov, but something that was characteristic of the whole Soviet bureaucracy.

"Comrade Leonhard, here is the address of your temporary accommodation," said the secretary. "Our comrade chauffeur will take you there. He will fetch you every day at ten o'clock in the morning and bring you here. I will notify you of your destination as soon as we have got that far."

Still feeling quite dizzy, I went to the door. The

car was already waiting there and what a car it was! Not just one of the usual *emmochkas* (as the little M.1. cars for middlegrade officials were called in the Soviet Union), but a splendid great Zis—the make for senior officials. The chauffeur opened the door of the car and asked me for the address. Then we roared off. This was all a bit too much for a young man who had only just been recalled from compulsory deportation!

About ten minutes later we stopped in front of a fine new building. There were no nameplates on any of the doors in the whole house—only numbers. On the second floor, I found my accommodation. I rang, and then I could hardly believe my eyes. Before me I saw Greta Loberbauer, an Austrian girl from Children's Home No. 6, whom I had not seen for more than two years.

"Hallo, Greta! How wonderful to meet you here!"

"Hallo!" she said indifferently, but I didn't notice this in the pleasure of seeing her again. I began at once to tell her about Kazakhstan, and everything that had happened to me in my few hours in Ufa. By this time we had been joined by another of the Austrian *Schutzbund* émigrés. He greeted me without giving his name, and showed me all round. Every room was equipped only with a bed and a small chest of drawers. The place seemed to be specially intended for accommodating party members in transit for a few days. I began excitedly to go on with my story again, but Greta Loberbauer, whom I had known hitherto as a lively young girl, said nothing and only nodded her head without interest from time to time. At last I began to notice this.

"Well, what have you been up to all this while?

What are you doing here, and what are you going to do next?"

She was silent for a moment. Then she said hesitantly, "I don't exactly know."

By this time the other boy from the *Schutzbund* had rejoined us.

"You shouldn't talk so much," he said significantly, though at the same time his tone was friendly.

It was not long before I realised that my friends had formed habits in their present way of life which were completely different from my own up till now. Of course, I had always known when I was a student and a member of the *Komsomol* that there were certain things about which one did not talk, but all the same I had always felt myself free to talk about anythink else that lay outside these fields. Gradually, I learned that different standards prevailed here: it was clear that what one did not talk about covered a much wider field.

Ufa could justly be described at that time as the Comintern Town. The Comintern was the only important organisation that had been transferred to Ufa. The Bashkiria Hotel, the largest and most modern in the town, had been requisitioned for leading Comintern officials. Here were to be found Dolores Ibarruri, the Secretary-General of the Spanish Communist Party; Wilhelm Pieck and Walter Ulbricht from the leadership of the German Communist Party; Koplenig, Fürnberg and Fischer from the leadership of the Austrian Communist Party; André Marty, whose reputation at that time stood very high, and Anna Pauker, who at that time was the leader of the Rumanian Communist Party; also Manuilsky and Vilkov of the Russian Party, who controlled the

general political and organisational leadership of the
Comintern. Dimitrov, who was at that time Secretary-
General of the Comintern, came to Ufa comparatively rarely for short visits. The other principal
officials of the Comintern were also often on the
move—sometimes to Kuibyschev, where many government offices and the radio station were, and sometimes to the Party schools scattered over various
parts of the country, or to prisoner-of-war camps
where conferences were to be prepared or held.

Apart from the Bashkiria Hotel, the residence of
the principal Comintern officials, and the Pioneer
Palace which now served as the Comintern office,
there were two other large buildings in Ufa reserved
exclusively for the Comintern. The former Geological Technical School on Lenin Street served as
accommodation for the middle-grade officials, as
well as for the family dependants of senior officials;
and the building which had formerly been the Agricultural Economy School on Stalin Street—not
nearly such a fine building as the Geological Technical School, to say nothing of the Bashkiria Hotel
—provided accommodation for junior colleagues as
well as for the family dependants of middle-grade
Party officials. This was where what might be called
the "Comintern proletariat" lived—disabled veterans
of the Spanish Civil War who could no longer be
used for political work; family dependants of comrades who were by this time working at different
schools or engaged in clandestine activities behind
the German lines; lower-grade clerks and bottle-
washers of the Comintern organisation.

The standard of living of the staff of the Comintern was as discriminatory as their accommodation.

All officials who were directly employed in the Comintern took their meals three times a day in the office building, the former Pioneer Palace. The most senior officials, apart from living in splendour in the Bashkiria Hotel, also had large parcels of what was called *payok* brought to their homes: *payok* meant the regularly distributed packets of food over and above the normal ration. Other members of the Comintern were provided from a "reserved" shop on the ground floor of the Bashkiria Hotel, and there they could get a shock-worker's ration card and other special allocations from time to time, besides their ordinary food. Thus all Comintern workers were graded according to their political usefulness in a carefully constructed hierarchical system, which applied to all questions of accommodation and rationing.

A Peculiar Voyage

I stayed in Ufa about a week, during which for the first time in ages I lived without a care in the world. At intervals I met other friends from the *Schutzbund* Home of earlier days, or from the Austrian section of the Comintern, all of whom behaved in the same way as Greta. None of them uttered a word about what they were doing there, where they had come from, what they were going to do next. I tried to imitate their behaviour, but so far it was beyond me. I had been a student for so long, I had been through so much in Karaganda, and I was so excited at meeting old friends; and besides I was so new to the *apparat* that I was often indiscreet and talkative in spite of all my good intentions.

After about a week, the secretary told me that I was to leave for the School the following morning with two other comrades. I was to report to her at ten o'clock.

Punctually at ten o'clock I was there. There were already two other comrades in the room besides myself, but she spoke only to one of them: "We think it would be a good thing for you to set out for the school to-day with these two comrades. Here are your tickets."

She handed me a sealed envelope. The other two shook hands with me, without introducing themselves, so I did the same.

"The car is there. You can be on your way. I hope you have a good journey."

The elder of the other two led us to a fine Zis car, and said something to the chauffeur which sounded to me like *pristan* (harbour). Sure enough, about a quarter of an hour later, we had reached a harbour in the Belaya River.

"We are going by this steamer," said our conducting officer. A few minutes later the steamer moved off.

Time passed.

My two companions spoke little. By this time I had also had sufficient experience not to be too cheerful or talkative.

About six hours later, our ship came to a stop again. The name of the place was announced loudly and unmistakably: Kushnarenkovo. Our conducting officer frowned at this. Obviously, he didn't like to hear the name of the place shouted out, but it was too late to do anything.

"I suppose we might as well get ready," he said. Without a word we picked up our cases. We disembarked, tired by the long journey, but nevertheless full of excitement about what was going to happen next.

The little village of Kushnarenkovo, as I later learned, lay about forty miles north-west of Ufa. It was not on any railway line. The only means of communication with it in summer was by ship and in winter by sledge. No doubt it was an ideal place for a political school which needed to attract as little attention as possible and to keep its pupils cut off from all contact with the outside world.

After walking on foot for about half an hour we found ourselves at the bottom of a hill. "I think we'll go up the hill," said our conducting officer; and silently we did so.

The Comintern School at Kushnarenkovo

After another quarter of an hour we came in sight of a group of large, rather dilapidated buildings, which obviously had once been a farm. Apart from the central building, there were two or three others to be seen. I was just thinking that we could not yet have reached the end of our journey when our leader said: "I think we will go in here."

He waved a hand vaguely in the direction of the principal building. At the entrance we received our final instruction: "You had better report to the secretary's office."

Silently we went up to the first floor. He told us to wait, and went into the secretary's office, and came back after a few minutes. He made a sign to his younger companion, who went in while I waited outside. A few minutes later he came out and gave me a sign to indicate that now it was my turn. Inside the room I was received by a secretary. The usual game of question and answer was repeated once more. After this introduction, which was already irritatingly familiar to me, the secretary looked me straight in the eye and said:

"We have certain special rules in this school. First of all, you must never leave the school grounds without special permission. I should like to impress on you from the start that any infringement of this rule may bring very severe consequences. Secondly, it goes without saying that you must never give the slightest indication in your letters of where you are living. There must be no further mention of the Comintern School, either in your letters or on the envelope."

This was something quite unheard-of for an innocent student like myself. "Yes, but what addres am I to give then?" I asked.

"You should write on the envelope: Bashkir A.S. S.R., Kushnarenkovo, No. 101 Technical School for Agricultural Economy. That is all that is necessary." (This regulation was soon to become even more drastic: a few weeks later, we were forbidden to write any letters at all.)

After a short pause she gave me a pentrating look and went on: "And now for the most important point. You are not permitted to give your real name to anyone, or to mention any facts whatever about your previous life. I should like to impress on you that conformity to this rule is absolutely imperative. No one, not even though you may perhaps have known them in the past, is allowed to know your real name." There was another short pause and then she asked in a slightly friendlier tone: "Now, what name would you like to choose?"

"Linden," I said.

She made a note of the name and finished the interview by saying: "All right, then: from now on, you are Linden. You must forget your real name and remember all the time that your name is Linden for the whole of your period in the school. That will be all for now. You can go and eat, and after you have eaten I will show you where you are to sleep. Tomorrow morning the Director will see you and tell you about everything else."

There was no one in the dining-room when I came in. The food was very good, but by this time my enthusiasm was already waning. How quickly one gets accustomed to good things! I was thinking—when just at that moment the door opened and an old friend rushed up to me.

"How wonderful to see you here!" he cried, delighted. It was Jan Vogeler.

I had been in the same class as Jan in the Karl Liebknecht School at Moscow, and I had always liked him. He was the son of the German painter, Heinrich Vogeler from Worpswede, who had emigrated to the Soviet Union. In the autumn of 1941 he had been deported to Kazakhstan, and died at the beginning of 1942 of the terrible hardships and deprivations there. This had happened more than six months earlier, and I assumed that Jan must long since have heard of his father's death, but to all appearances this had not altered his political attitude in the least, as was the case with many young people in the Soviet Union. Jan was a keen member of the *Komsomol* and spoke about the Soviet Union with great enthusiasm. He began to tell me at once: "Do you know where I have been? No, you couldn't possibly guess . . ." I was unable to get a single word in. "A little while ago I was at the front. There must be very few Germans who have gone there. I must have been extraordinarily lucky, somehow or other. I was an interpreter: I even interpreted once for Marshal Zhukov."

I listened to Jan with interest, but at the same time I was wondering how to get him off this subject so as to learn something about the school. The opportunity came earlier than I expected, for suddenly Jan clutched his hair in despair.

"Oh, my God, I oughtn't to be saying anything about my past! Please don't tell any one what I've told you—by the way, what's your proper name here, so that I shan't make a mistake?"

"I'm called Linden. And you?"

"Danilov. Jan Danilov."

It was a peculiar thing—hardly had he mentioned his new Party name than he underwent a complete transformation. He answered my questions cautiously and hesitatingly.

"The school—yes, there's a lot to tell you about it. We're divided into groups by nationality. There are general lectures for everybody and then lessons and seminars separately for each of the national groups. The German section is under Klassner: Klassner is what he is called here—I don't know what his real name is."

In a few seconds Jan had changed from an enthusiastic member of the *Komsomol* into a Party official, exercising complete control over himself and choosing his words with scrupulous care.

A moment later the secretary came into the

dining-room. "Comrade Linden, I will now show you the room where you are to sleep."

She then took me to the ground floor, where the classrooms were for the separate sections. At the end of a corridor a rickety old wooden staircase led up to the first floor. We went along a narrow corridor. The secretary pointed to a door and said: "That's the school library and reading-room."

She stopped in front of the last door and said: "Here it is." Looking in, I saw a large room with about fifteen beds in it. The secretary led me up to a primitive wooden bed and said, "Here is your place. Report to me to-morrow morning, please, and I will take you to the Director."

I sat down on the bed and reflected in astonishment over the events of the last few days, and wondered anxiously what the Comintern School had in store for me. Suddenly I saw my good friend Mischa Wolf from Moscow, whom I had met only a few weeks before in Alma Ata. I was about to rush up to him with a cry of "Mischa!" when I remembered that, of course, he would have another name here and one must not say anything about one's previous friends. By this time he had noticed me too, and came slowly towards my bed.

"Förster," he said, and stretched out his hand to me with a show of indifference.

"Linden," I replied.

"Good, here you are! You'll soon be at home here, I'm sure."

"Yes, I'm delighted to be at the school."

We said nothing more. We conformed strictly to the rule, absurd though it obviously was, since we

had known each other since 1935, which was eight
years ago. We undressed in silence. There was an
empty bed between us. I was curious to know who
was my next-door neighbour. Was he a German? I
asked. Mischa nodded. I put my things away in the
cupboard without noticing that my next-door neighbour had now come up beside me. Suddenly I looked
up at him. It was Helmut Gennys, whom we used to
call Helmerl at the Children's Home. He had been
my closest friend.

Helmerl came from East Prussia, where his parents
had been Communist Party officials. For years we had
done our exercises together at the same desk in the
Children's Home. We had read much the same books
and gone for long rambling walks together through
Moscow, talking together for hours. He knew the
whole story of my life and I knew his, as is bound to
happen with two inseparable young friends between
fourteen and seventeen years of age. We had prepared ourselves together for joining the *Komsomol,*
and been admitted into it at about the same time. In
recent years we had seen less of each other: he had
finished the tenth class at school just when the war
broke out.

In a meaningful tone, he said, "Zahl—Peter Zahl."

"Linden—Wolfgang Linden," was my reply. Then
somewhat timidly I began, "How long have you been
here?"

"Since . . . for quite a time."

I had not expected my reunion with my friend
Helmerl, now Peter Zahl, to be quite like this. But
there it was. Helmerl conformed strictly to the ritual
of the school—he always stuck to the Party line—
and I had no alternative but to conform to it too. I

had been longing until now to find out what it was like in the school, but if even Helmerl wouldn't tell me anything, then I could hardly expect to find out from anybody else.

In the morning we were woken up by a loud bell. Everyone rushed to get up. "Morning games!" Helmerl shouted to me.

All the members of the course, including the instructors, gathered in the great courtyard of the building, divided up by nationality. The leaders of the groups carried out a quick roll-call, almost like a military parade, while the rest of us stood at attention like soldiers. Every day began with morning games, including gymnastics, Swedish drill, running and jumping. The results were carefully noted down. Clearly great importance was attached to physical exercises.

After a substantial breakfast I went to the secretary's office, and a few minutes later I was summoned before the Director. All I knew was that his name was Mikhailov—or rather, that this was the name by which he was known in the Comintern School. It was not until some time later that I learned that Mikhailov was a Bulgarian. He had mastered several languages, and during the Spanish Civil War he had held important posts in the Party training system, particularly in the training of political commissars. He had also been editor of the Spanish newspaper *El Comisario*.

This time we did not have the usual game of question and answer. Our conversation was more like a friendly chat. He asked me casually about my activities in the *Komsomol* and about my studies; he even wanted to know how I had found the journey.

Only after that did he broach the subject of the Comintern School, and here he seemed to be particularly interested in the state of my political education.

"Have you been through the chief works of the classical writers on Marxism-Leninism?"

"Yes, of course."

"What books of Lenin have you studied so far?"

"At the Academy, and also in my spare time, I've already read a whole series of his works: *What Is To Be done? One Step Forward, Two Steps Back; Two Tactics for Social Democrats in the Democratic Revolution.*"

He interrupted me, and in a friendly tone put me a rapid series of questions about the books I had named. I answered his questions briefly as he put them. I only got stuck over the answer to one question: "What ideological trend was Lenin attacking in his pamphlet *What Is To Be Done?*"

For anyone who knew the Soviet Union, it was a ridiculously simple question, but at that particular moment the answer to it suddenly slipped my mind.

He smiled: "Well, of course, you know perfectly well. It was against the Economists."

I did in fact know it, and quickly explained what it was all about, but he waved me aside.

"That's enough for now. You will be going into these things in much greater detail here." Then he turned to another subject. "As you will already know, this is a School of the Comintern. We train the cadres for different countries. Are you willing to undertake missions in Germany?"

"In Germany?" It was all rather new to me, and I did not know what exactly he meant. Clandestine

work? Work among the German prisoners-of-war?
Political work after the defeat of Hitlerite Germany?

"Of course I am!" I replied.

He looked at me gravely. "Comrade Linden, it is
the duty of every pupil at this school to prepare himself for work in his own native country and to feel
a sense of responsibility towards his own people. You
must understand that your assignment will be in
Germany, and that you will have to devote yourself
primarily to German questions."

Our conversation was at an end. He gave me another friendly handshake and wished me good luck.

In the next few days I learned the basis on which
the Comintern School was divided into separate
national sections. It was an interesting fact that in
the year 1942 the officials there came only from
countries with which the Soviet Union was at war,
or which at that time were dominated by Hitler:
Germans, Austrians, Sudeten-Germans, Spaniards,
Czechs, Slovaks, Poles, Hungarians, Rumanians,
Bulgarians, Frenchmen and Italians. Each group
had its own instructor and a leader selected from its
own ranks. The largest group were the Spanish, who
numbered thirty or forty students. The average group
—for instance, the Germans, Austrians, Sudeten-
Germans and Bulgarians—consisted of fifteen to
twenty people, and the other groups were smaller
still. British and Americans were not represented
in the Comintern School. There was one Yugoslav, who was attached to the Bulgarian group, and
one Argentine woman, who was the wife of an
Argentine Central Committee official. She had taken
part in the Civil War in Spain and was now also
working with the Spanish group.

Instruction generally took place separately in the individual national groups. Joint lectures for the whole school were arranged only for particularly important subjects. Even the three German-speaking groups—the Germans, Austrians and Sudeten-Germans—studied separately. The separation of the Austrians was not surprising, for it was already clear at that date that Austria would again become an independent state; but it also appeared that no decision had yet been taken over the future of the Sudeten-Germans in Czechoslovakia, otherwise there would hardly have been a separate Sudeten-Germany group in the Comintern School.

It was only some weeks later that I learned that there was another group at the school besides the twelve which I have mentioned. A little apart from the other buildings of the school stood a smaller building, which was fenced off and which none of us was allowed to enter. It was so completely barricaded-off that at first none of the students knew what went on or who was the instructor there. Gradually one isolated piece of information leaked out: Korean Communists were being trained in this building. They lived entirely by themselves and never once took part in any of our joint occasions. The explanation of these exceptional security measures was not difficult to guess. The officials who were being trained at the Comintern School came only from those countries with which the Soviet Union was in a state of war, or which the Fascist Axis powers had occupied. As everyone knows, the Soviet Union was not at war with Japan until 1945: the two powers had even concluded a non-aggression pact and were enjoying normal diplomatic relations. Consequently, the training of Koreans who were being prepared for the ultimate struggle against the Japanese occupation had to be conducted in circumstances of extreme secrecy.

It was not only the "course-students," as they were called in the school, but also the instructors who had cover-names, so that during the whole time I was studying there, and even for many years afterwards, I did not know who the instructors really were. Apart from the German group, I was only able to recognise two of the instructors after 1945 from photographs, by which time they had come to occupy senior positions in the Government and Party. In this way I learned that the leader of our Polish group was Jacob Berman, who was later a member of the *politburo* of the Polish United Worker's Party and Deputy Prime Minister of the Polish People's Republic. Jacob Berman had studied at Jura University in Warsaw in his youth, and he had joined the Polish revolutionary student movement at an early age. Soon afterwards he became a member of the Polish Party leadership. After the dissolution of the Comintern in the spring of 1943, he played an important part in the foundation of the Union of Polish Patriots in the U.S.S.R., and the Polish Kosciusko Division trained in the Soviet Union. In 1944, he was the Deputy Foreign Minister in the Provisional Government at Lublin.

The leader of the Austrian section of our school was another whom I recognised later from photographs in the press. He was Franz Honner, who had been a member of the Socialist Party since 1918 and transferred to the Communist Party in 1920. After the rising of February, 1934, he was interned in the concentration camp at Wollersdorf, from which he succeeded in escaping to the Soviet Union. During the Spanish Civil War he was in the Austrian battalion of the International Brigade, and after the fall of the Spanish Republic in 1939 he returned to the Soviet Union. In May 1943, when the Comintern was dissolved, and our school with it, he went to Moscow and later became a leading member of the Austrian Free Battalion within the Yugoslav Partisan Army. After 1945, Franz Honner was for a short time Minister of the Interior in the provisional Austrian Government.

Of the other instructors, apart from those in the German group, of course, I have never heard anything more since I left the school. But one thing is clear in any case: the instructors were senior and highly-qualified officials of the Communist Parties in their various countries, and they should all be holding high positions to-day, unless by any chance they have fallen victims in the meantime to one or other of the many purges.

The German Group

The leader of our group, and our principal instructor, was a well-built man of about forty, with slightly greying temples and dark eyes, who spoke with a Southern German accent and was known as Klassner. Klassner was a typical example of the intelligent Stalinist. He had an exceptionally wide knowledge covering not only the field of Marxism-Leninism, the history of the Comintern and the German Communist Party, but also German history and philosophy. Over and above that, he had spent many years in a special study of the Balkans. Nothing could disturb his cool sense of superiority. He was capable of sacrificing his best friend or his closest colleague without hesitation if the leadership required it of him. His self-control never wavered, and it would have been impossible for him to express himself unreflectingly or inexactly. He chose his words with precision, and one could be sure that they did not deviate by a hair's breadth from the official Party line.

His intelligence was so much above the average that he was able instantly to recognise the slightest indications of an ideological shift and react to them accordingly. If the Party line changed, he was ready from one day to another to adjust his opinion, and with crystal-clear logic to defend the truth of the exact opposite of what he had said the day before. He was an outstanding teacher who made his wide theoretical knowledge unreservedly available for the purpose of justifying, elucidating and propagating the directives supplied to him from above.

I did not know at that time what his real name was; it was not till some years later that I learned it was Paul Wandel. He came from Mannheim and had been to the Lenin School in Moscow. After that he had worked in the *apparat* of the Comintern as a colleague of Wilhelm Pieck, mainly in the Balkan section. His first post after 1945 was as President of the Central Department for People's Education, and later he was Minister for People's Education in the Soviet Occupation Zone of Germany. In 1952 he was promoted to become chief of the office of Co-ordination and Control for Education, Science and Art. In July, 1953, he became Secretary of the Central Committee of the S.E.D.

The Deputy-Leader of the German section of the

Comintern School was Bernhard Koenen, a veteran working-class official who had acquired his knowledge the hard way. He had been a member of the Social Democratic Party since 1907, and in 1917 he had transferred to the Independent Social Democratic Party (U.S.P.). When the Revolution broke out in November 1918, he was chairman of the Factory Committee of the Leuna Works.

Bernhard Koenen remained a member of the Independent Social Democratic Party of Germany from 1918 until he transferred to the Communist Party in 1920. He had played a prominent part in the revolutionary struggle in the period between 1919 and 1923, including the rising in Central Germany in 1921 and the short-lived Workers' Governments of Saxony and Thuringia in 1923. In contrast with Klassner, one could see in him the real working-class revolutionary—a type that was now poles apart from the cold, calculating Stalinist *apparatchik*. When there was a shift of policy he was not always successful in adjusting himself to the new Party line without showing his feelings, as Klassner was so adept at doing.

One scene I shall never forget. I had been instructed by Klassner to translate into German the principal articles in *Pravda* for the benefit of Bernhard Koenen and his wife Frieda (who was also at the Comintern School), as well as other older comrades who knew very little Russian. One day I had to translate an article in *Pravda* which dealt "with the immemorial common struggle" of the Russians and Poles and other Slav peoples against the Germans. Unhesitatingly I translated: "There has been from the earliest time a brotherhood in arms against the

Germans, the vicious hereditary enemies of the Slavs."

Bernhard Koenen looked at me in horror. "Stop, stop! You've translated that wrong! That can't be right! Translate it again."

I read out the same phrase again. This time Bernhard Koenen was uneasy.

"Is there nothing there about German imperialism or the ruling classes of Germany?"

"No, Bernhard. What is written here is simply about the Germans."

"That is impossible!"

Without a word I showed him the passage in question in *Pravda* and some other passages at the same time which also spoke in the same way about the Germans as the "immemorial hereditary enemies" of the Slavs.

Bernhard Koenen had gone pale. He said nothing more. It was indeed hard for him as a veteran working-class revolutionary to turn himself into a Stalinist official, compelled unconditionally to defend Soviet directives.

During the great purge of 1936-38 Bernhard Koenen had been arrested by the N.K.V.D., and had lost one of his eyes in prison. Thanks to someone's intervention, however, he was set free again, and thereafter he went on serving Stalinism. In 1945 he became the first secretary of the regional headquarters of the S.E.D. in Sachsen-Anhalt. In 1953 he was sent to Prague as Ambassador for the Soviet Zone, which undoubtedly meant a step down for him.

Apart from our two principal instructors, Paul Wandel (Klassner) and Bernhard Koenen, we had also a woman assistant who was known at the school as Lene Ring. After 1945 I met her again in the Soviet

Zone under the name of Lene Berg. She was first an instructor at the Karl Marx Political Academy of the S.E.D., and thereafter she was Bernhard Koenen's right hand in the regional headquarters of the S.E.D. in Halle.

Our German group consisted of eighteen or twenty "course-students." Only a few of us were veteran officials who had belonged to the German Communist Party before 1933. These few included "Otto" from Hamburg, and "Willi" from Berlin (whose real names I never discovered), both formerly members of the League of Red Front Fighters (R.F.B.). They had fought together in the International Brigade in Spain. Another was Arthur (whose real name was Heinz Hoffmann): he had been political Commissar of the 11th International Brigade in Spain. After 1945 he became a Lieutenant-General and Chief of the People's Militia and Deputy Minister for the Interior in the D.D.R. Another was Lene Berner, who had been in the clandestine organisation of the German Communist Party since before 1933. She had also been active in the Comintern and had carried out special missions as far afield as Japan. After 1945 she was an instructor in the S.M.A. School, and later in the Society for German-Soviet Friendship in East Berlin, and after that in the Foreign Ministry of the D.D.R.

Most members of the German group in the school were young members of the Party or *Komsomol* like myself, who had been brought up in the Soviet Union. I met many of my old friends from the Karl Liebknecht School and Children's Home No. 6 again here. Apart from Mischa Wolf, Helmut Gennys and Jan Vogeler (whom I now had to keep on reminding myself to call Förster, Zahl and Danilov respectively), another old friend whom I met again to my surprise was Marianne Weinert, the daughter of the well-known Communist poet, Erich Weinert, whom I had got to know as a child in Berlin in 1932 among the artistic colony of Breitenbach Square. Others were Emmi and Else Stenzer (now known as Stern), the two daughters of one of the Reichstag Deputies of the Communist Party who were murdered by the Nazis.

Outside the German and Austrian groups I knew nobody; but on the third day I saw an extraordinarily pretty Spanish girl whose face seemed to me familiar. She also seemed to recognise me. She was Amaya Ibarruri, the daughter of Dolores Ibarrur, the Secretary-General of the Spanish Communist Party, who had risen in a few years from a minor Party post to become the best-known woman in Republican Spain under the name of *La Pasionaria*. After the defeat of the Spanish Republicans she had come to the Soviet Union with her son and daughter. Her son had joined the Red Army and fell at Stalingrad in November, 1942. Her daughter was studying with us at the school, where she was known as Maya Ruis.

The daughter of *La Pasionaria* was not the only prominent personality among the students. In my dormitory I noticed a young comrade who had lost an arm. He knew Russian well and he told me once in the dormitory—contrary to all the rules—that he had been fighting at the front as early as 1941, and it was there he had lost his arm. He seemed to be the only one who did not let himself be got down easily, and refused to take everything seriously; but he seemed to be allowed a certain amount of licence, which was a surprise to me. As soon as he came into the room, everything became more cheerful and relaxed. No sooner had he arrived than the cry would go up: "What's new, Zharko?" I also told him something about myself, and it was not long before he told me openly who he was: the son of Tito.

Our Education in the Comintern School

It was just as difficult to find out what we were supposed to learn in the school as it had previously been for me to find out where I was going. Generally we were only told what the immediately following parts of the syllabus were to be. It was only at the end of a series of lectures, which generally lasted two or three weeks, though sometimes substantially longer, that the next subject was announced to us. In the course of the ten months that I spent at the school, we went through the following subject: the history of the German Communist Party; the history of the Soviet Communist Party; the Weimar Republic; Fascism; the character and course of the Second World War; political economy; dialectical and historical materialism; the history of the Communist International; and a summary of the history of Germany. Each subject consisted of a series of lectures, most of which were given by Paul Wandel, or occasionally by Bernhard Koenen or Lene Berg. Besides these, a few historical subjects were given by a Hungarian woman Party member.

General lectures for all groups usually took place in the library or dining-hall. There was no large lecture-hall. This was how the history of the Communist International was dealt with, for all of us together. The lecturer in this series was our Director,

Comrade Mikhailov, who lectured in Russian. All those who knew Russian as well as their native language, which meant generally the younger members, sat in the front rows, while the older comrades sat at other tables where the lecture was translated into Spanish, German, French, Italian, Rumanian, Czech, Slovak, Polish and Hungarian. As the members of each national group sat at a table together, this was not particularly disturbing, and after a short time the translating system was working well. Afterwards seminars on the subject were held separately by the instructor of each national group with his students. The history of the Communist International was the most interesting of all the subjects.

The development of the Communist Party in each individual country, the battles and other events of the Revolution from 1919 onwards, were so strikingly depicted to us that we almost believed we had taken part in them ourselves. The Spartakist rising, the struggles in the Ruhr and in Central Germany, the revolutionary events in Poland, the gigantic wave of strikes in Italy in 1920, the accession to power of Mussolini, the struggle in Bulgaria in 1923, the period of so-called "relative stabilisation" from 1924-1929, the world economic crisis, the accession to power of Hitler—all these historic events were depicted to us in detail in the lectures, although (as I was to discover later) in a Stalinist presentation which entirely falsified the facts.

Of the subjects we dealt with in the German group, I was most interested in the political and ideological dispute with Nazism. The other subjects such as dialectical and historical materialism, political economy and so on, I had already been through at my Soviet Academy in a course of lectures on the fundamentals of Marxism-Leninism. On the other hand, the study of the political dispute with the Nazi ideology was something entirely new for me. In a long series of lectures in the Comintern School we were given the history of the N.S.D.A.P., the Hitler Youth Movement and the rest of the Nazi organisations, as well as biographies of the Nazi leaders. The emphasis here was laid on analysis of the substance of Nazism and the reasons for Hitler's seizure of power. We studied the ideology of Nazism in detail—the racial doctrine, the theory of "living space," the Nazi treatment of history and so on—and we did so in the light of the Nazis' own literature. We studied all these things so thoroughly that when I first met real Nazis after 1945, I was astonished to discover that I was much better informed about their doctrines than they were.

Again and again we were astonished at the relative breadth and detachment with which we dealt with Nazism and the Nazi ideology in the middle of a war which was a matter of life and death. Often one of us was required to expound in front of the group various doctrines of the Nazi ideology, while others had the task of attacking and refuting the Nazi arguments. The student who had to expound the Nazi arguments was told to set them out as well and clearly and con-vincingly as he could, and his performance was actually assessed more favourably the better he repre-sented the Nazi point of view.

Occasionally Klassner himself took over the role of Nazi spokesman; and as he set out the arguments very skilfully—probably more skilfully than most Nazis could have done themselves—it was often not

AT THE COMINTERN SCHOOL

easy to find ways of refuting them. There were limits,
however, to this latitude of outlook. We got not only
Nazi literature to read, but also the manifestos and
proclamations of bourgeois and Social Democratic
parties in different countries, as well as the encyclicals of the Pope; but however much we were allowed to familiarise ourselves with other political
ideologies (obviously in the certainty that there was
no danger involved so far as we were concerned, because none of us could have been influenced for a
second by these points of view), nevertheless we were
strictly debarred from reading any publications of
Communist opposition groups. At this point tolera-
tion came to a full stop.

It is true that we heard the names of Brandler,
Thalheimer, Ruth Fischer, Maslow, Korsch, Katz
and other opposition figures who had left the German
Communist Party along with their followers in the
1920's, or had been expelled from it and had built up
opposition organisations. But what these groups and
trends were really after was something we never heard
a word about. The same was true of the opposition
groups within the Bolshevik Party. We were never
given a single line to read from the original writings
either of the Workers' Opposition under Shlyapnikov and the Democratic Centralist Group under
Osinski, or of the followers of Trotsky or Bukharin.
This fact particularly struck me in our lessons and
seminars on Trotskyism.

Our instructor, Klassner, became quite unrecog-
nisable when he was dealing with this subject. Uncontrollable hatred filled his voice, and instead of
expounding the relevant arguments, his lecture became a flood of abuse—something unique in our

lectures at the School. Then we were given the literature on the Trotskyist argument, which consisted of a cyclostyled document, carefully put together out of Lenin's statements against Trotsky (naturally omitting his far more numerous statements in favour of Trotsky), together with extracts from Stalin's writings. The document contained not a single line written by Trotsky or any of his followers. None of us knew at that time what Trotsky had actually written; and whereas all the other seminars generally reached a respectable level of discussion, the seminar on Trotskyism was confined to furious partisan denunciations.

At that time I was unable to account for these facts, although the reasons for them were really not far to seek. Statements and expressions of opinion by the opposition were withheld from us precisely because they comprised views which were really dangerous to Stalinism. The Stalinist leaders were very well aware that there was no risk whatever involved in putting into our hands speeches by Hitler or Goebbels, or manifestos from the bourgeois parties, or encyclicals from the Pope, because it was certain from the first that none of them would have the slightest influence on us. On the other hand, books by Trotsky and manifestos by anti-Stalinist organisations, which could criticise and attack the Stalinist system in the Soviet Union from a Marxist point of view, would at least have made some impression upon us.

"Current Political Questions"

Apart from our theoretical political instruction, a very large proportion of our time was devoted to current affairs. It was an unwritten law that "theory must be linked with practice." On this basis there were frequent sessions on current political questions, in which each group had to deal with the current situation and with the tasks confronting Communists in the country under consideration. We had to learn how to compose, within an hour, a "politically correct" leaflet on any subject set us. The subjects chosen for the purpose were by no means easy. For instance, at the beginning of October, 1942, Goering's declaration on the increase of the food ration in Germany was read out to us. We were then given the task of composing a leaflet on this question with the object of destroying any possible illusions which might be created among the population.

Our leaflets were read out one by one on each occasion at a special seminar, and discussed in detail. Last of all came the critical verdict of our instructor. After doing many such exercises, which were very carefully discussed, it was not long before in fact we were in a position to compose fluently-written topical leaflets on any subject.

It was not only our own leaflets that we discussed, however. We also received all the leaflets put out by the political section of the Red Army for dropping over the front line. We were required to analyse these Red Army leaflets with care and to be unsparing with our criticisms. For me, this was something entirely new. In the Soviet Union up till now, I had never been asked to give my own opinion on matters laid down from above.

We now regularly read through the Soviet leaflets and discussed them. We expressed our opinion that

they were very feeble—a view which was later confirmed again and again as the numbers of prisoners-
of-war increased. It led eventually to a complete
transformation of Soviet propaganda, and to the
foundation of the National Committee for Free
Germany.

We also read eagerly the leaflets written by German
soldiers and officers who had been captured or deserted. They spoke an entirely different language.
This was particularly noticeable in a brochure produced by Captain Dr. Ernst Hadermann under the
title, "The Word of a German Captain." The same
was true of a leaflet composed by Heinrich Count
von Einsiedel, a great-grandson of Bismarck. Both
were among the founding members of the National
Committee for Free Germany.

Our practical instruction was not confined to the
composition of leaflets. We also learned how to produce leaflets in strictly clandestine circumstances.
Within the school, which was itself so secret, there
was also an even more secret little chemical labora-
tory. We were only allowed to enter this cubicle
when the subject of the period was the production
of clandestine leaflets. Instruction in this subject
took place twice a week in Russian. We were initi-
ated into all the methods of producing clandestine
leaflets from the most primitive of all (by means of a
lump of clay, with which it is possible to produce
not more than about a hundred copies of a short
text in large capitals), up to the most complicated
photographic methods, which make it possible to
produce any number of leaflets or newspapers, including drawings and caricatures, in a very small
but easily legible format.

Every method was explained to us in detail, including the ways of manufacturing the materials that might be needed, and then each of us had to produce leaflets in practice. The instruction was extremely detailed, but we were not allowed to make notes: we had to keep everything in our heads. As none of us, to the best of my knowledge, was sent to take part in any clandestine work after the dissolution of the Comintern, the graduates of our course must to-day presumably have only a faint recollection of those interesting hours of instruction in which we learned so many things which none of us were ever to put into practice.

Apart from instruction in current political questions, which was designed to prepare us to understand the situation in Germany and to equip us for our future tasks there, periods were also inserted in the curriculum whenever necessary on "current politics," in which we dealt with the Soviet Union. Current politics were not, as one might imagine, merely a kind of press review, or a general survey of the events of the day in the U.S.S.R., but a thorough discussion of important political measures taken in the Soviet Union, which we had to study and on which we were subsequently required to "adopt an attitude."

It was the duty of every student in our group on the course to "adopt an attitude" towards every question that was raised, even when other speakers had already said everything that could possibly be required on the subject. In this way, everyone was trained to be able to react immediately in a politically correct manner to every question in Soviet politics. We were thus all in a position, in the absence of directives, to be able to adopt the correct attitude and to propagate it on our own initiative.

Thus the union between theory and practice was achieved in a double sense. On the one hand we were trained to apply our theoretical knowledge to the country in which we were later to work; on the other hand we were equipped, both by our study of the history of the Communist Party of the Soviet Union, and also by the habit of discussing the most important measures put into effect in the Soviet Union, to be able in future not only to follow events in the U.S.S.R. accurately and continually, but also to be able to elucidate and popularise the measures taken by the Soviet Union anywhere in the world and to defend them against criticism.

The Secret Information Bulletins

About one-third of our working time was spent studying by ourselves. Generally, we found our sources in the library where most of the writings of Marx, Engels, Lenin and Stalin and a sufficient quantity of other source material was to be found. The most important texts were available in translations into all the languages needed in the school, but in a few cases we had to make do with Russian editions. One of the younger students on the course was then required to translate the material for the older ones.

However, the library was by no means confined to texts of Marx, Engels, Lenin and Stalin and other Party literature. It also contained cyclostyled information bulletins. They were not intended for general circulation and were stamped "Secret" or "Top

Secret." These information bulletins, which came out daily, contained the most important radio commentaries and articles from the foreign press, arranged by countries. The bulletins were presumably produced in the Comintern at Ufa. Every copy was numbered. We were only allowed to look at them in the reading-room, and every member of the course had to sign a receipt for them.

When I read one of these bulletins for the first time, I had quite a considerable shock. Though I had already appreciated from the Sunday lectures in the District Committee at Karaganda that the lecturers knew more than what was to be learned from the Soviet press, I had never discovered where they got their knowledge from. Now I knew. I remember very well the feelings with which I held one of these secret information bulletins in my hands for the first time. There was a sense of gratitude for the confidence placed in me, and a sense of pride at being one of those officials who were sufficiently mature politically to be trusted with the knowledge of other points of view. Other young officials must have thought and felt the same thing, and no doubt the graded privileges of information were for many officials an attraction as strong as titles, orders and material inducements.

The information bulletin which was issued in the Comintern School was limited to foreign countries, or more accurately, to allied and neutral countries. It contained the speeches of leading statesmen of these countries which were reproduced only briefly or not at all in the Soviet press; and also important articles from the American, Scandinavian, British and Swiss press, reports of Party meetings of every kind of political party in allied and neutral countries, and the more important radio commentaries.

While these bulletins were available to all students on the course, our German group also received an additional regular bulletin which was also cyclostyled and also, of course, stamped "Secret." This contained extracts from letters sent by German soldiers and officers to their relations at home. The material was in all probability put together by the "Central Political Administration of the Red Army of Workers and Peasants" (Glavpurkka). These bulletins appeared in two editions, the first containing extracts from letters by German soldiers and officers to their families, the other containing extracts from letters sent by the German civilian population to their relatives at the front. Obviously full and careful use was made of every letter which fell into the hands of the Red Army as it advanced.

All statements touching on political themes were arranged together in cyclostyled bulletins, in which we would generally find the following headings: statements about the war in general; about rations; about bombing; about foreign workers in Germany; about relations with prisoners-of-war; and with Germany's allies (the Italians, Hungarians, Japanese and so on); and conditions in the occupied countries. These statements were in no way "doctored" for propaganda purposes, and pro-Nazi statements were recorded just as carefully as anti-Nazi statements. Generally speaking, however, there were few very clear professions of political feeling to be found in these letters.

Only once was there a minor sensation. A soldier

had written to his wife at home: "I'm fed to the teeth with this war." A censor had added in the margin of the letter: "So am I."

Every extract was accompanied by the name of the writer and the addressee, together with the place and date, so that it was possible for us to make accurate, if cautious, analyses of the atmosphere in different parts of Germany.

Apart from the general information bulletins which I have mentioned, and these extracts from letters, we also received regularly, again in the form of a bulletin, all the official material about Hitlerite Germany, including decrees by the Hitler régime and all speeches by Hitler, Goebbels, Himmler, Speer, Baldur von Schirach, and so on; also Goebbels's articles in *Das Reich*, Fritzsche's radio commentary and other important commentaries from the Nazi press; and all articles of substance from the neutral and allied press about the situation in Hitlerite Germany. Obviously, we were not the only recipients of this material, for when I met some of the senior Soviet officers of the Political Administration later, in May, 1945, in Berlin, I was astonished to find how well-informed they were about Germany. No doubt they had been studying the same material during the war.

Natural Relaxation and Organised Social Activities

Up to the time when I joined the Comintern School, I had looked upon myself as a good and diligent student, but I soon realised that even the most assiduous study at the Soviet Academy came nowhere near the standard set at the school. We had lectures from early morning till after midday. After lunch, we had a bare hour free. From then until dinner our time was filled with seminars or study on our own, generally under the supervision of the leader of the group or the instructor in charge of the class.

At the beginning of the course we had to attend a lecture on morals. The basic rules were so severe that even strict schoolmasters of the old school shook their heads doubtfully. We were told first that for the duration of the course no student or lecturer was allowed to take a drop of alcohol. There were no exceptions even on the holidays of May Day, the 7th November, and New Year's Day. It was made unmistakably clear to us that anyone who tried to get himself so much as a thimbleful of alcohol would be severely punished. It was not enough, however, simply to announce this ban; it was also justified on political and ideological grounds—both as a matter of general principle and also with detailed accounts of shocking examples, to show how clandestine groups had been broken up as a direct result of the minutest quantities of alcohol, how Party members had ended on the scaffold, and even entire revolutionary movements had suffered disaster. The whole picture was so dramatically presented to us that one could almost believe the failure of the Revolutions between 1918 and 1923 in various European countries to have been due entirely to the fact that this or that official had had a glass of wine on New Year's Eve.

We were not only forbidden alcohol, but also any kind of intimacy with the other sex. This, too, was justified on ideological grounds. In one lecture we were told how a large clandestine group in Italy had been broken up because its leader had fallen in love. He had to travel by train to Paris with a false identity card one day, and he was under strict instructions to visit nobody before he left. In spite of this he had visited his girl-friend and had been caught there by the police. He himself was sentenced to fifteen years' imprisonment and the other members of his group were later discovered and arrested. In fact, even the most innocent contacts, such as a brief stroll around the courtyard in front of the school, were reported if they happened more than once, and made the subject of detailed criticism and self-criticism.

It was not easy to conform to these rules, especially for the younger men and women in the Party between the ages of 18 and 25; and these composed more than half of the students. Moreover, there were some extremely attractive girls in the Italian group, and even more in the Spanish group. On top of everything else, the central building of the school was surrounded by dozens of lilac bushes, and when their scent floated in through the open windows in the spring, it was exceedingly hard not to be allowed to see the lovely Spanish girls. A charming Polish student who fell in love with the Argentine girl, Raquel, went through the ordeal of criticism and self-criticism and declared that he would reform, but Zharko, Tito's son, who had fallen in love with an enchanting Spanish girl, refused to give way and was expelled from the school.

Our working time was so full up that the only free time we had was on Saturday afternoon and Sunday. At the week-ends we were allowed to do whatever we wanted—except to drink, fall in love, leave the school compound, admit our real names, tell anything about our previous life, or write anything about our present life in our letters.

It was clear, however, that the school authorities recognised that a little gaiety and relaxation was needed, and a resolution was passed to this effect. The immediate result was a meeting of the group to discuss the theme of "relaxation." Klassner gave us an address in which he spoke of the danger of overwork, the impossibility of comrades sitting till two o'clock in the morning in the reading-room, the uselessness of excessive strain, the need for free time and such things as communal singing and organised amusement; so after that we had "organised amusement," which took the form of social evenings and recreational meetings of the group.

It was laid down in detail where and when we should assemble for an evening's amusement and what form the evening's amusement should take. "It is of the highest importance that we should meet together sometimes outside working hours," explained Klassner. "The struggle in Germany requires of us not only political and organisational skill, but also a close contact with the German people, with their habits and manners. With this object in view, we will devote our evening's entertainment to learning German popular songs and singing them together."

The result was a model of the realisation of theory in practice. We now met regularly, either in the seminar room or out of doors in fine weather, and we sat down and waited for further instructions on our evening's entertainment. We had not long to wait, for as soon as we had sat down—after all, time devoted to entertainment must be utilised as rationally as possible—we were given the texts of German folk songs, which were then duly sung by all of us; rather timidly by the older comrades, but well and truly by the younger ones, who had never heard a German folk song before.

So there we sat, a few minutes after we had finished taking a machine gun to pieces or hearing a lecture about the Chinese Revolution, and we sang:

"Under the eaves of the roof, under the eaves of the
   roof,
 A sparrow is nesting with its young,
 And when evening comes, when evening comes,
 The whole nest begins to sing:

 Sing! sing! sing! sing!
 Open up, Julia—open up, Julia,
 For I have been waiting so long!"

We sang in the grave and disciplined manner which was expected of us in everything, but on this occasion it did not seem right. We received a new directive from Wandel: "Comrades, you must sing more gaily and cheerfully." As with all directives, we were urged to put this one into effect as quickly as possible, so we intoned again as brightly and cheerfully as we could: *hum! hum! hum! hum!* Finally, we were required to learn the texts by heart.

The German group's "organised amusement" was sheer torture. Time after time I could hardly wait for the end of it and longed to get back to seminars or the library.

One by one we learned probably a dozen German folk songs. We were assured again and again that our links with the German people would be all the stronger for them. Dutifully we plunged into our new task. Regretfully, however, I had to admit later that the German folk songs which we had so laboriously learned in Bashkiria were very little help to me in my relations with the German people, for in May, 1945, when I came back to the devastation and destruction of Berlin, none of the Germans I came into contact with was interested in folk songs. Fortunately, it was not long before a new tactical line was announced in the context of "organised amusement." From now on the evenings were no longer devoted exclusively to the learning of German folk songs, but also to giving the older Party members an opportunity of telling us their experiences.

These evenings soon became a regular feature of life in Kushnarenkovo. Bernhard Koenen was the one who told us most about his exciting life. He told us about the Revolution of 1918, and the Central German uprising of 1921; about the events of 1923, and May Days which he had passed in different countries. It cannot always have been easy for him to do this, because naturally he had to adapt the presentation of his experiences to the new political line, and this involved retouching his story to conform with the version of events which was now current— though this, of course, I was not aware of at the time. Dutifully he scattered derogatory remarks about Brandler and the Trotskyites throughout his personal reminiscences, just as our instructional periods prescribed. Apart from our instructors, some of the older students on the course were also required to give occasional accounts of their personal experiences. I shall never forget the story of a veteran Party member from France who had only arrived in the Soviet Union at the end of 1940, shortly before the outbreak of war. He had not officially belonged to the Party, but he had clearly had special tasks to carry out. He spent three hours telling us how he had had to fend for himself all alone during the German occupation in 1940, without any support from the clandestine Party organisation, with which he was not even allowed to make contact. He was, moreover, the only member of our group who occasionally dared to express criticisms on certain points about the school: for instance, on the subject of our military training and on Martin Grünberg, who as he said, "behaves as if he were chief of staff here without having the slightest clue to what it is all about." He appeared to be perfectly sure of himself, perhaps because he believed he had powerful protectors; but he was mistaken.

A few days later he was removed from the school. Was it because he failed to conform to the directives in his narrative, and told us things perhaps which he should never have mentioned? Or were the critical opinions he expressed to blame? Or had something happened to his protectors? We never knew. We were simply told briefly by Klassner that he had left the school: he had never properly joined the Party in any case, and there had been suspicions of him from the first. Six months later I met him again in Ufa and was horrified to realise what it meant to have one's connections with the Party severed in the Soviet Union.

My First Self-Criticism

The summer of 1942 in Ufa had given me a clear indication of the difference between the life of a privileged official and that of an ordinary person. It was quite clear to me that much that I had been able to say and do as a Soviet student or a member of the

Komsomol was no longer permissible in my present environment. On my arrival at Kushnarenkovo I had made up my mind to adjust myself to the new way of life. It was by no means only a matter of refraining from saying anything about my past, or from mentioning my real name. That did not turn out to be at all difficult. What caused much more difficulty was a fact which no one had ever told me, and which I was now to learn for myself: that every word is politically significant.

That sentence is not lightly set down. It means exactly what it says. Every word is politically significant. This was something entirely new to me.

When one was a student and a member of the *Komsomol* in the Soviet Union, it was good enough in normal times—the years of the purges from 1936-1938 being naturally an exception—to stick to the correct line when talking of political affairs, to voice no opinion on any subjects that had not yet been dealt with in *Pravda,* and to present one's political views in such a way that even the stupidest and most malicious listener could not distort them into anti-Soviet utterances. Apart from this, there were contexts of a completely non-political character in which one could say more or less what one wanted.

The difference between my previous life and the life which now awaited me was one which I had not completely understood in my first few weeks at the school. When talking of non-political subjects, I used to say freely and cheerfully whatever came into my head. So did all the other younger Party members in our group. We were all fundamentally in accord with the system, but that did not prevent young students like ourselves from criticising certain aspects of it here and there, and even making jokes on some subjects. Above all, it did not prevent us from feeling completely free and uninhibited when talking of non-political subjects, just like any other young people of our age anywhere else in the world. But it was just this that was forbidden, and this was the beginning of the criticism and self-criticism of which I was to be the first victim.

We were frequently made to undertake manual work, usually on jobs which had to be done in the vicinity of the school. Occasionally we were required to do agricultural or other labour outside the school grounds. One afternoon we were called together accordingly and told: "This afternoon's lessons are cancelled—our group is to unload a cargo steamer."

Half an hour later we were on board the ship, where we had to unload huge bags of flour. Otto, from Hamburg, who was as strong as an ox, missed no opportunity of teasing us younger ones because we could only carry one sack at a time, whereas he could easily handle two. One of the younger members of our group named Stefan, who was small and feeble and short-sighted, suffered particularly from Otto's ridicule. Stefan had guts enough to stand up to Otto, however, and the result was a fight in which Otto hit the wretched little Stefan in the face with his powerful fist. I was standing close by and I let myself go in a fury of indignation.

After lunch the following day, the three of us were notified that we were required to report to the Director at 7 o'clock. I presented myself without any anxiety, imagining that Otto was going to be severely ticked off and that I was required only as a witness. But things turned out quite differently.

As I came into the Director's room I had a surprise. Two long tables were set at right angles to each other. Besides the Director sat the Chief of Cadres—a man we seldom saw and still more seldom heard speak—and also a woman official who was said to be a member of Dimitrov's secretariat, together with Paul Wandel, and most astonishing of all, Emmi Stenzer, a blue-eyed girl of nineteen who was totally ignorant of all matters connected with political theory, but was very good at forming "people's committees" on them. There was a grave and solemn silence. It might have been an investigation by the Inquisition.

Against the wall stood a couch and three chairs. We were told coldly, almost in a whisper: "You can sit on those chairs."

Silence followed for several minutes: nothing whatever happened. An oppressive feeling came over me, although I still assumed that the discussion had nothing to do with me. After some time, Mikhailov said in a voice that was entirely unfamiliar to me: "I think we can now begin."

Paul Wandel was the first to speak. He reconstructed the whole incident, and to my surprise I began to realise that the episode of the sacks of flour was really a matter of serious political importance. My surprise was even greater, however, at finding that Klassner's account of the matter put the blame considerably more on the victim, Stefan, than on the aggressor, Otto. Stefan was accused of having been provocative.

"The behavior of our younger comrades seems to require a thorough review," I heard Paul Wandel

(Klassner) say. As he went on, my name was more and more frequently mentioned. His tone became sharper and sharper, but there was no anger in it and his voice was never raised. He spoke coldly and factually in clear, precise language. The others followed one after another, but I had difficulty in following what they said. All I heard over and over again were the words: "behavior unworthy of a Bolshevik . . . lack of serious-mindedness . . . presumptuous arrogance."

I sat dumbfounded. I had never known anything like it before. What made it worse was the complete calm with which everything was conducted; the pauses in which not a word was spoken, while the nightmare atmosphere in the room never lifted for a second.

I could not make up my mind what to think. What could it all mean? What was it all leading to? Why had I never been told anything before? What was going to come next?

About an hour had already passed since we began, and still nothing concrete had been said about what I had really done. Yet already I was beginning to feel myself guilty. I felt that I must have done something wrong, but the very fact that I did not know what it was made me feel even more helpless. Nor did I yet realise that this was only the beginning.

After a short pause—one of those ghastly minutes of silence—I heard the words: "I think Comrade Emmi Stenzer would like to say something."

The girl got up. She was no longer the helpless creature I had seen in the seminars when she was unable to answer political questions. She rose confidently, calmly, with a complete sense of her own power. Automatically she imitated the cold, severely factual tone which the others had used before her. She had a piece of paper with some notes on it in front of her. From time to time she picked the paper up, and then went on speaking. Her notes were the points of indictment against myself.

I was in such a state of excitement that I could not follow everything, but there was one thing which I have never been able to forget from that day to this— the exact detail in which the indictment was formulated against me. Every opinion that I had expressed at any time or in any place from the first day of my arrival in the school had been carefully noted down to be used against me as evidence now.

"On the 23rd September at 11.30 in the morning, as we were coming out of the seminar room, Linden said . . ."

"On the 27th September at 6 o'clock in the afternoon, as we were leaving the folk singing, Linden stated . . ."

It was all so petty that anyone who did not know the atmosphere at this kind of school would only have laughed at it. The remarks quoted had not the slightest connection with politics.

Suddenly Emmi raised her voice. "When the lecture about Alexander Nevsky was announced, Linden told us that this was a question which interested him very much and he had studied it in some detail at the Institute in Karaganda. He was anxious to see whether the lecturer would have anything new to say."

The prosecutors put on a solemn face at this, and eagerly made notes. The woman sitting at the table shook her head dubiously. It was clear that this re-

mark was one of grave significance. There followed
a number of other remarks that I had made. I tried
desperately to remember the points in the indictment,
but the whole atmosphere had had such an effect on
me that I was unable to do so. The indictment seemed
to be endless.

"When we came back from woodcutting on the
evening of the 6th October at about 7.30, some comrades from the Spanish group passed by us. Linden
then said to Förster that some of the Spanish girls were
very pretty." There was more scribbling at the tables,
and the eagerness with which the prosecutors made
notes showed that this remark, too, was one of exceptional gravity.

At last the indictment came to an end. Otto was
now quite at his ease on his chair. The whole thing
seemed to be over now as far as he was concerned.
Stefan, who was sitting next to me, looked at me from
time to time with anxiety in his eyes, although his
name was now very seldom mentioned. Next there
spoke in turn the woman from the secretariat of the
Comintern, the Chief of the Cadres, and Mikhailov
himself. The points in the indictment recited by
Emmi Stenzer were now only occasionally mentioned
in their speeches; they served simply as starting points
for the main indictment.

To-day, when I look back on this first evening of
criticism and self-criticism, I no longer find any
difficulty in understanding the system. Every kind of
remark—innocent, trivial, completely non-political
—was exaggerated and distorted on a gigantic scale,
so as to reveal peculiarities of character and political
notions. Then these political notions, which one
had never formulated, were equated with political

actions which one had never committed, and so finally the monstrous consequences were brought to light. This was achieved in something like the following way:

"Comrade Linden says that he has already studied the question of Alexander Nevsky at Karaganda. He says he was anxious to see what viewpoints the speaker would have to bring up. What is the significance of that? The significance lies in his belief that he already knows everything and that he has no need to learn anything new. This is an expression of the kind of presumptuousness which had already brought about the downfall of many Party officials in the past."

There followed examples, tragic and shocking examples in the clandestine struggle, of the way in which personal arrogance had caused officials to neglect security measures, so that trusted comrades had fallen into the hands of the enemy; examples of the way in which difficulties had been underestimated through arrogance, with the result that important tasks had not been fulfilled, and even that "if one follows the matter out to its logical conclusion, the officials concerned can be said from an objective point of view to have been accessories to the murder of trusted comrades and in that way to have served the enemy."

It was the same with my remark about the pretty Spanish girls at the school.

"One has only to look at the facts. In the middle of the war, when we are engaged in a life-and-death struggle against the Fascist criminals, when the entire Soviet people is sacrificing everything to achieve victory in the struggle for freedom and national independence, the Party gives Comrade Linden the opportunity of studying and preparing himself for the struggle ahead under ideal conditions. The Party has a right to expect that Linden's every effort will be directed to that purpose, that all his strength will be devoted to that goal; that every minute will be used for his studies and that all his thoughts will be concentrated on the coming struggle. And with what are Linden's thoughts in fact occupied? He is thinking of pretty Spanish girls and thus setting the interests of his own ego above the interests of the Party. Once again, it is not the first time that it has happened."

There followed further examples, each as shocking, startling and tragic as the other: of clandestine officials who had forgotten their duty through love affairs and thus gambled away into the hands of the enemy not only themselves, but also the whole of their clandestine group; examples from Italy, from Hitlerite Germany, from Franco's Spain and from Horthy's Hungary followed one after another.

Each time the conclusion was recapitulated, that this was the consequence of arrogant personal opinions. It all seemed so logical that by this time I felt myself guilty of having committed the same crimes. This impression was all the stronger because I had never yet experienced anything of the kind. At Soviet schools I had always been a model pupil and twice received certificates of merit as an exceptional scholar. As a student, I could point to more than one examination which had earned me a scholarship. As I had had no previous experience of criticism and self-criticism, and as there had never yet been a single critical remark about my conduct here at this school, the present massive indictment was a shattering blow.

At last, Mikhailov, the last to speak, had finished. Suddenly I heard him say: "Comrade Linden will now speak."

I remember making a few disconnected remarks to the effect that I considered the criticisms justified and would try to improve myself. I could not make a consecutive speech—I simply stuttered.

Then came the summing-up, again by several speakers. The keynote was the same as before; Linden's statement is an evasion—Linden has not grasped the kernel of the problem. His statement shows his superficiality. It would be premature to believe a statement of this kind, made on the spot. There then followed further examples—examples of officials who had been accused of some fault or other and had made an immediate, facile confession of their fault, but had not made any real change, and had continued on the same pernicious path as before. Suddenly, completely to my surprise, I heard Mikhailov's voice: "I think we can now close."

No conclusion had been reached, no resolution passed, no measures had been decided upon. I was not even given the slightest indication what I now had to do. After lasting several hours, this terrifying session had ended just as unexpectedly as it had begun.

It was now night and all was quiet in the house. Everyone had gone to sleep. Slowly I climbed the rickety staircase to my bedroom. For hours I could not get to sleep. I had no idea what the whole thing meant. Would I be removed from the school? Would I be dismissed from the *Komsomol*? Would I be sent back to Karaganda? I was not so much disturbed by my immediate personal fate as by my sense of guilt and the apparent impasse in which I found myself. I was sincerely prepared to admit my faults; but now I had done it—and that too was wrong. Restlessly I turned over from side to side in my bed. Just what was I to do? Never before, not even in the Kazakhstan desert, had I felt so helpless as I did that night in the Comintern School.

Next day the usual instruction went on. Nothing seemed to have changed at the school. No one seemed to know anything about last night's session of criticism and self-criticism in the Director's room. I found it hard to follow the lessons, but I knew that since the evening of criticism and self-criticism, my conduct was going to be even more carefully watched than before. I wrote out my lessons, but it was nothing but a mechanical process. My thoughts were still back on the previous evening and on what the future had in store for me. The only thing that I was clear about was that the episode was not yet closed.

On my left sat Emmi, who seemed completely unmoved by anything. I suddenly found myself surprised by the thought that the way she had behaved, noting down everything so precisely, was something contemptible. Without any intention on my part, my thoughts went farther: was this, after all, the right way? Was it really necessary to use such methods to train Party members into officials? Certainly, I thought, I have many faults and of course the Party at the school has not merely the right, but the duty, to help me to overcome my faults and my weaknesses. But is this the way it ought to be done, in an atmosphere grimmer even than that of a court of law? Would it not have been possible to do it differently and to give me some friendly advice from time to time?

I recoiled from my own thoughts, but it was now impossible to suppress them. Is our whole relationship at the school what it ought to be between Party members? There came back into my mind other critical thoughts, which I had had earlier in the period of the purges. Critical conversations came back to me, and I was frightened of myself. If I had already expressed critical thoughts like these, what was the end likely to be?

I made up my mind in future to be much more cautious in what I said and to keep it to the minimum necessary. I would think out every sentence and every word before I uttered it. But again there came doubt. Must it be so? Was it really honest? If not, what ought one to do? How could one be honest if every innocent word, looked at objectively, was to be treated as a hostile utterance?

Again I shrank back from my own heretical thoughts. The previous evening, my admission of guilt had been completely honest. I was convinced that evening that the criticism directed at me, severe as it was, had been completely justified. I had been really anxious to improve myself, but the statement I had stammered out in all sincerity had been rejected. If that evening of self-criticism had gone just a little differently, if everything had been cleared up by my admission, possibly my heretical thoughts would never have arisen, or anyway not until much later. Possibly, in that case, that evening would have contributed, as it did with so many Russian and non-

Russian officials, towards turning me into an unreasoning and compliant tool of the Stalinist Party leadership. But as it was, the evening had achieved the opposite.

True, I was still completely involved in the system. I wanted nothing more passionately than the victory of Soviet arms. I still believed firmly that Socialism had been realised in the Soviet Union, and that such of its manifestations as were unattractive to me personally were not the result of the system, but were explicable by the fact that it was in such a backward country as Russia that the Socialist order had first been established. I already saw these faults and defects quite clearly, but I did not yet see that they were linked by a logical connection. To me, they were still lapses by local officials; the childhood diseases of a new society; measures that had to be accepted as an inevitable consequence of backwardness; episodes of an essentially transitory character. But although this evening of self-criticism did not rob me of my faith in the Soviet Union, nevertheless it did contribute towards reinforcing my critical attitude.

The most important consequence of that evening was that, from then on, I reflected carefully upon every word and sentence I uttered, and quite consciously kept my thoughts to myself on many questions, to conceal my real feelings and opinions. But at that time my acceptance of Stalinism had much greater weight than my sense of criticism. What was likely to be the result, however, when more and more critical opinions intruded on the thoughts which I kept to myself and cautiously suppressed? To-day I believe that this was the beginning of a road

which was to lead seven years later, after a severe
internal struggle, to my break with Stalinism and my
escape from the Soviet Zone of Germany.

My reflections in the morning made me feel somewhat calmer and more secure. In the afternoon it
was announced that that evening a period of criticism and self-criticism would take place in our
German group. Nothing was said about the subject,
but the same solemn atmosphere prevailed as in the
Director's room the day before. The result was again
an extreme accentuation of the tension and nervous-
ness of everyone present.

First Wandel began to speak. The whole story was
repeated: the description of the episode on the
steamer, the shifting of the burden of guilt on to
Stefan and myself; and finally the main barrage of
criticism was again directed at me. Although this
was the second time I had heard the whole story, I
was just as tongue-tied as before. The critical reflections of that morning receded farther and farther
into the background as every minute passed, and soon
I felt again as helpless and guilty as on the previous
evening. But it was not exactly the same. There were
moments when I was not so completely the prisoner
of events, for this time I did not lose my head, and I
even felt a recurrence of my heretical thoughts.

Wandel spoke for about an hour. He explained that
this complex of questions was so important as to require a further serious discussion of them in the
framework of the whole group. There followed the
same equation of trivial, insignificant utterances
with political theories and actions. At the end of his
speech he mentioned that the previous evening Linden

had made an entirely unsatisfactory statement, and that now it was the duty of all members present to "define their attitude."

One after another all the members of our group then spoke. Everything went exactly according to plan. Even my best friends had now to condemn me —and they did so. The substance of the matter had been precisely prescribed in Wandel's speech, and every member of the group conformed to it. Only in the tone of their remarks was there some variation. Some of them wanted to exculpate themselves by condemning me even more severely than Wandel himself had done. Others linked their accusations against me with a personal self-criticism in which, although they had not been required to do so, they convicted themselves of similar faults. One of the students tried out of friendliness to spare me by not mentioning me at all, treating the matter entirely theoretically; thus he began with a general disquisition on the danger of defects of character—but he did not get away with it. He was sharply interrupted by Wandel and accused of deviating from the serious questions which were now under debate. Thus even this loop-hole was closed.

Several hours passed. Finally the moment came when I had to speak myself. This time I spoke more calmly and factually. I admitted my fault again, but I added at the same time that it was my intention to reflect seriously and in greater detail on the whole matter. On the first point, I was being quite honest, but the second was a tactical move which I felt myself obliged to make. After all, I already knew from the previous evening that an immediate admission of my faults was not well received. The evening then came to an end with a statement and a few closing words from Paul Wandel.

Once again no decision was reached. I still did not know whether everything was now finished or whether further measures would follow. Before long, however, it became quite clear that everything was in fact now finished. It was the first case of criticism and self-criticism in our group. In the following weeks and months we had many further examples of this performance, until finally practically every student had been through the mill of criticism and self-criticism.

The first self-criticism was responsible for a change not only in myself but in all the other students of our group. We became more serious, and above all more cautious in everything we said. There was no more of the boisterous greeting, the uninhibited story-telling, the happy shouting. Although we were still young people between nineteen and twenty-two years of age, we behaved like staid veteran Party officials, coolly and thoughtfully choosing their words. Probably my own behaviour now was indistinguishable from that of the official I had met in Ufa, whose conduct had struck me as inexplicable only a few weeks before.

The Struggle Against Sectarianism

At the end of October, 1942, all groups were informed that in the next few days we were to have an important visit. A member of the Central Committee of the Communist Party of the Soviet Union would be giving a lecture on the international situation.

The reading-room, in which communal lectures

generally took place, was filled to capacity. As usual, the translators sat at tables at the back, and in the front rows were those who knew Russian as well as their native languages. We could tell from the atmosphere that something very important was about to happen. We were not to be disappointed. It was noticeable that the lecture once more extolled the firm, unbreakable common alliance between England, the U.S.A. and the Soviet Union and at the same time denounced "sectarianism." We had sufficient political training to recognise that here was a new political line and an explicit directive for the whole of our future instruction at the school.

From that day onwards, every lecture and every seminar contained repeated references to the greatest of all dangers: "sectariansim." The following definition was given at the Comintern School of the concept of sectarianism: "Sectarianism is a damaging political and ideological notion in the working-class movement which seeks to deny the need for a policy of alliances between the working class and other strata and thus to isolate the Party from the masses."

At the beginning of November, 1942, the Allies had landed in North Africa. In the middle of November began the Red Army's offensive at Stalingrad, which was to be a turning point of the war. After these events, and especially from the beginning of the year 1943, scarcely a day passed at the school without a storm of abuse being hurled at sectarianism. It was not only the alliance between the Soviet Union and the western allies that was constantly extolled at the school and presented as the foundation of Soviet policy; there was also continual emphasis on the need for creating an alliance between all political forces in every country against Hitler. At this stage, so we were told, it was not merely a matter of advocating one's own political objects, but above all of mobilising every conceivable political and military force for the struggle against Hitlerite Fascism. It was precisely by setting aside its distinctive objects and by showing itself to be the most vigorous of all forces in the struggle against Hitler that the Party would later achieve for itself a decisive influence. It was hammered into us again and again that nothing could be more dangerous than presenting excessive demands or isolating oneself from potential allies. The most difficult situations and the remotest events from the past were resuscitated in order to equip us for the struggle against sectarianism.

I shall never forget the seminar we had on the subject of the history of the Chinese Revolution from 1925 to 1927. We had listened to an extremely interesting lecture, after which we were engaged in discussing the subject in seminars. There was a flood of questions: about the Kuomintang and its composition; its political objectives; the social forces on which it rested; the contradictions within these forces; the relations between the Communist Party and the Kuomintang; and the role of Chiang Kai-shek. During the seminar Mikhailov came into the room, sat down beside Wandel and took part in the discussion. Anyone else who had been listening would probably have concluded that we had mastered the subject, for Wandel's difficult questions were generally answered well and thoroughly, but Mikhailov did not seem to be satisfied. Impatiently he turned to

Wandel and asked: "Excuse me—may I intervene for a moment to put a question?"

"Of course," replied Wandel.

"Comrades—it is not enough that you should know the answers to all these questions. Of course it is important; but there is something else more important still. The events in China between 1925 and 1927 have taught us a great many lessons. These lessons will only be correctly understood, however, if one puts oneself in the situation as it was at the time, in order to learn how to make correct decisions in similar situations."

We all nodded our heads, though nobody knew what he was getting at.

"You all know the general situation as it was at the time. The Chinese Communist Party was formally allied to the Kuomintang, but it was obvious that the days of this alliance were numbered. The break might come any day. Now, I would like to draw your attention to one of the elements in the situation at that time. The Communist Party in Shanghai had very great influence on the workers. Moreover, the workers had weapons. There was thus a sense in which the Party represented an armed force. Meanwhile, the armies of Chiang Kai-shek were approaching the town—they might enter it any day. What was the Chairman of the Shanghai Communist Party to do? Should he welcome Chiang Kai-shek's army as allies? Should he let speeches of welcome be made and leaflets of welcome be distributed? Or should he summon the workers in the town to oppose Chiang Kai-shek's armies and thus himself demolish the alliance, which was bound to break down shortly in any case?"

Mikhailov had risen to his feet while he was speaking. He now paused for a moment and then suddenly hurled the question at us: "And you—what would you have done?"

We all thought feverishly. It was indeed a very complicated question. Finally one of us spoke. "In my opinion it would be right to maintain the alliance faithfully so long as one could be sure that it was a genuine alliance. But knowing as one did at that time that Chiang Kai-shek might betray the common cause at any moment and was already getting ready to strike, the right course was to protect the Party and the workers who sympathised with the Party. In no circumstances should the workers and Communists of Shanghai be surrendered to Chiang Kai-shek—all the more so since they had weapons and were able to defend themselves."

The student looked questioningly at Mikhailov, who said nothing. His face was expressionless. Then he asked: "Does everyone share this opinion?"

Another student spoke: "I am not quite sure, but I think that despite everything, the Chairman of the Shanghai Communist Party should have welcomed Chiang Kai-shek's troops in a friendly and brotherly spirit, even in spite of the danger that Chiang Kai-shek would break the alliance and that the actual effect would be to help Chiang Kai-shek to occupy an important city. The alliance should have been respected, so that it would have been clear to everybody in China that it was not the Communists, but Chiang Kai-shek, who had broken it and who had been a traitor to the revolution. No doubt this would have brought great temporary difficulties upon the Party and might even have cost heavy sacrifices, but in the long run a policy of this kind would probably have proved right, in spite of everything."

Most of us thought this was going too far. We looked anxiously at Mikhailov, but again he said nothing. He went on waiting.

Finally Emmi spoke. She smiled craftily and said: "I think one ought not to decide in favour of either solution. The Party leaders could have acted as follows. On the one hand they could have issued an official proclamation of the Government and welcomed the entry of the Kuomintang troops as friends; but at the same time they could have put out leaflets to the workers warning them that treachery was imminent on the part of Chiang Kai-shek and advising them to be on their guard and never to let their weapons out of their hands, because they might be needed any day for a settlement of accounts."

At this Mikhailov's face became grave. Weighing his words and speaking slowly, but in a tone that was for him unusually sharp, he said: "The last proposition is unacceptable. The case described is one that poses not a question of tactics but a question of strategic orientation, and Comrade Stenzer ought to know the difference between them."

This was not the end of the discussion. Practically all the students in our group had their turn one after another, but they introduced nothing new in substance. The most that they produced was only a variation on the first two contrasting opinions. After a while Mikhailov rose again: "Comrades," he said, "the second speaker is substantially correct. The general political alliance is of more importance than the fate of individual decisions. Even when an alliance is in danger, one must never in any circumstances be the first to break it. Even under the threat of partial defeats and sacrifices, one must never lose sight of the strategic object of the union, since in the long run it will be to the political advantage of the Party that the first defection from an existing united front should be made by the other party and not by ourselves."

Such was Mikhailov's reply at the end of 1942, in conformity with the strategic line which had been announced at the time. But I am not so sure that the result would have been exactly the same a few years later.

The struggle against sectarianism, however, was carried on not only in seminar periods about far-distant China in the year 1927. It was to raise its head only a few weeks later in a question of acute current interest.

A special lecture was arranged unexpectedly for the whole school, and it was to lead to highly significant consequences. Mikhailov delivered a lecture against sectarianism. Although this subject was certainly no longer new to us, we detected something unusual in the occasion. We were not kept long on tenterhooks. Suddenly Mikhailov raised his voice and said: "My reason for emphasising this point is that only a few days ago we had a case at this school which showed that sectarianism had by no means been defeated—a case so serious that we intend to deal with it in the presence of the entire school."

We were all tense. Everyone knew that the decisive words were now to come. Mikhailov waited until the last interpreter had finished at the last table, then he went on: "Sectarianism has gone so far in the Italian group that it has reached a point of serious political shortcoming. A member of the Italian group stated at one of the seminars that it was important to give guidance to the Italian partisans about finding safe hiding-places for their weapons, in order to ensure that in the event of Italy being liberated by Anglo-American troops, the weapons of the Italian partisans should not fall into British or American hands."

Most of us were astounded, for the discussion of such matters sounded like music belonging to the remote future. Soviet troops were still standing before Stalingrad; Allied troops had only just landed in North Africa; the struggle of the Italian partisans had barely begun. What had occurred in the Italian group was nevertheless taken very seriously by Mikhailov. "The greatest danger that confronts us to-day is sectarianism—the danger of isolating the Party and separating it from other patriotic forces. For this reason opinions of the kind expressed cannot be too severely condemned, for they drive a wedge into the unity of the anti-fascist front. They weaken the anti-fascist struggle and, objectively considered, they are tantamount to assisting Fascism. Anyone who expresses the opinion that the Italian partisans ought to hide their weapons from the Allies of the Soviet Union is doing nothing less than performing a service for Hitler."

This incident in the Italian group was used to initiate a carefully organised campaign against sectarianism in all the national groups of the school. But some five years later, the comrade who found himself then denounced as a pro-fascist was vindicated on the highest authority. In September, 1947, at the conference which founded the Communist Information Bureau (Cominform), the Italian Party was specifically blamed for not having hidden its weapons, but having carried out the orders of Moscow.

A Political New Year's Eve

So the year 1942 drew towards its end, with the dismantling and re-assembling of machine guns, with the organised study of German folk songs, with the after-effects of criticism and self-criticism, and with the struggle against sectarianism. Only a few more days separated us from New Year's Day. We had been informed that New Year's Day would be celebrated by each group separately. When I happened to hear Paul Wandel telling one of our older comrades something about organising New Year's Eve, I had no difficulty in imagining the form our celebration would take, but my imagination fell far short of reality.

On New Year's Eve we met punctually in our bleak, cold seminar room. The evening went just like a seminar, the only difference being that the tables were slightly differently arranged for the celebration and covered with tablecloths. In addition we had a pumpkin which was shared out among the members of the group. The girls had made tea, but we were strictly forbidden to taste alcohol. In spite of the bleakness of the seminar room and the unusual character of the celebration, with a pumpkin and tea, we soon achieved a cheerful atmosphere. It was entirely unorganised, however, and therefore could not last long.

"I think we can now begin our evening's entertainment. Comrades may sit at the tables."

Obediently we sat down, feeling just as if we were at the seminar. The organised New Year's Eve then went according to plan. Wandel gave a signal to one of the older Party members, who thereupon stood up and recited a poem about the revolutionary struggle, which had not the slightest merit of any kind. Then he sat down. Wandel again gave a signal. A second member began to read out an extract from a book. The prevailing atmosphere now was no longer that of a seminar: it was more like the silence which accompanies a lecture. One felt as if one ought to make notes, and it seemed a pity that there was no paper or pencil available. When the second comrade had finished, a third stood up, again with a poem to recite.

Suddenly something completely unforeseen happened. The door opened. The comrade with the poem came to a stop. We could hardly believe our eyes. Mikhailov, the Director of the school, came into the room dancing and singing. He looked in some surprise at our dumbfounded faces as we sat solemnly round the table. We in turn stared in amazement at our Director hopping and singing.

Mikhailov was the first to recover himself. Realising the effect he had created, he put on a grave face, such as was clearly required at the German group on New Year's Eve, and sat down at the table and waited in silence for what was to come next. By this time our histrionic comrade had recovered from his horror and was continuing with his recitation. Highly disciplined as we all were by this time, we still could not entirely follow what he was saying. Fortunately he soon finished.

Nobody knew now what the next step was to be. No doubt Wandel had organised a few more jacks-in-the-box and everything was perfectly planned—except the arrival of the Director. Questioning looks were exchanged between Wandel and Mikhailov. Wandel's dedication to the Party line was clearly too much even for Mikhailov. When he saw that there was to be no relaxation of the atmosphere for the German group, even on New Year's Eve, he adapted himself to the occasion and gave us an address—but in a manner so uninhibited, so different, and in a way so human, that it was like nothing I ever heard before or since, even in Europe.

He spoke of the dangers and the splendours of revolutionary life. At the end of his brief address, he took a box of matches out of his pocket. "Perhaps," he said, "the best way I can make clear my thoughts and feelings at this moment is by a concrete example."

With that, he took out a match, and struck it. The match burned out in a few seconds, leaving only a little ash behind. Mikhailov looked at us amiably and a little thoughtfully.

"Isn't the life of an ordinary man just like that? He gives out a little flame at first, and then a bigger flame, and finally burns out. All that remains is a little useless ash. Man lives, works, establishes a family, brings children into the world, dies and is mourned at best by the members of his family and a few of his friends: a futile, superfluous life. When we look at our own life by contrast—a life of experience, danger, travel, imprisonment; with responsible tasks, with membership of the great family which we call 'the Party,' with a clear and firm objective as the cornerstone of a new world, with countless comrades to mourn us at our death—is that not something very,

very different from the futility of a spent match?"

We were all enthralled. Never before had anyone at the school spoken to us like this.

Mikhailov looked attentively at us, at each one in turn. "You may think on what I have said, now and then, perhaps," he said, "especially when you are in difficulties. It helps. But now you must have at least one evening of real fun the night before the New Year. I am sure you will forgive me if I now go and visit the other groups."

There was no more fun, however. A few of us were commissioned to go to the other groups and carry them our good wishes. I had the Bulgarians to visit. There too, I had to admit the atmosphere was far from unconstrained. When I came back to the German group it was just eleven o'clock, but our New Year's Eve entertainment was already at an end.

I was not really sorry for it. I went out for a short walk and tried to find an answer to the question, why an evening's entertainment at the school should be so stiff and impersonal? At the time I still believed that this was an isolated phenomenon confined to our school, and that it was the exceptional condition there which prevented friendship and cheerfulness from emerging. It was only later that I realised that these phenomena were by no means limited to our school. Other evenings' entertainments with senior officials—especially those who had spent many years in the Soviet Union—took almost exactly the same course.

It was not until after my break with Stalinism that I realised that this phenomenon was a necessary consequence of the system itself—a consequence of the

criticism and self-criticism which compelled every
official to weigh and reflect on every word; a consequence of unconditional subordination to the leadership; of the veto on free discussion, the complete
segregation from ordinary people, and the purges
which annihilated all the humanity in human beings.

For some of us the New Year's Eve celebration had
a serious aftermath. A few days later the whole school
was summoned together again. It appeared that on
New Year's Eve four young Spaniards had procured
a little alcohol and were proceeding to empty the
flask together. They were caught right at the
outset, when two of them had already drunk a small
glass, one of them half a glass, and one nothing at all.
The whole episode had already been dealt with at two
sessions of criticism and self-criticism in the Spanish group. A decision had been taken there to expel
the four young Spaniards from the *Komsomol,* of
which all were members. Now the case was brought
before the whole school in order to serve as a lesson
and a warning for others. Again came the indictment
and the recitation of examples, which to me were
already familiar enough. At the same time the Soviet
Komsomol was held up to the Spaniards again and
again as a shining example, although everybody present certainly knew well enough that thousands of
members of the Soviet *Komsomol* each drank more
alcohol every day than the four accused young
Spaniards together had tried to drink on New Year's
Eve.

The expulsion of our four Spanish alcoholics was
officially confirmed. About three and a half months
later they were readmitted to the *Komsomol,* having
behaved themselves in an exemplary fashion in the

meanwhile. Not all disciplinary measures turned out so fortunately.

The Dissolution of the Comintern

Nine months had passed since my arrival at the Comintern School. The course had begun in August, 1942; the date was now May, 1943. None of us knew how long our studies were to last, for as each subject came to an end, a new one was announced.

We had only one clue to rely on, which was the series of lectures on the history of the Communist International. For this subject was not taken consecutively, but worked through as a separate series, parallel to the general instruction. It was therefore clear that it would only be concluded when the course itself came to an end.

By the middle of May we had gone through the history of the Comintern up to the year 1934. This made it fairly easy to calculate that we must have at least another three to four months in the school. We had heard from some of the students on the course that it had been reduced in duration by a year while the war was on, so we were ready to see ourselves stay at Kushnarenkovo until August or September, 1943. This was certainly also the school authorities' plan, until it was unexpectedly and completely disrupted by higher direction.

It happened on the 16th May, 1943. I was on my way back to the courtyard after a seminar when I saw a dozen of my fellow students gathered in the anteroom of the school. I noticed my friend Peter Zahl with a horrified expression on his face.

"What's up?"

"The Comintern has been dissolved!"

I was speechless, and at first I could not take anything in.

"That's impossible!"

"Well, read this!"

By this time some of the others had read the text to its conclusion. They went off without saying a word; then I and some of the other newcomers had an opportunity to read it. There on the blackboard in the ante-room of the Comintern School building I read the decree dissolving the Comintern. The crucial passage in this important decree read as follows:

"The whole course of events in the last quarter of a century, and the collective experience of the Communist International, have decisively shown that the form of organisation chosen by the First Congress of the Communist International to unite the working class, which corresponded to the requirements of the early period of the re-emergence of the working class, has more and more obviously outlived its usefulness, in the light of the growth of this movement and the growing complexity of its problems in every country. This form of organisation has in fact become a hindrance to the further strengthening of national workers' parties. The World War unleashed by the Nazis has still further accentuated the difference in conditions in different countries, by bringing out the sharp line of division between those countries which acted as carriers of the Nazi tyranny and the freedom-loving peoples which are united in the mighty coalition against Hitler.

"On the basis of the considerations adduced above, and having regard to the growth and political maturity of the Communist Parties and their leading cadres in the various countries and to the fact that during the present war a number of component sections have raised the question of dissolving the Communist International as the main centre of the International Workers' Movement, the Presidium of the Executive Committee of the Communist International, not being in a position to convene all its members to secure approval section by section on account of the circumstances of the World War, permits itself to submit the following proposal:

"The Communist International is hereby dissolved as the main centre of the International Workers' Movement, and the component sections of the Communist International are relieved of the obligations which they undertook on the basis of the statutes and decrees of the Congresses of the Communist International.

"The Presidium of the Executive Committee of the Communist International calls on all members of the Communist International to concentrate all their strength on giving general support and active cooperation in the war of liberation of the peoples and states of the anti-Hitler coalition in order to accelerate the destruction of the mortal enemy of all working people, German Fascism and its allies and vassals.

"Signed by the Members of the Presidium of the Executive Committee of the Communist International: Gottwald, Dimitrov, Zhdanov, Kolarov, Koplenig, Kuusinen, Manuilsky, Marty, Pieck, Thorez, Florin, Ercoli."

Like everybody else, I was at a loss to know what to say. The Communist International—up till a few minutes ago our highest organised authority! The decree dissolving the Comintern was not published in the Soviet newspapers. The signatories represented the Communist Parties of eight countries: the Soviet Union (Zhdanov and Manuilsky); Germany (Pieck and Florin); France (Thorez and Marty); Bulgaria (Dimitrov and Kolarov); Austria (Koplenig); Czechoslovakia (Gottwald); Finland (Kuusinen); and Italy (Ercoli, which was the Party name for Palmiro Togliatti in the Soviet Union).

Even the leaders of other Communist Parties who were then in Ufa or Kuibyshev (for instance, the Spanish leader Dolores Ibarruri; the Rumanian leader Anna Pauker; and the Hungarian leader Rakosi), were not brought in to sign the documents, because the twelve signatories were not acting as representatives of the Communist Parties in their own countries, but as members of the Presidium of the Executive Committee elected at the last Comintern Congress. Evidently the decree must have been composed so quickly and at such short notice that it had not been possible even to inform the leaders of the other Communist Parties, or to ask them to give at least their formal consent.

The news naturally enough spread rapidly throughout the whole school and led to a lot of excited running to and fro. It was not until midday that it became known that Mikhailov, our Director, had gone to Ufa and would be coming back in the next few days. Meanwhile our instruction continued, but we paid only half-hearted attention to it. Three days later Mikhailov came back from Ufa. Immediately a general meeting of the school was summoned on the subject of the dissolution of the Comintern.

We had often had special lectures before now and we knew that they always led to some important announcement; but never had the excitement been so tense as it was this morning. Mikhailov began with the statement that two false points of view must be rebutted in considering the dissolution of the Comintern. First of all there was the assumption voiced by the Nazi, that the dissolution of the Comintern was no more than a trick, a manœuvre, and that in reality the work of the Comintern would go on.

"The dissolution of the Comintern is not a trick and not a manœuvre," said Mikhailov. "It is a fundamental decision which will be implemented immediately. You will all of course readily understand that the Comintern School is also dissolved, just like all the other institutions of the Comintern *apparat,* as it existed hitherto. The second false theory about the dissolution of the Comintern, which has been spread by certain circles in the West, holds that it is a concession on the part of the Soviet Union to our Western Allies. This view also has no connection with reality. Questions like the dissolution of the Comintern do not depend on temporary considerations of foreign policy, but are of a much more fundamental character."

Mikhailov then went on to elucidate the official explanation of the dissolution of the Comintern. He explained that the real ground lay primarily in the fact that the form taken by the Communist International up to now had outlived its usefulness. It was hampering the struggle of the Communist Parties in the common anti-Fascist front and was no longer adapted to the changed tasks which confronted Communists in various countries.

"In the early years after the foundation of the Comintern," Mikhailov explained, "the tasks of

Communists in other countries, apart from a few national peculiarities, were by and large the same. If we compare that situation with the present day, we can see the fundamental difference. The task of the Communists in England and America to-day is to support the efforts of their countries in the war. The Communists of Germany and Italy, on the other hand, have to do everything they can to bring about the destruction of Fascism. The Communists in the occupied countries have another task again—to set themselves at the head of a national patriotic anti-Fascist front and to liberate their countries from Fascist oppression. Even this brief examination is enough to show how different are the various tasks to-day."

Mikhailov showed that the development which had now led to the dissolution of the Comintern was the logical continuation of the policy which had been adopted as long ago as the Seventh Congress of the Comintern in 1935. Since that Seventh World Congress, a series of examples had shown that a comprehensive organisation such as the Comintern tended to act more and more as a drag, making it difficult for the Communists to evolve new political forms. The history of the workers' movement had shown that at a certain stage of their evolution, international organisations are an absolute necessity, but at other times they could prove to be a hindrance in the evolution of workers' parties in individual countries.

"The establishment of the First International in 1864 was a great step forward. In the course of the next decade its task was fulfilled. The next thing was to develop the component sections into powerful workers' parties in their respective countries. The organisational constitution of the First International then proved to be a shackle which had to burst asunder before this task could be carried out. Again, the foundation in 1919 of the Third International, bringing together on an international basis all those revolutionary groups which took their stand on Marxism, was at that time a vital event in the international workers' movement. To-day, twenty-four years later, when powerful Communist Parties exist in practically every country in the world and when the conduct of the struggle requires increasing independence, the Comintern too has fulfilled its function and its retention would be nothing but a shackle on the further evolution of the Communist Party."

At the same time Mikhailov warned us, however, against underestimating or depreciating the importance of the Communist International. The Communist International had achieved outstanding work. Its dissolution did not mean that its foundation or its activity as a whole were in any way wrong, but only that in the present period new forms must be found in each individual country for the Communist movement. Mikhailov went on to indicate that the dissolution did not represent in any way a repudiation of the spirit of internationalism, which must now and always continue to be an inseparable element in the Communist Party's struggle. The dissolution of the Communist International would open up new possibilities and new perspectives for the Communist Parties of all countries, enabling them to carry out their task more successfully in their respective countries and to continue the great patriotic anti-Fascist struggle.

When the applause subsided, Mikhailov announced that he would gladly answer questions and remove any uncertainties. A young Spaniard took the opportunity to ask: "What will happen to the Young Communist International? Is it also dissolved, or will it possibly continue to function?"

Mikhailov answered without hesitation: "No official decree about the dissolution of the Young Communist International has yet been received, but one can safely assume that its activities will also be terminated. All the arguments which pointed to the dissolution of the Comintern are naturally valid also for the Young Communist International. I certainly need hardly remind our Spanish comrade that the successful youth organisation known as the J.S.U., the United Socialist Youth of Spain, does not represent Communist Youth in the usual sense of the word but is rather a new form of youth organisation. Nobody should be left in any doubt that in the course of the struggle against Fascism in the occupied countries, or those under the control of the Axis, such as Poland, France, Czechoslovakia, Austria, Hungary, Rumania, Bulgaria and so on, and probably even in Italy and Germany, new youth organisations will come into existence, no doubt to some extent on the model of the United Socialist Youth of Spain; but undoubtedly they will be even wider, and will unite all progressive, anti-Fascist young people. The retention of the Young Communist International would be a great handicap to this development. A step in a new direction has already been taken, too, by the establishment of the anti-Fascist Youth Committee in Moscow."

"Comrade Mikhailov, what will become of the

periodical *Communist International?* Will it be
stopped? Will there be another international periodical?" asked one of the older Party members.

Mikhailov's answer was that publication of the
periodical *Communist International* would obviously
be stopped. Whether a new international periodical
would take its place, he could not yet say. He
thought this probable, however, although it would
certainly have a different character.

Mikhailov was to be proved right. A few weeks
later there appeared in Moscow, in Russian and English, a periodical called *War and the Working Class.*
Its name was later changed to *New Times.* The foreign language editions were constantly extended:
to-day it appears in nine different languages.

The last question was: "Is there any definite directive to show how the dissolution of the Comintern
will be put into effect administratively, and when
we can expect the dissolution of our school?"

"The dissolution of the institutions of the Comintern has already begun as an immediate sequel to the
announcement. It is to be expected, however, that
the technicalities will take a few weeks more to put
into effect. The preparatory measures for the dissolution of the Comintern School have already been ini-
tiated simultaneously, too, but they too will probably
need a few weeks more. Until then, instruction will
continue and the subject of the dissolution of the
Comintern will occupy a central position in all
parts of the syllabus. Examinations will still take
place at the end of the course, but the future work
of students on our course will no longer be prescribed by the Comintern, but by the leadership of
the Party in your respective countries."

The Last Days of the Comintern School

The dissolution of the Comintern was variously received at our school. It goes without saying that there was no one who voiced any dissentient opinion against the dissolution of the Comintern, even indirectly. On the other hand, it was unmistakable that the reactions of the older and younger students on the course to this event were very different, not only during the first few days after the dissolution, but also during Mikhailov's lecture. The older comrades who had been Party members or officials for many years, or even decades, sat listening with grave faces; even a few hours earlier the Communist International had still been the summit of everything in their lives. Perhaps at this moment they remembered the words of Dimitrov at the Reichstag Fire trial, that "the programme of the Communist International was the highest of all laws and the Control Commission of the Communist International was the highest of all courts." Perhaps, too, they remembered Stalin's oath over Lenin's grave: "We swear to you, Comrade Lenin, that we will not spare our lives in our efforts to strengthen and extend the league of workers of the whole world, the Communist International." And now from one day to the next there was to be no more Communist International!

For us younger ones, however, the blow was not so hard; and we represented more than half the number of those taking part in the course. We had grown up at a time when the Communist International had long ceased to have the prestige and significance and influence that it had had in the 1920's. Its dissolution seemed to us to be a logical continuation of what we had learned at the Comintern School; indeed, there

were some younger ones among us—and I was one of
them—who looked upon the dissolution of the Comintern as in a sense a positive advance. It was with
some sympathy and even enthusiasm that I read again
and again the passage in the decree of dissolution
which set out the argument that the Party in each
individual country must now tread its own path:

"The profound difference in the paths of historical development in every country in the world, the
diverse character and even contradictions in their
social organisations, the difference in the level and
degree of their social and political evolution, and
finally the difference in degree of consciousness
and organisation of their workers, require that the
solution of the problems which the working class has
to face in each individual country should also be
different."

We younger ones were satisfied to read that the
victory over Fascism could "best and most fruit-
fully be achieved by the vanguard of the workers'
movement of every country in the framework of
their own state," and that the Party in each individual country—as it had already been put at the
Seventh World Congress—"must in making its decisions on every question, start from the concrete situation and the specific conditions which prevail in
that particular country."

This phraseology led me to hope that after Fascism
had been conquered the Communist Party of Germany would no longer be so closely linked with the
U.S.S.R., and would be free in some matters to strike
out in a direction of its own. I think similar thoughts
were shared by the younger Party members in many
other groups. They too were certainly fundamentally

in accord with the system in the Soviet Union, but they cherished the hope of later being able to alter many things for the better in their own countries. I could not guess at the time that, only a few years later, Moscow's control over the Communist Parties would grow even stricter and closer. But although I was convinced of the rightness of the decision, I nevertheless had serious doubts whether the grounds stated were the real ones that had led to the decree of dissolution. The Comintern School was less than forty miles from Ufa. The school authorities were in the closest daily contact with the Comintern. It was easy to see that this decree must have been drawn up literally overnight, otherwise we should certainly have been given some preparation for such a step in the Comintern School, at least indirectly. A lecture on the history of the Comintern had been scheduled for us on the very day on which the decree of dissolution was announced on the radio. Only a few days earlier, we had had a detailed talk on the great significance of the Comintern in the struggle against Hitler.

It was therefore quite certain that the dissolution was a case of a decision very suddenly taken. Probably it emanated from Stalin himself, and had been decided much less on grounds of historical experience than on considerations of Soviet foreign policy.

A couple of days later I was going for a walk with a fellow student. He was one of the few whom I suspected of having never belonged to the category of "150% Communists."

"Extremely interesting, this dissolution of the Comintern, isn't it?" he said, giving me a slight wink.

"Yes, and particularly how suddenly and unexpectedly the decision came," I replied. This reply at once served as a bridge to further conversation, which by no means exactly followed the Party line.

"You know, Linden, whatever people say, I am still convinced that this is a concession to England and America. Perhaps the decision was actually taken at their request."

There was clearly some fear that many students on our course might secretly cherish similar opinions. This may have been the reason why for weeks on end the subject of the dissolution of the Comintern was repeated again and again in innumerable seminars. All the arguments in the decree of dissolution and Mikhailov's speech were analysed to the last detail, in a way which must be almost unimaginable in non-Soviet countries. Every single phrase was explained and elucidated, and examples from recent years were once more elaborated and examined in detail to show why even the First International, seventy years ago, had proved itself after a certain time, in spite of its exceptional positive importance, to be a drag on further progress.

When three weeks had passed since the dissolution of the Comintern and we had examined this single subject again and again from every point of view, the day finally came for which so many of us had long been eagerly awaiting. The announcement was made at a general meeting of the school: "Instruction is now at an end. The task of all comrades in all groups is now to prepare themselves for the examinations which will take place in the near future."

For the first time in the school, we had something like free time. It is true that we were given whole lists of subjects for the examinations to guide us in our preparations; but how we were to do it was left entirely to ourselves. I was by this time so accustomed to a life in which every minute was filled that the last few weeks of preparation for the examinations (which were also our last few weeks at the school) seemed to me like a pinnacle of freedom. We were allowed to spend these lovely warm June days doing our studies in the open air. Finally, in the middle of June, 1943, the time came: examinations took place daily in the different groups; our German group had its turn among the first.

At a table in our seminar room sat the instructors with the seminar leader of the group—Paul Wandel (Klassner), Bernhard Koenen, Lene Berg (Ring) and also Mikhailov, as well as one or two instructors from other groups who knew German. One after another the students on the course were called up. Each one had to go up to the table and take a paper containing the examination questions. There were four or five questions on each paper, one being on the category of subjects which we had been doing for some time at the school:

1. Philosophy (i.e., dialectical and historical materialism); political economy; or other theoretical questions of Marxism-Leninism.
2. History of the Communist Party of the Soviet Union; or of the Comintern.
3. History of the German Workers' Movement; or current questions on the present anti-Fascist struggle.
4. General politics (i.e. primarily Fascism and the situation in Hitlerite Germany); or fundamental political questions of the struggle

against Hitler (e.g. refutation of the Nazi ideology, strategy and tactics, united fronts, popular fronts, etc.).

The examination was not particularly severe, but perhaps it was influenced to some extent by the dissolution of the Comintern. At least it showed, however, how much had been stuffed into us in the relatively short period of eleven months.

It lasted about eight hours. After that, for the first time in almost a year, we had nothing whatever to do except to enjoy to the full the almost excessive free time which was now for once allowed us. Instructors and students in all groups on the course were now waiting only for one thing—the order for the final dissolution of the Comintern School, and their transfer to new political work.

Special Commission in Ufa

On one of these days of unaccustomed holiday, something happened which only a few weeks earlier I would have regarded as practically impossible. "Tomorrow there will be a general excursion for the whole school," we were told. "We shall spend the whole day in the sun by the Belaya River, relaxing and bathing."

This was the first time, apart from three working expeditions, that we had been allowed to leave the school compound. So we lay on the river bank, we bathed and sun-bathed, and we made the most of the wonderful day. But there is also another reason why this day by the Belaya River has remained in my memory.

A friend and I were lying a little apart from the

group. Suddenly we saw a peasant woman coming towards us, and before we had thought out what we were to do if she spoke to us, she had reached us and was asking: "You must be from the school, aren't you?"

We muttered something unintelligible.

"Well, of course, you mustn't say. And anyway, I know you are from the foreigners' school. They're daft, the Soviet authorities—they give you foreigners everything and we have to go hungry. But they don't get anything out of it back there, anyway! When you get out, you won't be on their side, anyway!"

We looked at each other, but said nothing. The peasant woman went placidly on her way, walking quite fast. But her bold words had served to remind me that I had now spent eleven months in a completely separate world, utterly out of touch with the life of ordinary people. To-day I regard this complete isolation of the responsible official class as an important characteristic of the Stalinist system. It explains many aspects of the Stalinist official's way of thinking and behaviour.

A few days later, when I lay reading in a field in the neighbourhood of the school building, I suddenly heard my name called.

"Linden! Linden!"

"What's up?"

"You're to come to the Director at once!"

Somewhat uneasily, I went along. Was I in for another bout of criticism and self-criticism? Had my fellow student reported our brief conversation about the dissolution of the Comintern? But he had himself gone much farther than I had! When I entered

Mikhailov's room, there were already seven of our comrades sitting there, all from different groups.

"We have two comrades still to wait for," said Mikhailov.

Two minutes later the other two came in. It did not look as if it was to be a session of self-criticism. Next to Mikhailov sat an official whom I had never seen before at the school.

Mikhailov began without further ado. "Comrades, we have invited you here because we have chosen you for a special task. As a result of the dissolution of the Comintern, it has become necessary to put in order the Comintern archives, which are in a rather chaotic state as a result of the evacuation. We have chosen you for this task, not only because in our view you have the political qualifications needed for working in the archives, but also because you all have necessary foreign languages for the work. I need hardly remind you that nothing whatever must be said about this assignment. You will travel to Ufa with our comrade here. I think it can be managed to-morrow morning."

And so the next morning the trucks arrived to take us all to Ufa—ten students, the official and two stenographers. Everyone else remained behind at the school. I did not know whether I should ever see the school again, or what would happen to us after the completion of this mission. As we drove off, I took a last look back at the school, where I had learned so much of interest, but where also I had been through those terrible hours of criticism and self-criticism. Within eleven months I had been transformed there from a lively, open-minded student and member of the *Komsomol* into one of those Party officials who weigh every word they utter.

A few minutes later the school lay far behind us, as we were driven towards an undertaking which I looked forward to with eager curiosity. It was my first mission for the Party.

In Ufa we were not driven to the Comintern building. Instead, we stopped in front of the Hotel Bashkiria—the hotel which used to house the leading members of the Comintern, none of whom were now left in Ufa. Our conducting officer led us upstairs to a room that had been reserved for us. As much at ease as if he were himself the manager of the hotel, he opened the door to the dining-room and invited us in.

"This is where you will take your meals," he said, and at the same moment a neatly-dressed maid came into the room and began to serve us.

Our food at the Comintern School had not been bad, but what we were now offered was beyond all our expectations. After the meal we were given good cigarettes, and we made ourselves comfortable.

"Now perhaps we can have a talk about our work, if our comrades have no objection," said our conducting officer. There was no objection, and he went on: "Every morning after breakfast you will be taken by car to the Comintern archives. The archives are on the fourth floor of a school: the place is strictly guarded, of course. You can only enter and leave it together, and even then only with this pass." Each of us was then given a pass, which had already been prepared. Our conducting officer went on politely: "I think it wouldn't be a bad thing to go to the archives now. There I can explain the work to you in detail; then you can set to work to-morrow morning. Are there any questions?"

There were certainly many things I would have liked to know, but, of course, there were no questions. "Then we're all set," he said.

Three private cars were waiting for us. We drove across the town until we reached a new building, four stories high. On the top floor we were met by a sentry. We showed our passes, and were led into a large room in which lay a huge pile of sacks. The sacks were about five feet long and nearly two feet wide. It looked as if they were filled with files or folders. We soon discovered that there were two more little rooms, also filled with sacks.

Our conducting officer led us into a corner and explained: "When Moscow was evacuated there was not sufficient time to arrange the Comintern archives systematically. The files and folders of the archives of the various national Communist Parties were simply packed in sacks, and these were provisionally numbered so that at least we know where to find the archives of a particular Party; but nobody knows what is contained in each individual sack. Your task will be to open the sacks, to look through them, to number the folders according to their contents, and to prepare an inventory of the contents of each sack, which you can then dictate to the stenographer. This will at least make a rough survey possible of the contents of the archives. When we come to look through the material later, we shall then be able to find our way around on the basis of your lists."

I looked somewhat doubtfully at the quantity of

sacks which were stacked up in the huge room. We had an immense task in front of us.

"Our idea is to divide up the archives by countries. Each of you will take the material of one Party to work through. I will now give you the break-down, which is as follows."

He took a paper out of his pocket and read out our Party names, followed by the countries and the numbers of the sacks each of us had to work on.

"Comrade Linden—Communist Party of the U.S.A. and half the material of the Communist Party of Great Britain."

Now I was really beginning to enjoy the work. It would indeed be highly interesting to read the material in the archives of these Communist Parties. But perhaps our companion suspected what I was thinking . . .

"I must emphatically warn you," he said, "that nobody engaged on this work must allow anything about it to get out. I should like also to warn you that every piece of paper, however unimportant it seems, must be put back in the sack from which it was taken. It goes without saying that not the smallest scrap of paper must be taken out of this room. Finally, I should like to stress that your work does *not* consist of reading the material in the archives, but simply of sorting it. None of you is authorised to read a word of the material in these archives."

Not even the rigour of my past training could prevent me from wondering how one was to establish the contents of entire sacks full of documents if one was not allowed to read the documents; but I refrained from saying anything.

Our Work in the Comintern Archives

After a good night's rest, we began our work in the Comintern archives the next day. Each of us first set about collecting together the sacks belonging to his Party. After looking through the first few sacks, I was compelled ruefully to admit that the task was more difficult than I had thought. The confusion was appalling.

Were the others finding the same thing? In spite of the strictly conspiratorial atmosphere, we naturally showed each other how things stood with our particular material. It was generally agreed that I had by far the hardest task of all: the Communist Party of the U.S.A. was readily conceded first place for chaos and confusion. The sacks belonging to my American comrades contained not only whole bundles of Party documents which had simply been stuffed in without even a file-cover being put round them, but also the remains of cinema advertisements, old numbers of the *New York Times,* broken pencils and every kind of rubbish that had not the slightest connection with the archives.

"Our American comrades must have been damned hard-pressed for time, if that's how they sent their archives to Moscow!" said one of my colleagues with a smile.

The same utter confusion did not prevail with the British Party. Here at least all the papers had been collected into folders; and even if nothing was written on the outside of the folders to show what they contained, nevertheless it all looked comparatively well arranged. But this was nothing in comparison with the archives of the German Communist Party.

We had never thought such a thing possible; the papers were not only arranged in folders, but every folder had a complete list of contents attached to it.

"Well, you are lucky! you certainly picked an easy job," said one of us to the comrade who had been chosen to sort out the material of the German Communist Party. The latter only groaned: it was true his sacks were well arranged, but to make up for it he had three times as many as we had for the other parties. No Party had sent such copious material to Moscow as the German Communist Party.

Gloomily I went back to the material sent in by my American comrades, and tried desperately to bring a little order into the confusion of Party documents, broken scissors, old newspapers, india rubbers and indelible pencils. Our conducting officer watched us at work. When he passed me and saw the depressing situation in which my American comrades had landed me, he shook his head thoughtfully. "You'll never be finished like that. I think in this case we must confine ourselves to a rough description. The main thing is to get the papers quickly into the folders, so that at least things are a little more orderly. If it's not clear at once what the subject is, you can easily write 'Miscellaneous' on the folders, because we must get the whole job done in a few days."

It was not until I had been working hard for several hours putting the Party documents into folders as quickly as possible according to their headings, writing on the outside of the folders and putting them back in the sacks again, that I infringed the strict ban on reading anything for the first time.

Among the various American newspapers, I suddenly discovered one called *The Militant*. I took it to be a bourgeois newspaper and was about to put it back in the sack again without further thought when suddenly I was struck by seeing the sign of the hammer and sickle on the front page of the paper and the slogan: "Proletarians of all countries, Unite!"

Could this be a Party newspaper? But there had never been any mention of such a newspaper during lectures on the American Party in the history of the Comintern. Yet I supposed it must in fact be a Party newspaper, until I saw a large headline on the first page:

"Rakovsky's Surrender, by Leon Trotsky."

I could hardly believe my eyes: an article by Trotsky! So this must be a Trotskyite newspaper! I could not have been more startled if I had found a packet of dynamite.

I looked round quickly. There was nobody near me. Curiously, I ran quickly through Trotsky's article. I cannot describe how startled I was by it.

Rakovsky? I had come across the name occasionally in Lenin's writings, and I knew that he had been condemned in the spring of 1938. I had of course had my doubts for some time already whether the victims of the purge from 1936-1938 were really counter-revolutionaries, but so far my suppositions had been merely instinctive. I had never been able to find out anything more reliable. Now I was reading about the fate of this revolutionary and about the political struggles of the opposition against Stalin's "faction" (an expression which was itself a complete novelty to me); but still I could not understand why Trotsky spoke about a "surrender." Then I saw that Rakovsky had admitted his errors and returned to the Communist Party of the Soviet Union.

Things like self-criticism and the recognition of the rightness of the Party's policy formed part of the vocabulary which I had hitherto learned. It was quite a discovery to find this procedure described as "surrender"; but in this case wasn't Trotsky right? Had it not in fact been a surrender? By this time I had wasted almost a quarter of an hour reading the American Trotskyite newspaper and I had to catch up again. I went on working more quickly than before, still hoping, however, that another copy of *The Militant* would fall into my hands. I duly found a second one in the same sack. Again I read quickly through the most important passages. After that it became a rule for me to work without stopping until *The Militant* turned up again, and then to interrupt my work for three or four minutes' reading. Probably I was not the only one who read Trotskyite publications in these archives.

There is a simple explanation for this interest. The bourgeois newspapers which came into my hands while sorting the Comintern archives, just like the extracts from the bourgeois press in the bulletins which we had read at the school, contained nothing that could really interest us. They dealt with things that were so remote from our life and our problems, and they used expressions which were so entirely meaningless to us, that we could hardly summon up any interest in them. The Trotskyites, on the other hand, wrote in our own language, using our own terminology and dealing with things about which I had already had doubts of my own, so that my excitement and interest in this case can easily be understood.

With every day and every hour that passed I found myself regretting more and more that everything had to be done at such a furious pace. There were so many things that I would have liked to have read—protocols on sessions of the Central Committee, struggles with the factions, justifications for the expulsion of leading Party officials—but unfortunately there was not the slightest possibility. I had to open the sacks, put the material in folders, and write on the outside "Trade Unions" or "Miscellaneous" or "Party 1921-1923" at the pace of a Stakhanov. With every day that passed, we were urged more and more often to pay less attention to accuracy than to speed. All that the lists needed to show was what was in every sack, and there was no point in an exact inventory.

Within three weeks, despite all the difficulties, our work came to an end. Our conducting officer thanked us. Anxiously we waited to see what would happen to us now.

"Comrades, the idea is that you should stay temporarily in Ufa for a few days longer, and have a bit of a rest. You will stay on in the Hotel Bashkiria and be looked after there. As soon as a few other matters have been settled, we shall travel to Moscow together, and there you will be put at the disposal of your own Parties."

A Glimpse of Ordinary Life

To Moscow! My joy knew no bounds at the thought of being able to return to the capital after the last two years and all that had happened in them. However, we still had a few days to wait.

Ufa had changed again in the last year. Senior officials and their closest colleagues had by this time gone back to Moscow. By July, 1943, only the middle grades and the "proletariat" of the Comintern still remained in Ufa, all of them waiting eagerly for the opportunity to return to Moscow.

One day as I was walking through the streets, I noticed what appeared to me to be a market. I felt curious and went nearer. A terrible sight confronted me. Dozens of people, many of them clothed only in rags, had gathered there to exchange a part of their miserable rations for other things. One old woman, who could hardly stand on her feet for hunger, was holding in her trembling hands a piece of black bread for exchange, and an old man was trying to exchange two lumps of sugar for some bread. Another man was offering two cigarettes for sale at six roubles each. The utter destitution which I saw in the market of Ufa served to remind me in a blinding flash how incredibly well-off I had been all this time. In a few months I had almost completely forgotten that such poverty existed. My memories of Karaganda, and of the time when I had lived just as miserably myself, had entirely faded.

Two days later I had another meeting in Ufa which again severely shook me. I had left my hotel after a sumptuous lunch when I saw an old man of poverty-stricken appea......ce in tattered clothes coming toward me. I had already put my hand in my pocket to find some money when he spoke to me:

"Good afternoon, Linden."

This was a shock: how did this unknown man know my Party name? Then I looked more closely at him. He was one of the students from our group on the course, the same who had told us in such detail one afternoon about his clandestine activity during the occupation of France, and had afterwards suddenly been removed from the school without any explanation. This had happened more than six months earlier, and to judge from his appearance, he must have gone through a terrible time since then.

"Well, haven't you a piece of bread for me?" He looked at me imploringly.

"No, I haven't for the moment, but when I come back from dinner I will bring you something. It isn't allowed, but I will try and bring you as much as I can without being noticed. You must forgive me though—it will hardly be possible to bring anything with me except just bread."

He made a gesture. "My dear Linden, you don't have to apologise. The others don't even give me bread: they won't even speak to me any longer. And most of them turn away and won't talk to me when they see me in the street. If you can give me a little bread, I shall never forget it—I shall be eternally thankful to you."

From then on I always took some bread with me, in order to slip it to him in the evening at some remote spot. He thanked me every time, but said extremely little. I only learned that after his expulsion from the Party school, he had got no more help from any quarter. A Party member who had carried out special missions for the Party for years on end was thus cast off and left to his fate—an example of the iron ruthlessness and logic of Stalinism towards any human being it no longer needed.

But in spite of these experiences at Ufa, I was still far from condemning the system as a whole. I still believed that these were failings of individual officials, or relics of the Russian past. The Stalinist ideology was still so deeply ingrained in me that not even these experiences, nor the indescribable difference between the life of an official and that of an ordinary man as I had seen it so strikingly at Ufa, could yet shake me in my loyalty.

The weeks of July, 1943, which we spent in Ufa brought a series of exciting events. Mussolini was overthrown; Italy was on the eve of withdrawal from the war. Everyone hoped that the war was now approaching its end. On 21st July, came a new surprise. On the third page of *Pravda,* with great prominence, there appeared a manifesto from the National Committee for Free Germany, addressed to the *Wehrmacht* and the German people. To our astonishment we learned that on 12th-13th July in the neighbourhood of Moscow, a conference had taken place between German prisoners-of-war (including both soldiers and officers) and German émigrés. At this conference a National Committee for Free Germany had been elected and at the head of it was Erich Weinert, whom I knew well, together with Major Karl Hetz, and Lieutenant Heinrich Graf von Einsiedel as vice-president.

I read their appeal with burning interest, and

ticed at once that it was even more widely framed than the appeal of the so-called "West German Peace Conference" which we had studied in such detail at school. Baron von Stein, Ernst Moritz Arndt, Clausewitz and Yorck were held up as examples in this appeal, which included no socialist demands even by implication and never so much as mentioned the existence of German Communists.

The objects of the manifesto, so far as concerned the reconstruction of Germany after Hitler's downfall, were limited to the demand for a strong democratic constitution ("having nothing in common with the futility of the Weimar system"); the complete abolition of all laws based on national and racial hatred; a re-establishment and broadening of political rights and social services; economic and commercial freedom (including a guarantee of legitimately acquired property); the immediate liberation and compensation of victims of the Hitler régime; and finally a demand for a just and ruthless trial of war criminals and those responsible for the war, which was, however, to be linked with an amnesty for all those adherents of Hitler who dissociated themselves from him in good time by practical steps such as joining the movement for a Free Germany.

I could still form only an imcomplete picture of this National Committee, and I still did not know that the colours black, white and red had been adopted as its symbol, since these were not distinguishable in *Pravda's* reproduction; but naturally I was passionately interested in the National Committee for Free Germany, and there was nothing I desired more earnestly than to collaborate with it. My wish was to be fulfilled more rapidly than I could have thought possible on this 21st of July.

The following afternoon we were summoned and told that we were to travel to Moscow the same evening. Karaganda, the Comintern School, my work in the Comintern archives—all this lay behind me. I was all eagerness for what lay before me. The very next day we arrived in Moscow.

CHAPTER SIX

The National
Committee for Free Germany

BACK IN MOSCOW at last! How often in Karaganda
and Kushnarenkovo had my thoughts gone back to
Moscow! I had left the city in September, 1941, in a
guarded train full of compulsory deportees. Now in
July, 1943, I was returning as a graduate from the
Comintern School, ready for action in the political
field.

Cars stood waiting at the station for our group.
We had no idea where they were to take us. It was
only when we were on our way across Moscow that
our escort explained: "We shall stop at the Hotel
Lux, where you will live for the time being. In the
next few days you will be told all about your future
work by representatives of your respective parties."

The Hotel Lux! The celebrated Hotel Lux on
Gorky Street (formerly Tverskaya Street) had been
the home of Comintern officials and staff for twenty-
five years. In 1940 or at the beginning of 1941, if I
had wanted to visit anyone at the Hotel Lux, I should
have had to go through a security procedure every
time. Every visit was a great event for me at that date
—and now I was going to live there myself!

The Hotel Lux, Moscow

At the Hotel Lux each of us was provided with a pass bearing his photograph. This was what was known as a *propusk,* and it had to be shown every time one went into the building. The hotel was a world apart. Things were so organised that its occupants hardly needed to come into contact with any outside bodies. Apart from the special "reserved" dining-room, there was also a special laundry and special tailors' and cobblers' shops, as well as a special clinic or out-patients' department, all of which were available only to the occupants of the Hotel Lux. We were restricted to a special "reserved" shop in the immediate neighbourhood of the hotel. Comintern workers who lived in the Hotel Lux—after the dissolution of the Comintern they were known as "representatives of foreign Communist Parties"—were conveyed to their places of work and brought back again in groups by special buses, so that we used the public transport only on the rarest occasions. There was also in the hotel a special branch of the militia and the army, which dealt with all questions of registration for military service and demobilisation, so that if anyone was called up by the army all the necessary steps to secure his release were taken at once without any need for him to do anything himself.

When I came to the Hotel Lux in July, 1943, most of the leading officials had already returned from their places of evacuation. I now saw more of Wilhelm Pieck, Walter Ulbricht and Anton Ackermann; also Anna Pauer, who was at that time Chairman of the Rumanian Party, Jacob Berman, who had been an instructor at our Comintern School and was a leading Polish Party official, and Erno Gerö, a member of the Hungarian Party *politburo*; and the leading Austrian officials, Koplenig, Fürnberg, Ernst Fischer, Zucker-Schilling, and Franz Honner.

At this time a great many younger officials were living in the Hotel Lux besides the members of the former Comintern *apparat*. Most of them were sons and daughters of officials—émigrés who had grown up in the Soviet Union like myself and had later been trained for political work. There were even a few young Spaniards at the hotel at this time. They had come to the U.S.S.R. during the Spanish Civil War and had grown up in Spanish Children's Homes and later gone to the Comintern School or other political schools. I also met a few young Germans there, including Peter Florin (the son of the party leader Wilhelm Florin, who died in 1944), as well as two young Canadian girls; and finally a number of young officials of various other nationalities, most of whom had grown up in the International Youth Home at Ivanovo.

Most of the occupants of the hotel worked in what was called "Institue No. 205," a sort of successor organisation to the Comintern, which was established in a gigantic group of modern buildings hermetically sealed from the outside world at Rostokino, in the neighbourhood of the agricultural exhibition. It was the same building in which the Comintern had had its headquarters from 1940 to 1941. Of course, the work had changed since the dissolution of the Comintern. All that was done here now was editorial work for the broadcast transmissions of the various so-called clandestine stations, of which there was a whole series. Among them, for instance, were the

German People's Broadcast, the Free Austrian Broadcast, the Spanish Anti-Franco Station, and transmissions to the various countries occupied by Hitler. A number of the occupants of the Hotel Lux did not work at Institute No. 205: they were editors, scriptwriters, announcers and monitors in Moscow Radio, or lecturers and instructors at the prisoner-of-war camps, and especially in the anti-Fascist schools.

The evacuation at the end of 1941 had almost completely emptied the Hotel Lux, but now it was full again. As a precaution, the neighbouring buildings round the courtyard had already been evacuated and put at the disposal of the foreign officials. These were not so comfortably equipped, and were earmarked for staff below V.I.P. status. There were no single rooms in these buildings. People were accommodated three, four or even five in a room.

I was put in one of the neighbouring buildings. In spite of the dissolution of the Comintern, our room had a highly international character. I was billeted with a Turk, a Spaniard, a German and a lively Portuguese called Ferreira, who was the only Portuguese in the U.S.S.R. at the time: he used to draft the Portuguese broadcasts for Moscow Radio.

At the Hotel Lux I met Hans Mahle. As always he was in good form and greeted me with delight.

"So here you are in Moscow again! The Karaganda period's over?"

"Yes, I've been here a few weeks now and I'm just going to get an appointment."

He gave me the first issue of a paper called *Free Germany* and to my astonishment I saw that the front page carried a border in black, white and red at the top and bottom. I was absolutely dumbfounded and asked: "Tell me, Hans, is this black, white and red accidental or has it got some symbolic significance?" For all the struggle against sectarianism, I had never expected to see Moscow tolerate the colours black, white and red.

"No, it isn't an accident. The Free German Movement isn't a continuation of the anti-Fascist movement in the usual sense: its object, as you perhaps have seen from the Manifesto, is to unite all our forces against Hitler, including the German Nationalists, the Conservatives and even the National Socialists—at least those who have gone some way in opposition to Hitler."

I showed interest, and this led him on to talk more about it.

"Before the establishment of the National Committee there was a series of important discussions. Originally, a black, red and gold flag was planned for the Free German Movement, but then our Soviet friends had second thoughts. Manuilsky in particular spoke against it. 'The black, red and gold flag,' he said, 'was reminiscent of the Weimar Republic—a period of weakness and crisis and mass unemployment: this would be a handicap to the Movement. The black, white and red flag would be better, because it was popular with the officers' corps of the *Wehrmacht* and would therefore contribute towards making possible the creation of a really broad national movement!"

As I was about to take my leave, Hans Mahle detained me. "The question of your future job will soon be settled. The steamer from Ufa is due the day after to-morrow, and then we shall summon a meeting of all the students of the German group from the Comintern School."

The steamer from Ufa now became the principal topic of conversation at the Hotel Lux. Everybody knew what it meant: the eventual return of the last of the Comintern officials and workers who had been evacuated to Ufa, as well as the graduates of the Comintern School in Kushnarenkovo. Some of us went down to the landing stage to meet the steamer, which to our general amazement arrived on time. It was a great reunion.

On the ship's rail I saw Bernhard Koenen. He gave me a friendly wave and asked: "Well! what's the news in Moscow?"

"The first number of the newspaper *Free Germany* is just out. And the Movement's got a flag."

"What sort of a flag?"

"Guess, Bernhard!" I replied, and waited anxiously for his answer.

He thought for a moment. "It certainly won't be a red flag—probably the National Committee will have decided on a black, red and gold flag."

"You're wrong," I said with a light laugh. "The National Committee has chosen a black, white and red flag."

Bernhard became serious and said: "That's silly—it can't be so! One shouldn't joke about that sort of thing."

"Yes, Bernhard, that's exactly what it is. The National Committee really has chosen a black, white and red flag."

At that Bernhard became really cross. He thought his ex-pupil from the Comintern School was perpetrating a bad joke. He turned away with an angry look on his face. I don't know what he said or thought when he discovered that Free Germany really had adopted the colours of Kaiser Wilhelm's *Reich*.

A few days later, the German graduates of the Comintern School were summoned to a room in the Hotel Lux. The conference was opened by Hans Mahle, who was at that time responsible for the junior officials. We knew that our future appointments were to be decided at this conference, so we were in a serious mood as we sat around him. He was just going to begin with a political introduction when his eye fell on me.

"There's no need for you to take part in this session. Your case has already been decided. You are to work in the National Committee for Free Germany."

I was overjoyed. This was exactly what I had wanted. Hans Mahle thrust a piece of paper into my hands, on which was written "Filipovski Street."

"That's the address," he said. "You're to report to Major Pieck."

Until that moment I had no inkling of the existence of such a person as Major Pieck, but I had learned not to ask questions. I took my leave of the graduates of the German group, and a few minutes later I was on my way to my new place of work: the National Committee for Free Germany.

Institute No. 99

The house had an abandoned air. There was no sign to show where to go. Could this really be the home of the much-advertised National Committee for Free Germany? Hesitantly I went up the staircase. There were no indications anywhere, no nameplates to identify the occupants or the offices. On the fourth floor a door stood wide open. Immediately past the entrance there was a young Soviet officer sitting at a table.

"What do you want, Comrade?" he asked me in Russian.

I stammered a moment. "Actually, I'm looking for the National Committee for Free Germany," I said hesitantly.

"Come in here. This is where it is."

Astounded, I entered the ante-room. A Soviet officer in the uniform of a major came to meet me.

"Major Pieck," he introduced himself.

"Wolfgang Leonhard," I replied, for the name Linden now belonged to the past. This Soviet Major Pieck, who I learned only afterwards was the son of Wilhelm Pieck, spoke in German. I was very much taken aback, because this was the first time that I had ever seen a German in the uniform of the Soviet Army.

"I've heard of you. I'm very pleased to see you here. I'll introduce you at once to Comrade Karl Maron."

Major Pieck led me down a corridor, on either side of which there were four or five rooms. Most of them stood empty. Obviously the organisation was only beginning to be built up.

In the last room there were a few tables and chairs. Behind a mountain of manuscripts and innumerable packets of cigarettes sat a pleasant-looking, rather corpulent man of about forty. This was Karl Maron. If anyone had told me then that Maron was to become, a few years later, the Chief of the People's Police of the Soviet Zone of Germany, I should have laughed out loud, so inappropriate was his appearance.

He was reading a newspaper. He offered me a cigarette, looking as if nothing could disturb his calm.

Major Pieck disappeared, and in his place there came in a cheerful-looking man who introduced himself as Kozlov and told everyone diffidently that he was absolutely at their disposal to carry out their slightest wish or need, in so far as it was of a technical or administrative character. It soon turned out that Kozlov was far from being so unimportant as he appeared. He was a senior Party official, charged by the Central Committee of the Bolshevik Party with the task of controlling our organisation and establishing proper contact with Soviet bodies.

A few days later another Russian turned up: a silent, fair-haired young man, who did not introduce himself and spoke little. It was not difficult to make out that he was the Chief of Personnel. The rumour soon got around that his name was Vorobev; at least that was how he was known to us. Nothing much more was found out about him, for like most Soviet Chiefs of Personnel he did not let himself be seen about much, and he preferred to deal with personnel matters behind locked doors.

The rooms were soon all occupied. Émigrés came to join us almost every day. Typewriters clattered, reports were written, files were opened and the incessant coming and going was sufficient to show that an important new body was in process of development. Rooms were allotted, two of them being reserved for the principal members of the National Committee: one to be occupied by Erich Weinert and the other by Walter Ulbricht. The rest were occupied by the editorial staff of the newspaper

Free Germany and the radio station, together with the secretariat of the National Committee proper.

There were no difficulties in the process of establishing and equipping ourselves, apart from one small incident. One day loud shouts of abuse were to be heard from a neighbouring room. We asked what was up and Karl Maron, with a cigarette in his mouth, replied indifferently: "That's Walter Ulbricht."

I went into the corridor and saw what had gone wrong. It was all on account of a desk. To be precise, Ulbricht's table was not big enough for him. However, the incident was quickly dealt with. The obliging Kozlov had already appeared. "My apologies, Comrade Ulbricht, it is simply a technical oversight."

I thought I detected an ironic smile. The same afternoon a larger desk was already there for Ulbricht.

A few days later we were summoned one by one to Vorobyov. Each of us was given a printed card, on which was our name and nothing else except the words "U.S.S.R. Institute No. 99" in large letters.

"This is for any dealings you may have with Soviet offices or authorities. If any Soviet officials ever ask where your place of work is, you should not mention the National Committee, but always Institute No. 99."

So for the Soviet authorities we were Institute No. 99. But what was our relation with the National Committee proper? I was only able to form a clear picture of this some weeks later, after we had begun work. At Lyunovo, the official location of the National Committee for Free Germany, were to be found the German soldiers and officers who had adhered to the National Committee, or were members of it. They too had with them, among other things, an editorial staff for a newspaper and a radio; but in Moscow, where we soon became accustomed to calling our place of work the "Town Editorial Office" or the "Town Committee," our staff consisted exclusively of German émigrés. Presumably most of the members of the National Committee at Lyunovo knew of the existence of the Town Committee, but had no knowledge of its activities. It was not long before I realised that the real work of political editorship went on in our offices and not at the official location of the National Committee.

"You are to work on the editorial staff of the newspaper. The editor-in-chief will be here to-morrow. You will report to him at once," said Maron in an off-hand way.

"Who is the editor-in-chief?"

"Rudolf Herrnstadt."

Rudolf Herrnstadt? I had never heard the name until this moment. Knowing the more important party documents as I did, I was sure that he had never signed a party manifesto. What is more, his name was not even to be found under the appeal to the German people on 30th January, 1942, which had been signed by all the prominent émigrés, nor was it among the signatures of the manifesto issued at the establishment of the National Committee.

The following morning I knocked on the door of the editor-in-chief. He began the interview by saying: "So you are Wolfgang Leonhard?" He used the plural form of "you," and involuntarily I started. It was the first time that a German émigré in the Soviet Union had addressed me in the plural.

"Have you ever worked on a newspaper before?"

He put the question with polite condescension, and there was an ironic undertone in his voice.

"No, I have only just finished studying at a political school, where we did not get much journalistic training."

I had chosen the expression "political school" because I did not know whether I ought to mention the Comintern School in the presence of a man who seemed to have the appearance of a bourgeois. It was all exceedingly peculiar.

"I am not interested in political schools. I asked you about work on a newspaper."

"No, I have never worked on a newspaper before."

"You will have a lot to learn. Work on a newspaper is very difficult and responsible. I assume it is quite clear to you that you will have to begin from the very bottom?"

Herrnstadt was polite and cold. He continued to use the plural form of "you" throughout. He never spoke either of the struggle for the liberation of the German working-class or of the Party. He behaved exactly as I had imagined the editor-in-chief of a capitalist paper would do. I was completely bewildered.

Finally Herrnstadt began to speak about my own work. "You will act as liaison with the press, read proofs, help the Russian compositors with the setting up, and in particular you will be responsible for all the information bulletins that come in."

We received every day whole bundles of material from the radio monitoring service at Institute No. 205, the successor organisation of the Comintern. These contained all the communiqués and commentaries broadcast both by the Hitler *bloc* and also by the anti-Hitler coalition. There were also the special bulletins, which I already knew from the Comintern School, including the so-called "Red Bulletin" containing the broadcasts from Hitlerite Germany. It goes without saying that I was forbidden to utter a word to anyone about the contents of these information bulletins.

Shortly after I had begun this work, Herrnstadt sent for me one day. "We need some detailed material on certain economic questions relating to Germany, and I would like to ask you to collect this material for us. You will see from this list what the subjects are."

At first I was completely at a loss, for the list contained subjects of a highly detailed and specialised character.

"Don't worry. There is any amount of material at Institute No. 205 on all these subjects. All you need do is report to Mrs. Gertrude Keller, who will give you the necessary directions."

Herrnstadt had already telephoned to Geminder, who was at that time Chief of Institute No. 205, to tell him I was coming. Geminder was one of the most senior and important Party officials. No one could enter or leave Institute No. 205 without a pass signed by him, or without his personal permission. (Even the most complete pessimist could not have guessed at the time that nine years later, in October, 1952, Geminder would be executed with Slansky in Czechoslovakia as an "enemy of the people.")

On the following day, when I entered Institute No. 205 with a pass signed by Geminder in my hand to make my way to Gertrude Keller, I was still in considerable doubt whether I should be able to get to-

gether all the material in the short time available.
However, my doubts proved unjustified. The huge
halls contained a remarkably complete library of all
important political and economic writings published
outside the Soviet Union, carefully arranged by
countries and subjects. Another room was full of
filing cabinets containing newspaper cuttings, also
arranged by countries and subjects. Gertrude Keller
had a whole staff of colleagues who were responsible
for individual countries and areas. Among them were
some graduates from the Comintern School.

"Please go and take a seat in the reading-room. My
colleague who is responsible for Germany will bring
you all the newspaper cuttings from the German,
Allied and neutral press on the subjects you are interested in at once."

Sure enough, I was provided with everything in a
few minutes. I could not help being astonished at the
abundance of the material and the accuracy and
completeness with which it was assembled, as well
as the superb organisation and the speed with which
it was served up to those who wanted it. Obviously
there were no limits to the financial means and professional experience available. This impression was
only confirmed again and again by the frequent visits
which I made to Institute No. 205 in the course of
the following year. (I have not so far seen in West
Germany any institute containing anything like so
much material about the Soviet Union and the countries of the Eastern *bloc,* or so well equipped and
organised, as this Soviet Institute No. 205 with its
collection of material on non-Soviet countries.)

I had to go there almost every week from now on,
to dig out and put together relevant material for our

newspaper. This was the most interesting of all my activities, because it gave me the opportunity to form a picture of Germany more accurate than anything published in the official Soviet press. Moreover, I liked the atmosphere better in Institute 205 than in Institute 99, where the editorial staff of *Free Germany* consisted in the early months only of four men, whom I soon got to know more intimately.

Lothar Bolz was the author of all articles on Germany, most of which appeared unsigned. He was very industrious at his work; he read carefully all bulletins containing extracts from Hitler's press and based his articles on these. He seemed to know Herrnstadt personally from some earlier period, for of all the editors he was on the closest terms with him. Like everyone else who had been a long time in the Soviet Union, he spoke very little about himself, but from the occasional remarks he made it emerged that he had previously been a lawyer in Upper Silesia and had already lived many years in the Soviet Union. He had worked on the editorial staff of the German-language *Red News* in Leningrad and the *German Centre News* in Moscow, as well as teaching German and German literature at Novosibirsk. But his name was never to be found in official party announcements. The fact that his articles appeared unsigned in the newspaper gave the impression even at that date that he was not to become a public figure. It could hardly have been foreseen at that time that he was later to become the leader of the National Democratic Party in the Soviet Zone, as well as the Foreign Minister of the D.D.R.

Number two in the editorial staff was Alfred Kurella. He was not with us all the time; he generally came when difficult questions arose. He wrote little himself. His main talent seemed to lie in editing the articles written by officers of the National Committee from Lyunovo, and in giving shape to the paper and elaborating the political line. This was generally discussed in Rudolf Herrnstadt's room, frequently to the exclusion of the rest of the editorial staff.

Karl Maron's sphere of activity on the other hand was clearly defined. He wrote military commentaries for the paper, which generally appeared over his own name. The comparatively wide freedom of expression which was allowed us was particularly marked in his commentaries. They departed considerably from the stereotyped official Soviet analyses; they often contained forecasts, and were among the most valuable contributions to the newspaper.

Although Maron, Bolz and Kurella were entirely competent in their respective roles, there was no collective editorship as such. It was unmistakable that Herrnstadt alone held all the strings in his hands.

Rudolf Herrnstadt spoke little about himself. When I read his first articles, I was enthusiastic. They were somehow completely different. When I gave expression to my enthusiasm, the other members of the editorial staff smiled and explained that he had previously been the Warsaw correspondent of the *Berliner Tageblatt*. But what he was up to in the Soviet Union was something about which not only I but all my editorial colleagues were completely in the dark. All I knew was that he was married to Valya, a pretty Russian girl who had studied like myself at the Moscow State Academy for Foreign Languages. In contrast to the rest of the editorial staff, he did not live at the Hotel Lux, and his connections seemed to be less with the leaders of the K.P.D. émigrés than with Soviet official quarters direct.

In the course of the many years which I had now spent in the Soviet Union, I had often before encountered officials of this impersonal type. Generally speaking, they were people who one could see at first glance had reached their high positions through sheer ruthlessness. They were never distinguished either by a high level of education or by exceptional intelligence. What constantly astonished me about Herrnstadt was his mixture of western appearance, western clothing, western manner of writing, and exceptional intelligence, with an icy hardness which was only lightly concealed by his exaggeratedly polite manners and behaviour.

At first I had the impression that our newspaper was not subject to any kind of censorship, a fact which seemed to me incomprehensible at the time. But although we enjoyed a comparatively generous freedom of expression judged by Soviet standards, this did not in fact mean that there was no censorship at all.

At the beginning of September, 1943, Herrnstadt sent for me one day.

"I would be glad if you would take these proof sheets to the Hotel Lux and have them read through." He gave me the number of a room.

"Who should I have them read by?"

"Ask for Erno Gerö."

I could not have been more surprised. I had imagined that our newspaper would be censored either by Division VII of the Political Administration of the Red Army (which was responsible for propaganda to the German *Wehrmacht*) or, by a representative

of the Foreign Division of the Central Committee
of the Bolshevik Party. Now I learned that a member
of the inner leadership of the Hungarian Party in
Moscow had the final word on what was published in
the newspaper of the German National Committee!

From then on I was to have frequent meetings with
Erno Gerö, who was forty-five years old at the time.
Occasionally he paid a visit to our editorial offices,
and the way Herrnstadt behaved towards him made
it clear to me that Erno Gerö was at that time a man
of exceptional influence. It was his habit to give the
most important political directions in a quiet con-
versational tone. Often they were buried in asides and
only indicated by a slight emphasis. I was continually
struck by the way he would pick up our proofs, often
setting aside whole sheets without paying any attention to them, but immediately picking out the most
important political points. Then he would occasionally strike out a word with a smile and substitute another with a slightly sharper or weaker nuance. I
remember to this day the brief conversations we had
with each other, and the revelation of his exceptional
knowledge of German problems, his emotional pene-
tration and his political sensitiveness, which I could
also detect time and again in his censorship of our
newspaper.

Erno Gerö had lived in the Soviet Union since
1923 and he had there played a leading role in the
apparat of the Comintern. He was in Spain during
the Civil War and subsequently returned to the
Soviet Union. During the Second World War, apart
from his role in the leadership of the Hungarian
Party, he not only served as political adviser to the
National Committee for Free Germany, but also un-

doubtedly played an important part in laying down the policy of Communist Parties in other countries. From 1945 on he was continuously a member of the inner circle of the Hungarian Party leadership, besides holding various important ministerial posts in the Government. It is highly probable that the activities of Erno Gerö, who has one of the ablest brains in Eastern Europe, were even subsequently not confined to Hungary.

I was soon able to satisfy myself that our newspaper was carefully followed in even more exalted circles. The name of Manuilsky was frequently mentioned. This was not surprising, since Manuilsky had for many years played a leading part in the Comintern, and during the war he had always been responsible for the final decisions taken in Ufa. But probably even Manuilsky was not our most senior counsellor. One day, when there was an exceptionally difficult question to be settled arising from an article by a German general, Gerö happened to be on a visit to us. He shook his head with a smile and said: "A tricky point!" Then in the course of further discussion he mentioned a name which at that time belonged to the very highest circles—Shcherbakov.

Colonel-General Alexander Shcherbakov had been the successor of Khrushchev at the head of the Moscow Party organisation; and only three years later, at the Party conference in the spring of 1941, he was nominated as a candidate member of the *politburo* along with Malenkov. This meant that he belonged to the highest circles of the Soviet Party leadership. It can be assumed with some certainty that at that time he was already concerned with questions of foreign policy. During the war he was the Chief of the Political Administration of the Red Army, and at the same time head of the Soviet Information office which issued a daily *communiqué* from the front. He died on the 11th May, 1945—two days after the end of the war. It was officially announced that he had succumbed to a heart attack. Eight years after his death, on 13th January, 1953, it was alleged that Shcherbakov had been killed by a group of Kremlin doctors by faulty treatment and the use of improper drugs. This announcement was repudiated a few weeks later on 4th April, 1953, and the arrested doctors were released.

Uncertain though the causes of his death may be, the fact is beyond doubt that during the war Shcherbakov occupied a position of predominant importance. As Chief of the Political Administration of the Red Army, it goes without saying that he had an important voice in the decisions made on the most important questions of foreign policy. Although his name was rarely mentioned among us on the editorial staff, it is nevertheless certain that the National Committee's most important political questions were in the last analysis decided by him.

An Armistice Offered and Withdrawn

The newspaper *Free Germany*, with its black, white and red border and its constant references to Tauroggen, Yorck, Clausewitz and von Stein, was produced on a press located immediately opposite our building and bearing the name *Iskra Revoluitsii* (the "Spark of the Revolution"). It did not take me many days to realise that my function as liaison with the press offered me the opportunity of an insight into an interesting and little-known part of the National

Committee's activity. I could see what alterations Herrnstadt introduced in the articles. More than once I was a witness of far-reaching changes in the text, generally made at the last minute and obviously on directions from the highest authority. Significant things began to happen right from the first few weeks of the foundation of the National Committee. At the end of August, 1943, in one of the first issues of the paper, the title page was to have carried a prominent display of greetings from various prisoner-of-war camps to the National Committee. Naturally, these were not spontaneous statements but texts devised and drafted at the very highest level. From there they were transmitted to the "activists" in the prisoner-of-war camps who were then to issue them as messages of greeting to the National Committee.

I noticed to my astonishment that all the messages of greeting referred to the National Committee as "the nucleus of the new German régime of the future." Although I had already seen that the National Committee enjoyed support at a very high level, I was nevertheless surprised to see expressions that went so far. The newspaper was just about to go to press when Herrnstadt sent for me and said: "Please give instructions to the press not to start printing yet, and ask them to give you back the last proofs. There are a few more minor alterations to make." He spoke in an indifferent tone; it seemed a little too indifferent.

Half an hour later I took the proofs back to the press again. The minor alterations proved to be highly significant. Herrnstadt had deleted all passages referring to the National Committee as "the nucleus of the German régime." While the Russian compositors and setters were cursing over the readjustment that had to be made at the last minute, I wondered to myself what could have happened at the end of August, 1943, to bring about such a sudden down-grading of the National Committee.

This was not the only curious thing that happened during the first few weeks of the National Committee. In the second half of August we were told at Institute No. 99 that on the 1st September, 1943 (the fourth anniversary of the beginning of the war), a League of German Officers was to be founded, comprising particularly all those officers of middle and senior rank, including generals, who were not yet ready in July, 1943, to join the National Committee and who took the view, as we then put it, that our sights were set too high. Everything was ready for the foundation of the League on 1st September. But then it was unexpectedly postponed, and nothing more was said of this League of German Officers. There were no explanations of the postponement. Ten days later there was another turn of the wheel, and on the 11-12th September, came the sudden, almost precipitate, foundation of a League of German Officers under the presidency of General von Seydlitz.

At first I believed that the postponement of the foundation of the League was due to technical reasons, but at just about the same time there came a third event which made me think again. It was in the first half of September, 1943. Herrnstadt gave me an article with the title "Armistice—the Need of the Hour." An armistice? I could not help starting. The official slogan of the National Committee at that time

was the overthrow of Hitler and the withdrawal of
the German Army to the borders of the *Reich*. Nothing whatever had been said about an armistice up till
that moment. I read the article through carefully
with great attention. There were two places in it
where the word "armistice" was mentioned, and
throughout the article struck a completely different
note from that to which we were accustomed. It was
not primarily addressed to those generals and other
officers who had taken up an attitude in opposition
to Hitler; on the contrary it was virually an offer of
an armistice, however indirectly made, to the official
authorities of Hitler's Government. It was obvious
that a leading article of this kind could only have
been inspired by the highest authority. I waited anxiously to see what would happen next. The article
remained unaltered, however, and went through two
proof-readings by Herrnstadt. The making-up was
completed, and that night printing was to begin. Suddenly Herrnstadt came into the press at about midnight. A few minutes before the time of going to press
he took away the proof of the first page, again mur-
muring to himself something about "minor alterations."

When the page came back, the title of the leading
article was changed. Herrnstadt had removed all
references to an armistice and substituted new
phrases of an entirely different kind. All that night,
as I worked with Karl Maron on the making-up and
waited for the first complete copies, I reflected on
these curious alterations. Had there really been a possibility of an armistice with Hitler's Germany? At
the time I rejected these speculations as too fantastic. It was not till many years later that I learned

that in the first half of September, 1943, conversations had in fact taken place in Stockholm between representatives of the Soviet Union and Hilterite Germany on the subject of an armistice.

The soundings which took place in Stockholm at that time must have had their influence on the political line of the National Committee. The situation presumably made it impossible for the National Committee to be represented as the nucleus of a future German Government, and consequently all indications to this effect had to be deleted. The postponement of the foundation of the League of German Officers must also have had some connection with it. The article prepared by Herrnstadt for the newspaper *Free Germany* was obviously intended to reinforce and underline still further the Soviet Union's offer of an armistice. As soon as the negotiations were broken off, no doubt Herrnstadt was instructed to withdraw his article and alter it. As he was one of the few émigrés who had connections with the higher Soviet authorities, it is even possible that he was at least partially informed about the peace feelers.

Herrnstadt took away with him the proof of the original article. So vanished the only printed evidence which might have corroborated the fact, now known only from individual memoirs, that soundings took place in Stockholm in the autumn of 1943 for an armistice between Hitlerite Germany and the Soviet Union.

The First Months of the National Committee

Looking back, it seems to me that the most important period of the National Committee lay in its first few months—approximately up to the conference at Tehran at the end of November, 1943. With the foundation of the League of German Officers on 11-12th September, 1943, a whole crowd of generals and other senior officers had come near to accepting the objectives of the National Committee. It is true that the League of German Officers was by no means a mere appendage of the National Committee, at least to begin with; it had a certain independence and even an executive committee of its own. In contrast to the National Committee for Free Germany, which was intended to provide the leadership of a movement, it was possible to join the League of German Officers as an ordinary member.

On the 14th September, 1943, a plenary session of the National Committee was held to co-ordinate activities. The Presidium of the National Committee was enlarged to include the principal figures of the League of German Officers. General Walter von Seydlitz, the President of the League, and Lieut.-General Edler von Daniels became Vice-Presidents of the National Committee. Major-General Dr. Korfes, Major-General Martin Lattmann and Colonels Luitpold Steidle and van Hooven joined the National Committee as representatives of the League of German Officers. The Committee now had more than fifty members.

The importance of the National Committee was increased by the addition of former German Generals and the enlarged representation they brought with them. I could see from Erno Gerö's frequent visits that there was much interest in it on the Soviet side. Its increased importance was testified also by the messages of greeting from allied and neutral foreign countries.

In the early months there was a substantial difference between the propaganda of the National Committee for Free Germany and the League of German Officers on the one hand, and that put out by Division VII of the Political Administration of the Red Army on the other. While Division VII was urging German soldiers and officers to suspend hostilities, there was nothing of the kind in the National Committee's propaganda. On the contrary, the National Committee's principal theme at that time was the overthrow of Hitler and the organised withdrawal of German troops to the boundaries of the *Reich,* in order to provide an acceptable starting-point for the conclusion of peace with the allies.

From 28th November to 1st December, 1943, a conference of the "Big Three" at Tehran was taking place, and this led to still closer relations between the Soviet Union and the Western Powers. We could soon detect from the Soviet press and from political propaganda within the Soviet Union that relations with the western allies had become more intimate since the Tehran Conference, and this fact also had an effect on the political line of the National Committee and its activities.

As early as December, 1943, it was frequently to be heard said among the town editorial staff and at the Hotel Lux that the political line followed by the National Committee so far had proved itself unworkable and no longer corresponded to the current situation. A plenary meeting of the official National Committee thereupon decided on a change of the political line. This meeting took place on 5th January, 1944.

Weinert presided and announced: "We are now entering upon the second stage. In this stage we must organise the struggle of the soldiers, the home front, and the people on the broadest possible basis. The situation is changing and our watchword must change with the times. For the present, work at the front is of the most urgent importance."

Wilhelm Pieck followed with an announcement of the new political line: "It is senseless to expect a military or industrial leader to emerge in Germany to foil Hitler at this ultimate stage in his criminal career. It is exceedingly doubtful whether anyone in a position of responsibility in Germany's army or economy could prove strong enough for the purpose: they have already let Hitler go too far. We must therefore create the forces that are to save Germany out of the German people—out of the workers, the peasants, the intellectuals. We must mobilise and organise the struggle on the part of the German people. These are the words, and this is the appeal, that we must direct to the front line troops: Suspend hostilities, come over to the National Committee!"

With this the whole nature and purpose of the National Committee was radically altered. Up to the Tehran Conference it had been a body whose task was to address appeals or letters to army leaders, calling on them to withdraw their troops to the frontiers of the *Reich* and so to create the possibility of an honourable peace for Germany. The new political line adopted at the beginning of January 1944 shifted the emphasis to propaganda for a popular uprising against Hitler in the rear and desertion to the National Committee at the front. The National Committee now set itself to demonstrate that the military situation in Hitler's Germany was hopeless and therefore called for a suspension of hostilities. As far as the individual soldier was concerned, this meant in practice allowing himself to be taken prisoner in order to save himself for the reconstruction of the new Germany.

Desertions to the National Committee were now announced regularly in prominent positions in the paper. Most cases at this time, of course, were only desertions by individuals or small groups, but a few weeks later the course of events at the front presented the National Committee with an important opportunity.

This came with what was known in German *communiqués* from the front as a "pocket" west of Cherkassy. At the end of 1943 the Dnieper Line, on which Hitler's headquarters rested such high hopes, had been overrun by the Soviet armies on a very broad front, and at many points they had penetrated far westwards. In spite of this, on Hitler's orders, ten divisions under General Lieb continued to hold fast on the west bank of the Dnieper. It was not difficult to foresee that these groups could be encircled and cut off with the greatest ease. This duly happened in the last days of January when the spearheads of the Second Ukrainian Front, advancing in the south, joined up with the front operating in the north.

The manœuvre led to the encirclement of a force of seventy to eighty thousand German soldiers and officers, according to figures published at the time in the Soviet Union, in the area of the town of Korsun, west of Cherkassy. On instructions from the highest authority, General von Seydlitz and Dr. Korfes, together with a number of other German officers of the National Committee and a Soviet General, travelled to the front in a special train in the hope of influencing developments. General von Seydlitz addressed a personal letter to General Lieb, and the encircled troops were flooded with leaflets and appeals. However, all this propaganda by the National Committee and the League of German Officers had only a negligible effect.

Conditions were admittedly not favourable, since a German relief army had fought its way to a position only a few miles off and there was thus the chance of breaking out. I later learned from a member of a deputation from the front that a large proportion of the surrounded troops in fact succeeded in fighting their way out again.

However, official Soviet propaganda said nothing about the break-out: it announced that 55,000 German soldiers had been killed and 18,000 had surrendered. The newspaper *Free Germany* also adopted the Soviet version, though in different words. It added that, of those who had been taken prisoner, about half had declared their adherence to the Free Germany movement after their capture. But even this statement was described to me by a deputy from the front, in private conversation, as exaggerated. It was impossible to gloss over the fact that in spite of the direct participation of senior members of the National Committee and the League of German Officers, in spite of broadcasts, newspapers, leaflets and direct propaganda at the front, the Free Germany movement had suffered a set-back.

Broadcasts on the "Free Germany" Radio

In course of time the tasks of the Town Committee of Institute No. 99 became so extensive that the office was too small for us. It was the ambition of Kozlov, our intermediary with the Russian authorities, to make his institution (as he called it, although he took no part in the real work) as large as possible. "I'll do something," he told us encouragingly.

A few days later Kozlov came back radiant with delight. "We've found something abolutsely splendid," he told us triumphantly. We were invited to make an inspection at once, and a quarter of an hour later we found ourselves to our astonishment standing in front of an imposing building at No. 3 Obucha Street.

This house was also in the centre of the town, not far from what was known as the A-Boulevard. It must obviously once have been the villa of a merchant or a senior official. It had very spacious rooms with large windows and a garden all round it. An impressive drive, by Moscow standards, led up to the entrance. I already knew the house from the time when it had served as a home for émigrés up to the beginning of the war in 1941. German and Austrian émigrés had lived in it uninterruptedly for many years. As some of them had now been forcibly deported to Kazakhstan and others had been evacuated to Tomsk, the building was left almost empty.

Soon after we had moved in, there were a number of changes in the editorial staff. Two newcomers joined us, Willi Eildermann and Peter Florin.

Willi Eildermann had recently come from North Africa, where he had been interned after fighting in

Spain. After the allied landings he had been released and joined the British Army, where he remained for a time. Then an agreement was reached which enabled him and some others to come to Moscow via Tehran. I met him again later as an S.E.D. official in Berlin. He also belonged for a time to the editorial staff of the S.E.D. periodical, *Unity*.

I already knew Peter Florin, the son of Wilhelm Florin, a former member of the K.P.D. *politburo*. We had gone to the Karl Liebknecht School together and been quite friendly for a time. After 1945 I met him in the Soviet Zone as editor-in-chief of the S.E.D. publication *Freedom* at Halle. Since then he has been further promoted to become head of a department in the Ministry of Foreign Affairs in the Soviet Zone of Germany, as well as Chairman of the Foreign Affairs Committee of the People's Parliament.

In the middle of May, 1944, I ran into Anton Ackermann, who was at that time in charge of the radio editorial staff. "We've been thinking you might come and join us on the radio editorial staff and work as an announcer," he said. "You'll certainly find the work more interesting than what you're doing now on the newspaper."

"Of course, I should very much like to come," I said, "but I don't know whether Herrnstadt will allow it."

Anton Ackermann smiled. "If you agree, there will certainly be no difficulty. I've already spoken to Herrnstadt about you."

"There'll be no hold-up on my side. As far as I'm concerned, I should like to join the radio at once."

"Good—then come along with me now. We're taking a car to the radio station and you can have a look at everything straight away."

I had assumed that we would be going to the Moscow Radio Committee, but instead we took the opposite direction. A quarter of an hour later the car stopped in front of a new house at 34 Shablovka Street. This building was also surrounded by a garden, and wired off and guarded. Our papers were examined at the porter's lodge, and only then did I realise where we were—at the first television studio in the Soviet Union. So far as I know, it had been established in 1938-39, since when television broadcasts had been made from it, though originally on a very restricted scale. At the beginning of the war even these were suspended. Now the place was used for broadcasts by the National Committee for Free Germany.

I was shown around by Anton Ackermann and Fritz Heilmann, our radio announcer, who had formerly been a Communist Party provincial deputy in Thuringia.

"Now, Wolfgang," Ackermann asked me, "wouldn't you like to have a try at once?"

"What, on the air right away?"

So shortly before the next transmission I took my seat in the studio beside Fritz Heilmann. He hastily gave me a few essential instructions. A few minutes later a little red light went on. I heard the tune of "God who created iron"—the invariable introduction to our broadcasts. After that came the clear voice of Fritz Heilmann: "Attention! Attention! This is the National Committee for Free Germany calling! We speak in the name of the German people! We call for the salvation of the Reich!"

After Heilmann had given the news, I read the military commentary. When I had finished Ackermann gave me a friendly smile. "You see, it went splendidly," he said. "You have the right voice for broadcasting. If you like, you can begin to-morrow morning. To begin with you'll sit in with Fritz Heilmann, and as soon as you've learnt all the tricks you can take part in the broadcasts." And so I became an announcer for the Free German Radio.

My new chief, Anton Ackermann, was a man of entirely different character from Rudolf Herrnstadt. He often inquired in a friendly way how I liked my new job and it was not long before he invited me to join in the editorial work. "If you like, you're welcome to take part in editorial conferences," he said. "That will help to give you the picture, and perhaps before long you can start writing articles and commentaries yourself."

Of course I agreed, and from then till the end of the war I regularly took part in editorial conferences. In contrast to Herrnstadt's autocratic method of controlling the editorship of the newspaper, the system of work at the radio station was truly collective.

Anton Ackermann, though he was in charge of editing and himself wrote the most important commentaries, never asserted himself as our boss, but enjoyed all the more authority for that very reason. Everyone accepted his status without question, recognising his abilities to be of a higher order than those of any of his colleagues. He was not yet forty years old at that time. He had been born in December, 1905, at Thalheim (Erzgebirge) and had begun his active career in the Youth Movement. In 1926 he joined the K.P.D. Soon afterwards he was working in the sub-district headquarters of Plauen-Zwickau, where his obvious ability led to his being sent to Moscow in 1928 for further political education. In October, 1935, he was elected to the Central Committee and the *politburo* at the so-called Brussels Conference. He was in Spain during the Civil War and returned to the Soviet Union in 1940. He was one of the signatories of the K.P.D. proclamation, the Manifesto to the German People, and the appeal launched at the foundation of the National Committee. Immediately after the foundation of the Committee, he had been put in charge of editorial work at the radio station.

The brief daily commentaries on the military situation were written by Kurt Fischer. He had joined the K.P.D. as a young man, and spent the greater part of his life in the Soviet Union. He was not a member of the official party leadership, and he seemed to have had little connection with the German Party for many years. Even during the period when he was working in the National Committee, he did not live at the Hotel Lux. In the Soviet Union he had pursued a military career: it was even said that he had passed the Staff College of the Red Army and that he had carried out many special missions, in China among other places. He was very secretive and irritable. One could see that he often found it difficult to restrain himself and subordinate himself to Ackermann. I remember often thinking that if Fischer ever had power in his hands, I should not like to be under him; and my prognostications were to prove justified. After 1945 Fischer became Minister of the Interior in Saxony, and he used this position not only to pursue a merciless vendetta against the opposition, but also to seek his own financial advantage and to eliminate personal enemies whom he thought dangerous.

Most of the brief commentaries on other subjects were written by Fritz Erpenbeck, a gifted and versatile journalist who had once published in the Soviet Union a novel about the First World War called *But I Would Not be a Coward*, as well as another which attracted much attention, *The Founders*. After 1945 Erpenbeck worked as a free-lance journalist on various newspapers and periodicals. Later he was appointed head of the Directorate of Pictorial Art and Music in the Soviet Zone Aritstic Commission.

Fischer and Erpenbeck concentrated principally on the editorial work in our town editorial office. At the same time, liaison between the radio editorial staff and the official National Committee at Lyunovo was the responsibility of Max Keilson, who was later editor-in-chief of the S.E.D. newspaper *Vorwärts* in Berlin, and Gustav von Wangenheim, who was for a short time after 1945 in charge of the German theatre. Finally, the other members of the editorial staff were Lore Pieck, daughter of Wilhelm Pieck, who was originally responsible for compiling the broadcasts, but later also joined in the editorial work; and Hans Mahle, who was in charge of the apparatus for recording broadcasts prepared in Lyunovo. We also had two American jeeps at our disposal for communication between the National Committee at Lyunovo and the broadcasting station at Shablovka.

Most of the current material, whether news or

commentaries, was written at our town editorial
office at No. 3 Obucha Street, while the more important broadcasts, such as appeals, proclamations
and weekly commentaries, were composed in collaboration between ourselves and the members of the
National Committee and the League of German Officers at Lyunovo. The same was true of the sermons
which were broadcast every Sunday alternately by
Kayser, a Roman Catholic in the German Army
Chaplain's Department, and Schroeder, an Evangelical priest in the same department. Later they
were joined, among others, by Dr. Ludwig for the
Catholics and Dr. Krummacher, a member of the
High Consistory, for the Evangelicals.

With the advance of the Soviet Armies and the
constantly increasing number of generals and other
officers joining the National Committee, more and
more people were taking part in the broadcasts. From
the conduct of Ackermann and the other members
of the editorial staff on the radio station, it was
clear that what we were trying to do was not to im-
pose the outlook of the émigrés on our new comrades
from Lyunovo, but to learn from their experience—
since they knew the Nazi system at first hand—and
thus to work out a common platform on which we
could all take part in the struggle against Hitler together.

Possibly our collaboration would have been closer
and better if Ackermann and his colleagues on the
town editorial staff had enjoyed complete freedom
in reaching their own decisions; but all radio contributions, just like all newspaper articles, were subject to Soviet censorship. This censorship was certainly not nearly so severe as it was for official broad-

casts on Moscow Radio or for the German People's Station operated by German members of Institute No. 205 (which was at that time the official station of the leaders of the K.P.D. in exile). Nevertheless, even in our case not a single sentence could be put on the air that had not previously passed the censorship.

After the editing was completed, the radio announcer had to submit the whole of the broadcast material to the censorship, so every other day I had to take our American jeep, with the manuscripts clutched in my hand, to the Political Administration of the Red Army, which was established during the war in a large building on Arbat Square. There the material was looked through by Colonel Braginsky, who was then head of Division VII (the division in charge of propaganda in the languages of the Axis powers). Before the war he had been a professor of oriental languages; in addition he had a fluent knowledge of all the west European languages, and was one of the most highly educated men I ever met in the Soviet Union. Like Erno Gerö, he had an extraordinary flair for what was important. He picked out the most important passages in a moment, and the whole process lasted only a few minutes.

On the rare occasions when Colonel Braginsky was not there, his work was taken over by Frieda Rubiner. She was a veteran member of the Communist Party, who disliked being reminded that in the early 1920's she had translated books by Trotsky, Bukhairn and Radek into German. She had lived in the Soviet Union for a very long time. During the war she was one of the few Germans who worked in the Political Administration of the Red Army. She

composed leaflets and appeals; and under the pseudonym of F. Lang she was responsible for the pamphlet entitled "The Truth about Soviet Russia"
which had a very wide circulation in prisoner-of-
war camps.

Of all the broadcasting stations at that time, ours
was probably the most primitive. Apart from the
studio, all we had for our transmissions was a small
recording apparatus and a few blank discs. That
we nevertheless succeeded in putting out transmissions which were noticeably more interesting and
lively than those on the official Moscow Radio, and
in some respects as good as the transmissions of the
Western Allies, was due primarily to the fact that
under Ackermann's leadership we evolved an excellent co-operative system of work, and established a
close and friendly relation with members of the editorial staff at Lyunovo. I firmly believed at that time
that this collaboration with our new comrades on
the National Committee would not only continue
after the destruction of the Hitlerite system, but
would grow closer and stronger. These hopes were
to prove illusory, like so many of the things I believed
in in 1944.

High Hopes in the Komsomol

Apart from my new friends at the Hotel Lux, it was
not long before I renewed contact with members of
the Soviet *Komsomol*. In Moscow I had come across
Jan Vogeler again. He lived at the Government House
(*Dom Pravitelstva*), a gigantic residence for officials on the bank of the Moskva River. In his company I frequently met Russian and foreign members
of the *Komsomol*. Most of them were students who

were interested in literature, philosophy and politics, among them some from the famous "IFLI" (Institute for Philosophy, Literature and History), an academy which was in great demand among young people in the Soviet Union, but which one could only get into by an exceptionally tough examination. Often, too, Jan had students of the educational and legal faculties as his guests, or members of the *Komsomol* who were being trained for special tasks —for example, as partisans behind the lines.

Our discussions were extraordinarily interesting and sometimes lasted the whole night. At that time we all cherished high hopes that victory over Fascism would bring about something entirely new in Western Europe—that a gigantic social revolution would be accomplished. We believed in a great revival, a *Renaissance*—some of us even used the French term—and in an evolution of new Socialist movements and the establishment of new socialist states, which in many respects would be different from the Soviet Union. This last idea, of course, was generally expressed in somewhat veiled terms.

After the first announcement, with salutes of guns and fireworks, of the victory of the Red Army at Kursk and Orel at the beginning of August, 1943, it became the custom to announce such victories in the same way as well as with special *communiqués*. On the occasion of a specially important victory, thousands of people would throng the streets in a state of jubilant excitement, confident that now the worst of the danger was over. Soon people became quite accustomed to these celebrations, which they took as proof that the war had entered its last phase.

At the beginning of April 1944, Soviet troops

reached the River Pruth, and thus were on the Soviet frontiers. Whereas in the first two years of the war the situation at the front had been the principal subject of conversation, it was different nowadays with the advance of the Red Army. People's interest turned more and more to the political changes that were now coming about, and to the changes that could be looked forward to after the war.

Would not life in the Soviet Union itself also change after the war?—we asked ourselves. This was a subject to which we came back again and again in our discussion. Our hopes had become far stronger by this time than when I first heard them expressed in the autumn of 1941 at the Udarnik Cinema. Certain relaxations in the system were already noticeable. Generals and officers who had been arrested and deported were released again in the course of the war, and even partially restored to high command. In conversation the years of the purge were no longer unquestioningly defended as they had been earlier. The censorship of art and literature became less severe.

A Soviet film was shown at that time which contained one very interesting detail. There was a scene of a conversation between a Soviet party official and a man who was not a member of the Party. The conversation turned on the horror of the war, and the non-member remarked how fine it would be if one could get back as quickly as possible to the pre-war situation. The Party official replied: "Yes, certainly, but there cannot be just a simple return to the past. We have learnt from experience. We were often too severe in the pre-war period."

When I saw the film, the title of which I have

unfortunately forgotten, I noticed at once the strong impression this little scene made on the audience. Another symptom, or so it seemed to us, was the relatively large number of foreign films we could now see in Moscow. Among them were *The Thief of Baghdad* and the American feature film *Sun Valley Serenade*, as well as a number of American films which dealt in part with life in the Soviet Union, such as *Mission to Moscow* and *North Star*, which depicted life on a Soviet collective farm, and a documentary film called *The Campaign in Russia* produced by an American Army Propaganda Unit.

The fact that by this time one could see foreign films and buy foreign periodicals in Russian freely on the streets (such as *America* and *British Ally*, the latter of which seemed to me much the better adapted to the Soviet mentality) was taken by us as a sign that there would be other changes too, and that life in the Soviet Union was bound to be less restricted after the war. Then, at the beginning of June, 1944, came the invasion of France by the Western Allies. I happened not to be on duty at the radio station that day. I was at Institute No. 205, where everything was in a state of joyful and excited confusion. Everywhere people were tuning in to western transmissions. Doors were left open and in the corridors one could hear the latest *communiqués* about the progress of the invasion. The news was given great prominence in *Pravda*. It was rare that an event taking place outside the Soviet Union was so prominently displayed.

As I went back to town from Institute No. 205, the invasion was the chief subject of conversation everywhere. British and American officers who were in Moscow at the time were congratulated by people in the street. During these days one could even see people making the famous victory sign which Churchill had so popularised in the West.

Soviet newspapers were full of praise for the Western Allies. On 11th June, 1944, a document was published in the Soviet press of which no subsequent mention was ever made: it was a list of the deliveries of military supplies by the Western Allies to the Soviet Union from 1st October, 1941, to 30th October, 1944. We were astonished to read what America alone had delivered to the Soviet Union, including 6,430 aircraft, 3,734 tanks, 82 torpedo boats and small destroyers, 206,771 vehicles, 22,400,000 rounds of ammunition, 87,900 tons of explosive, 245,000 telephone instruments, 5,500,000 pairs of boots, and more than two million tons of food. These were only a part of the gigantic quantity of supplies which the Soviet Union had received from the U.S.A., England and Canada. Everywhere people were saying that at last, with the publication of this news and the opening of the second front, relations with the Western Allies were satisfactorily settled and a joint post-war policy after the fall of Hitler was assured.

The approach of the end of the war; the government proclamation that the advance of the Red Army into other countries would not lead to any change in their internal system of Government; the landing of the Allies in the west; Stalin's interview about the invasion; the publication of the immense material help supplied by the Western Allies; the appearance of the periodicals *America* and *British Ally* in Russian; the regular exhibition of foreign films; the relaxation of the censorship; the new attitude towards the purges of 1936-1938; the rehabilitation of some of those who had previously been denounced as enemies of the people—all these things combined to build up a widespread wave of hope among the Soviet population. It was the hope that, after so terrible a war, everything would somehow or other be different.

Moscow and the 20th July, 1944

I had just left the studio after a transmission when the telephone rang. Kurt Fischer was at the other end. He shouted excitedly down the phone: "Just got news of an attempt on Hitler! Be prepared for a complete recasting of our broadcasts up to mid-day to-morrow! The scripts will be coming in up to the minute."

Not even the outbreak of war on 22nd June, 1941, had excited me so much as this news. At last! I thought. Now the struggle against Hitler had broken out into the open, even in Germany itself; the war would come to an end and Germany would be spared an occupation! The aims of the National Committee had proved justified and people in the Soviet Union like Ehrenburg, who identified all Germans with the Nazis, had been proved wrong. Even the Russian radio engineer, a girl who was usually not much interested in politics, was quite excited this time. She had only one comment on the news: "Now the war will be over! How lovely it will be!"

We switched on our receiver to listen to reports from all parts of the world. I knew nothing yet for certain; I knew nothing of the failure of the attempt. Meanwhile, the editorial staff had been called together again. Only an hour later—an incredibly short time in Soviet conditions—the first commentaries reached the broadcasting studio.

I particularly remember an outstandingly good article by Fritz Erpenbeck depicting in vivid terms the need for united action by all Hitler's enemies. The article called upon Social Democrats and Communists to discard all their doubts about the Prussian Generals and to make common cause with them. It appealed to generals not to neglect any of the forces that were ready to support them in their struggle.

These were the most stimulating hours and days in the life of the National Committee. It goes without saying that we wished success to the men of the 20th July with all our hearts. We realised perhaps even more clearly that Hitler's enemies in Germany that only the removal of Hitler's régime by German forces could offer a chance of preserving a united independent Germany. The official Soviet press also published detailed reports on the 20th July, but the great prominence given to the news only went to show that people in Moscow had allowed themselves exaggerated hopes.

It happened that on the evening of the very day when the news of the 20th July was published, there was a meeting of the *Komsomol*. There was a new recruit to be admitted on this occasion. As always, questions were put to the new recruit by members of the *Komsomol* group to test whether her political knowledge was sufficient to justify her admission to the *Komsomol*. The first general political questions she answered hesitantly and uncertainly. Suddenly, somebody asked: "What do you know about the latest political events in Germany?"

With great enthusiasm, she recounted in a few words what had appeared in *Pravda* about the 20th July. As she got into her stride, she even began treating reports which appeared in *Pravda* as speculation in foreign circles as though they were established facts: "In Germany an opposition Government composed of generals and anti-Fascists has taken over power, and peace negotiations will shortly take place between the new Government and the anti-Hitler coalition." For her too, as for many other people in Moscow at that time, the wish was father to the thought.

In the next few days, the real situation became clear, at least so far as it was possible to know anything at all at that time. When it became known that the attempt had failed and that the conspirators and their adherents had been arrested and executed, our disappointment was all the greater. After the defeat of Germany, the conspiracy of the 20th July was never mentioned again in the Soviet press. In our broadcasts and the newspaper *Free Germany*, on the other hand, a series of contributions subjected the movement to analysis.

The men of the 20th July were represented in all these contributions as models of courageous and determined action, and high tribute was paid to them. Critical comment was limited at that time to the suggestion that the men of the 20th July had omitted to establish firm links with the numerous formation commanders who were ready to collaborate in a revolution. The emphasis had been laid on the reserve army. So far as the front line troops were concerned, however, the conspirators had confined themselves to cautiously sounding the opinions and attitudes of senior formation commanders. This reticence in dealing with the army at the front had its origin in the fact that there were differences of opinion, or at least a lack of clarity, among the opposition generals about the question how the end of the war was going to be brought about. It was decided that the army at the front should not be brought into action immediately, in order not to lose its potential value as a force in being when the peace negotiations eventually took place.

The National Committee emphasised that this tactic must in retrospect be regarded as mistaken. If firm links had been established from the beginning with the numerous formation commanders who were ready to work for a revolution, then the operations of 20th July might have proved successful, even after the failure of the central attempt at the Führer's headquarters. It had also been a mistake to restrict contacts with the civil population to leading figures in the administration, business and industry, since success was unthinkable without the collaboration at least of powerful workers' groups and representatives from the key points in industry and the transport system.

This was how the movement of the 20th July was judged in Moscow at that date. Ten years later, however, in July, 1954, the men of the 20th July were misrepresented and abused by the press of the Soviet Zone. The S.E.D. periodical *Unity,* in its issue of July 1954, declared that the men of the 20th July were trying to salvage as much of German militarism and imperialism as still could be rescued. It said that even at that time their allies were the "reactionary circles of American imperialism" and their object was alleged to be primarily that of enabling "re-actionary German monopolistic capital in league with a reactionary corps of generals, to continue the war against the Soviet Union, the leading power of workers and peasants, in common with the re-actionary forces of British and American im-perialism."

"The men of the 20th July," according to the S.E.D. central newspaper on the 20th July, 1954, "were without exception not enemies of Fascism in principle. They were blood of the blood and flesh of the flesh of German imperialism. The attempt to glorify the conspirators of the 20th July as men en-gaged in the struggle against Fascism cannot blind us to the fact that their object then, as to-day, was and is, one of hostility to the people and the nation."

Such is the change in Moscow's evaluation of the movement of the 20th July.

The events of 20th July were not the only excite-ment of that period. The invasion in June had torn a great gap in the Western front; the allies were ad-vancing through Italy; at the beginning of July, 1944, began a great Soviet offensive, which led in a few weeks to the complete collapse of the German cen-tral front and cut a gap in the neighbouring fronts. Then on 8th July, 1944, came an almost incredible event.

We learned that Vincenz Müller, who was at the time acting as Commander of the 12th Army Corps on the central front, had accepted an ultimatum from the Red Army and issued on his own authority an instruction to his troops trapped in the eastern enclave near Minsk to surrender. "After many weeks of severe fighting, our situation has become hopeless.

We must put an end to the useless bloodshed. I therefore order that the battle shall cease at once. Local groups of 100 or more should be formed under the leadership of officers or senior non-commissioned officers. The wounded should be collected to join them."

This order was printed in the newspaper *Free Germany* and frequently read out over the radio. Both in our office and at Lyunovo, all was high excitement. General von Seydlitz announced in his commentary: "General Müller is the first German general who has deliberately acted against an explicit, categorical order from Hitler and has thereby saved the lives of thousands of German soldiers for the rehabilitation and the future of Germany. We salute this pioneering and truly patriotic act of our German colleague."

It was only later that I learned from a member of the National Committee's delegation at the front that both we and General Seydlitz had been misinformed. "The facts about Vincenz Müller's surrender and his famous order were not correctly given. Vincenz Müller was taken prisoner just like all the other generals, and it was only after his capture that he wrote this famous order. The Russians circulated it among the trapped armies in the general confusion."

"Yes, but didn't Vincenz Müller agree to it?"

"Of course he did: this was his great political opportunity. He took advantage of it at once. As soon as he saw how immensely it advanced his own reputation, he himself began to persuade other generals to make proclamations against Hitler. He convinced and converted them so fast that people who had been anti-Fascist for years could hardly believe their eyes and ears. In October he was converted to Catholicism by a priest in the Army Chaplain's department. In November, he reported for an anti-Fascist course, and by the time he reached Lyunovo in December— he was a fanatical devotee of the Party line."

In contrast to many other generals who had decided to join the Free German movement only after long and painful conflicts, which did them all the more credit and meant that they were by no means becoming mere puppets of the Russians, there is not the slightest doubt that Vincenz Müller put himself at the service of the Soviet Union as a matter of deliberate calculation. His rapid change of heart and devotion to the Party line did not pass unnoticed. Soon after his return to Germany in the autumn of 1948, he was rewarded with the post of Deputy Chairman of the National Democratic Party and the rank of a General in the People's Police.

The events round about 20th July, the shootings and the reign of terror, resulted in many generals and officers who had previously taken a hostile or neutral attitude towards the National Committee now deciding to abandon their reservations and to take an active part in the struggle against Hitler. For many of them these events were the last straw which persuaded them to come over, especially because quite a number of the generals who were then Soviet prisoners-of-war had lost close friends or acquaintances among the victims of the 20th July.

As a result of the collapse of the German central front in July, 1944, some twenty more German generals became prisoners of the Soviet Army in the course of less than three weeks. Seventeen of them signed an appeal addressed to the German Army in

the East as early as the 22nd July. By the end of July
the gossip in the Hotel Lux had it that Paulus too
was now going to collaborate. Finally, on 8th August,
1944, on the very day when Field Marshal von Witz-
leben was executed in Berlin, a declaration by
Paulus came into my hands at the broadcasting
studio.

It struck me that the final date of his statement
had evidently been added at the last minute. The
date "August '44" had been typed in, but the actual
day, 8th August, had been added subsequently by
von Paulus in his own hand. On that evening I was
able to announce the declaration by Paulus, which
had been recorded on a disc like the statements of
all the generals and officers at Lyunovo:

"Attention! Attention! You will now hear General
Field-Marshal Paulus, the former Supreme Com-
mander of the Sixth Army. Here he is! . . . General
Field-Marshal Paulus."

There followed a brief statement, of which the
following is the text:

"At Stalingrad the Sixth Army fought to the last
under my command, obedient to the orders of Adolf
Hitler. We fought in the hope that our sacrifice
might enable our leaders to bring the war to an end
that would not prove totally disastrous for Germany.
This hope has not been fulfilled. Recent events have
made the continuation of the war nothing but a senseless sacrifice for Germany. The Red Army is advancing on a wide front and has reached the borders of
the *Reich* in East Prussia. In the west the Americans
and the British have broken through the German
defences and are advancing through open country

in France. Neither in the east nor in the west has Germany the necessary reserves to restore the situation. The crushing superiority of the enemy in the air and at sea makes the situation still more desperate. The war is lost for Germany. This is the situation to which Germany has been brought by the political and military leadership of Adolf Hitler, despite the heroism of her army and her entire people. Add to this that the conduct of some of Germany's representatives in the occupied areas towards the inhabitants has filled every true soldier and every true German with disgust. It must bring upon us the bitter reproaches of the entire world. If the German people does not itself denounce these policies, it must carry the full responsibility for them. In these circumstances I regard it as my duty to declare to my fellow prisoners-of-war and to the German people as a whole that Germany must renounce Adolf Hitler and establish a new political leadership, to end the war and to bring about conditions that will make it possible for our people to survive and to enter into peaceful and even friendly relations with our present enemies."

I was still deeply impressed by this declaration when I sat down in the restaurant of the Hotel Lux on the following day. I would never have believed a year earlier that the former supreme commander at Stalingrad could bring himself to such a denunciation of Hitler. Paulus's declaration was naturally the chief subject of conversation at the Hotel Lux, but enthusiasm was soon to be damped. The main tenor of the conversation that day in the Hotel Lux was to the effect that it had taken Paulus quite long enough to make up his mind about his declaration.

It was already August, 1944, and only a matter of a few weeks before the Red Army troops would cross the German borders.

The invasion, the 20th July, the collapse of the central front, and Paulus's declaration had set the ball in motion. The Soviet offensive continued uninterrupted through the autumn of 1944. More and more new German generals were taken prisoner, and in contrast to their predecessors they did not need any very lengthy political treatment. Most of them had recognized the hopelessness of the situation in Hitlerite Germany, and were often ready to sign appeals and to join the movement for a Free Germany after only a few days of captivity. There were so many generals writing in the newspaper *Free Germany* that the prisoners-of-war in the camps used to call the National Committee's organ the "Generals' Advertiser." One appeal succeeded another, and practically every one was signed by generals.

Finally, on 8th December, 1944, the famous "Appeal of the Fifty Generals to the People and Army" was published. About eighty German generals were prisoners-of-war in the Soviet Union at this time. Fifty of them had joined the League of German Officers (which at this time numbered 4,000 enrolled members) and therefore also the Free Germany Movement. All fifty of them signed the final warning to end the calamitous war:

"Germans! Our deep concern for the future of our people compels us German generals, together with many hundreds of thousands of soldiers and officers in Russian prisoner-of-war camps, to address you, men and women of Germany, at the eleventh hour. The hour of our collapse under the crushing superiority of our united enemies draws nearer every day. The war is lost, but in spite of that Hitler seeks to continue it. Our people must not succumb. Therefore this war must be brought to an end immediately. People of Germany, rise up and save yourselves by taking action against Hitler! Germans, restore the honour of the German name in the eyes of the world by an act of courage, and thus take the first step towards a better future!"

This appeal by the fifty generals was scattered over the front in millions. For weeks on end we repeated it over the radio again and again, sometimes supplemented by brief individual statements of the signatories to explain why they had declared themselves for the overthrow of Hitler and the ending of the war, and why they had joined the Free Germany Movement. It seemed impossible to increase the pressure any further. Here were fifty generals appealing for the downfall of Hitler and the end of the war. This was at once the climax and the end of the movement for a Free Germany.

On 12th February, 1945, when the decisions of the Yalta Conference were published, there was nothing more for the National Committee to do except to announce: "All that remains for us is to hope that the complete and richly deserved destruction of Hitlerite Germany which is now in progress will stir forces in the German people which will help us, after a ruthless purge of our house and a bitter reparation, to win an honourable survival and a place for ourselves in the community of nations."

It was clear that the National Committee had not achieved its object. After the appeal of the fifty generals there were no more political declarations of any importance. It was now beyond the possibility of doubt that our work on the newspaper and at the broadcasting station went on only as a matter of routine, while the important political decisions from now on were taken at other levels.

Our Directives for Germany

"A training course for our future political tasks in Germany will begin in the next few days."

Of course we had often discussed what it would be like when we could at last return to Germany, but so far this had been nothing but wishful thinking. With the prospect of training for our future tasks, a feeling of homesickness for Germany welled up in me. Generally speaking, this homesickness was confined to the older émigrés. Among the younger ones there were many who would brush aside any mention of Germany. "Oh, Germany! I'd rather stay here," they said. In some cases the process of Russianisation had gone so far that they would always talk Russian even among themselves, and had long regarded the Soviet Union as their real home. But I was not like them. I was longing to be able to go back to Germany as soon as possible and to take up political work there, so I was in a tremor of expectation over the beginning of the training course, which was to deal with the tasks that lay immediately before us in Germany and the essential directives for them.

A few days later about a hundred and fifty German émigrés gathered to take their seats together in the building of the Moscow Committee of the Party. Among them I met several more graduates of the Comintern School: Mischa Wolf, Jan Vogeler, Emmi Stenzer, Hellmut Gennys, Marianne Weinert,

Heinz Hoffmann and a number of other émigrés whom I did not know. Some of my colleagues on the newspaper and at the "Free Germany" broadcasting station were also taking the lectures. The introduction was given by Wilhelm Pieck.

"We shall meet once a week for a lecture followed by a discussion," he said, "to give ourselves the opportunity of going over again all the political problems that are likely to be of importance in our future political work in Germany."

On the first two evenings of the course we heard lectures from Wilhelm Pieck on the general nature of our tasks, and from Walter Ulbricht on the objectives of the anti-Fascist democratic forces. On later evenings there were talks by Hermann Matern about the lessons of the K.P.D.'s struggle in the period of the Weimar Republic, and from Anton Ackermann about the struggle against Hitlerite Fascism in the years 1933-45 and the conclusions to be drawn from it. Edwin Hörnle gave a talk about agricultural problems; Rudolf Lindau (who was known as Paul Gratz in the Soviet Union) spoke on the lessons of the November Revolution of 1918; and there was another lecture dealing with the future tasks of the trade unions.

The keynote of our training was the following. The defeat of Hitlerite Fascism had been achieved not by an internal rising of the German people, but by the armies of the anti-Hitler coalition. Whereas in the countries occupied by Hitler, resistance movements of varying degrees of strength had carried on an active struggle, this had not been the case in Germany. From an objective point of view the German people had made itself an accomplice in the crimes of Hitlerite Germany. It followed as a logical consequence that Germany must be occupied by the powers of the anti-Hitler coalition.

The task of the anti-Fascist democratic forces would be to support the activities of the occupying powers in the struggle to destroy Nazism and militarism, to re-educate the German people and to carry through democratic reforms. The guarantee of victory over Hitler was the unity of the anti-Hitler coalition, maintained primarily by the U.S.A., Great Britain and the Soviet Union.

Our political task was not to consist of establishing socialism in Germany or encouraging a socialist development. On the contrary, this must be condemned and resisted as a dangerous tendency. Germany was on the threshold of a bourgeois-democratic transformation, which in substance and content would be the completion of the bourgeois-democratic revolution of 1848. The policy was therefore to support this process and to repudiate every kind of socialist slogan which under present-day conditions could be nothing but pure demagogy. By insistence on such slogans the idea of socialism could only be discredited.

It is an interesting point that during this course we were given very detailed instructions on how to answer criticism which might come in future from the left. In one country after another, we were told, the working classes had proved to be particularly liable to such tendencies. For instance, in Bulgaria there had been far-reaching "leftist deviations" which had only been overcome by the direct intervention of Dimitrov. We were told that it was highly probable that we should come upon such tendencies and ideas in Germany too, to the effect that "now was the time to introduce socialism." We would probably even find ourselves reproached with having formed a united front with former Nazi generals in the National Committee. Our answer to that should be: "What matters is not whom one joins, but with what object one joins them."

If we were told that our policy of collaboration was the same as that of the right-wing social democratic leaders after 1918, then our reply must be: "The right-wing social democratic leaders joined General von Epp in the struggle against the workers. We have joined General von Seydlitz in the struggle against Hitler. That is the difference."

The claims of those whom Hitler had oppressed must be vindicated from first to last. We must have the courage to take a dispassionate view of the facts. After all that had happened, those who had been oppressed and maltreated must have guarantees against a repetition of such a horror. It must therefore be the task of German anti-Fascists and democrats to come out in favour of the frontiers demanded by the subjugated peoples, including the Oder-Neisse line, and also for the reparations which they demanded. This must be treated as a debt of honour on the part of the German people.

The occupying powers were coming to Germany, we were told, to uproot Fascism and militarism and to initiate the preliminary stages of a democratic revival of the German people. The measures which the occupying powers would eventually take were not yet known in detail, but it could be confidently assumed that, in addition to the trial of war criminals, there were plans for measures against monopolistic capitalism and for land and school reform. Our task must be to collaborate in these reforms in precise conformity with the Allied directives, and to see that they were punctiliously carried through.

As soon as German political organisations were promoted, it would be decided to create a broad anti-Fascist democratic mass organisation under the title of the "*Bloc* for Militant Democracy," a broadly-based, anti-Fascist, democratic mass organisation. I was naturally all the more astounded when a few weeks later measures were taken in Berlin in direct contradiction to our directives.

All our discussions now turned more and more on our return to Germany and our future work there. Our preparations were speeded up. Memoranda were prepared at the National Committee and the anti-Fascist schools, particularly in the sphere of popular education. There were even complete manuscripts ready for school history books, which were to be printed later in Germany after the defeat of Hitler.

The hope that the end of the war was near could be felt everywhere. And to the German émigrés these were also days of hope for an early return to Germany. To our older colleagues, this meant a return to the home they had left thirteen years before—a home which in spite of every book they had read and every lecture they had heard in the interval still remained in their mind's eye just as they recalled the Germany of 1933. For those of us who were younger and had left Germany as children, such recollections had almost entirely faded. It was a journey to a country to which we belonged, but which had in store for us nothing but the new, the unpredictable and the un-known.

A Farewell Dinner at William Pieck's

"Congratulations, Wolfgang! You are to go back to Germany with the first group," Anton Ackermann told me after a radio transmission in the middle of April, 1945.

Two aircraft carrying the first twenty German émigrés were to fly as soon as possible to the Soviet occupied area. One group under the leadership of Ulbricht was to operate in the area of Marshal Zhukov's army group, which was advancing directly on Berlin; the second group under the leadership of Anton Ackermann was to operate in the area of Field-Marshal Konev's army, which was approaching Dresden from the direction of Czechoslovakia; but the exact composition of the two groups was not yet known.

A few days later Anton Ackermann told me that I was destined for the Ulbricht group. "There will be ten of you, and at the end of April you will fly in the general direction of Berlin. We will probably set out for Konev's area a day later from here. You'll be told in the next few days where you should report to complete the formalities."

I was naturally delighted to be in the party on the first aircraft, but at the same time I was disappointed not to be able to fly with Anton Ackermann, for whom I had so much respect. I did not know Ulbricht well, and I found him rather unsympathetic.

Now began a busy period. I was on duty every other day as usual, for twenty-four hours from midday, for the radio broadcasts. The rest of my time was filled up with formalities and discussions. Two days later the "Ulbricht Group," as we were now called, was introduced to Ulbricht himself. He did not seem at all impressed or pleased; at least he gave no sign of it. He addressed us as if it were a prefectly matter-of-fact affair to be returning to Germany after so many years.

On 27th April we were presented to Ulbricht again for a brief talk.

"Everything ready? Everything completed?" he asked. This was the first time I had ever seen him smiling and friendly. "Probably we shall fly on 29th or 30th April. Before then we shall be having a farewell dinner with Wilhelm Pieck. Now, another practical matter——" He opened his brief case and took out a bundle of bank notes, which he distributed among us. "Here's a thousand roubles each as pocket money," he said. It was a sum far in excess of a month's wages for a worker at that date; and this distribution of money was not the end of the matter. "And now here are two thousand German *Reichsmarks* for each of you for your first expenses in Germany." Again we were given a bundle of newly-printed notes. This time they were Allied occupation marks produced by the Americans. We had heard about the occupation currency before now, but this was the first time we had seen it.

On the 29th April we were summoned to see Ulbricht for the last time. Our talk was again a very brief one. "Everything is settled. We shall be flying off to-morrow morning at seven o'clock, and leave for the airport in a bus. Everyone is to bring a small case containing just the bare necessities. This evening we are invited to Wilhelm Pieck's."

Pieck's rooms were furnished just like all the others in the Hotel Lux. The only difference was that he had several rooms at his disposal instead of only one.

In comparison with living conditions for the ordinary Soviet citizen and many German émigrés they could be called comfortable, indeed even luxurious. Looked at through western eyes they might suggest the home of a skilled worker in Western Germany. However, they would have made a modest, even shabby, impression in compariosn with the villa which Wilhelm Pieck occupied in Berlin-Niederschönhausen after 1945.

In the living-room there was a round table at which we took our seats. In front of each chair stood a small glass of vodka. I had been afraid that the occasion would be very official. At heart, I was even prepared for a political lecture or an organised "evening's amusement" such as we used to have at the Comintern School. But this time I was pleasantly surprised. The evening was cheerful, friendly and informal. It seemed we were now at a level in the official hierarchy at which one could meet without official addresses and proclamations. During the course of the evening we even talked occasionally about our future work, but we did so freely in our own words and not in the jargon of official Party directives. Then our glasses were filled with vodka for a toast in honour of the day.

"To our future work in Germany!" said Wilhelm Pieck, hearty and friendly.

"To your early arrival in Germany, Wilhelm Pieck!" one of us replied.

He laughed. "Yes, yes," he said, "I shall soon be back!"

We parted after about an hour. Wilhelm Pieck shook each of us by the hand: "Till we meet again soon in Germany."

Ulbricht reminded us once more to be at the side entrance of the Hotel Lux punctually at six o'clock in the morning. I was still dizzy with excitement when I got back to my room. For a long time I could not sleep. It was my last evening in the Soviet Union.

CHAPTER SEVEN

With Ulbricht to Berlin

AT SIX O'CLOCK in the morning of 30th April, 1945, a bus stopped in a little side street off Gorky Street, in front of the side entrance of the Hotel Lux. It was to take the ten members of the Ulbricht Group to the airport. We climbed aboard in silence.

The streets were still empty as we drove down Gorky Street, across Pushkin Square in the direction of the airport. It was a fine spring morning. The whole town was already decorated for the 1st of May with flowers, stickers and slogans. A quarter of an hour later our bus stopped in front of the buildings of Moscow Airport. As usual we had to pull up at the gates.

"*Propusk* (permits)!" the sentry called out sharply. Ulbricht proffered him a paper.

"All right!" the sentry replied, and let us through.

We were politely conducted to a transport aricraft standing by itself some distance off. It was an American Douglas. We made ourselves as comfortable as possible in it. A few minutes later the engine started.

With the exception of Ulbricht no one knew exactly where we were to land. We only knew that our flight was in the direction of Germany and would end in an area under the command of Marshal Zhukov. About the details of our work, we were equally in the dark. All we knew was that, according to our directives, we had a political mission to carry out, the target of which was Fascism and its remnants, and the purpose of which was the transformation of Germany into a democracy.

The Ulbricht Group

I had made the acquaintance of most of the members of the Ulbricht Group only in the last few days. Walter Ulbricht, the head of our group, was at that time fifty-one years old. He had been born in Leipzig and was a joiner by trade. According to his own account, he had joined the Social Democratic Party in 1912 at the age of nineteen, and from 1916 onwards he had taken an active part in the *Spartakusbund* in Saxony. From 1928 to 1933 he had been a K.P.D. deputy in the German *Reichstag;* from 1929 he was the District Secretary of the K.P.D. for Greater Berlin and Brandenburg; in 1933 he took refuge in France and became a member of the leadership of the Communist Party in exile in Prague and Paris; and during the Civil War he was in Spain, where he became notorious (though this I only learned later on) for the liquidation of anti-Stalinist revolutionary combatants in the Spanish Republican Army. On the downfall of the Spanish Republic he returned to France, and from there went to Moscow after the fall of France in 1940.

His strong points were his talents as an organiser, his phenomenal memory for names, his skill in foreseeing each successive change in the Party line, and his tireless industry. He never seemed to be exhausted even after the longest day's work. I seldom saw him laugh, and I do not remember ever having detected any signs of personal emotion. Being entirely innocent of theoretical ideas or personal feelings, to the best of my knowledge he never failed to carry out the directives transmitted to him by the Soviet authorities with ruthlessness and skill.

Richard Gyptner, who had been born in Hamburg, was an admirable assistant in his pedantic way. His frail constitution made him more suited to clerical than official duties in the Party. He was a man entirely without humour. His most prominent characteristics were his pedantry on paper and his careful attention to his clothes; these seemed to be the strongest feelings he was capable of. I do not recall him ever showing lively enthusiasm, enthusiastic emotion or uncontrollable anger. He therefore found no difficulty in accepting and passing on every contortion of the Party line, with no more embarrassment than if it were a matter of methodically filing the appropriate Party documents. He spoke little of himself, but we knew that he had spent many years as a member of the leadership of the Young Communist International and that he had been for some time active in the Comintern *apparat* in Moscow and later at Institute No. 205. In 1946, Richard Gyptner became head of the Central Secretariat of the S.E.D., after which he held a senior post in the People's Police and later became head of the section in the D.D.R. Foreign Ministry dealing with foreign capitalist countries.

Otto Winzer, who was known in Moscow under the pseudonym of Lorenz, resembled Richard Gyptner in many respects. What distinguished him was a keener brain, which enabled him not simply to pass on directives but to give them a sharper and more aggressive edge, to railroad them through regardless of personal considerations, and occasionally (though not very profoundly) to justify them ideologically. More than any other member of the Ulbricht Group, Winzer represented that cold, acid type of Stalinist official who would remorselessly carry through every directive and whose long apprenticeship in the *apparat* had cut him off from all contact with the real life of the workers' movement or the ideals of Socialism and the brotherhood of nations. From 1945 onwards, Winzer scaled the highest rungs of advancement accessible in a career in the East. In May, 1945, he took over the Culture and Popular Education section in the Berlin Municipal Council. From 1946 to 1950 he was the head of the press and radio department in the Central Secretariat of the S.E.D., and for a time also deputy editor-in-chief of the newspaper *Neues Deutschland*. In October, 1949, he was promoted to be *chef de cabinet* of Wilhelm Pieck, the President of the D.D.R.

In contrast to those I have mentioned so far, Hans Mahle, who was now thirty-three years old, had survived a long apprenticeship in the *apparat* without losing his natural spontaneity. He could still laugh and enjoy himself and talk to ordinary people; he even had a vocabulary going beyond the Party jargon for expressing personal thoughts and feelings. Of all the members of our group I found him the most sympathetic, for his work had not dried him up or inhibited him as a human being. His reactions to events and personalities were always spontaneous, and he was capable of exercising his own initiative and judgment on them, though naturally only within given limits. In the summer of 1945 he was appointed manager of the East Berlin Radio, and later general manager of all radio stations in the Soviet Zone of Occupation. At the beginning of 1951 his career ended in an abrupt downfall and it was only some time afterwards that he reappeared in the relatively subordinate position of editor-in-chief of the Schwerin *People's News*.

Gustav Gundelach also came from Hamburg. At fifty-eight he was the oldest member of our Group. He was a worthy working-class official who had acquired his experience the hard way. It was not often that I saw him as cheerful as Hans Mahle; he was silent, almost reserved, but not for that reason unfriendly. His calm manner was neither phlegmatic and pedantic like that of Gyptner, nor cold and forbidding like that of Winzer. He was keen, industrious and reliable. In the summer of 1945 Gundelach was appointed President of the Central Directorate of Labour and Social Welfare in the Soviet Zone of Occupation. In April, 1946, he was sent to reinforce the Communist Party of Western Germany in his native town of Hamburg, where he soon afterwards became a municipal councillor. Later he was given a leading position in the West German Communist Party, and on 14th August, 1949, he entered the first German *Bundestag* as a Communist Party Deputy.

Karl Maron, who was forty-four at this time, was already known to me from the editorial staff of the newspaper *Free Germany*, and I had always been on good terms with him. His versatility was astounding. After many years' activity in the sport movement, he next wrote the military commentaries in the publication of the National Committee. In June, 1945, he was first appointed Deputy Lord Mayor of Berlin; later he was Chairman of the S.E.D. Group in the

Berlin Town Council; in November, 1948, he was municipal councillor for economic affairs in the East Sector of Berlin; in November, 1949, he became deputy editor-in-chief of the Central S.E.D. newspaper, *News Deutschland;* and after that he was Inspector-General and Chief of Staff of the German People's Police. It is quite possible, and even probable, that during his meteoric career Karl Maron developed into the same type of which Ulbricht, Gyptner and Winzer are the most striking examples.

Walter Koppe—a squat, bald-headed little man of fifty-three—occupied a position somewhat apart. He came from Berlin and spoke pure Berlin German. Considering his appearance and his age, he had an astonishing vigour, but he had very little understanding of political or theoretical questions. Personally not unsympathetic but politically incompetent, Walter Koppe's first post in June, 1945, was as Vice-Chairman of the K.P.D. in Berlin, where his official position was organising secretary. It was not long before he was released from this post. While he held it he spent his time in long, detailed conversations with Berlin officials about life as it used to be, instead of giving them their directives for the immediate tasks in hand. In 1947 he was appointed financial secretary of the Karl Marx Academy of the S.E.D. Party, a post for which his practical mind and organising gifts well suited him. Three years later he was appointed financial secretary of the Forst-Zinna Administrative Academy, where he still was at the time of writing.

Fritz Erpenbeck, the Communist writer and journalist from Mainz, who was forty-eight years old, was the only one of us all who was not immediately given a definite assignment in 1945 and had no precise function. Erpenbeck wrote copiously and busily and was always about the place, whether at editorial conferences of newspapers or periodicals, at the Cultural League and in the theatrical world, or at lectures on films or the visual arts. He was lively, expansive, interested in everything, well-educated and obviously delighted with his free-lance role. But the more firmly the system became established in the Soviet Zone, the more difficult it became for him to lead this unattached life.

And so I come to myself. At the age of twenty-three I was the youngest member of the Ulbricht Group, and I was the only one who could not point to many years of Party activity. Probably I had been chosen for the Ulbricht Group because I had grown up in the Soviet Union and represented the younger generation, which was generally promoted more quickly than in the west to occupy important positions at an early age. Obviously the coming generation was a matter of keen interest for the German Party—as had already been shown by the relatively large number of younger comrades at the Comintern School. Possibly, too, I had been chosen because, after all, I had already been a member of the *Komsomol* for more than five years and had graduated from the Comintern School. I was deeply interested in politics and eager to advance my political education, as the expression was in the Soviet Union. Moreover, by that time I spoke fluent Russian without a trace of an accent. Other members of the Group understood Russian but they could by no means speak it accurately or easily.

Finally there was another young German attached to our Group, not as a political member but as a specialist secretary. He was quiet and silent, and might almost have been a cadre-leader. He seldom took part in our conversations, but he did his work well. I met him again later as an office manager in the provincial government at Potsdam.

The ten members of Ulbricht's Group were the first German émigrés to return to the Soviet occupied area of Germany. It was now their task to lay the political groundwork for further developments.

Bruchmühle, the Political Centre of Zhukov's Army

After an hour and a half's flight, we came down on a little landing ground obviously intended for emergency landings by military aircraft. A few minutes later a car drove up, from which a Soviet officer climbed out and greeted Ulbricht warmly. Then a truck arrived, and the Soviet officer was somewhat apologetic. "You must forgive us, Comrades, for only being able to provide you with a truck. At your next stopping place you will all be given private cars."

After two hours' drive, we stopped again in a small village in front of the Soviet Headquarters. Two young officers met us and invited us to lunch.

"We're always delighted to entertain foreign guests," said one of the officers, in a friendly and even respectful tone. "In the last few days we had some Polish officers, and now we are particularly pleased to be able to welcome members of the new German Government."

I almost gasped. What was it he had said? The new German Government? Hans Mahle was sitting beside me and we looked at each other in embarrassment. What were we to do? We couldn't, after all, leave him under the delusion that we belonged to a new German Government, but we had no authority to tell him that we were only the Ulbricht Group.

One of us waved the compliment aside and gave the Russians to understand that we were not the new German Government, but this only convinced the officer all the more firmly that we were, and he became even politer and more deferential. As we left the headquarters, we found American and German cars waiting for us. The cars carried little red flags and Soviet Army signs; the chauffeurs were in Soviet uniform. Soon we reached Küstrin (now known by the Slavonic name Kostrzyn in Soviet *communiqués*), which had been reduced to a desolate pile of rubble. There was a brief halt. Ulbricht exchanged a few words with our Soviet conducting officer, who said something to our drivers, and then the journey went on.

What had the next few days in store for me? I could hardly wait to talk to real Germans again— Germans who had lived their whole lives here—and to see Berlin again, and to revisit the places where I had passed my childhood. Then suddenly my reverie was interrupted.

"We've arrived," said my driver. We were in a neat little German town about twenty miles east of Berlin: Bruchmühle.

At that time Bruchmühle enjoyed a very special position, since the political staff of Marshal Zhukov's army was established here. It was under the direction of General Galadzhiev, Marshal Zhukov's political Chief of Staff. All other troops had been evacuated from the village. The population must have been through a terrible time on the first arrival of the Red Army, but now they were enjoying a privileged position, at least for a few weeks. There were almost no private soldiers in the little town, but one saw a great many officers of Galadzhiev's staff, almost all of whom spoke German and regarded it as their principal task to establish friendly contact with the population. There was also an editorial office where German-language leaflets were produced.

Shortly after our arrival we were received by some of General Galadzhiev's colleagues. As it was already evening, it was decided to postpone all discussions till the following day. We were billeted in a new house, which had been evacuated for us.

The following morning, 1st May, 1945, was a beautiful spring day, and I felt happier than ever before in my life. At last I was back in Germany! There was nothing yet to weigh on my mind. I knew nothing of what was going on there at that time. I was in Germany—and yet in a sense I was not really there. All I had seen of Germany up to that morning was nothing but fine streets, tidy houses, and liberated foreigners at the hospital headquarters—nothing else. We were called together early that morning, and an officer handed each of us a document. The first glance at mine was enough to show me that it was something important and valuable. Over the signature of the political Chief of Staff of Zhukov's army, General Galadzhiev, it stated that Wolfgang Leonhard was a representative of the Supreme Political

Administration in the areas occupied by the armies of the first Belorussian front.

We were then invited into the officers' mess of the Supreme Political Administration. We were given tickets from which I saw that we were entitled to the rations of a Soviet major. Each of us was at once given a large packet of cigarettes, and an officer who introduced himself as a representative of the political staff undertook in a friendly tone to look after our practical needs.

"Comrade Ulbricht had a talk with General Galadzhiev last night and left early this morning for Berlin. He will be back by this evening. Some of General Galadzhiev's close colleagues would very much like to have a talk with you, however, and would be glad if you could see them at four o'clock."

After breakfast I went back to my new room. Shortly afterwards there was a knock on the door. A woman of about thirty entered shyly and rather nervously.

"I'm supposed to keep everything tidy here. Can I do your room?" she asked.

"Thank you very much, but there is no need for it. I'm used to doing everything myself."

When she heard me speaking fluent German, she looked at me in amazement. I invited her to sit down and rest for a minute, hoping at last to have an opportunity of a conversation with a real German.

She seemed unable to grasp what on earth was going on. Here were Germans arriving suddenly in cars, being warmly welcomed by Soviet officers and fed in Soviet officers' messes, and living in a house requisitioned by the Soviet Army! My suggestion seemed to have shocked her. She became very nervous, and quickly left the room. I could not help being reminded of the way people behaved in Moscow at the time of the purge in 1936-38.

I could not understand it. Why was she so nervous? The war was almost over, and the hard times were past. She ought to be happy, I thought. I had heard nothing yet about looting and rape and suchlike things.

I spent my first morning in Germany going for a walk with Hans Mahle and Fritz Erpenbeck. Unfortunately, almost the only people we met were Soviet officers. Then suddenly we saw our housekeeper again, and this time we succeeded in getting into conversation with her. We soon came to the questions which interested us so passionately: the Nazis, the war, the end of the war, the present situation, the Russians, and the future.

She seemed to have nothing to say about the Nazis or the war. She said she was glad there was going to be peace again. "Only you must understand, after all," she said, somewhat hesitantly, "that in the last few weeks we've been through a terrible time."

"What did the Nazis do to you?" one of us asked.

"But . . . I didn't mean exactly the Nazis. You must realise that when the Russians arrived here . . ."

Then her story began. It was a story which I was to hear repeated in dozens and hundreds of different versions and variants during the next few days and weeks. By this time Maron and Winzer had also joined us. They had clearly been looking for real Germans, too. She went on with her description, and when she began to talk of the cases of rape a cold shiver went down my back. Could such things really have happened? I was shaken, but I firmly believed that these could only be regrettable isolated cases.

Before long the conversation turned into a political discussion. It was a curious situation for a future general supervisor of broadcasts in the Soviet Zone, a future Inspector-General and Chief of the People's Police, and future *chef de cabinet* to the President, to find themselves trying in vain, with every argument they could muster, to persuade a simple German woman of the correctness of our viewpoint. She listened patiently to it all, and it was probably the only occasion when such an intensified political treatment had been devoted to a single German housewife; but nothing could get her to change her ideas, for these were the result of her own experiences.

"You can't tell me anything!" she said at last, almost crossly. "I know very well that the Nazis are bad, but you know it's not so good with the Russians either. You'll find it out in good time." One or two of us chuckled.

On our way back to lunch we were talking about the picture she had drawn. Our opinions were divided. "Straight Nazi propaganda," said one of our '150-percenters.' "She's undoubtedly an active Fascist—probably even belongs to the Nazi underground movement."

Another of our group took a less extreme view. "She may not be an active Fascist, but just a stupid housewife who has been taken in by the Fascists' atrocity propaganda."

The conversation left me very thoughtful. I believed her, and in my heart of hearts I had reconciled myself to the fact that she was really telling the truth. I tried to put my mind at ease by admitting to myself it was possible, after all they had gone through in this terrible war, that individual Red Army soldiers in individual units had behaved in this way.

In the afternoon we had an invitation to visit some of the senior officers of the Political Administration. The conversation was on a high political level. The political officers had undoubtedly been carefully trained for their task in Moscow. They knew German history better than many Germans, and in particular they had a very exact knowledge of the recent past. They knew about the parties in the Weimar Republic, the composition of parliament, the strength of the groups within the parties, the election results from 1918 onwards, and of course, the history of the K.P.D. But did they know what was going on in the minds of the Germans to-day? Did they know what the German population was thinking and feeling? I do not know, for there was no mention of it in our hours of conversation. We talked about the policy of the Party in the past, about the Brussels and Berne Conferences of the K.P.D., about the National Committee, and above all, about the need to carry through to its conclusion the bourgeois-democratic revolution of 1848, and the prospects of Germany's development in the future. The thought struck me that our discussions were often conducted in a vacuum, and that they had little or no contact with reality.

In the evening Ulbricht returned. He had spent the whole day in Berlin, but he told us very little. "You will see for yourselves," he said.

Later on, when we were sitting together, Ulbricht at last told us something about our plans. "Our task will be to build up German agencies for self-government in Berlin. We shall tour the various districts of Berlin to try and pick out those democratic anti-Fascists who are best suited to build up the new German régime. The best thing will be for us to divide ourselves up and each take over a particular district in Berlin. We can then meet in the evenings, and each report on his district."

"When do we start work?"

Ulbricht's answer was short and sharp. "To-morrow."

To-morrow—that was the 2nd May, 1945. It was the day on which the Wehrmacht capitulated in Berlin. On the same day, the Ulbricht Group started work.

My First Meeting with Berlin Communists

On the morning of 2nd May a column of cars set out from Bruchmühle through Kaulsdorf, Biesdorf and Friedrichsfelde towards the town centre of Berlin. In them sat the members of the Ulbricht Group and a few Soviet political officers from General Galadzhiev's staff. Our cars made their way slowly through Friedrichsfelde in the direction of Lichtenberg. The scene was like a picture of hell—flaming ruins and starving people shambling about in tattered clothing; dazed German soldiers who seemed to have lost all idea of what was going on; Red Army soldiers singing exultantly, and often drunk; groups of women clearing the streets under the supervision of Red Army soldiers; long queues standing patiently waiting to get a bucketful of water from the pumps; and all of them looking terribly tired, hungry, tense and demoralised. It was a sharp contrast to what I had seen in the little villages east of Berlin. Many people had put on white armbands as a sign of surrender, or red ones to welcome the Red Army. A few of them had even taken the double precaution of putting on both a white and a red armband. Similarly, white or red flags waved from the windows. It could be seen that the red ones had been recently converted from swastika flags.

Our conducting officers showed us how to get to the headquarters at Lichtenberg, which had been established to begin with in a boarding-house. Our welcome was brief: the commander had his hands full of work. Officers were coming and going, and reporting in short, sharp, telegraphic phrases what was going on in their district. We entered the room to find a Soviet officer in the middle of a furious tirade about the conduct of Soviet troops. That was how I came to hear the first complaints about the behaviour of the Red Army in Berlin—the first, that is, from the Soviet side.

The Commandant was already in the picture about the Ulbricht Group and was obviously delighted to have some help in creating a German administration.

"A German administration—no, we have no such thing yet, but we shall be very glad if you could come here to-morrow or the day after to help us in establishing one." Ulbricht agreed.

Shortly afterwards we continued our journey. Ulbricht decided that for the time being our group should work in pairs. Members went off in the direction of Kruezberg, Treptov, Tempelhof and other districts. I was the only one left.

"Where am I to go?"

"You stay with me," said Ulbricht. "We are going to Neukölln."

Ulbricht stopped the car in front of the open door

of a badly-damaged boarding-house in Neukölln. We could hear an animated discussion going on in the entrance hall. We knocked on the door and went in. Some of those inside were so absorbed in their discussion that they did not even notice us. Suddenly one or two of them leapt up and cried: "Ulbricht!" He was surrounded in a moment, and the surprise and joy of his comrades was reflected in their faces. Ulbricht on the other hand remained severely practical. He greeted them—I thought rather coolly—and introduced me as his colleague. Two or three minutes later the discussion was continued, but henceforth Ulbricht took the lead.

I now had an opportunity to look round. We were in a simple room of a worker's house. An oil lamp stood on the table—there was of course no electric light at that time. On chairs or on the floor or the sofa sat twelve Neukölln Party members. The whole atmosphere was entirely different from that of meetings of the Soviet *Komsomol* or Party. It was like the pictures I had formed to myself of meetings at the time of the October Revolution and during the Civil War in Russia; and this was how I had wished real Party meetings to be.

One could feel the genuineness of the enthusiasm combined with a healthy realism. Without waiting for directives, the Party members had immediately realised that the first thing was to organise a supply of food and water to alleviate the most urgent needs of the population, to create a functioning administration and to overcome chaos and starvation. Brief, clear-cut proposals came from all sides; they were discussed and frequently supplemented by counter-proposals; and so decisions were reached. Someone was noting down the details: names of Party members to be looked out and called upon; rough plans for organising working parties to unload and distribute food, for contacting engineers and mechanics to get the light, water and gas put in order, for organising more working parties to clear the wreckage, for writing out identity documents—all done without any agenda or excitement or unnecessary talk. More was accomplished in half an hour than in all the endless meetings I was used to in Russia.

The only thing I disapproved of was Ulbricht's manner and the way he behaved towards his comrades. While the first few minutes of this *ad hoc* Party meeting were enough to convince me what a very great deal we had to learn, coming from Moscow in total ignorance of everything, Ulbricht behaved like a dictator.

Insensibly the subject changed from the pressing needs of the moment to political questions, the struggle of our Party colleagues during the Nazi period, and the general political line for the present and future. When it came to the conduct of the members of the Party, Ulbricht came to life, and one question followed quickly upon another. "How did so and so behave?" "And so and so?" "Where was so and so?" "What did so and so do?" The names were rattled off without a pause, for Ulbricht had them all in his head. Later on I was to be even more astonished at his phenomenal memory for names.

The way he put his questions was not exactly like a police court hearing, but it was very different from the tone which I would have expected of an émigré returning after twelve years to meet the survivors of his party who had spent years living under the Nazi terror. When he came to laying down the current political line, he did it in a tone which permitted no contradiction. His manner left no room for doubt that the Party's policy was to be settled by him, and not by the Berlin Communists who had been working clandestinely under such difficult conditions.

On our way back, I reflected on this first meeting with the German Communists. Were there not really two different sorts of Communists? Hitherto I had mostly had to deal with officials who were distinguished, apart from a few exceptions, by their hard, impersonal manner and their constant repetition of Party phraseology. How different I found these Communists whom I had met on my first evening in Berlin! They were lively, they were in touch with reality and ordinary people, they were enthusiastic and ready for self-sacrifice.

That evening, when the other members of Ulbricht's Group had returned to Bruchmühle, we had our first conference. Each of us reported briefly on his experiences, and our secretary got his first instructions: to draw up a record of our conferences with several copies, so that from the start a complete report would be available on every district of Berlin.

The first conference was conducted in a relatively informal manner. From the next day onwards our work was to become more organised. Every district of Berlin that had to be covered was to be visited by one or two comrades. A few days later we were to be replaced, so we had to make a clear report on the general situation, to locate the active Communists, Social Democrats and independent anti-Fascists in the various districts of Berlin, and to find out enough about them so that we could hand over a list of suitable names for administrative posts to the respective district commanders. We were also to pick out and nominate district mayors and deputy-mayors.

We flung ourselves into the task of finding the anti-Fascists needed to form an administration with great energy. We had two sources of information to rely on: the Party officials whom Ulbricht and one or two members of our group knew previously, and the lists of names which reached us every day from the political officers on the district commanders' staffs.

Within a few days we had established in every district of Berlin a sort of active nucleus, mainly composed of former K.P.D. members and officials, who for their part brought in other anti-Fascists. The work gathered speed every day. More and more anti-Fascists put themselves at our disposal, enabling us to use them as a basis on which to build up the local administration.

Appointment of the Mayors and Local Administrations

In the early days of May, the Russian Commandants had established Mayors and local administrations of their own. Their appointments were often entirely capricious. In many cases the Commandants did not understand German and were in a difficult situation—how were they to proceed? They found their own solution to the problem (and this is by no means intended as a criticism)—they simply appointed those who stated that they were anti-Fascists, or victims of the concentration camps, or old Communists. One Commandant, on receiving the order to establish local Mayors in office, simply

went out into the street and seized by the arm the first
passer-by whose face he liked for some reason, saying:
"Come here! You now Mayor!"

Luckily he picked on a good one: his particular
Mayor proved very competent. Unfortunately the
same was not true everywhere. In many cases the so-
called anti-Fascists, concentration camp victims or
old Communists turned out within a few days to be
either opportunists, or incompetent, or creatures of
dubious antecedents, and in some cases even active
former Nazis. Our task was now to put right the
defects in the administrations which chance had
thrown up, and to appoint competent anti-Fascists.

Ulbricht gave us our new directives. Every local
administration was to be under a Mayor and two
Deputies (of whom the senior Deputy was also to be
responsible for questions of personnel). There were
to be a series of specialist departments for food, social
and economic questions, health, transport, distribution of labour, popular education and finance, and an
adviser for religious questions. Ulbricht explained:

"The local administrations must be established on
correct political principles. One cannot have Communists as Mayors, especially at Wedding and in
Friedrichsheim. In working-class districts the Mayors should as a general rule be Social Democrats.
In the bourgeois quarters—Zehlendorf, Wilmersdorf,
Charlottenburg and so on—we must appoint a
bourgeois member of the Centre, the Democrats or
the German People's Party. Best of all if he has a
doctorate, but he must also be an anti-Fascist and a
man we can work well with."

"What about the other posts?" interjected somebody.

"As Deputy Mayor, and for food, social and economic questions and transport, we had better take Social Democrats who know something about municipal politics; for health, doctors with an anti-Fascist record; for posts and communications, qualified non-Party experts. At least half the posts must in any case be held by members of the bourgeoisie or Social Democrats."

Our faces grew long at this, for so far we had met practically no one but Communists, and we had no idea where to find Social Democrats and representatives of the bourgeoisie at such short notice.

Ulbricht went on: "And now for Party members. The senior Deputy Mayor, who will be responsible for questions of personnel, and the official responsible for popular education, must both be our men. You will also have to find one completely reliable comrade in every district whom we shall need to build up the police. This applies to all districts. In many of them we will limit the appointment of our own people to these posts. In the working-class districts of Wedding, Friedrichsheim, Neukölln and Lichtenberg we can perhaps put in one or two more of our own people."

"And the adviser on religious questions?"

"There you must find anti-Fascist priests. We must get good co-operation with them—that's very important."

There was some discussion of Ulbricht's directives, particularly on the question how so many representatives of the bourgeoisie and even of the churches were to be found at short notice. But after about half an hour Ulbricht interrupted the discussion. In typical Saxon style he gave us his final directive: "It's quite clear—it's got to look democratic, but we must have everything in our control."

Everything was indeed perfectly clear. The districts of Berlin were then divided up. I was secretly hoping to get a district where a Social Democrat was to be made Mayor, for in those days of May 1945 it was easier to turn up a Social Democrat than a bourgeois. But I was to have no such luck. My assignment was Wilmersdorf of all places—a district where we had to have a bourgeois at the top.

So next morning I was standing in front of the headquarters in Berlinerstrasse wondering what to do. There was a huge crowd in front of the headquarters, where a ground-floor window stood open. In the room sat the Commandant and in the street immediately in front of the window stood a young Soviet girl in uniform. People wanted answers to every kind of question from the Commandant. His answers were often obscure, and the girl's translations still obscurer. The whole business served very little purpose. I took a quick decision to join the interpreter and help her. A few minutes later I too was surrounded by the inhabitants of Wilmersdorf.

A man of about forty-five came up to me and asked, "Could I speak with you alone a moment?"

We moved to one side. "Forgive me for troubling you. I observed that you were well-informed about the situation and that you could speak Russian fluently. This is the position: I was arrested in connection with the conspiracy of the 20th July, and I was in a concentration camp until a few days ago."

He showed me his papers, and after a few questions it emerged that he had previously been a member of the Democratic Party. During Hitler's time he had joined one of the opposition groups. It was clearly a bourgeois opposition group—exactly what I was looking for!

He had one or two practical questions to put, which I answered at once. Then he thanked me and was about to take his leave.

"Now you must forgive me for troubling *you* so directly," I said hastily. "Would you be willing to take a leading position in the new local administration? We are looking for qualified anti-Fascists, and from our brief conversation I have formed the impression that you will serve our purpose very well."

He smiled amiably but with a deprecating gesture of the hands.

"No, I don't think that's for me. I would hardly fit into an administrative post. But if administrative talent is what you want, I have a good friend with plenty of administrative experience. He used to be a senior civil servant and was a member of the German People's Party. He was bitterly opposed to the war and they arrested him after the 20th July. He would certainly be interested."

"Where does he live?"

"Not far from here. Perhaps about a quarter of an hour."

I indicated the car which I had at my disposal. "Would you mind going there with me straight away?"

So off we went on the search for a Mayor for Berlin-Wilmersdorf. The little villa in front of which we halted had a somewhat neglected appearance. An elderly man of friendly appearance who had obviously seen better days opened the door to us. He introduced himself as Dr. Willenbucher.

We soon got into conversation, and within ten minutes I had already privately taken the decision that Dr. Willenbucher was to be Mayor of Wilmersdorf. I liked him from the first moment, and besides he corresponded exactly to Ulbricht's directive. He came from a bourgeois background, he was a member of a bourgeois party, he was an anti-Fascist, he had a doctor's degree and, what was also important although it was not explicitly mentioned in the directive, as a retired senior civil servant he had many years' experience in administrative matters.

"Would you be prepared to accept the post of Mayor of the Wilmersdorf district, if the occupation authorities agree?"

He drew himself up and seemed to grow several inches taller.

"It would be an honour for me to put my modest administrative experience at the service of the public."

The absurdity of the situation did not escape me. Here was a twenty-three-year old Communist who had grown up in the Soviet Union and spent three days in Germany, appointing a former civil servant as Mayor! Now there was the other side to be dealt with—the Russian Commandant. But that proved easy. He was delighted to be released from the disagreeable task of finding yet another German mayor in the general confusion. "Bring your mayor here at once," he said, "we'll have a drink together and appoint him at once."

A few minutes later I was back at Dr. Willenbucher's. His appearance was now completely changed. He had put on his best black suit, he was no longer bent, and there was a new dignity in his walk. He raised his eyebrows in pleased surprise at being invited to get into my car. The Commandant, having already been briefed by me that the new mayor was a bourgeois who attached importance to the formalities, did his best.

"I am delighted, Herr Doktor Willenbucher, to have the pleasure of welcoming you."

"The pleasure is entirely mine," replied Willenbucher modestly.

We sat down in what was relative comfort for those days in May, 1945, and for form's sake the Commandant put a few more questions. A few minutes later he announced in somewhat solemn tones that he hereby appointed Dr. Willenbucher to be Mayor of the district of Berlin-Wilmersdorf. An aide had by this time brought some glasses and vodka, and the atmosphere was becoming extremely friendly. The Commandant raised his glass and drank to the success of the new German local administration of Berlin-Wilmersdorf.

Before the day was over I had composed a list of candidates for the most important posts in the Wilmersdorf local government, in strict conformity with my directives. The Deputy Mayor and the official responsible for public education were both Communists. Control of the police was in the hands of a reliable former K.P.D. official. Several other officials were non-members of the Party—either Social Democrats or bourgeois.

"O.K., and many thanks," said the Commandant; and so the local administration of Wilmersdorf went to work.

Local administrations were similarly set up in all

the other twenty districts of Berlin during the first ten days of May by ourselves and the active Party members working with us. We had not the slightest difficulty with the Russian Commandants. On the contrary, they readily signed all the lists we put forward, and we had so many invitations to meals from them and were compelled to drink so much that we used to say jokingly to each other: "It's easy enough to appoint a Mayor, but how can one get out of all the drinking with the Commandants?"

H.Q. at No. 80 Prinzenallee

One morning in the second week of May we received instructions not to drive back to Bruch-mühle that evening, but to take our cars to No. 80 Prinzenallee, Berlin-Lichtenberg, as a new house had been put at our disposal there. Our new head-quarters was about half-way between two under-ground stations, Lichtenberg and Friedrichsfelde. It was a fairly large new building, considerably more spacious than our house in Bruchmühle. We each had a room to ourselves. The offices were set up in the rooms on the ground floor, and the work began to get more organised. Stenographers and secre-taries joined us as our responsibilities grew wider every day.

I had to travel constantly to Karlshorst in the eve-nings with Ulbricht, where a representative of Marshal Zhukov's staff would discuss the details of our work with us. Although Ulbricht, unlike Wil-helm Pieck, knew Russian well, he made me trans-late for him. Probably the Soviet officers also knew German well, so the only purpose of interpreting between the two parties to the conversation was to give each of them more time to think out the answers.

One evening, after a conversation with a Soviet General, we were conducted into a large room where we were told that Marshal Zhukov wanted to talk to us. Marshal Zhukov and Ulbricht greeted each other in a way which implied that this was not their first meeting. Ulbricht introduced me as his colleague, and we were invited to sit down.

I had expected to listen to a political discussion, but politics were hardly mentioned at the meeting. The Marshal inquired about Ulbricht's health, and asked whether his wife was still in Moscow and when she would be coming to Berlin. The rest of the conversation, too, turned mainly on private affairs. It was only after a quarter of an hour that Zhukov turned to another subject.

"There have been a few incidents recently in Berlin which point to activity on the part of the Nazis—definite, though not serious. I think our German comrades ought to be a little more watchful in this respect."

Ulbricht was on the defensive. "Comrade Zhukov, there have been not a few cases in which our comrades have reported active Nazis to your Commandants, and all they've done is set them free again at once."

"That's very interesting," said Zhukov. "I must find out about it at once." He picked up the telephone and called General Serov, who was responsible for security matters in Berlin at that time, and later became Chairman of the Committee for State Security in the U.S.S.R.

"I have Comrade Ulbricht with me," he began, and went on to describe what Ulbricht had told him. After a little while Zhukov said into the telephone: "Oh, yes, yes, I understand. Good!" The conversation ended, but Zhukov did not tell Ulbricht what Serov's reply had been. Instead he put a totally unexpected question.

"How are things getting on with the school reforms? Are the plans ready yet? Have you put in hand any of the preparatory work?"

Ulbricht seemed to be taken aback, and I could see from his reply that apart from preparations in Moscow nothing had yet been done in this field.

"This is a matter to which I attach great importance," said Zhukov. "It wouldn't be a bad thing if our German comrades were to get to work on it soon."

Marshal Zhukov's hint was not ignored. The appointment of Otto Winzer, whom Ulbricht obviously looked upon as one of the most effective members of our group, to be responsible for public education in the local government of Berlin, was probably due among other things to this observation of Zhukov's.

We were so deeply involved in our work that we hardly noticed the surrender of Nazi Germany and the Soviet troops' victory celebrations. It was on that very same day that Ulbricht assigned us a new responsibility.

"The local administrations can wait for the time being. We must form a municipal government for the whole of Berlin, and this has top priority now. If necessary, we can even take people away from the districts and put them to work in the municipal administration."

"Are we all going to be on the new job?" somebody asked.

"No, that won't be necessary. It'll be enough if Maron, Gyptner and Winzer concentrate on it, but if it becomes necessary we can bring in the rest of you too."

The rest of us assumed that our activities would continue as before, until Ulbricht gave us a new directive. "There'll have to be a change now in our work in support of the local administrations. We shall have to restrict ourselves exclusively to the districts to the north-west, south-west and west of Berlin. About a month from now we must count on the arrival of the Western Allies, and by that time the local administrations must be functioning in their districts unchallenged."

So from now on our work was confined to the districts which were shortly to be occupied by the Americans, British and French. By this time we had good bodies of activists to rely on everywhere. Our work now consisted of supporting already established local administrations, clearing up any complications that might arise for them with the Russian Commandants, and carrying out an occasional shake-up to replace inadequate officials by stronger ones.

I was on the move day in, day out. I got to know dozens of people of every type, and my note-book was full of the addresses of anti-Fascists of all descriptions, including the names of professional administrators, technicians and engineers. Besides our current work, part of our group was also busy with preparations for establishing the city administration in Berlin. Ulbricht had many private conversations on the subject with Maron, Winzer and Gyptner. Apart from these daily discussions, every Sunday morning from the middle of May onwards there were larger conferences in which between eighty and a hundred active Communist functionaries took part, most of them being members of the local administrations. In this way we received an accurate picture of the situation in Berlin every Sunday. Ulbricht always gave out his directives after the reports from our party colleagues from the various districts.

Generally the proceedings of these conferences were serious and practical. On one occasion, however, our Sunday morning conference was interrupted by peals of laughter. An old Communist Party official from Wedding, who still spoke the pure Party jargon of the 1920s, was reporting on work in his administrative district, but without a word to say about his own activity.

"What are you doing yourself, then?" asked Ulbricht. "You keep on telling us about other people. What's your own function?"

"I'm responsible for religious questions."

General consternation.

"How did you get that job?"

"Plain enough, Comrade Ulbricht. When we divided up the posts, I naturally took that one, because after all there had got to be someone to keep an eye on the priests. There are some very crafty fellows among them sometimes, after all."

Peals of laughter; but Ulbricht was furious.

"You must resign at once! That's a post for a priest —we have to co-operate with progressive elements in the Church these days. We can't allow you to make havoc of our Church policy!"

The laughter froze at Ulbricht's angry tone. Our colleague from Wedding looked round helplessly, puzzled. It was obvious he no longer understood what was going on and could not even begin to grasp what was meant by "progressive elements in the Church." However, Ulbricht did not consider it necessary to give a mere working-class official from Wedding even the briefest exposition of the Party line; he simply confined himself to the reprimand.

Another incident was more serious. On one occasion there was direct, open and explicit opposition to one of Ulbricht's directives on the part of several Berlin officials. The Sunday conference was nearly at an end. Current reports and directives on work in the local administrations were over.

"Are there any more questions?"

"Yes, there are!" said a Party member from the farthest corner of the hall. "A question has been put to us by some doctors—men with an anti-Fascist background—about what course they ought to take with women who have been raped and come to them for abortions. I've promised the doctors a reply. We need a clear definition of the proper attitude to this question of abortion in such cases, from our own point of view."

He was immediately supported by another voice: "The question's very urgent. It's being talked about everywhere. We must give officials responsible for public health a clear directive. In my view, abortion ought to be permitted officially in such cases."

Voices of assent could be heard from all over the room, but Ulbricht interrupted the discussion by saying sharply: "There can be no question of it! I regard the discussion as closed."

However, the Berlin Communists in May, 1945, were by no means servile automata, and they did not regard the discussion as closed at all. For the first time in my life, I saw something happen which up till then I had regarded as practically impossible; there were open cries of protest against a senior Party official.

"You can't do that! We must discuss it!"

"We have a moral obligation to define our attitude on the question."

"We must give working-class women the right of abortion."

"We can't just go on avoiding every unpleasant question."

Ulbricht stood facing them with an angry frown. One speaker followed another. Before long it was no longer a question of simply permitting abortion. What was demanded was more fundamental: it was that a clear and public attitude should be taken towards the excesses of the Soviet Army. There must be no more evasion of the subject. As German Communists, we must at least explicitly dissociate ourselves from what was going on, and if necessary openly condemn it. Finally, when the excitement had somewhat subsided, it was Ulbricht's turn to speak.

"I repeat," he said sharply, "I regard the discussion on this subject as closed. It is quite impossible for us to adopt the attitude that abortions are permissible if the pregnancy results from these incidents. People who get so worked up about such things to-day would have done much better to get worked up when Hitler began the war. Any concession to these emotions is, for us, quite simply out of the question.

I regard the question as closed, and I will not allow the debate to be continued. The conference is adjourned."

The conference broke up, muttering angrily. The Berlin Communists present, who had been brought up in a strict Party discipline for years if not decades, had shown themselves courageous enough to speak against a Party directive, but not strong enough to prevail against it. The delicate question was never raised again at any subsequent meeting.

Special Missions

"You must go to Reinickendorf as a matter of urgency to-day—everything else can wait," I was told one morning.

"What's up, then?"

"I don't know. Hurry down to the office and see Ulbricht and the Soviet liaison officer. They'll tell you."

The Soviet liaison officer gave me the explanation: "This is what it's about—there are said to be Trotskyites at Reinickendorf, and the local Communists are beginning to show Trotskyite tendencies."

I was extremely surprised to think that in May, 1945, a few weeks after the destruction of Hitlerite Fascism, when the basic minimum conditions of existence had still to be established for the population, I, of all people, had to go and hunt out some Trotskyites or other. I was just going to ask whether the Trotskyites could not wait until the following day, when the Soviet liaison officer went on: "The matter is of extreme importance—very high authorities have expressed interest in the question, and I have to make a report this afternoon."

Two minutes later I was sitting with the Soviet liaison officer in a car on its way to Reinickendorf. My mission inspired no enthusiasm in me. If anyone had to be ferreted out, I would have preferred it to be Nazi leaders rather than Trotskyites. So on the way I worked out a plan in my head, which would enable me at least to deal with the matter as quickly and as painlessly as possible.

"Perhaps it would be a good thing if I have a talk first alone with our comrades in the District Administration?"

The Soviet officer agreed.

Arriving at the administrative offices in Reinickendorf, I went at once to the Deputy Mayor, since this was the post occupied by our most active Party colleague. As it seemed to me really too ridiculous to come to Reinickendorf merely to inquire after Trotskyites, I started off with a general conversation on the situation. Finally I came to the point.

"There's just one other thing. Our Soviet friends have heard there are some Trotskyites here in Reinickendorf. They want to know whether it's true or not. It seems to me unlikely in any case, but I just wanted to inquire about it."

"Oh, that business!" my colleague replied with a smile. "Yes, that happened almost a week ago. There were a few Party members who had a meeting, and Trotsky was mentioned in the course of their discussion, but everyone present spoke out against him without hesitation."

"So on this I can report that there is no Trotskyite

organisation here, or anything else of the kind, and the whole business obviously rests on a misunderstanding?"

"Of course—it was a matter of no significance whatsoever."

We parted. The Soviet officer appeared to be as pleased as I was that everything had been cleared up. "I will put the matter in my report just as you have described it to me."

I agreed at once. On the way back, however, I could not help having further thoughts. There had in fact been a private discussion between a number of Party members at which Trotsky's name had been mentioned; and the fact had somehow immediately got up to the highest Soviet authorities, where so much interest had been aroused that the liaison officer to the Ulbricht Group—himself a senior political official—had had to take the thing up as a matter of immediate urgency!

My next special mission was regarded as so important that this time I was not sent on my own. It was again the Soviet liaison officer who was the first to broach the matter. "It's a most important, most urgent matter, comrade," he told me gravely. "It's been reported that Berlin Radio still has a number of recordings relating to Molotov's conversations in Berlin in the autumn of 1940. These recordings are said to be at present in a secret archive section of the radio building in Masurenstrasse, in Charlottenburg. Charlottenburg is due to be occupied by the British. I need hardly tell you how extremely important it is that these recordings should not fall into the hands of the western allies."

This special mission really made an impression on us, and I could not help catching my breath.

The liaison officer went on: "So I would like to propose that two members of the Ulbricht Group should come with me at once to the radio building and try to find out, with the help of Hans Mahle, where these recordings are. Once that's done, it will not be part of your task to take possession of the material; all that's necessary at this stage is to locate it."

Ulbricht thereupon appointed Gyptner and myself for this job, and half an hour later we had reached the radio building in Masurenstrasse with the Soviet liaison officer. When we tried to enter the archive section we were stopped by Soviet soldiers in uniform.

"You can't enter this department," we were told, in Russian. After a good deal of persuading and displaying his documents, our companion was allowed to talk to the *nachalnik* of the special guard. This was an officer wearing, if I remember rightly, the blue cap of the N.K.V.D., the Soviet Security Service. He was unyielding. "I have instructions to let no one in."

Then our companion whispered something to him, and they went off by themselves for a few minutes.

"Everything's arranged, we can go back now," said our companion eventually. "I apologise for having inflicted this business on you, but it was put to me by my superiors as a matter of the highest urgency. Now it seems that the matter has already been taken care of: the recordings were found a few days ago by another party, and they've been seized."

It was not difficult to guess whom the other party

comprised. Anyway, they had certainly worked quickly—obviously, more quickly than the political administration of the Red Army.

Berlin's City Government is Born

"These are the food rations to be distributed from May 15th onwards," Ulbricht told us, giving each of us a list. "The ration cards are being printed now."

We observed that the new food rations were substantially the same as those in the Soviet Union. In Germany, too, there were big differences between the rations of heavy workers, workers, officials and the rest. The daily ration varied between 300 and 600 grammes of bread; between 20 and 100 grammes of meat; between 7 and 30 grammes of fats; between 15 and 25 grammes of sugar. Only the potato ration (400 grammes a day) and the substitute coffee ration (100 grammes a month) were the same for all inhabitants of Berlin.

The new system of rationing and distribution, if it were to function properly, presupposed a central administration for Berlin. So on the following day Ulbricht told us: "We must now set about finally establishing the Berlin City Government. We know enough people by this time."

Our discussion was so casually conducted that I still believed we were only making a temporary plan.

"Well, first of all the Lord Mayor. You all know Dr. Werner. How would it be to have him?" said Ulbricht.

Maron, Gyptner and Winzer did not seem very enthusiastic. "I don't know, Walter," said somebody, "Dr. Werner doesn't seem to me quite the right sort of man. Besides, he's too old."

"I've heard it said that sometimes he's not quite right in the head," said one of the men we were intending to put in the City Government.

"That doesn't matter," said Ulbricht. "The Deputy will be one of our men."

Thus the Lord Mayor of Berlin was decided upon. Fortunately Dr. Werner proved the doubts expressed about him to be unjustified, since he turned out to be a man of great energy.

"Now, the most important thing is the first Deputy Mayor. You would be the best person for that, Karl," said Ulbricht, turning to Maron.

Maron's face registered astonishment. He was not at all pleased. "But I have never done anything of the kind," was his reply.

"You'll soon learn the job," Ulbricht told him.

"All right," said Maron, "but only if young Wolfgang comes along with me."

"No, we can't let Wolfgang go into the Berlin Administration with you. He stays here for the time being to deal with current business."

So the Deputy Lord Mayor's appointment was fixed too. The subsequent course of the discussion made it clear that the administration of Berlin was to be made up on the same pattern as that of the district administrations, with the possible difference that "our people" (as Ulbricht liked to call them) were to be rather more strongly represented in the City Government. One name followed another, and our list grew longer and longer. It took about an hour before each of us had the names of all the intended members of the Berlin City Government in writing in front of him. The three most important posts were to be held by "our people." In this context "our people" meant not simply Communist Party officials, but those of them who had emigrated to the Soviet Union: Karl Maron as first Deputy Lord Mayor, Arthur Pieck as Chief of Personnel, and Lorenz (Otto Wenzer) as the official responsible for public education. In addition to these three Moscow officials, who held the really key positions, there were two other Communist Party officials: Ottomar Geschke and Hans Jendretzki, who had been many years in a concentration camp. It was significant that both of them held relatively subordinate positions, responsible respectively for the distribution of labour and social welfare, which clearly brought out the difference in prestige between Communist Party officials from Moscow and those who had stayed in Germany.

The third Deputy Lord Mayor, who was also Chief of the Planning Section, Paul Schwenk, was another of the Moscow émigrés. At the time when Ulbricht appointed him he was actually still in Moscow and, as we learned later, was himself very surprised at his appointment. He arrived in Berlin by air a few days afterwards.

The fourth Deputy Lord Mayor, Karl Schulze, and the official responsible for trade, Joseph Orlopp, were counted as Social Democrats. The Lord Mayor, Dr. Werner; the second Deputy (who was also responsible for food), Dr. Hermes; the official responsible for health, Professor Sauerbruch; Scharoun, who was responsible for building; and Dr. Landwehr, who was responsible for economic questions—all these were regarded as bourgeois: so was the priest, Buchholz. Two other officials, Ernst Kehler (information and communications) and Engineer Jirack (responsible for communal enterprises), were labelled non-Party and were expected to behave accordingly, although all of us knew that Jirack had previously been a member of the Communist Youth Organisation and Kehler had studied at the Anti-Fascist School in the Soviet Union.

The City Government was thus composed of seven bourgeois, six Communist Party officials, two Social Democrats and two non-Party members. In contrast to many later bodies and organisations which were supposed to be above party, the Berlin City Government in May 1945 may not have looked very democratic, but it was so in practice; for the bourgeois and Social Democrats in the Government, as I was able to infer from remarks made by Maron and Winzer, were not men of straw but very much personalities in their own right, with the highest professional qualifications. They behaved very conscientiously and showed a large measure of independence.

The composition of the City Government was announced on the 17th May, in the only two newspapers then appearing in Berlin—the *Tägliche Rundschau* and the *Berliner-Zeitung*. The new Government took office at a ceremony in the building in Parochialstrasse, which had been partly rebuilt. The room was decorated with the slogan: "Unity against Fascism is the Guarantee of the German People's Rebirth." Colonel-General Berzarin, who was at that time Commandant in Berlin, called upon the Berlin City Government to restore the normal life of the City of Berlin as rapidly and effectively as possible.

In his speech in reply, the new Lord Mayor said:

"To-day there is hardly any branch of our economic and social life that does not have to be entirely rebuilt anew. Hitler turned Berlin into a city of chaos. We shall make Berlin a city of progress." Dr. Werner ended his speech with the words: "We are grateful to our anti-Fascist comrades, who defended and fought for our ideas even under the Nazi domination. A new spirit of honourable love and harmony must, and shall, permeate the German state. Our unity against Fascism has led us to our initial clear-cut successes. It is the guarantee of the newborn German people."

These words of Dr. Werner's undoubtedly corresponded to the hopes cherished by every anti-Fascist at that date. I too was moved as I heard them. But it was only a few days before things began to happen in flagrant contradiction to Dr. Werner's hopeful words about unity against Fascism.

The Dissolution of the Anti-Fascist Committees

"There have been various offices, committees and organisations set up recently," said Ulbricht at one of our routine conferences, "calling themselves Anti-Fascist Committees or Anti-Nazi Groups or Socialist Offices or National Committees or suchlike."

I had seen such offices again and again on my travels through Berlin. I took it for granted that the task Ulbricht was about to assign to us was to make contact with them and support their work. "It has been reported," he went on, without saying how or by whom, "that these bodies have been created by the Nazis. They are in fact cover organisations, whose object is to frustrate the development of democracy.

We must break them up at all costs. It's a highly important task, and you must all find out, without fail, where these committees have been established in your respective districts. You must then ensure their immediate dissolution."

I thought this statement by Ulbricht rather curious, but I assumed that he had unexceptionable information. Besides, such tactics on the part of the Nazis were by no means impossible. Had not the Seventh World Congress of the Comintern, in the summer of 1935, required the German Communists to join Nazi organisations, in order to disrupt them from within? Possibly, I thought to myself, this was what the Nazis were now trying to do. In the Ulbricht Group we greatly overestimated the influence of the Nazis at that time. Nevertheless, my earliest direct contacts with members of these spontaneously established Anti-Fascist Committees had persuaded me that there were no Nazis in them at all, only Party members who had worked clandestinely in Germany. I was soon left in no doubt at all that they were not camouflaged Nazis but straight Party members and anti-Fascists.

Clearly my colleagues received the same impression, for all our reports agreed on this point. However, Ulbricht did not allow this to have the least influence on him; he rejected every attempt to put in a good word for the committees. "They are to be dissolved, and at once," he repeated abruptly. "We cannot allow the errors of the Greek Party to be repeated here in Berlin. In Greece members of the Party collaborated in committees like these while their enemies set about establishing control of the Government."

Bring the kind of official who thinks for himself about political decisions, I could not help detecting the contradiction in Ulbricht's argument. The committees were to be dissolved in the first place because they were allegedly cover organisations for the Nazis; and in the second place because they diverted Party members from establishing themselves in the administrations; and the errors of the Greek Party were thus to be avoided. Throughout the whole campaign against the Anti-Fascist Committees, Ulbricht alternated between the first argument and the second. Only one thing remained fixed, which was the rigour and determination of his directives to break up the Anti-Fascist Committees and to nip in the bud any new creations of the same kind.

From the first I regarded this directive as a mistake, but I was sufficiently disciplined to carry it out against my own inner convictions. In doing so, however, I always took care to carry out the dissolution with the greatest possible circumspection and to incorporate as many Party members as possible in our own administrations. I had a special feeling of regret in particular over the dissolution of one outstandingly effective Anti-Fascist Committee in Berlin-Charlottenburg, which had established its office in the Kurfürstendamm, near the Uhlandstrasse underground station. There was a board hanging at the entrance to the building with the inscription "National Committee for Free Germany," in the same lettering which had been used for the title heading of the newspaper we published in Moscow. There were even the black, white and red stripes as well, and the sign could only have been painted by somebody who had seen our newspaper, *Free Germany*.

I asked to see the Chairman, but the man I spoke to shrugged his shoulders. "Can't be done," he said. "You can see for yourself, he's extremely busy."

There was no point in beating about the bush or playing at hide-and-seek here. "I come from the Ulbricht Group. I was working for the National Committee for Free Germany in Moscow until a short time ago."

At that I was greeted with enthusiasm: "That's wonderful!"

I was immediately received by the Chairman, who made an extremely good impression on me. The word quickly got round that someone from the National Committee in Moscow had arrived, and soon all the more important members of the committee assembled.

"We used to listen regularly to the Free Germany broadcasts," said the Chairman, "and we copied out and reproduced the most important bits." In the course of a short talk I was able to satisfy myself that this was not an invention, as was so often the case at this time, but corresponded to the facts. Everyone present knew the names of the members of the National Committee, and they were even able to recall many of the broadcasts in detail.

"Our National Committee used to take the general proclamations and commentaries of your committee as basic guidance to apply to the particular, concrete situation in Berlin. Of course," he added, almost apologetically, "we had no generals here, but at least we were in contact with other circles of the 20th July."

It became evident that the anti-Fascist members of this National Committee had been putting into practice, in an admirable way, the basic principle of a broad united front of all anti-Fascists against Hitler. Among the leaders were former members of the K.P.D. and S.P.D., as well as bourgeois and religious circles all working in harmony. The Chairman was a former official of the Socialist Workers' Party (S.A.P.), a small but active party created in 1931, which had devoted itself particularly to the creation of a united anti-Fascist front, even before Hitler seized power.

Immediately after the capitulation of the *Wehrmacht* in Berlin, this organisation had set to work on the most pressing tasks without waiting for any directives, not even ours. Engineers, technicians and specialists were recruited to arrange for the provision of gas, water and electric current; the clearing of rubble from the streets was organised; hospitals and schools were got going; in brief, everything was done which needed to be done at the time.

For me this was an unforgettable encounter, and it made me sad to think that possibly Ulbricht was going to destroy even this vigorous and admirable organisation. "I shall do everything I can to prevent it," I thought to myself, and I told my new friends nothing yet about Ulbricht's directives.

At Prinzenallee that evening, I made a report in which I emphasised the positive aspects of the committee as altogether exceptional. But it was no use. "That show on the Kurfürstendamm must be closed," said Ulbricht. I tried once more to speak up for my anti-Fascist friends, but it was in vain. "You will go back there again to-morrow morning,"

said Ulbricht, "and tell them to close down their
activities. We do not need any committees. If you
really think that there are good people in it, then we
can take a few of them into the Charlottenburg administration."

So the following day 1 made my way back to
Charlottenburg. The Chairman of the committee
had by this time invited in all his active colleagues,
as well as a group of people involved in the 20th
July. There were about forty present, all of them
waiting eagerly to hear what the representative of
the National Committee from Moscow had to say.
It was unfortunate that I was announced with so
much ceremony, and that it was stated in the course
of the introduction that the speaker was to explain
the basic principles that would guide the future
activity of the Free Germany Movement.

Here was an appalling situation. In my heart of
hearts I was firmly convinced that this anti-Fascist
organisation ought not only to be given the right to
continue its activities, but to be still further rein-
forced by the adherence of expatriates such as ourselves. On the other hand, there was Ulbricht's firm
directive not to allow any such organisations to continue, and to dissolve all those that existed. My Soviet
training was far too strong to allow me to entertain
the thought of disregarding the directive and acting
in accordance with my own conviction and conscience. I was determined, however, to carry out
Ulbricht's directive with all possible caution and
circumspection, and not to give offence to the anti-
Fascist members of the committee, and to incorporate as many of them as possible in our own administrations.

"Does this mean that our National Committee must be dissolved?" asked an elderly gentleman, who had been introduced to me as a professor, when I had finished speaking. His voice was quite calm, but one could see how much he dreaded the answer, "Yes."

"I find it really painful to have to tell you this, because I am quite convinced of the excellent work of your organisation, but our instructions do not permit the continuation of any such organisations at all."

"But we are not just *any* organisation, we are an anti-Fascist coalition, formed with the object of taking an active initiative, as Germans, not only in solving the most urgent problems of the day, but also in the political and spiritual re-education of the people on democratic lines," said another voice, this time more bitterly. "All we want, after all, is to carry out the principles laid down by the allies for the struggle against Fascism and the democratic re-education of our people."

I could see his point. "We ought to be delighted about such organisations and welcome them, support them and participate in their work," I thought to myself; but what I said was:

"I understand what you are thinking, but I should like to draw your attention once again to the fact that we anti-Fascists have a duty to carry out the instructions of the occupation authorities. I should also like to emphasise that the dissolution of your organisation does not in the least entail the interruption of your activity as individuals. Your work must simply be carried on in other contexts. You know that anti-Fascist administrative authorities are now being set up everywhere, but there is still a considerable shortage of able anti-Fascists, so it would be perfectly possible for all of you to get yourselves incorporated in the new administration."

Again I saw disappointed faces, and I could share their feelings. These people had no wish to become Government officials. They had banded together, despite all previous divergencies of outlook, in a common struggle against Hitler, and a close corporate spirit united them. Now, with the destruction of Fascism, they wanted to carry on the work together for a new Germany in a vigorous anti-Fascist organisation; and it was at this very moment, when their first object, the destruction of Fascism, was achieved, that their organisation was to be broken up. Their disappointment was great; and so was mine.

I returned to Prinzenallee with a heavy heart, and found the session just beginning.

"Well, what's the situation with that comic show in Charlottenburg?" asked Ulbricht. "Did you break it up to-day?" All Ulbricht's contempt for any independent initiative from below could be detected in his question. I reported what had happened, and indicated that they had definitely accepted their dissolution but needed two or three weeks to carry it out.

"Two or three weeks!—they're mad!" snorted Ulbricht. "To-morrow we'll send them somebody else from the Party!"

Ulbricht duly sent one of his most narrow-minded *apparatchiks*, and it was not hard to imagine what happened then. The job was completed a few days later. The committee was broken up, and the majority of its members retired into private life, bitterly disappointed. Later on I met some of them, who joined the Government service and carried out their duties conscientiously, but there was no trace left of the fire, the enthusiasm, and the initiative they had shown before.

The fate of the Charlottenburg committee was only one example among many. Dozens of similar committees and groups and bodies, which had been created on their own initiative from below in Berlin, were broken up simultaneously; and this happened not only in Berlin but in all the major towns of the Soviet Zone, as soon as the Government authorities were established. Later on, it happened even in the area occupied by the Western Powers.

I shall never forget a brief encounter which took place at this time between Ulbricht and a Party member from Brandenburg.

"Well, how are things in your local administration?" Ulbricht asked his colleague with interest, but somewhat condescendingly. His colleague reported briefly on the activity of the Administration, adding with a certain pride: "And we have also founded an anti-Fascist organisation."

"How's that?—what've you done?" asked Ulbricht angrily. His colleague showed him some printed membership books of an anti-Fascist action group, with a programme somewhat similar to that of the National Committee.

Ulbricht was furious. "Who allowed you to do that? How dare you do a thing like that? Your anti-Fascist action group must be broken up at once, and the membership books must be destroyed! You're supposed to wait for instructions from the Central Committee."

Shocked by the violence of Ulbricht's tone, his colleague tried to justify himself. "But Comrade Ulbricht, we had no intention of anticipating directives from the centre." He pointed to the membership cards and went on: "We expressly inserted the word 'provisional' in front of our programme. Our membership books, too, are labelled as temporary."

"Provisional or not, the whole show must be broken up, and that forthwith!"

Later I learned of similar happenings in Thuringia and Saxony. In Thuringia a United Socialist Party, with the title of "The Workers' Party" (P.D.W. had been formed by former concentration-camp victims immediately after their liberation. They too were broken up. When the S.P.D. and the K.P.D. were established from above in the middle of June, only half the former members of the P.D.W. joined them. Many others, including those who had been most active in the P.D.W., abstained because they did not want to return to the old parties.

In Dresden an organisation was set up under the name of the Anti-Fascist People's Committee, and it was joined by twenty to thirty thousand members. After the re-establishment of the old parties, seven thousand of them joined the K.P.D. and three thousand the S.P.D. All the rest, who were only too ready to collaborate in an anti-Fascist People's Committee, but did not wish to opt for a particular Party, withdrew in disappointment back to private life. There were no doubt similar examples in many other places. In this way, every initiative from below was nipped in the bud between the beginning of May and the middle of June.

At the time I regarded this merely as an error in

one particular limited context, and I tried to justify it, exactly as I had previously tried to justify negative tendencies in the Soviet Union as temporary errors. It was not until my break with Stalinism that I really understood the significance of the directives at that time against the spontaneous creation of anti-Fascist committees. It was not an error in a limited context but an essential feature of Stalinist policy. It was impossible for Stalinism to permit the creation by independent initiative from below of anti-Fascist, Socialist or Communist movements or organisations, because there was the constant danger that such organisations would escape its control and try to resist directives issued from above. The dissolution of the Anti-Fascist Committees was therefore nothing other than a disruption of the first emergence of what might prove to be a powerful independent anti-Fascist and Socialist movement. It was the first victory of the *apparat* over the independent stirrings of the anti-Fascist, left-inclined strata of Germany.

Wilhelm Pieck and the New Line

During the first weeks of June, we members of the Ulbricht Group were abruptly taken off our work. One morning several large private cars stopped in front of our house at No. 80 Prinzenallee. The officials from Moscow had arrived: Wilhelm Pieck, Fred Oelssner, Paul Wandel, Johannes R. Becher, Edwin Hörnle, Marthe Arendsee, and a number of others whom I did not know personally. With them came a number of graduates from the Anti-Fascist School, who were now more or less well known. I particularly noticed Bernhard Bechler, a former major on the General Staff, who had been re-educated in the Soviet Union and was regarded as completely loyal to the Party line, so that he now even took part in confidential conferences. Not long afterwards he became Minister of the Interior for Brandenburg.

There was little time for greetings or personal conversation. Private sessions, at which only Ulbricht took part from our group, began immediately after their arrival. Little rooms were permanently reserved for these sessions.

It was not difficult to see that the significance of these conferences went far beyond Berlin. The day after the arrival of the top officials from Moscow, they were joined by Anton Ackermann, Hermann Matern and Kurt Fischer from Dresden as well. These were members of the Ackermann Group, which had left Moscow one day after us, to be installed in the operational area of Marshal Konev, where they were to carry out the same tasks that were assigned to us in Berlin.

After sessions lasting almost two days, we were allowed to know their decision. "There will be no unified Socialist Party: both the K.P.D. and the S.P.D. will be re-established as independent parties. The Communist Party of Germany will be founded in a few days' time, and preparations must be made at once for the issue of the Party newspaper. The creation of bourgeois parties is to be encouraged, and they must correspond to the former Democratic Party and the former Centre. After that, we must establish a democratic anti-Fascist *bloc* of the new parties. To begin with, all our efforts will have to be devoted to the foundation of the Communist Party.

Once it is founded, the next thing will be to set to work on training, and then preparations for the land reform will have to be set in motion: it must be introduced in the summer of 1945."

Our house at No. 80 Prinzenallee had always been a scene of busy activity, but now it became like a beehive, with one conference following another. New cars were provided to maintain liaison between our chief officials and the executive officials in the various localities. Within two days of his arrival, Fred Oelssner dictated the first training manual for members of the German Communist Party, which was not yet in existence. All its members were to be made familiar with the new line as soon as it was founded.

"Training is the most important thing now," said Oelssner. "We must do more training than we've ever done before. It's already been decided that meetings of Party members are to take place once a week exclusively for the purpose of training. We must prepare our comrades for carrying out their new tasks, which are entirely different from those before 1933."

The following day there was a conference attended by some of the chief officials in Berlin, Brandenburg, Potsdam and other towns. At this conference we were told that the principal task at the moment was preparing for the foundation of the Party. "In a few days' time, an order from Marshal Zhukov will be issued, permitting the existence of democratic anti-Fascist parties. We must lay the foundation stone even before then. Every day is precious. Immediately after permission is made official,

we will come out into the open with a proclamation
of the foundation of the K.P.D."

The creation of independent Communist and Socialist Parties was in direct contradiction with the
directives which we had received in Moscow in
March and April, 1945. It did not escape me that
there were other respects too in which the new directives which Wilhelm Pieck had brought with
him were in conflict with those which we had received in the spring of 1945. At that time we had
been told that political activity on the part of the
German people could only be developed initially in
the context of a large-scale, comprehensive anti-
Fascist movement under the title of the "*Bloc for
Militant Democracy.*" Now, on the contrary, what
was talked of was the foundation of political parties.
Earlier, again, it had been said that land reform could
not be undertaken before the beginning of 1946. Now
we were to carry out the land reform immediately
after the foundation of the Party in the summer of
1945. Even at the beginning of May, after our arrival
in Berlin, we had still been told that only anti-Fascist
newspapers which were above party would be permitted during the initial period. Now, on the contrary, we were given a directive to prepare a Party
newspaper.

The Re-establishment of the K.P.D.

Our top officials from Moscow had brought with
them not only the new directives but also the text
of the proclamation to be issued on the foundation
of the new K.P.D. Two days after their arrival there
took place the first large-scale meeting of the execu-

tive leadership of the Party. It was in one of the premises then under our control—if I remember rightly, at the corner of Prinzenallee and Hohenlohestrasse. Those present included about eighty Party members whom we had recruited for our work during the past four weeks.

There was an atmosphere of extraordinary excitement, because the rumour had already got around that the re-establishment of the K.P.D. was to be announced that day. After a brief introduction, Ulbricht read out the proclamation with which the K.P.D. was to come out into the open on its foundation in the next few days.

The crucial paragraphs of the inaugural proclamation were as follows:

"Simultaneously with the destruction of Hitlerism, we must also carry through to completion the tasks of democratising Germany and of transforming the bourgeois democratic system, which were begun in 1848; and we must completely eradicate the remains of feudalism and destroy the tradition of reactionary Prussian militarism, with all its economic and political accretions. We take the view that the method of imposing the Soviet system on Germany would be wrong, since this method does not correspond to present-day conditions of development in Germany. We take the view rather that the overriding interests of the German people in their present-day situation prescribe a different method for Germany, namely the method of establishing a democratic anti-Fascist régime, a parliamentary democratic republic with full democratic rights and liberties for the people."

Ulbricht then began to read out the charter of

the K.P.D., which was summarised under ten headings. These did not go beyond a general anti-Fascist programme. Marx and Engels were not even mentioned: the term "Socialism" did not occur.

First and foremost came the demand for the complete eradication of the relics of Hitler's régime, a purge of active Nazis from all official positions, and the punishment of all major war criminals; also for efforts to combat starvation, unemployment, and lack of housing; and for a transition to a normal existence and a restoration of production.

There were one or two surprises, as when Ulbricht read out the phrase: "Complete and unrestricted development of free commerce and private enterprise on the basis of private property."

Three further principles were the restoration of democratic liberties; the restoration of self-governing democratic institutions; and the democratic election of representatives from the manual workers, clerical workers and officials, together with the introduction of scales regulating conditions of pay and work. Besides this, there were also demands for the confiscation of all property belonging to Nazis and war criminals, the transfer of this property into the hands of self-governing institutions, a land reform, and the transfer into the hands of self-governing institutions of all businesses which had been abandoned by their owners.

The last two clauses of the proclamation were concerned with neighbourly co-existence with other peoples and recognition of the duty of reparation. The burden of reparation was to be equitably distributed, so that the rich carried the greater part of it. The proclamation ended with the statement that this programme of action could serve as the basis for the creation of a *bloc* of democratic anti-Fascist parties.

When Ulbricht finished reading the proclamation, at first all was silence in the hall. It was easy to see that, in particular, those of our comrades who had stayed in Germany through the Nazi period (and they were the majority in the audience) had expected something more from the proclamation. At that time free discussion still took place among Communists in Germany, and Party members would state their opinions without mincing matters. An official from Wedding spoke as follows:

"Comrade Ulbricht, right and necessary though this programme may be, on which point all of us here are in agreement, there is one point which is not clear to me. In what respect does it differ from the programme of any democratic party you care to name?"

Ulbricht grinned, and replied in a blunt Saxon accent: "You'll soon see, Comrade! Just wait a bit!"

After these words, which were spoken with a wink, our directives followed. First came the formation of a reliable corps of officials in the various districts and quarters of the town; then arrangements to ensure that Party meetings were summoned immediately after the issue of the proclamation; finally, the organisation of the meetings and the choice of leaders to be put before each meeting. All this was to be done, however, without causing too much stir before orders were issued by the Soviet occupation authorities permitting the formation of democratic anti-Fascist parties.

"How long have we got? When will parties be officially permitted?" people asked.

"We reckon the order will be issued on 10th June. We shall come out with our proclamation the following day, and probably the first number of our central newspaper, the *Deutsche Volkszeitung*, will appear on 13th June."

This meant that we had only three or four days. The Party meeting broke up and members went off to their own quarters of the town to get everything ready.

We were all required to speak at the first Party meetings. I shall never forget the inaugural meeting held in one of the quarters of Charlottenburg, at which I was the speaker. There were about a hundred and twenty Party members present, and one could see on their faces the pride and satisfaction and joy they felt at being members of the Communist Party again. At the end of my talk a discussion began, and soon there was mention of the excesses of the Red Army, which were then causing the Berlin Communists so much anxiety. At that moment, a member in the far corner got up to speak. He spoke vehemently about things which he himself had seen, about the damage done to German Communists by the conduct of the Red Army, and about the inevitable conclusions which German Communists must draw from this behaviour. This sort of language was quite new to us, and there was tense excitement in the hall. It may have been this atmosphere which led the speaker, from his deepest inner conviction, to express what he really thought: "And I tell you we've got to establish Socialism in

Germany without the Red Army and, if necessary, even against the Red Army!"

For a few seconds we all sat dumbfounded. Then one or two timid protests were heard from different directions, and then some more forcible ones. The Chairman immediately cut short the discussion of this theme, by calling on me to speak. I spoke with complete loyalty to the Party line.

"I hope that the opinions expressed by our colleague do not correspond to the view of those present. It is not our task to discuss the conduct of troops belonging to one of the occupation authorities, but only our own practical affairs."

At this there was loud applause from most of the audience and the discussion returned to Party commitments in the district. It was only on my way home that the phrase used came back to my mind: "We've got to establish Socialism without the Red Army and, if necessary, even against the Red Army!"

"Against the Red Army" was of course wrong, I thought that night. These words were due only to our colleague's excitement; but what about "without the Red Army?" After all, why not? Had it not been my own hope too that the development of Socialism in Western Europe would take a different course from that in the Soviet Union? Hadn't I formed this opinion as early as the spring of 1943, when the Comintern was dissolved? But I had little time to reflect on the matter, for the next few days were to eclipse everything that had hitherto seemed so eventful during these last few weeks in the Ulbricht Group.

When Marshal Zhukov's permission for the formation of democratic and anti-Fascist parties was issued on 10th June, the text of our proclamation was already set up and could go to press at any moment. Ulbricht turned to Erpenbeck and myself and said: "You'd better both be ready to work for a time on our new paper as long as we can spare you; but, Wolfgang, you mustn't stay there too long— there's another job waiting for you to do in the Party."

We went at once to the press, which was in a badly damaged building in the centre of the town. While we were getting things ready, Ackermann visited us shortly before the actual printing was to begin.

"Dahlem's coming to Berlin in the next few days. His signature has to be added to the proclamation."

"In which position?" (We had lived long enough in the Soviet Union to know that the order of names was not unimportant.)

"He's to come third, immediately after Ulbricht and before me."

Of the sixteen signatories of the proclamation, thirteen had spent the whole Hitler period as émigrés in the Soviet Union. Chief among them were Wilhelm Pieck, Walter Ulbricht, and Anton Ackermann. Among the former members of the Central Committee who had come back from Moscow there was also Hermann Matern, a former Communist provincial deputy from East Prussia; Gustav Sobottka, a former Communist provincial deputy from the Ruhr; Edwin Hörnle, a former Communist national deputy from Stuttgart, who was specially concerned with agricultural questions; the poet Johannes R. Becher; Elli Schmidt, formerly the wife of Anton Ackermann, who had signed the proclamation with her Moscow pseudonym of Irene Gartner; Marthe

Arendsee, a pleasant woman who had formerly been a militant colleague of Clara Zetkin; and Bernhard Koenen, who had once been my instructor at the Comintern School. From the Ulbricht Group only two, apart from Ulbricht himself, appeared as signatories of the proclamation: Otto Winzer and Hans Mahle.

In addition to the thirteen émigrés, there were the signatures of three Central Committee officials who had been active either clandestinely in Germany or in concentration camps. Two of them, Ottomar Geschke and Hans Jendretzki, had joined the Ulbricht Group early in May; the third, Franz Dahlem, had been released from a concentration camp by the Americans and was to join us in the next few days. Later developments were to show that a number of the signatories of the proclamation, such as Sobottka, Hörnle, Michael Niederkirchner and Marthe Arendsee, had been chosen principally because they were well known to Communists in Germany from the period before 1933. Later on, however, they were to play no role of any significance in the development of the Party.

The proclamation was hardly in the press before we had set to work on our next task, which was the issue of the *Deutsche Volkszeitung*. Paul Wandel, Fritz Erpenbeck and myself went off as soon as the printing presses were running. Our car stopped in front of a ruined building in the centre of the town —in Mauerstrasse, if I remember rightly.

"Is this where our editorial offices are to be?"

It did not look very cheerful. Consisting of a few bare rooms with a few tables and chairs and no windows, it had a wretched appearance. We had hardly inspected the rooms before we were greeted by a colleague who had been appointed a few days earlier to deal with the technical problems of the new newspaper. He seemed to be fairly competent. Thanks to him, the rooms were furnished to some extent the same day, and even bookcases and typewriters suddenly appeared in adequate quantities. An hour later we were joined by two typists, who had no doubt also been organised by our taciturn but energetic secretary for "technical matters."

Work could now begin. We quickly agreed what everyone was to write. My task was simply to read through the last year's issues of the newspaper *Free Germany*, and select from it anything that might be useful. No more than an hour later, a clatter of typewriters served to show that the editorial staff of the central newspaper of the K.P.D. was already in action.

It had been arranged that the first number of the *Deutsche Volkszeitung* should contain the inaugural proclamation of the K.P.D. On the same day I was given my first important editorial task: "We must print some opinions on the K.P.D. proclamation tomorrow, or the day after at the latest. Go round Berlin and note down what people are saying about the proclamation—but we don't want statements from Party members: just interview ordinary men in the street. There's a car you can take down below."

"At least it should be easier to interview men in the street than to appoint mayors," I said to myself as I set out.

It was only when I had gone a little way that my optimism was somewhat damped. What was I actually to do? Should I simply confront people with

a blunt question? After all, this was the first time in
my life that I had ever been a reporter—but a Party
job is a Party job. Wherever I saw people standing,
I stopped the car, boldly overcame my shyness, and
asked what they had to say about the inaugural proclamation of the Communist Party. The answers were
hopeless:

"What proclamation? What Party?"

"Never heard of a proclamation."

"What!—another Party? I had my bellyful of the
last lot."

"I'm not interested in proclamations. I'd like to
know where I can get some potatoes."

"Haven't you got anything better to do, young
man?"

Back in the car, I noted down all the replies; but
I might as well not have bothered. After I had spent
three hours going round six districts of Berlin to get
the required statements from people about the proclamation of the K.P.D., I gave it up in despair and
stopped despondently in front of the Charlottenburg
Town Hall. There I met one of the officials of the
district administration whom I had appointed myself, and told him of my predicament.

"Is it people with names and addresses you want
opinions from? Not Party members, just ordinary
people?"

"Yes—and if possible they ought to include mid-
dle-class people."

"O.K. I'll see to it."

Soon the answers he collected began to arrive.
He had taken my suggestion about the middle classes
too literally, and now I was sitting in the editorial
office anxiously studying a heap of opinions, all fa-

vourable, from master butchers, small industrialists, and craftsmen—from the neighbourhood of the Kurfürstendamm of all places—who seemed to be enthusiastic about the inaugural proclamation of the K.P.D. In a state of gloom, I wrote a long introduction and a long postscript, setting out everything that these people ought to have stated but had failed to. The article appeared under bombastic headlines, but my mind was made up never to be a reporter again.

The official announcement of the inaugural proclamation of the K.P.D. took place on 12th June, 1945, in the Great Chamber of Berlin Town Hall. About two hundred people attended on this occasion, including practically all members of the municipal administration and a number of other anti-Fascist officials. It was the first official political occasion in Berlin since the end of the war.

Walter Ulbricht and Gustav Dahrendorf were announced as speakers. Walter Ulbricht made a short speech welcoming the legalisation of democratic anti-Fascist parties and proposing the ten-point proclamation of the K.P.D., as a programme of action for the common front of democratic anti-Fascist parties. Next Gustav Dahrendorf, as representative of the future S.P.D., was called upon. In a brief and vigorous speech, Dahrendorf expressed the general desire of active anti-Fascists to create a united Socialist Party. Unfortunately, however, he went on, this was not possible because the representatives of the Communist Party had refused. What they wanted first was a period of political clarification before the question of unification could be posed. On this basis, the S.P.D. was going to reconstitute itself as an in-

dependent party, and it would come out in the next
few days with an inaugural proclamation.

There then followed a discussion, in which everyone who spoke expressed himself in favour of the
formation of a United Socialist Party. I returned to
the editorial offices and wrote out my report for the
Deutsche Volkszeitung. However, all references by
the speakers to the need for a United Socialist Party
were deleted.

The first official conference of executives of the
K.P.D. (our meetings with Communist officials at
Prinzenallee between the beginning of May and the
middle of June being regarded as purely informal)
took place on the 25th June in the building of the
Metropole Theatre in Berlin. It was summoned as a
conference of executive officials in Berlin, but more
than a third of the Party members taking part in this
conference came from the province of Brandenburg.
An hour before the conference began, there were
happy scenes of reunion on all sides. Comrades who
had not met for years flung their arms round each
other. I myself saw all the new friends I had made in
the course of innumerable meetings and conferences
since the early days of May, 1945. As I was going
through the Great Hall looking for a seat, my friend
Roman Chvalek signalled to me, and I went and sat
beside him.

Then the first meeting of executive officials of the
K.P.D. opened with some classical music, played
by the theatre orchestra. This had certainly been
organised deliberately, to serve as an example to Party
members for future Party conferences and demonstrations. It was as if to relegate to the past the rather
rowdy character of pre-1933 K.P.D. meetings, and

to emphasise the new and more serious line of 1945.

In moving terms Ottomar Geschke declared open the first conference of executive officials of the K.P.D. to be held in Greater Berlin since 1933. I saw tears in the eyes of Roman Chvalek sitting next to me; and it was with difficulty that he controlled his sobbing. It was the same with several others, especially those who had spent the Nazi period in concentration camps. Ulbricht, on the other hand, showed no signs of emotion. I sensed a sharp contrast between the dry tone of his speech and the feelings of most of our colleagues present.

He spoke about the conditions which had made possible the victory of the Soviet Union in its struggle against Hitlerite Germany; he explained that the Soviet Union was the most advanced state in the world from the political, economic and military point of view. He particularly emphasised the need for a recognition of guilt and responsibility on the part of the German people, if it were to break with the reactionary past and find a new path. He referred bluntly to the cession of the territories east of the Oder-Neisse line and told us to consolidate our co-operation with the Allied occupation authorities. He defined the fundamental orientation of the party, in conformity with the directives we had already had in Moscow, and the task of completing the bourgeois-democratic revolution of 1848 and establishing a democratic anti-Fascist régime. In doing this he set himself in opposition to the views of those workers who wanted to establish Socialism immediately. He spoke of the serious desire to create a new relation of mutual trust between Communists and Socialists, but expressed himself against the immediate formation of a united socialist party. Before that could happen, certain pre-requisites were necessary, in particular an informed comprehension on the part of the most advanced forces in the working class and the labouring population of the meaning of Socialism in the Soviet Union and the Marxist-Leninist philosophy of life.

Ulbricht then gave a new definition of the Communist Party, which I knew to have been worked out by Fred Oelssner. Instead of the old formulæ current before 1933, which spoke of the Party of the "revolutionary proletariat," the terms now used referred to a National Party, the Party of the People and the Party of Peace. The Party was to include the best men and women of all classes in the active population, and all sincere opponents of Fascism. Ulbricht was critical of the fact that in many areas comparatively few Party members had been admitted, and in many cases the Party leadership had set up impossible conditions for admission to the Party: this was a grave mistake. Unmistakable sounds of astonishment were to be heard in the hall as Ulbricht declared: "In admitting people to the Party it must not make any difference at all whether the anti-Fascists concerned are Catholic, Evangelical or Jewish in their religius affiliations."

When Ulbricht had finished his speech and the International had been sung, many of those present raised their fists in the old salute of the Red Front, which Party members had used before 1933. Ulbricht, together with his colleagues on the Presidium and those present who were already familiar with the new line, did not do so. Many others thereupon lowered their arms again. It was a small but typical example of the change which had taken place in the K.P.D. since 1933. What had been a revolutionary party of the opposition, with the dictatorship of the proletariat as its objective, had now turned into a party bearing the authority of the state, which was about to embark on an anti-Fascist democratic system aimed at achieving parliamentary democracy.

CHAPTER EIGHT

An Official
in the S.E.D. Central Secretariat

ONE SUNNY MORNING in July, 1945, twelve large heavy lorries were standing in front of No. 80 Prinzenallee. They were to remove the essential furniture to equip our new Party building. The original intention had been to re-equip the former Karl Liebknecht House as the Central Party Headquarters of the K.P.D.; but this proved impossible, so the decision fell on a larger building at No. 76-79 Wallstrasse, in the centre of Berlin.

On the first floor were to be the officers of the four most senior officials—Wilhelm Pieck, Walter Ulbricht, Franz Dahlem and Anton Ackermann. The carpenters were already at work. Wilhelm Pieck, who had once been a joiner, and was not yet President but only an official, and visibly delighted to be back in Berlin, had put on overalls and was helping them himself. I have rarely seen him so happy as at that time.

Within a week the removal from No. 80 Prinzenallee to our new Party building was complete. The allocation of tasks followed almost at once. Of the "big four," Wilhelm Pieck was responsible for overall control and general political questions; Walter Ulbricht for economic questions, agriculture, trade unions and official administration: Franz Dahlem for Party organisation; and Anton Ackermann for culture, the press, education, public relations and Party training.

Even before the building was completely ready, Anton Ackermann sent for me one day and said: "We thought of making you deputy head of the Press Office of the Central Committee. Would you like that?"

"Yes, of course, very much. Who is to be the head of it?"

"We haven't got one yet, so for the time being you will be alone there."

I got the impression of being in charge of a section which was given responsibility for everything that other sections did not want to undertake. It also became the general practice to send my way Soviet representatives who wanted a general look at things—and there were not a few of them. Several times a day I had to explain patiently to visitors the significance of the inaugural proclamation, the objectives of the United Anti-Fascist Democratic Front, the reconstruction of the trade unions and the general policy line. Besides this, I had to take part in conferences, carry out special missions, travel with Ulbricht or Ackermann, translate internal documents from Russian, and prepare reports for the Central Office or drafts of speeches.

One afternoon Ulbricht sent for me. "Arrange your work so that you can be entirely free tomorrow: you're coming with me to Brandenburg."

When I arrived at the Central Committee building the following morning, Ulbricht was ready to start. He introduced me briefly to two senior Soviet economic officials: "We're going with these two comrades."

A few minutes later we were on the road, in the two magnificent cars which were then at the disposal of the Central Committee. Ulbricht briefly explained our purpose while we were on the way. "There are a few questions we have to look into about delivery targets for agricultural produce, and land reform."

At various places in the province of Brandenburg, notably Kyritz, we had talks with the Commandants, the Mayors and the agricultural economic experts. I was amazed to see how well-informed Ulbricht was on the minutest details of the regulations governing delivery of produce in the Nazi period; but I was still more astonished to see our two Soviet companions, both of whom spoke fluent German, open their brief-cases and put on the table bundles of proformas, instructions and documents bearing on the same subject. There was a particularly animated interchange with two experts of the former National Agricultural Board. Ulbricht was familiar with every last detail; one question followed another, and the ex-officials of the National Agricultural Board answered briefly and to the point. Ulbricht seemed to be entirely in his element, as always when he was dealing with the practical matters of organisation.

Before we left Kyritz there was a last conference between Ulbricht and the two officers.

"Things are quite clear now," said one of the two officers. "We can submit the appropriate proposals. Perhaps it wouldn't be a bad thing, though, to stop in one or two of the smaller places, and have a

talk with a few of the peasants about the land reform."

So on the way back from Kyritz to Berlin, we
stopped in one small village, where the mayor was
rather taken aback by his distinguished guests.

"Could we get all the villagers together?" asked
Ulbricht.

"Of course."

"How long would that take, approximately?"

"Our village isn't a big one—they could all be here
in a quarter of an hour."

Within twenty minutes the villagers were assembled. A few of them mumbled something which
sounded like "Good day." Most of them just looked
at us with distrust.

Ulbricht put a few questions about the harvest
and the delivery regulations, but only two or three
of those present replied, and that after long hesitation,
monosyllabically. Several of them looked suspici-
ously at the two Soviet officers standing in a corner
of the room. It was only when these two smiled in a
friendly way, put a number of questions in fluent
German, and offered the peasants cigarettes, that
they began to take part more readily in the general
conversation. Gradually the villagers began to talk
of their own accord, about the productivity of the
soil. Then Ulbricht steered the conversation towards the real object: the land reform. He spoke of
the redistribution of the great estates, and explained
that the peasants would be getting more land.

"Now, let's hear what you think of that?"

They looked at us doubtfully again. At first there
was complete silence. Finally, one of the villagers

made a start: "Yes, it wouldn't be bad to have some more land."

When the mayor had explained the proposal again, a few of the other villagers expressed their agreement. The more silent ones let it be understood, by nodding their heads, that they too agreed. It was not exactly how I had pictured to myself the enthusiastic assent of the peasants to the land reform, but at least everyone present had expressed his agreement after a fashion.

I would gladly have stayed longer with the villagers, but Ulbricht looked at his watch, and the two Soviet officers also wanted to be on the way. I had expected that we would stop in other villages to test the feeling, but Ulbricht and the two Soviet officers did not regard that as necessary. We arrived back in Berlin in the evening, and within a few days I realised that as a result of this trip the introduction of the land reform in the Soviet Zone of Occupation of Germany had been decided upon.

"To-day we've got to work overtime," Ackermann said to me, a few days later. He gave me a Russian typescript to translate, and asked me to have each page brought to him as soon as it was ready. It was the draft law on land reform, and it was to come into effect immediately the law was promulgated. The process was to be completed by the end of October, 1945.

About two weeks after the proclamation of the land reform, there was a meeting of the Central Committee, with an enlarged attendance which included myself. At that time the *apparat* was still small, and business was conducted without much formality. Twenty-five to thirty officials sat round

the table in the middle of the committee room of the
Central Committee, with Wilhelm Pieck and Walter
Ulbricht at the head. The chief subject of the meeting was the land reform. Officials reported one after
another on the situation in their particular districts.
There were no reservations about what was said in
this circle: one got an unvarnished picture of
what was happening, both in areas where the land
reform was going through successfully, and also of
defects, mistakes and failures.

I recall an altercation that occurred after about
two hours' discussion. My former instructor at the
Comintern School, Bernhard Koenen, who was at
that time Party Chairman in Sachsen-Anhalt, had
finished his report on land reform, and then went on:
"In conclusion, I should like to submit a rather important request, which is directly connected with
the land reform. At the Leuna Works there are two
plants due to be dismantled which are essential for
the production of artificial manure. I should like
to ask whether it is not possible to arrange for these
two plants to be exempted from dismantling."

"This meeting has nothing to do with dismantling," Ulbricht interrupted him.

"But I really must draw your attention to the importance of this type of production in relation to the
land reform. Very thorough precautions have been
taken to ensure that nothing can be produced having even the most indirect connection with war
material. The workers themselves have given under-
takings to this effect at their meetings."

"I have already said that this question is irrelevant
here!" said Ulbricht, this time in a sharper and more
peremptory tone.

Still Bernhard Koenen would not let himself be silenced. "It isn't so—we must reach a solution of this question here. I have solemnly promised the workers to make every effort to see that these two workshops, which have nothing to do with war production and are exclusively devoted to artificial manure . . ."

But Ulbricht would not let him finish. "I don't want to hear anything more on the subject—we will deal with it elsewhere in another context!" he shouted menacingly.

Bernhard Koenen said no more. The threat had worked. Nothing more was ever said about the two workshops at the Leuna Works.

The meeting went on, but this exchange of words impressed itself deeply upon my memory. Once again, as in 1942 over the self-criticism and the expulsions at the Comintern School, and in May, 1945, at the first meeting between Ulbricht and the Berlin Communists, I found myself on the side of the official who felt an affinity with the life of the workers, rather than on that of the *apparatchik* who simply carried out orders from above.

One day—I do not remember exactly when—Ulbricht sent for me and said: "To-morrow there's to be a conference at Karlshorst, at which the Prime Ministers of the provincial Governments and the heads of the central administrations will be present. I should like you to go there and take notes of what happens, and give me as exact an account as possible in the evening."

Ulbricht gave me a pass, and I was introduced to the Soviet Liaison Officer. Next day, after going through the various control posts, I was led into the meeting hall, where the conference had already begun. At the table on the platform sat Marshal Zhukov, surrounded by five or six Soviet generals, who became identified in the course of the conference as the Soviet plenipotentiaries in the different regions and provinces. There were thirty or forty people present, including the regional Prime Ministers and heads of the administrations.

A few minutes after my arrival one of the regional Prime Ministers got up to make his speech, and began: "I cannot begin my report without first expressing our gratitude to the illustrious Soviet Army . . ."

He was interrupted by Marshal Zhukov: "None of that please—we're not at a public meeting here! Please confine yourself to a report on your sphere of competence, so we can get on with things."

The Prime Minister swallowed and broke off. I was as astonished as he was. I had never before attended an occasion at which one was interrupted on referring to the heroic Red Army. The Prime Minister soon recovered himself and abandoned his further panegyrics. Zhukov and the other generals listened attentively, and occasionally Zhukov interrupted with questions. His favourite question was: "What exactly are you proposing to do to put it right?"

The next speaker was Ferdinand Friedensburg, then head of the Central Fuel Administration. At the end of his report he said: "I should like to draw your attention, Marshal, to one difficulty which is holding up our work. The production of fuel is being jeopardised by the Commandants not carrying

out standing instruction, but issuing other instructions of their own."

"What Commandants?" asked Marshal Zhukov.
"Do you mean the District Commanders?"

"No, I mean the Soviet Military Representatives
in the factories, who call themselves Commandants
and are treated as such."

"You can take my word for it, Herr Friedensburg,
that we will do everything possible to prevent ob-
struction by Soviet authorities in their spheres of
work and to ensure that the development of the fuel-
producing industries is carried out according to
plan. I shall find out exactly what the factory Commandants are up to."

His words made me thoughtful. I had no doubt
of his goodwill, but I also knew the structure of the
Soviet system well enough to be sure that there were
offices which were not subordinate to Marshal Zhukov's chain of command but to the appropriate
economic authorities in Moscow; and I also knew
of the antagonism between the different Soviet
authorities.

It was only a few days since I had been driving
through the Soviet Sector of Berlin with an officer
of the Political Administration of the Red Army. As
we passed a group of new residential houses he waved
his hand in their direction, and said: "That's where
the enemy lives!"

"Who—the Nazis?" I asked.

"No, worse still—our own reparations gang!"

Mass Production of Training Manuals

In the second half of October, 1945, I was sent
for by Franz Dahlem. "Fred Oelssner tells me that

our party training section is in difficulties," he said. "The comrade they've got to prepare the weekly training material is plainly not up to the job. The next booklet has to be ready in six days. Couldn't you write it, just this once?"

"What's the subject?"

"The title is *The 28th Anniversary of the October Revolution*."

"Fine—I'll do that."

Without dreaming of the consequences of helping them out in this way, I wrote the booklet they wanted and took the lecture for the training instructors in the Berlin Party organisation. As a result of doing both jobs satisfactorily, my future Party career was for the time being settled. From that day on I gave up my position as Deputy Head of the Press Section in the Central Committee, and was appointed as the editor responsible for the Party's educational material.

The task of Party training was under the general control of Fred Oelssner, who had arrived in Berlin in July, 1945, with Wilhelm Pieck. I had already met him in Moscow, where he was known as Larev and was working as editor-in-chief of German broadcasts on Moscow Radio. Like Ackermann, he had been at the Lenin School in Moscow.

My first discussion of my work with Fred Oelssner was brief.

"Your job is simply to see that the manuscript of the training booklet is ready on time every week."

"When will I be given the subject?"

"The subjects are settled at a general meeting with Ackermann, at which you will take part, about te~ days before each booklet goes to press."

So every week I had to devote myself to a new training subject. In rapid succession I wrote on the Party's work in the provinces, on the consumer co-operatives, on food policy, on equality for women, on school reform, on the establishment of the Party's organisation, and on the struggle against militarism and reactionary Prussianism.

After a time, Anton Ackermann took over the censorship of my work. Of all the censors I had so far experienced he was the most agreeable. As the booklets had to go to press every Monday morning, it soon became a habit for me to visit Ackermann at his villa in Niederschönhausen every Sunday evening to have dinner with him. He would look through the booklet and pass it for the press with his initials: "A.A."

Every Monday morning I was visited by a representative of the Dietz Publishing Company, who practically tore the manuscript out of my hand. Often he would prepare it for the press in my presence, and write at the top on the left the number 120,000, which was the size of the edition in which the training booklets were then produced.

Apart from the weekly evenings for training, there were also regional Party schools being set up in the autumn of 1945—in Mecklenburg, Brandenburg, Sachsen-Anhalt, Sachsen, Thüringen and Berlin. They were generally established in castles that used to belong to big landlords. These regional schools took sixty to eighty students on courses lasting four weeks.

The weekly evenings of training and the Party boarding schools had various different tasks, but they were contributing to a single unified policy. The evenings of political training were designed to re-educate the older members of the K.P.D., who had returned to the Party after 1945, to the new line and their new tasks; and also to familiarise the new and younger forces, now streaming into the Communist Party, with the Party's way of thought. On the other hand, the purpose of the Party boarding schools, which were steadily increasing in number, was to educate the new generation of officials.

One Sunday evening in November, 1945, I was with Anton Ackermann at Niederschönhausen. I noticed that as he went through the training booklet his attention was not entirely on it. He seemed cheerful and excited, and his thoughts were far away. After he had passed the manuscript for the press, he began to talk at once on the subject which was completely filling his thoughts at the time, and certainly not only then.

"We're on the brink of an important reformulation of some of our fundamental theses," he told me, and went on to speak of the new situation since the Second World War; of the possibility of taking new roads to Socialism, and of finding one's own road on the basis of present-day conditions instead of following the course of the October Revolution in Russia. He read me out the manuscript of an article half of which he had just completed that evening.

Ackermann's starting point was that Karl Marx had envisaged a revolutionary transition to Socialism only in the continental countries. In England and America at that date, on the other hand, he regarded a peaceful, democratic transition to Socialism as possible because these countries already enjoyed a bourgeois-democratic form of Government, without any marked degree of militarism or a vast bureaucracy. From these premises, Anton Ackermann drew the conclusion that it would be erroneous to deny "in all circumstances, in all countries, and at all times" the possibility of a peaceful transition to Socialism.

Ackermann went on to argue that in Germany since 1945 the possibility of such peaceful development did exist. His article concluded with an argument which I had long accepted, but had never dared to express openly: that it was imperative to take an independent road to Socialism, quite distinct from that of Russia. With a smile of satisfaction, Ackermann read out: "It was no less an authority than Lenin who emphasised that it would be a great mistake to exaggerate the general applicability of the Russian experience, or to extend it beyond more than a few features of our (i.e., the Russian) Revolution. In this sense we must unquestionably give our assent to the concept of a separate German road to Socialism."

Finally Ackermann indicated, if only in relatively cautious terms, some of the differences between Socialist development in Germany and that in Russia. Russia in 1917 had been far behind the more advanced countries. In Germany, on the other hand, it would be possible to restore a high level of production fairly quickly, and there was an incomparably greater number of qualified experts than in Russia in 1917. "This difference may work in the direction of making our labours relatively less severe in comparison with the sacrifices which had to be borne by the Russian people in order to achieve Socialism. These are circumstances in which the in-

crease of prosperity under Socialism can be ac-
celerated."

He went on to argue that in contrast with Russia
in 1917 the working class in Germany represented
the majority of the total population. "This will also
be of great importance after the victory of the
workers' forces in Germany, since it will mitigate
the domestic political struggle, reduce the burden
of sacrifices, and hasten the evolution of a Socialist
democracy."

This official change of the Party line on a question of such decisive importance enabled us to see
many things in a completely different light. We now
saw the interventions of the Red Army of Occupation, the dismantling, and the political control exercised by Soviet officers, as merely temporary manifestations of a period of transition which would last
only a few years. It was troublesome, but it would
soon be over; and then, so I hoped and believed, the
day would come when the occupying powers would
withdraw altogether and the German Socialists
would be free from foreign tutelage to find their own
road to Socialism, in accordance with their own
traditions and conditions.

My mind was still full of these new hopes as I
went back to my billet in Pankow at four o'clock
in the morning. At last, I thought, what I had always
longed for was now to become reality—an independent road to Socialism, free of the features which had
so often worried me in the Soviet Union. A few weeks
later, in December, 1945, Ackermann's article appeared under the title "Is there a separate German
road to Socialism?" The article had the effect of a
bombshell. Apart from a very small number of offi-

cials, who were 100% supporters of Moscow and who were entirely against the new idea, his thesis brought great relief to everyone. At last, we all thought, the way had been found. We had not, it was true, openly dissociated ourselves from measures taken by the Soviet occupation authorities, but something else had happened which we thought much more significant and profound at the time. This was a fundamental divergence from the course of development in the Soviet Union.

So Ackermann's Theses began their triumphant march through the Party.

The Campaign for Unity

The theory of a separate German road to Socialism played an important part, especially among officials, in the great campaign for unification in the Soviet Zone of Germany. At the time of the foundation of the S.P.D. and the K.P.D. in June, 1945, Ulbricht had rejected all proposals for a United Socalist Party on the grounds that organizational unification must be preceded by a process of idological clarification. Thereafter, both parties set about building up their organisational machinery. There was no doubt that we in the K.P.D. had the advantage. We had been able to set up our organisations in the towns and villages before the S.P.D.; our material resources were greater, and the circulation of our newspapers larger; and we had—what was particularly important in this early period of organisational work—more cars at our disposal, so that we were able to establish more rapid communication with the village organisations.

Soviet support was by no means limited to preferential treatment in the provision of technical assistance. The K.P.D. also enjoyed an unconcealed preference from the occupation authorities in political matters. On the other hand, Soviet officials would also intervene directly in the internal affairs of the S.P.D., to silence any critical or independent voice by means of political pressure and intimidation. Nevertheless, it was soon obvious that the S.P.D. was developing considerably more rapidly than the K.P.D. leadership had been able to do in June, 1945. The growth of the K.P.D. was unimpressive by comparison. In more and more villages our membership was being outstripped by that of the Social Democrats.

Eventually, in November, 1945, the great campaign for unification began. Unity became the universal slogan, and at every conference the question of unification was put at the top of the agenda. This was necessary because in the early weeks there was a good deal of hostility among members of the K.P.D. to the idea of unification with the Social Democrats and the creation of a united party. Our principal task in the training section was to bring our fellow members finally into line, all the more so because some of them were by no means enthusiastic about the new slogans.

The more disciplined members of the Communist Party adapted themselves fairly quickly to the new situation. For our younger colleagues there was anyway no difficulty about the new course: they quickly assimilated the idea of unity. But the Social Democrats at that time only agreed to unification on condition that the question should be put to a National Assembly of the whole Social Democratic

Party. Those members and officials of the K.P.D. who were accustomed to thinking independently found a new hope in the phraseology about an "independent German Socialist Party" and the explicit recognition of the right to free expression of opinion on the part of all Party members. One often heard it said at that time that in the new Party many things would be very, very different from the former K.P.D.

On 26th February, 1946, there took place a joint conference of the Party leaders of the S.P.D. and the K.P.D. in the Soviet Zone. At this conference, attended by thirty leading representatives of both Parties, it was decided to summon a Party meeting to carry out the unification on 21st-22nd April. At the same time a draft of the principles, objects and charter of the future S.E.D. was given out.

Our whole effort was now devoted to unification. The mass education unit, at that time under Rudolph Dölling (later head of the political administration of the People's Police) was strengthened, and leaflets and placards were printed non-stop. My training manuals were now confined to the one subject of unity. Not a single meeting or assembly or conference, whatever the purpose for which it was summoned, was allowed to go by without finally adopting a resolution demanding the immediate unification of the K.P.D. and the S.P.D. Stacks of these resolutions poured into the Central Committee and the editorial offices of the *Deutsche Volkszeitung*.

In the middle of the hectic excitement of the campaign for unification, all members of the staff of the agitation and propaganda section were suddenly summoned to Fred Oelssner. On the table we saw large coloured designs of the flag and badge of the future S.E.D.

"These are first suggestions for our new emblems," he said. "We commissioned a number of draughtsmen to design an emblem for the S.E.D., with a symbol of clasped hands." In front of us we saw eight or ten designs of a round badge, with clasped hands and the words "Socialist Unity Party of Germany."

"I have my doubts," said one of our officials who had been in a German concentration camp. "I don't like a round emblem. It might remind people of the Nazi symbol."

New instructions were given to the artists, and a few days later we found ourselves faced with another row of designs. The one we liked best had the clasped hands against a white background, but again we could not all agree. Otto Grotewohl, who used to paint in his spare time, proposed having a red flag in the background. The idea met with general approval, and again the artists set to work. At our next meeting the composition of the Party badge was at last agreed. In the middle there was to be a red flag on a white background, and in front of it the clasped hands in gold. Round the border on a steel-gray background, also in gold, were to be the words: "Socialist Unity Party of Germany." We now had a charter, a statement of our programme, and a badge. Only one thing was missing: the United Party. All efforts were now concentrated on setting up the S.E.D. throughout the Zone and in Berlin by the appointed date.

By this time opposition within the S.P.D. to an immediate organisational unification had become visibly stronger. Distrust of the K.P.D. was on the increase. Although open manifestations of this opposition were impossible in the Zone, in Berlin the Social Democrat opponents of amalgamation carried out a plebiscite of all their members. This was fixed for 31st March, 1946. The S.P.D. Central Committee of the day, under Grotewohl's leadership, had accepted unification and therefore rejected the plebiscite: and in the Soviet Sector it was actually forbidden by the Soviet Commandant. This last decision was criticised by some Communist Party officials known to me.

"There are naturally grave doubts in the S.P.D. about unification," said one of my colleagues, "but to veto such an expression of opinion will only sharpen the opinion against unification. Let our Social Democrat comrades decide the matter for themselves." I entirely agreed with him.

As a result of the veto, only 32,547 members of the S.P.D. in the Western sectors of Berlin were able to vote. The following were the results of the vote: 2,937 in favour of immediate unification of the S.P.D. and the K.P.D.; 14,763 for an alliance between the S.P.D. and the K.P.D. to guarantee a common effort and fraternal struggle; 5,559 against any unification or alliance. It was indisputable that the overwhelming majority of Berlin's Social Democrats had expressed themselves against immediate amalgamation.

When this result became known at the Central Committee of the K.P.D., we received instructions for a further intensification of the campaign for unification. Conferences and meetings followed each other in rapid succession. At many of them a real enthusiasm prevailed with a hope that the unhappy division would at last be overcome and that the new Party would unite the best traditions of both Parties. There was, it is true, also some pressure exerted on the many Social Democrats who were opposed to unification, but even we in the *agitprop* section of the Central Committee were left very much in the dark about these proceedings. At that time I only came to know of one case of the arrest of an opponent of unification from the ranks of the Social Democrats. This case, which took place in the district of Prenzlauer Berg, caused a very great stir among many officials of the Berlin Party leadership. "These Russians with their arrests! They do us nothing but harm. If a few odd officials don't want unification, one can just leave them aside for the time being. It won't take long for them to convince themselves of the justification for a United Party afterwards."

We still had great illusions at that date!

The Foundation of the S.E.D.

At ten o'clock on the morning of 21st April, 1946, the meeting to unite the two parties began in the Admirals-Palast in Berlin. More than a thousand delegates and hundreds of guests streamed into the building for the first joint party meeting of the Communists and Social Democrats. Thousands of people had gathered in front of the building, not as a result of any organisation on this occasion, but from spontaneous interest and sympathy. They waved and shouted encouragement at us. At last we were all in our places. Communists and Social Democrats sat mixed up together, greeting those they already knew and introducing themselves to those they had not previously met. The orchestra played the overture to

Beethoven's *Fidelio*. A few minutes later Wilhelm Pieck and Otto Grotewohl came on to the platform from opposite sides, met in the middle, and shook hands amid a storm of applause which went on for several minutes.

"As we came on to the platform," said Grotewohl, "I was struck by the symbolic significance of what we were doing. Wilhelm Pieck came from the left, I came from the right, but both of us came to meet here in the middle."

The delegates leapt to their feet and roared their applause. Whatever may have happened later, on this morning of 21st April, 1946, a real and spontaneous enthusiasm prevailed among them.

It was announced from the platform that Comrade Amborn from Lepizig would next make a presentation, together with a brief explanation. Towards the back of the meeting a delegate stood up and advanced slowly through the hall to the platform. In his hand he held a large wooden club of menacing appearance. When at last he reached the table on the platform, before the astonished eyes of the delegates, he solemnly presented the great stick to Grotewohl, who held out one end to Pieck, so that both of them were holding it simultaneously.

This was a memento of August Bebel, explained Amborn, the delegate from Leipzig. Bebel had cut the stick himself and had had it with him when he presided over the Erfurt Congress in 1890. At the end of the congress he had given it to Comrade Paul Reisshaus for safe keeping. Reisshaus had been an advocate of unity; he wanted to put the stick at the disposal of a Party Congress when, and only when, unity had been achieved.

"As Comrade Reisshaus's executor," said Amborn, "I felt it my duty to hand over this stick to this Party meeting, or rather to the new presiding authorities of the United Party." (Amborn, a veteran member of the Social Democratic Party, was arrested shortly after the foundation of the S.E.D. by the M.V.D. for the offence of "Social Democratism.")

Although this interlude was of course pre-arranged, Wilhelm Pieck appeared to be visibly moved. Did he recall his own youth in the German workers' movement? Did he still feel sentimental links with that period, despite all his re-education and Party discipline and life as an expatriate in the Soviet Union? I knew Wilhelm Pieck well enough to be able to distinguish between real and feigned feelings.

Next Grotewohl called upon Wilhelm Pieck to speak. Pieck listed all the reasons in favour of unification, and referred to the conferences and decisions which had preceded the present meeting. He said that the object must be a complete fusion, so that it was no longer possible to distinguish who was a Social Democrat and who a Communist. He called on all delegates and Party members to cultivate still further the spirit of comradeship, friendship and mutual tolerance.

Grotewohl also spoke without using the party jargon, which has nowadays become an essential element in the S.E.D. He spoke vigorously and without dogmatism of the present and future of Germany, with a flow of brilliant phrases. He explained that the S.E.D. rejected anti-Bolshevism but "this rejection is far removed from a surrender of our internal affairs to foreign influences." The loudest applause of the whole assembly was earned by Grotewohl's statement:

"I do not think it is presumptuous, and I do not think that the Soviet occupation authorities will take it amiss, if I make it clear at this point that, at least in the Soviet Zone of Occupation, the Socialist Unity Party which we have to-day created represents, thanks to its immense political strength, a guarantee of our stability in the Soviet Zone to an extent which makes us no longer dependent on the bayonets of the Russians."

The roar of applause and enthusiastic clapping which went on for several minutes at this, was an expression of the hope that with the foundation of the S.E.D., the German Socialists would soon be masters in their own house, so that they could then set out on an independent road to Socialism, founded on their own traditions.

Grotewohl laid special emphasis on the need for personal freedom in the new Party. He said that the Party had the duty to develop and encourage the free personality. "In no other German Party was there so warm and staunch a respect for human rights as in the Socialist Unity Party."

Then came the climax—the voting on the programme, the charter and the decision to create the S.E.D. By this time Ulbricht had taken the chair. In a loud voice, with his characteristically Saxon accent, he read out the resolution on unification:

"On the 19th-20th April, 1946, the Fortieth Party Congress of the Social Democratic Party of Germany and the Fifteenth Party Congress of the Communist Party of Germany decided by common consent to unite the two workers' parties. The Social

Democratic Party of Germany and the Communist Party of Germany constitute themselves henceforth as the Socialist Unity Party of Germany."

Thunderous applause at first prevented Ulbricht from going on. At last he succeeded in continuing: "All in favour of the resolution on unification, please show your cards." The vote of approval was unanimous. Together we sang the song, "Brothers, to the sun, to freedom." The S.E.D. was founded.

In the evening all the delegates and many officials gathered for a winding-up celebration at the Friedrichstadt Palace. This building, which could hold three thousand people, was filled to the last square inch, and hundreds of comrades stood at the entrances. Thus this day which had been so eventful for us came to an end on a note of hope. Everything seemed to point to the fulfillment of our wishes: the equal composition of the leadership; the admonitory words about comradeship and mutual confidence which Pieck had addressed to the Communists; Grotewohl's insistence on freedom of the personality in the new Party; the thesis of a separate German road to Socialism, which has now found its echo in the S.E.D. programme; and Grotewohl's hints of the possibility of an early end to Soviet occupation.

Little could I guess that evening that, of the participants at the assembly to unite the two parties, more than half would within a few years have been expelled from their posts, degraded, falsely accused, or eliminated by purges.

The First Elections

For the past four months our whole effort had been

exclusively devoted to making the unification a
reality. Now the Socialist Unity Party really existed.
What next?

Officials like ourselves, for whom life without constant political activity and campaigning was hardly
conceivable, began to have a feeling of emptiness.
For the first time, there was nothing for us to do apart
from routine jobs. Several weeks went by. In the
Party schools and subordinate Party organisations a
noticeable decline of enthusiasm was to be detected. For a Party such as ours nothing could be
more dangerous than a few weeks of peace, or the
want of an immediate task to keep everyone up to
the mark.

It was not till the second half of June that new
tasks came our way. In September the first local
elections were to be held, and then on 20th October,
1946, the elections for the provincial parliaments,
and in all four sectors of the City of Berlin.

As the date of the elections drew near, the S.E.D.
authorities published an announcement clarifying
their attitude towards what were known as "nominal
Nazis." This statement had been prepared a long
time beforehand. In private, the decisive argument
in the S.E.D.'s attitude was that we must not repeat
the errors of the Austrian Communist Party in the
elections of autumn, 1945, when our Austrian comrades had been carried away by their crude anti-
Nazism to the point of rejecting the great mass of
minor Nazis, and thus isolating themselves from the
population as a whole. Officially, however, the argument was that "the S.E.D. considers the time has
arrived to incorporate those who were nothing more
than simple members or fellow-travellers of the for-

mer Nazi Party into the democratic structure." This led, however, to a storm of angry protest in our own ranks, going far beyond anything we had expected. Whatever subject might be announced for discussion at Party meetings, without fail the first speaker would start angrily on the question of the Nazis.

There was only one thing to be done: education. At once the S.E.D. began to organise and encourage meetings with former "nominal Nazis." Many officials said that this was really going too far, but others were very favourably impressed by these meetings. They said there were some splendid people among them, who would do well with us—vigorous, constructive and not inclined to grumble.

Waldemar Schmidt, who had almost ten years of concentration camps behind him, came home one evening very amused from one of these meetings with "nominal Nazis."

"I've seen a lot in my time," he said, "but I should never have dreamed of anything like this. They're downright enthusiastic about the S.E.D.'s announcement. One of them made a very excitable speech and ended up with a slogan he had invented himself." Waldemar Schmidt looked at me and said with a mischievous smile: "You've made up a lot of slogans. What do you think his was?"

I suggested several possibilities, but he only shook his head. "No, our nominal Nazi's slogan was much better. He shouted out: 'Long live the S.E.D.—the little Nazi's greatest friend!' "

As soon as the uneasiness over our new Party line towards the "nominal Nazis" had died down, our Party members and officials turned all their efforts to the election campaign. Despite all their efforts, however, the S.E.D. received on the average less than half of the votes cast. Out of a total of 519 deputies elected to the regional parliaments in the Soviet Zone, only 249 belonged to the S.E.D. There was some help from the mass organisations, for 12 out of their 16 deputies were members of the S.E.D., thus bringing the actual total of S.E.D. deputies up to 261. This gave the S.E.D. a narrow overall majority in the regional parliament of the Soviet Zone. The electoral regulations provided that the next local election should take place two years later, in 1948, and the next district and regional parliamentary elections three years later, in 1949. "By the next elections, things will go better," said many of the more optimistic officials after 20th October, 1946: but there were no next elections. The elections of October, 1946, were the first and the last in the Soviet Zone at which a political choice was open to the electors. From that time onwards there were only single lists.

We realised that the regional elections in the Soviet Zone were only a preliminary. The real decision would be made at the Berlin elections on 20th October, 1946. I spent the night of the 20th-21st October at the editorial offices of *Neues Deutschland*. Every report came in here, and we could at once form the best possible picture of what was going on. In expectation of our victory at the elections, huge loud-speakers had been put up in front of the editorial building to publish the results to the crowds assembled outside. Soon the reports came in: one piece of bad news after another. Our faces became longer and longer. The announcer who was to publish the results to the crowds waiting outside was tearing his hair. Despairingly he tried to pick out from the flow of reports such as were favourable to the S.E.D. With every few minutes that passed, the situation grew worse. The first reports to be put together showed a catastrophic defeat for the S.E.D. and a gigantic victory for the S.P.D., which only six months before we had been referring to as the "Zehlendorf Hospital Club" and in the last few weeks as the "S.P.D. splinter."

We heard the final results in the early hours of the morning. The Social Democratic Party had received 48.7% of the votes; the Christian Democratic Union, 22.1%: the S.E.D., 19.8%; and the Liberal Democratic Party, 9.4%. The cause of our defeat was perfectly clear to me and to many other officials. To the man in the street, we were known as the "Russian" party. Theoretically, of course, we had evolved the line of a separate German road to Socialism, but only a narrow circle of the population knew or understood this. In practice, we had supported and defended all measures taken by the Soviet occupation authorities. They had supplied us with paper, vehicles, buildings and special food rations. Our leading officials lived in large country houses hermetically sealed from the rest of the population and guarded by soldiers of the Red Army. They travelled in cars which, in some cases, carried Russian marks of identification. The result of the elections was the logical consequence of our dependence on the Soviet occupation authorities. I told myself that the population of Berlin had not voted against us because we were in favour of Socialism, nor had they voted against Party members and officials who had done what they could, at considerable cost to themselves, to relieve the needs of the population. They had voted against us because they saw in us a Party dependent on the Soviet Union; and unfortunately they were not wrong.

Now only one thing could save us: a clear dissociation from the Soviet occupation authorities, and a public avowal of our intention from now on to function as an independent German Socialist Party. That night I hoped that perhaps the electoral defeat of 20th October would finally lead to our taking this step, and thus work eventually to our advantage. I hoped that the Party leadership would now openly recognise the real reasons for our defeat, and would draw the appropriate conclusions.

The Process of Sovietisation

The more I went on with my training and the more success I enjoyed in it, the stronger became my doubts about the S.E.D.'s policy since the electoral defeat of 20th October, 1946. The way they chose was not towards greater independence, but exactly the opposite; their links with the Soviet Union and the Soviet occupation authorities became stronger.

On 7th November, 1946, there were large-scale celebrations in the S.E.D. of the Soviet National Day. In contrast with 1945, this was the first such occasion when the speeches of the Soviet leaders were reproduced verbatim. On 5th December, 1946, Soviet Constitution Day was also treated in the same servile fashion. On 21st December, Stalin's sixty-seventh birthday, there appeared an article by Wilhelm Pieck in which it was stated that "the far-sighted genius of the Soviet Union's great leader shows the German people, too, their way."

In the middle of January, 1947, a further step was

taken. Marshal Sokolovsky and his Deputy, together with the head of their Political Administration, Colonel Tulpanov, invited the leaders of the S.E.D. —Pieck, Grotewohl, Ulbricht and Fechner—to take part in negotiations, the results of which were published on the 16th January. "The request of the Socialist Unity Party of Germany to bring the process of dismantling to a final halt has been granted. When the dismantling of the war industries in particular is complete, there will be no further dismantling."

Agreeable though this promise was for us—later it was to turn out that it would not be kept—I and several other officials still could not help reflecting on the fact that our Party leadership had yet again emphasised their close links with the occupation authorities in the submissive tone of their expressions of gratitude. There followed an official statement of thanks from Wilhelm Pieck, and then another from Ulbricht, and finally still another collectively from the Party leadership of the S.E.D. to the Soviet Occupation Authorities.

Henceforth, this became the common form. At the end of January, 1947, the leaders of the F.D.G.B. visited Sokolovsky. Again their requests were granted, and again there followed servile expressions of gratitude. The turn of the F.D.J. came next. Finally, even minor improvements in the supply of vegetables came to be solemnly introduced by negotiations and collective expressions of gratitude from the S.E.D.

Our thesis about a separate German road to Socialism still remained the official Party line, but what was it worth in the face of the adulation of Stalin, the telegrams of greetings and good wishes to the

Soviet Union, the petitions, negotiations and thanksgivings to the Soviet Administration? Gradually my doubts increased.

In August, 1947, I paid a visit to a friend of my childhood, Mischa Wolf, whom I had known at the Comintern School. He was now a commentator on foreign affairs for East Berlin radio under the name of Michael Storm. He had a still more important function as controller responsible for the principal political broadcasts. He had particularly good relations with very senior Soviet circles, and he occupied a luxurious five-roomed apartment in Bayern-Alee, not far from the radio building in West Berlin. Since I last saw him he had married Emmi Stenzer, the blue-eyed blonde at the Comintern School, who had reported things I said to the school authorities and thus been the cause of my first self-criticism.

"It's wonderful to see you again! You can come with us to our country house right away. We always spend our week-ends there."

An hour later we stopped in front of a fine villa in the neighbourhood of Lake Glienicke. It was the property of Mischa, who was then twenty-five years old.

As we walked along the shore of the lake, Mischa remarked to me casually: "It's really time you gave up that theory of yours about a separate German road to Socialism. The Party line is going to be quite different."

I laughed. "Mischa, with all respect to your position and your cleverness, I know a bit more about the political line than you do. After all, I work in the Central Secretariat and I write the Party manuals, which are authoritative for all members and officials of the entire Party."

˹ Mischa had lit a cigarette. With an ironic smile he went on: "There are higher authorities than your Central Secretariat." He was obviously teasing me in speaking of "your" Central Secretariat.

"But Mischa, this thesis about a separate German road to Socialism is expressly stated in the charter and programme of the S.E.D."

Mischa Wolf refused to be in the least impressed by the charter and programme of the S.E.D. "Then they must be re-written."

I gaped in astonishment.

"Wolfgang, I'm not telling you that this is going to happen to-morrow, I only want to give you notice in good time about certain modifications. We had a talk with Tulpanov about it just the other day. He told us—naturally in extreme confidence—that a stop will soon be put to the theory of a separate German road. If I were in your position, I shouldn't go on talking or writing too much about it. That will make the about-turn easier when it comes."

He spoke casually, without guessing that the abandonment of this thesis meant for me the destruction of one of my fondest hopes. For him, on the other hand, it seemed to be no more than a means to an end.

A few days later, on 20th September, 1947, I was sitting expectantly in the German State Opera. The second Party Congress of the S.E.D. was opened to the solemn strains of Beethoven. Anxiously I awaited the speeches of our chief officials. Wilhelm Pieck was to give the political report, Otto Grotewohl was to speak on some problems of German unity, and Walter Ulbricht was to speak on the political and economic development of the Soviet Zone. During the five days the Party Congress lasted, the thesis of a separate road to Socialism was not officially set aside, but the continual emphasis on the pre-eminent achievements of the Soviet Union was to me an indication of a tendency which I found disquieting and more than ever difficult to justify. In contrast with the period of 1945-46, our links with the Soviet Union were now openly proclaimed.

On the third evening of our discussions, Herman Matern stood up at the table on the platform and boomed down the hall: "It is now my privilege to convey to the meeting, in addition to many greetings from all over the world, the most important greeting of all." He then read out the Soviet message of greeting, which had been signed by Suslov, the Secretary of the Central Committee of the Communist Party of the Soviet Union.

All eyes were turned to the box in which Suslov sat as the guest of the Congress. He stood up and cried in German: "Long live the Socialist Unity Party of Germany!" When the applause at this had died down, Matern shouted from the table on the platform down the hall: "Long live the Communist Party of the Soviet Union! Long live its Central Committee! Long live its leader, Stalin!"

In the year and a half since the assembly to unify the two parties, the S.E.D. had greatly changed. At that first Congress a greeting of this kind would have been quite impossible.

On the Sunday after the Party Congress I was driving with a leading member of the S.E.D. in the

Soviet Zone, and we had an opportunity to talk without interruption. I decided not to let the opportunity pass.

"Between ourselves, you certainly know as well as I do that the process of dismantling is still going on full blast. The negotiations on halting it were conducted in the name of the Party, and we put it across to the public. You can well imagine what that means for us now. Isn't there in fact any possibility of really bringing the process of dismantling to a halt, or can't the Party at least officially dissociate itself from it?"

The party leader looked at me unmoved. "No, there is no possibility."

"And what have you to say to that?"

He drew a deep breath; it might almost have been a groan. Faintly the words came out, almost in a stammer: "They pay no attention to us."

By "they" he meant the Soviet leaders; but even in this conversation 'between ourselves' the self-discipline inculcated in every official by his training and years of Party activity still prevailed. "We'd better not speak about it."

A quarter of an hour later, however, we had touched on another delicate matter. This was the conduct of the Soviet troops, and the veto on the S.E.D. taking any attitude towards it on their own initiative. I tried again.

"I can understand the whole business perfectly. Things like this may happen in any occupation, especially given the composition of the Soviet Occupation Forces in Germany at the present time. Their best cadres were destroyed in 1941, and the majority of their troops come from remote villages.

They haven't had much education . . . but why can't one talk about them freely and openly, so as to explain the situation and to dissociate the Party from these incidents, and at the same time to save its reputation from being so severely damaged by them. If we don't talk about them, other people will, and they will use them to stir up nationalist trouble generally."

My interlocutor nodded and seemed to agree with me, but he said nothing.

"You have been to Moscow several times in the last year and a half. Has any attempt been made at least to open this question there?"

"Yes, an attempt has been made—with Stalin." He fell silent, but I did not let up.

"And how did it turn out?"

"Stalin replied with an old Russian proverb: 'In every family there is a black sheep.' He said nothing more. When one of us tried to put the matter more seriously and to hint at the consequences, he was interrupted by Stalin: 'I will not allow anyone to drag the reputation of the Red Army in the mud.' That was the end of the conversation."

I avoided any further delicate questions; but on that Sunday of September, 1947, I had at last realised how indissolubly we were now chained to the Soviet Union.

The Karl Marx Party Academy

It is the general practice in the Stalinist *apparat* that after a year and a half to three years in the same appointment, one is transferred by the Party leadership to a new and different job. I had been engaged for about two years at a stretch on the preparation of educational material for the Party and as a visiting lecturer at the Party Academy, the district schools of the S.E.D. and the central school of the F.D.J. (the Free German Youth movement), which was established in a villa at Bogensee that had formerly belonged to Goebbels. One day in September, 1947, I was summoned to see my immediate chief, Anton Ackermann, and Franz Dahlem, who was then in charge of cadres in the S.E.D. I guessed that I was to be assigned to a new post in the Party.

Both of them had much the same thing to say. "The leadership of the Party attaches great importance to broadening the work of the Karl Marx Party Academy, so the suggestion has been made that you should join it for about two years to reinforce the teaching staff. You can choose your own faculty. All right?"

"All right!" I was pleased by the suggestion. I would now have the opportunity, I thought, to devote myself to studying theoretical problems in peace, at a distance from day-to-day politics, without being obliged to spend my time popularising the political decisions and measures taken by the S.E.D.

At that time the Party Academy was at Liebenwalde, about twenty miles north-east of Berlin. From the outside, the group of buildings reminded me somewhat of the Comintern School at Kushnarenkovo. I was welcomed by Rudolf Lindau, who was at that time Director of the Party Academy. I had known him in Moscow under the party name of Paul Gratz, which he then used. In 1916 he had been a member of the founding committee of the *Spartakusbund,* and he had belonged to the K.P.D. since its foundation. During his period as an émigré in the Soviet Union most of his time had been devoted to preparing a history of the German Communist Party.

Rudolf Lindau greeted me warmly and briefed me on the work of the Party Academy. "Up to now our courses have lasted six months. We are just about to begin the first two-year course. However, the half-year courses will continue to be held, though in a slightly different form."

"A kind of abbreviated two-year course?"

"No, there is going to be an important difference. In the two-year courses we shall take young, promising Party members who joined us after 1945, and have already been through the local and district Party Schools and completed their courses. We shall train them up into officials with a sound theoretical background, ready for responsible Party posts. The half-year course, on the other hand, is designed primarily for older Party members who were active in the K.P.D. or the S.P.D. before 1933. There we aim to familiarise them with new political ideas and tasks, and bring them up to a higher level from a theoretical point of view. Particular attention will have to be devoted to Party members from Western Germany."

"From Western Germany?"

"Yes, about a quarter of the students on our courses, both the two-year course and the half-year course, are K.P.D. officials from Western Germany. We have taken over responsibility for their training. For obvious reasons, they are studying here under assumed names. The same applies to four Party members from Norway whose training is also the responsibility of our Party, since the Party in Norway only has week-end courses."

Rudolf Lindau then showed me the very comprehensive library, and took me to the teaching material section, where a number of the staff were engaged in producing instructional literature on a duplicating machine.

"All the instructional literature for our students is produced here," he explained. "Before every lecture the students on the course receive a brief duplicated summary of the lecture, which also includes a list of required reading on the subject. At the end of the lecture they receive the appropriate reading material, duplicated, from the issuing office of the library, and then they can go off for their private studies on the subject of the lecture, either in the reading-room or in their own rooms. The following day, or sometimes at later intervals, a three-hour seminar is held. Then every three months there are written examinations, and at the end of the semester there are both written and oral examinations on every subject."

The following day Rudolf Lindau introduced me to the Deans of the four faculties in the Party Academy. All four of them came from the K.P.D., for the Party Academy was one of the few institutions at that time in which parity had not been established between former Social Democrats and former members of the Communist Party. In order to give an appearance of at least token parity, the Director of the Party Academy, Rudolf Lindau, had as his deputy a pleasant, modest former Social Democrat called Paul Lenzner. Lenzner had previously spent many years in the cultural section of the S.P.D. and in the Teetotallers League. Obviously incapable of standing up to the Communist Party officials at the Party Academy, he had to confine himself to giving an occasional lecture and taking care of the school's cultural affairs.

Another former member of the Ulbricht Group whom I met was Walter Koppe, who had been relegated from political work since I last saw him to the post of financial administrator at the Party Academy. Here he felt more in his element, though he was still very insistent on being addressed as "Comrade Director."

After a certain amount of reflection, I decided in favour of the history faculty, and set about getting to know the method of work in what was called "forging the party cadres." It only took me a few days to observe certain differences from the Comintern School. The equipment of the S.E.D. Party Academy at Liebenwalde in 1947 could not have been improved upon—it was certainly even better than that of the Comintern School in 1942-43. We were extremely well fed, even in that period when the rest of Germany was starving. Every student at the Academy received pocket money, and his family or dependents received either their subsistence or the salary of the student on the course. At that time, in the autumn of 1947, the regulations were far less strict than in the Comintern School. Students on the course could write letters and visit Berlin at the week-end. Even on week-days, they were permitted to leave the school grounds. There were, of course, evenings of criticism and self-criticism, but there was no comparison between them and those which I had gone through at the Comintern School. Even the seminars were not so strictly conducted. Fallacious ideas and incorrect expressions were indeed sharply criticised, but at the time they still did not lead to immediate expulsion from the School and Party.

The Academy seemed to me almost liberal in comparison with the Comintern School. Students who were not in a position to make such comparisons and could not know what the Party Academy was going to be like in a few years' time, took a different view of it. A former Social Democrat groaned: "I feel as if I were in a strait-jacket here." He told me what the Social Democrats' educational institutes used to be like, and then I saw what he meant.

The difference between the Karl Marx Party Academy and the Comintern School lay not only in the relatively freer atmosphere of the former, but also in the method of study. In the S.E.D. Party Academy there was no training in military matters or in clandestine work. On the other hand, the purely theoretical studies were more comprehensive than in the Comintern School. In philosophy the students were given, to begin with, a general survey of the whole history of philosophy. The detailed treatment of Marxist-Leninist theory came only after that. Political economy included the study of Karl Marx's *Das Kapital* section by section, together with extracts from the economic writings of Hilferding and Rosa Luxemburg, Lenin's theory of imperialism, and the political economy of Socialism.

The history faculty, to which I belonged, was responsible for giving a general survey of world history. After this came the history of Germany, beginning with the establishment of Brandenburg, the evolution of the Prussian state, the role of Frederick II and the unification of Germany under Bismarck. The history of the German workers' movement was

not studied separately, but only in the framework of
the general history of Germany between 1848 and the
present day.

The lectures on basic questions of Marxism-
Leninism were very much like those in the Comintern School. The subjects were the same as in all
Party schools in the eastern *bloc,* from Eisenach to
Peking: classes and class struggle, the theory of the
state, formal and real democracy, the role of the
working class, Party theory, the struggle against opportunism, reformism and revisionism, strategy and
tactics, the peasant question, national and colonial
questions. Just as at the Comintern School, great
importance was attached to the study and refutation
of hostile theories and antagonistic points of view.

The study of hostile points of view was pursued
with particular keenness in the teaching of philosophy. Students learned in great detail how to refute
conventional conceptions of the alleged determin-
ism of Marxism. The relation between logic and
dialectic was exhaustively covered. Duplicated
material was regularly put out under the title of
"Contemporary Conceptions of the Marxist Philosophy," which consisted entirely of extracts from
bourgeois and social democratic writing.

As at the Comintern School, however, there was
one important exception. The library contained none
of the writings of Trotsky or Bukharin or other important opposition figures, nor books written by former Communist Party officials who had broken with
Stalinism; nor were any extracts from their work
circulated among the duplicated material. The
S.E.D. leadership in East Berlin in 1947 evidently
considered it just as dangerous to allow their writings

to be studied by students or instructors of the Party Academy as had the Comintern at Ufa in 1942.

Later things became even stricter. The very names of leading Communist Party officials who had subsequently broken with Stalinism were not allowed to be mentioned. On one occasion Arthur Dorf, an instructor in the faculty of Marxist-Leninist theory and a former combatant in Spain, mentioned in a lecture the name of Paul Frölich (a former colleague of Karl Liebknecht and Rosa Luxemburg, who had joined the opposition at the end of the 1920's). At this the Dean of the Faculty, Frieda Rubiner, leapt up to the platform like a fury and screamed: "I will not allow the names of Trotskyite traitors to be mentioned here!"

Lecturers for about three-quarters of the periods of instruction were provided out of the Party Academy's own resources. As each of the four faculties had three or four instructors and one or two assistants at its disposal, in addition to the Dean of the Faculty, every instructor had sufficient time to prepare his own lectures. Apart from ourselves, lectures were given by guest speakers from the Central Secretariat of the S.E.D., or from the editorial staff of the Party's theoretical periodical *Unity,* or from the University of East Berlin, as well as occasionally by leading officials from the satellite states. Sometimes the lectures by these guest speakers were fitted into our general programme of work; sometimes they dealt with entirely different subjects, which were regarded as important contributions to the general broadening of our studies.

There was also much interest in the additional "information lectures" given on international questions. At the time I joined the Academy there were already lectures on the situation in the Near East and on the Revolution in China, the latter given by an official who had just come back from China. A member of the Bulgarian Party leadership called Dramaliev gave a detailed report on the situation in Bulgaria, which went a good deal farther than what could be read in the press. Leading officials used naturally to speak a good deal more freely about particular questions of current policy in the S.E.D. as guest-lecturers at the Party Academy than at public meetings. This practice helped to give us a very clear picture of the situation in the Soviet Zone and of the difficulties within the Party—in some cases, we were actually requested not to take any notes.

A few weeks after I joined the Academy, in the late autumn of 1947, we were told one day at an instructors' conference: "There has been a proposal at a high level to enlarge and expand the Party Academy. Our present accommodation in Liebenwalde is not sufficient for the purpose. Work has already begun on the preparation of our new Party Academy which will be located at Klein-Machnow, near Berlin. The move will probably take place at the beginning of 1948."

One day at the end of December, 1947, Rudolf Lindau told me that he was going to visit the new building and invited me to accompany him. It was thus my good fortune to see, on that December afternoon, a sight that exceeded my highest expectations. There were five huge modern houses, with large windows, situated in a park; garages, underground passages to connect the five buildings, and hundreds of living-rooms done up in modern style, each for two or three students. Two smaller villas were reserved for the Deans of the Faculties. Each of the instructors had either a villa in Klein-Machnow if he had a family or, if he were single, a fine apartment in a new building.

We moved early in January, 1948. After the move, the activities of the Party Academy were expanded. The number of six-month courses for executive officials were increased; at the same time, various other short courses were introduced. At the beginning of 1948, less than three years after the capitulation of Hitlerite Germany, this huge complex of buildings, where hundreds of officials were trained simultaneously, seemed to us to represent the ultimate limits of what was possible. But it turned out to be only the beginning.

In 1949, the six-month courses for responsible officials were lengthened to nine months. In 1950, one-year courses were also introduced. In the autumn of 1950, the Party Academy began a special correspondence course which was constantly enlarged until, three years later, it had grown into a five-year correspondence course. In February, 1953, the first three-year course began, and from 1954 onward these three-year courses led up to a state examination. By that time the Party Academy had been granted the right of giving diplomas and promotion. These courses are now turning out every year, at an increasing rate, hundreds and thousands of well-trained officials, most of them convinced of the correctness of their outlook on the world.

CHAPTER NINE

My Break with Stalinism

AMONG OFFICIAL CIRCLES in the Eastern *bloc,* there is a special term for doubts and uncertainties and opinions that do not coincide with the official line: "political collywobbles." Most officials keep their "political collywobbles" to themselves; a few tell their best friends under the seal of secrecy. Naturally, the particular form of "political collywobbles" depends on the particular sector in which one is employed—the Party, the economy or the administration—as well as on one's political training and rank. Although these "political collywobbles" take very different forms among different categories of officials, there are two characteristics common to practically all cases: first of all, they have practically nothing to do with Western arguments or the Western attitude to life. They are rather an expression of opposition ideas and opinions within the system itself: an expression of the contradictions between the teaching of Marx and Lenin on the one hand, and the Stalinist theory and practice on the other hand. In the second place, these "political collywobbles" are never expressed or even hinted at in the presence of non-members of the Party. It can happen, and I have often seen it myself, that in conversation with people from the West an official who is wrestling with the severest internal doubts will

stubbornly, and apparently with complete conviction, defend the official Party line. His Western interlocutor then leaves him with the firm conviction
of having been talking to a 150% Stalinist. He sees
the whole conversation as a pointless waste of time,
whereas in reality that same official, who is already
at heart in opposition, will subsequently describe his
conversation in detail to a small circle of fellow
members of the opposition, and spend hours discussing it.

The "Collywobbles"

Busy though I then was, and fully occupied
though my day was with the Party's affairs, as was
the case with all officials at the time, nevertheless
it was impossible to prevent critical thoughts and
doubts rising continually in my mind. Again and
again, memories came back to me of painful and
unpleasant events which I had long kept in the background. I recalled the arrest of my mother, when I
had knocked in vain on her door. I recalled the anxious thoughts and fears of my Children's Home during the trials and arrests, and the terror of people
in Moscow in the years of the great purges, 1936-38,
and—even worse—their eventual indifference. I recalled the arrest of my friend Rolf in the dormitory
of the Children's Home in March, 1938. I recalled
the pact with Hitlerite Germany and the elimina-
tion of anti-Fascist literature which followed it.
I recalled the draconian penal regulations against
workers in the summer of 1940. I recalled the terrified face of the girl at school who told me, under
the seal of secrecy, that she had been compelled to
work for the N.K.V.D. I recalled the starving people

at Karaganda and Ufa, side by side with the privileged luxury of the official class, who remained entirely unmoved by their misery. I recalled the terrible
atmosphere in the evenings of criticism and self-
criticism in the Comintern School. I recalled the
tragic eyes and imploring hands of the official who
had been expelled from the Comintern School, when
he begged me for a crust of bread in Ufa. I recalled
the arrogant superiority of Ulbricht towards those
of his fellow Party members in Germany who had
been through the clandestine struggle there.

There were many other things which had oppressed me, and still did so, but I generally resisted
these memories and doubts, because they did not fit
in with the picture of the world that had been inculcated in me, and because I did not want them
to interfere with my beliefs, my activities and my
hopes. The further training progressed, the more I
had in my hands all the means necessary to resolve
my doubts and anxieties on a higher level by complicated theoretical considerations which went way
beyond the official propaganda prepared for the
masses. On the other hand, it was exactly this that
increased my doubts and anxieties; and I soon realised that I was by no means alone, and that the
most highly trained officials were often the very ones
who were furthest gone in heresy.

To-day, when I look back on those conversations
"between ourselves" at that period, I believe that our
"political collywobbles" can be summed up under
the following heads:

1. The dependence of the S.E.D. (or of the Stalinist Party in any other country) on the Soviet
Union and the Communist Party of the Soviet

Union, in contrast to the equality of status laid down by Marx and Engels for the Socialist workers' movement in each individual country.

2. The Stalinist thesis that the People's Democracies (that is to say, the Eastern satellite states) have to follow the example of the Soviet Union, in conflict with the principle stated by Marx and Engels that the evolution of each individual country towards Socialism should follow a course corresponding to its own economic, political and cultural conditions.

3. The principle enunciated by Stalinism of the continual reinforcement of the power of the state in the U.S.S.R. and the Eastern *bloc,* in conflict with the doctrines of Marx and Engels, that Socialist evolution should lead to the weakening and final "withering away" of the State.

4. The omnipotence of the nationalised direction of industry in the Soviet Union and the Eastern *bloc,* in conflict with the principle of Marx and Engels that Socialist industrial enterprises should be controlled by elected workers' committees.

5. The claim to infallibility of an omniscient leadership and the superstitious acceptance of Stalinist authority, in contrast to the readiness to approach problems with an open mind that we find in the writings of Marx, Engels and even Lenin.

6. The suppression of free opinion in the Party, which becomes particularly striking when we read in Lenin's writings of the free and open discussions which used to take place earlier in the Bolshevik Party.

7. The immense privileges of officials in the Party, state and economy, in contrast with the principles

of Marx, Engels and Lenin, which laid down that in a Socialist community no one should receive remuneration exceeding a worker's wage.

8. The continually intensified repression, in contrast with the principles laid down by Marx, Engels and Lenin, which treated restriction of freedom as merely a transitory measure aimed against the exploiting classes, to be abolished after they have been deprived of power, in favour of measures to secure the widest range of liberties for all workers.

For those of us who had been brought up in the East and imbued with its ideology, passages and quotations from the basic literature often meant more than our own most painful and personal experiences. They confirmed our doubts and anxieties, and proved the justice of our opposition tendencies. In the case of officials who had grown up in the Stalinist system, and been educated in its ideology, opposition took its origin from a Marxist standpoint; it was a defence of the doctrines of Marx, Engels and Lenin against the corruptions of Stalinism.

One of the outstanding evils, and one which was frequently the cause of "political collywobbles," was that of the privileges enjoyed by officials. My friends and I who had grown up in the Soviet Union had never known it otherwise, and at first we saw no problem in the preferential treatment given to governmental, economic and Party officials. It was true that as long ago as 1942 in Karaganda, I had thought it not altogether right that there should be such a vast difference in time of war between the great mass of the working class, including many Party members who were, in the literal sense of the word, starving, and a small number of Party officials who never knew what it was to have the least material anxiety; but then it was only the degree of the officials' privileges that I regarded as excessive, not the fact itself.

A single event made me change my mind. It was in October, 1945, at the beginning of the great campaign for unification. I was just coming out of my office to go to the dining-room of the Central Committee. On the steps I was accosted by a pleasant looking middle-aged man: "Excuse me, Comrade, do you work here?"

"Yes, in the *agitprop* section."

"That's good. I am a K.P.D. official. I have been invited here from the West. I have been given some chits for meals, but I don't know where the dining-room is."

"That depends on what sort of ticket you have."

He looked at me in surprise and showed me his ticket. It was Category III—a ticket for the less important members of staff. I showed him the way.

"But tell me—are the meals different for different members of the staff in the Central Committee?"

"Yes, of course. There are four different kinds of ticket, according to the class of work one is doing. The last two categories are for technicians and clerks."

"Yes, but . . . aren't they all members of the Party?"

"Yes, of course. They are all certified Party members, including the charwomen and chauffeurs and night-watchmen."

He looked at me in astonishment and said, "Different tickets—different meals—and they are all members of the Party!"

He turned and went without another word. A moment later I heard the creak of the front door. My comrade had left the Central Committee building. Thoughtfully, I crossed the courtyard to the dining-room. I went through the rooms in which Categories III and IV—the lower classes—were fed: and for the first time I had an uneasy feeling as I opened the door into the dining-room reserved for our category. Here, at a table covered with a white cloth, the senior members of staff enjoyed an excellent meal of several courses. Curious, I thought, that this had never struck me before!

My thoughts turned to the luxurious villas at Niederschönhausen where Pieck, Grotewohl, Ulbricht, Dahlem, Ackermann, and the others lived. I visited them practically every week-end. The whole quarter was fenced off, and the two exits were guarded by Soviet sentries.

"Well, I agree," I said to one of the senior officials who lived there, "I understand the need for security measures, but do they have to—absolutely *have* to—be Soviet soldiers? And of course, you need plenty of room to live in; but does it really have to be such a palatial villa? It's not a question of principle, but at a time when everything is short, preferential treatment may well provoke bitter feelings among the population."

The man I was talking to grew serious.

"I should never have expected such antiquated ideas from you. That is simply succumbing to hostile propaganda—it's nothing but a reversion to *petit bourgeois* egalitarianism. Why shouldn't our leading comrades live in these villas? Perhaps you would like to give them back to the Nazis?"

"I never said anything of the kind," I replied. "I

am just against these palatial villas at a time when everyone is in such need—in the middle of political controversies in Berlin, where everyone knows that the Social Democrat officials in the West are living on a much more modest scale, and old Kulz, of the Liberal Democrats, is living somewhere in three rooms of a lodging house."

"Sometimes I have the impression that in spite of your responsible position, you are something of a starry-eyed revolutionary idealist."

The words "starry-eyed revolutionary idealist" were spoken in the cold tone of superiority of an *apparatchik*. I said no more. The villas continued, of course; so did the Soviet sentries. Both of them were electioneering points for the S.P.D. in the Berlin elections of October, 1946.

These villas, and the hierarchical grading of the feeding arrangements, were not the only privileges enjoyed by senior officials. The building of the Central Committee in Wallstrasse had been specially equipped, as we came to know at the opening of a Rest Home reserved for members of the Central Committee *apparat*. It was at Bernicke, near Bernau, and it was very luxuriously fitted up for that date. It was surrounded by a huge park, and entirely cut off from the outside world. The feeding there was so sumptuous that it made even the rations at the Central Committee building appear poor by comparison. This was where we used to spend our leave.

Careful attention was paid to rank in the exercise of all these privileges. At first the Rest Home at Bernicke was used by all officials in the Central Committee *apparat*. Not long afterwards, however, a new distinction was introduced: an even more exclusive Rest Home at Seehof was established for the most senior members of the Central Secretariat.

There was also an exact gradation of rank in the distribution of the famous *payoks,* those great parcels of food, cigarettes, tobacco, drinks and chocolate which we received regularly in addition to our ration cards and our meals at the Central Committee. These *payoks* were not only for middle-grade and senior Party officials, but also for officials in the Government and economic administration, as well as for scientists, specialists, poets and artists: but they were on a sharply graduated scale. Everything depended on the function of the recipient and whether he was a V.I.P.

In Saxony, I met a Party official who worked in the Free German Trade Unions and was well acquainted with the situation in the factories. He trusted me, and was glad to have the opportunity of unburdening himself.

"Between ourselves, we feel our dependence on the Russians much more forcibly down here than you do in higher places, where things are done more politely. For instance, the trouble with these *payoks*——"

"I know what you mean—the workers are feeling bitter about them."

"Yes, they are, but that's not what I meant." He then went on to tell me the story of the fate of a *payok* official in his town.

A loyal party member who had spent years in a concentration camp had come back to his factory, where he was joyfully welcomed by his fellow workers. He soon got an official position again, and came to be regarded as the chief man in his factory. Then came the dismantling of German industry. The Russians told him that he must justify the dismantling to his fellow workers. They promised him that as soon as the dismantling was over, everything would be settled and the workers would be able to go on working unmolested. He believed it, and the workers trusted his explanations. The dismantling was carried out. The workers assumed that everything would now settle down, and they went back to work with great enthusiasm, recovered their machinery from somewhere or other and rebuilt the factory. It was not so good as before, but anyhow the factory was working. A few months passed. The Party official was called to see the Russians again. They told him his factory had to be dismantled again. He remonstrated with them, and reminded them of their promise on the first occasion. He spoke of his own reputation and the prestige of the Party. It was no use. The Russians insisted on the second dismantling. He refused to put their case to the workers. The Russian officer smiled maliciously and said: "If you aren't going to do it, I shall tell your fellow workers what you have been receiving in *payoks* and special privileges." With that, he pulled a list out of his pocket. Every single item that he had received in a year and a half was carefully enumerated. That was when he first began to realise what *payoks* meant. The following day he justified the second dismantling to his fellow workers, but he was no longer the man he used to be: he was completely broken.

It was this story that first taught me that the *payoks* were not merely a generous device for helping loyal comrades, and their purpose was not merely the well-being of the Party cadres.

Western Propaganda

It generally causes surprise in the West when I tell people that I read the most important Western newspapers every day from 1945 onwards. The immediate question is then: "Well, and what effect did they have on you?"

Unfortunately I can only answer, "None whatever. If one can speak of any effect at all—apart from a very few exceptions—then it would only be that reading these newspapers contributed to delaying my break with Stalinism."

Three quarters of the space in Western newspapers, which naturally have to adapt themselves to Western readers, are devoted to news which has no possible interest even to an opposition Party official. Most of the articles and editorials are written in a language which a well-educated official in the East can certainly understand, and which he can even think himself into, but which has no appeal for him at all.

"The unscientific phraseology of the Western press" was the phrase we used to use contemptuously whenever we talked about Western articles. Since every political expression such as "the people," "democracy," "freedom," "the nation," "socialism," and so on had a precisely determined meaning for us, any use of these terms which did not correspond to our definition was called "unscientific." We assumed it to have been written by people who had not, as we expressed it at the time, "the slightest basic political education."

Naturally, we paid particular attention to despatches and articles dealing with the Soviet Zone of Germany or the Soviet Union and the People's Democracies. Generally we could only shake our heads over them, and often we were exceedingly disappointed. There was usually not even any mention of the really significant events that were causing endless discussions amongst ourselves and on which we were passionately eager to read a serious Western commentary. "They don't even seem to know what's going on" was the main theme of our conversations when we talked to each other on the subject.

Nevertheless, in the West Berlin and West German newspapers frequent and detailed reports continued to appear, exulting over the faults and failures of local authorities in the Soviet Zone. Not a single one of my friends or acquaintances was ever encouraged in his opposition or stimulated to critical reflection by these articles. On the contrary, every one of us without exception felt outraged at the arrogance of their jokes against youthful mayors, whose inexperience had led them into difficulty, or against working-class officials in the administration who occasionally made mistakes on paper. Thus we constantly suffered a double disappointment. The great events which so stirred us, which occupied our night-long discussions and were responsible for our "political collywobbles" were not even touched on at all in the Western press. Instead, they trotted out all our relatively minor deficiences and inadequacies. This seemed to us entirely unjust, and the result was that we felt more in sympathy with the system for being subjected to such attacks.

What we wanted was to hear serious arguments which would help us in our own fundamental dissension. Instead of this, we got such irrelevancies as contrasts between the higher living standard of the working class in the West and that of a worker in the Soviet Zone, or in the countries of the Eastern *bloc*. "So they've found that out, have they?" was our reaction, "as if we didn't know it ourselves! Of course the standard of living is higher in West European countries than in the People's Democracies—it's perfectly obvious: historically, declining societies always have had a higher standard of living than those which are just coming into being."

The few articles which did try to discuss the problems of the Eastern countries in a somewhat more serious spirit ended all too often in a paean of praise for private enterprise or Western Christianity, but such arguments persuaded us of nothing, for in most cases where the younger and politically educated generation was in sharp opposition to the Stalinist system, this by no means implied approval of the Western system. Attempts to undermine the Stalinist ideology by propaganda in favour of the Western system were incapable of exercising any attraction worth speaking of on us. Although we were hostile to Stalinism we were not prepared to replace it with the obsolete conditions of capitalism, and we were on our guard against propaganda which appeared to us to imply the payment of compensation to the big landlords, the restoration of the factories to their previous owners, the reintroduction of the old political parties and the deliberate imposition of the Western system on the countries of Eastern Europe.

Particularly ominous, we thought, was the ironic tone in which Western newspapers and broadcasts spoke about things which were sacred even to those Party officials who were in opposition, like ourselves

—for instance, when the great Socialist October Revolution was referred to as a *Putsch,* or when Lenin was personally attacked or treated with contempt. Again, the frequent attempts which newspapers and broadcasts made to refute Marxism in tones of ill-concealed superiority made no impression at all on Party officials like ourselves. In most cases they were designed for the masses, and expressed in such crude terms that it was impossible to take them seriously.

Sometimes conditions in the Soviet Union were preferred to as the "realisation of Marxism." Our "political collywobblers," however, were in a state of grave and justified doubt whether the political evolution of the Soviet Union and the Soviet Zone could be reconciled with the principles of Marxism at all. And now here were the Western newspapers to confirm, even if from very different motives, that the official Party thesis was the correct one after all!

There were, of course, occasional exceptions, and these have always remained in my mind. One day when I was going for a walk in West Berlin, I found on a newspaper stall outside the Steglitz Town Hall a little pamphlet with the simple title "Trade Unions and Social Policy in the Soviet Union." The author was Solomon Schwarz, a name till then entirely unknown to me. On opening the pamphlet I saw the imprint of the *Neue Zeitung,* which was the official American newspaper in Germany until 1955.

"This must be the usual utter nonsense, published by the Americans," I thought. When I got back to my room in the Party Academy I got out some paper and my fountain pen, ready to note down all the errors which I was practically sure to find. Then I began to read.

There was no abuse and the language was straightforward, full of references, tables and statistical material. It was just the sort of thing we were used to among ourselves. I checked the figures and the references: they were correct. My fountain pen still lay ready, but with the best will in the world, there was nothing to mark. It took me two hours to read the pamphlet through. Apart from one or two question marks at certain phrases, there was nothing in the arguments, the statistical material or the quotations that I could counter out of the Soviet press. I had known it all before, but I had never yet read it in so concise a form, or seen the connection of ideas so clearly brought out.

A few months later another pamphlet was going the rounds among officials with opposition tendencies. It was an extract from Koestler's book, *The Yogi and the Commissar,* and it was also published by the *Neue Zeitung* under the title of "Soviet Myth and Reality." I found myself gripped by it at once, for the very first page talked about the October Revolution, but this time not treating it with hostility and contempt, as so often in Western writings. I therefore read the pamphlet through with interest. Much that I had hitherto suspected was here set out in coherent form. Here was a document which expounded the concept of Stalinism as the antithesis of Marxism; a document in which the present-day system in the U.S.S.R. was depicted not as the consequence of the October Revolution, but as evidence for the view that the Stalinist system had betrayed the achievements of the October Revolution and turned into its very antithesis.

Then came a third document from the West which showed me that we did not stand alone in the trend our thoughts were taking. It was a book by Paul Sering, under the title of *Beyond Capitalism*, with a sub-title: "A Search for a New Socialist Orientation." A good deal of the book dealt with the Soviet Union, and although many opposition officials would not have agreed with all its views, it made a deep impression on us, because within the range of literature that came into our hands at that time, it was the first attempt to make an analysis of the Soviet Union; to answer the question why the Soviet Revolution had led to this particular type of state, and show how completely it contradicted the original doctrines of the Marxist classics.

There were radio receivers in the rooms of many students of the Party Academy, and the instructors also had a good set. We listened to Western broadcasts quite often. One evening, three of us were sitting in my room and listening to a broadcast by the R.I.A.S. Practically every third word was "freedom." One of us was so bored that he got up and turned the radio off. "Why do they always go on about *freedom?*" he asked. "In the first place there is no freedom in the West, and in the second place, people in the West don't even know what freedom is."

We agreed with him. He was not one of the officials who were always loyal to the Party line: on the contrary, he belonged to the opposition. But what was generally forgotten in the West was that this opposition was conducted within our world of ideas, in our own terminology, and was concerned with our own problems. It had nothing to do with Western sympathies or Western conceptions of freedom. For us freedom meant insight into historical necessity. We were free because we were the only ones who possessed this insight on the basis of scientific theory; whereas people in the West who lacked this scientific theory and simply confronted historical evolution with an unreasoning, desperate opposition, to the point of being simply the playthings of that evolution—these were the ones who were unfree.

However, there were occasional exceptions in the radio broadcasts too. The first was a dramatisation of Koestler's book, *Darkness at Noon*. I had never heard of this book before, but as I already knew a pamphlet of Koestler's I turned on the broadcast. I was gripped from the very first words. It was a play about a veteran Bolshevik in an N.K.V.D. prison. When it was over, I took a walk for several hours to think about it. In the next few days I discovered that other officials had also listened to the broadcast and had also been impressed by it. From that day on I listened to Western broadcasts more often, but after a week or two I gave it up again. There was no point or sense in it, for that type of broadcast was only a rare exception.

As the newspapers and radio transmissions from the West entirely passed over the questions that were so important and decisive for us, we—that is to say the group of independent thinkers, including many Socialists affected by the disease of "political collywobbles" and probably thousands of other members and officials of the S.E.D.—were compelled to apply ourselves to the slow and painful task of working out our problems by ourselves, without receiving any stimulus from any quarter to help us in our discussions or in our efforts to build up something to set against Stalinism.

"What's up with Yugoslavia?"

On the 29th June, 1948, I went as I did every morning to the place where newspapers for the instructors and Deans of the Faculties were distributed. I had to wait a moment while Professor Victor Stern got his newspapers next to me. On top of the pile lay the *Telegraf* with huge banner headlines saying: "Stalin breaks with Tito—Tito accused of Trotskyism."

"What nonsense! The rubbish they go on writing! What's it mean 'Tito accused of Trotskyism?'—utter twaddle! Tito has just been eliminating Trotskyites from his Party leadership." Snorting angrily, Victor Stern folded up his newspaper and went away.

I ran my eyes quickly over the headlines of the most important Western newspapers and knew at once that this was no *canard* of the *Telegraf*. It was the explanation of some of the peculiar things that had been happening in the last few weeks, but there was nothing about it in the Eastern newspapers that morning.

I ran back to my room and read through the reports of all the Western newspapers with great attention. They were so abbreviated that it was impossible to form an accurate picture, but one thing seemed to be clear. The Cominform had passed and published a resolution accusing Yugoslavia of political shortcomings and deviations. From that moment I sat by the radio almost without a break. Two hours later I was joined by my friend Ilse, who was another of the "between ourselves" group, as we called ourselves. She worked in the building of the Central Secretariat on the editorial staff of the Party officials' periodical *New Way*. She had come from Klein-Machnow, where she had naturally heard everything, and had already been to visit friends on the staff of various newspapers.

"They haven't got the exact text yet, but it will be in our papers to-morrow morning. There's great excitement everywhere, but nothing definite is known yet."

We sat by the radio till late at night. Everything was still uncertain. The following morning, 30th June, 1948, the text of the Cominform Resolution finally came into my hands. I read the accusations against the Yugoslav Communists carefully through, and the result was that I felt even angrier than before at these crude charges which I knew to be completely groundless.

"Supporting capitalist elements in the villages!" I read in the Resolution, knowing that in fact the Yugoslav Communists had not only carried out land reforms with complete consistency, but had also been the first of the People's Democracies to institute agricultural collectives.

"Hostile attitude towards the Soviet Union!" I thought of what had appeared in Yugoslav publications about the Soviet Union, and how the Yugoslavs idealised the U.S.S.R., and how they always modestly rated their greatest successes below those of the Soviet Union.

At the allegation of a "military bureaucratic system in the Yugoslav Party" I could only laugh. That of all people the Soviet Party, in which the military bureaucratic system prevailed *par excellence*, and which contrary to its own statutes had not called a Party Congress since 1939, nine years ago, should assume the role of defender of Party democracy!

Then came another attack on the Yugoslav agricultural policy, this time for alleged "left deviationism." It was characterised as a policy of "adventurers," after the Yugoslav Communists had been accused a few paragraphs earlier of "taking up an opportunistic attitude." The whole thing was simply laughable.

"Who can take such a document seriously?— who can really believe it?" I wondered. But the next moment I found myself taking it seriously—not of course on account of the arguments contained in it, but rather because of the threats and warnings at the end of the Resolution: "The duty of all sound elements in the Yugoslav Communist Party is to admit their fault openly and honourably; or if the present leadership of the Yugoslav Communist Party proves itself unfit to do so, to remove them from power and to establish a new internationalist leadership of the Communist Party of Yugoslavia in their place."

That at least was clear—only too clear. The only country in Europe where a victorious revolution had been carried through in the last twenty years with a Communist Party at its head, was now to be coerced into obedience! I realised at once, knowing Soviet policy well enough by this time, that the real motive had nothing to do with the accusations contained in the Resolution, but lay in the fact that the Yugoslav Communists had openly tried to pursue a particular independent policy of their own. From the first moment, I took my stand with complete conviction on the side of the maligned and traduced Yugoslav Communists and against those whose views were represented in the Cominform Resolution.

I was not the only one. It luckily happened that day that I was working only in the morning, so I went to Berlin to visit my friends. All of them were talking about the Cominform Resolution. The Berlin blockade, which began in the course of the same few days, was hardly mentioned, although it was in Berlin that our conversations took place. Everything turned on one question: What would the Yugoslavs do? Would they submit and admit the errors which they had never made, and capitulate to the overwhelming threat, or would they take heart and fight the Resolution? Many of us were sitting by the radio and taking turns in order not to miss anything— waiting for the Yugoslav reply.

"Let's hope they refuse!" This was the keynote in the "between ourselves" group that day. In the evening my friend Ilse came from the Central Party Building.

"It's like a swarm of bees in a glass-house," she said. "Everyone is dreadfully excited. Some are on the Yugoslav side. Let's hope they refuse!"

We sat down by the radio again. Half an hour passed, then an hour. At last we heard the voice of the news announcer from London: "The Central Committee of the Communist Party of Yugoslavia has rejected the accusations of the Cominform as groundless." We could hardly contain ourselves for joy. At last, at last, a Communist Party had had the courage to speak up against Stalin's leadership! But then at once our anxieties began to find expression.

"Will the Yugoslavs be able to hold out? Certainly the Resolution won't be the end of the matter."

"Perhaps the Bulgarians or one of the other People's Democracies will take the Yugoslavs' side. The Poles might do so! Perhaps there will be internal disputes among the Parties in the Peoples' Democracies?"

We went on talking about it till late at night and tried to get Radio Belgrade, but without success that evening. In the next few days we learned that we had not been the only ones who had sat by their radio sets in a state of excitement, to convince themselves beyond doubt of the unbelievable fact that a Communist Party had repudiated a decree of the Cominform, and therefore Stalin with it.

One thing was still missing: the text of the Yugoslav reply to the Cominform. We finally got it three days later when it was published in the *Tanjug* bulletin. Hitherto this had just been one of the many press bulletins which lay about in the editorial offices of newspapers. Overnight, the bulletin of the Yugoslav news agency became the most exciting and important document ever distributed in the S.E.D. We were now able to read in black and white what had seemed impossible till that moment: the leadership of a Communist Party had refused to recognise a Resolution of the Cominform and simply declared it to be false. "The criticisms in the Resolution are based on groundless and inexact assertions, and represent an attempt to destroy the reputation of the Yugoslav Communist Party abroad and at home, and to provoke confusion among our own population and in the international workers' movement."

Calmly and factually every assertion in the Cominform Resolution was refuted in detail with a complete statement of facts. I was particularly interested in the reply to the accusation alleging that Soviet military and civilian specialists had been put under surveillance in Yugoslavia. The Yugoslavs not only rejected the accusation, but stated in reply that the Soviet Secret Service had been trying to infiltrate its agents into the fraternal Communist Party. A whole series of members of the Yugoslav Communist Party had indicated in statements made to their Party organisations that they had been baldly recruited as spies by representatives of the Soviet Intelligence Service. The Central Committee of the Communist Party of Yugoslavia took the view that such conduct towards a country where the Communists were the ruling party, a country which was on the road to Socialism, was something that could not be allowed. It could only lead to the demoralisation of the population of the Federal People's Republic of Yugoslavia and to the weakening and undermining of Party and State.

"That's something our own S.E.D. leadership ought to say once in a while!" was the ejaculation of an S.E.D. official who, like myself, had put a specially heavy mark against this passage.

The Yugoslavs concluded with a clear and categorical statement that they were not prepared to recognise the accusations in the Cominform Resolution, but that at the same time—and this for us was particularly important—they would continue to work for the establishment of Socialism with even greater perseverance than before.

Anyone in the West must find it difficult to realise

what an impression was made on us by the passages in the Yugoslav reply which condemned the habit of servile subordination and refused to admit errors which had never been committed. These were things on which the whole system of criticism and self criticism rested—indeed the Stalinist system as a whole. For me it was like a revolutionary banner as I read the words:

"The Central Committee of the Yugoslav Communist Party rejects the view that its refusal to discuss errors of which it is not guilty can in any way have damaged the unity of the Communist front. The unity of that front does not rest on the recognition of invented and fabricated errors and slanders, but on the fact of a Party's policy being or not being, in fact, internationalist. It is impossible however to pass over in silence the fact that the Information Bureau has done violence to the principles on which it was founded, which provided for the complete freedom of action of each party in respect of the passing of Resolutions. The Information Bureau now not only demands that the leadership of the Yugoslav Communist Party should admit errors which it never committed, but also calls upon the members of the Party to rebel against it and to destroy its unity. The Central Committee of the Communist Party of Yugoslavia can never allow its policy to become a matter of discussion on the basis of fabrications and uncomradely relations, and without mutual trust."

The reply of the Yugoslav Communists had the effect of a bombshell. Wherever I went everyone was talking about it. Many people would pull the *Tanjug* bulletin out of their pockets: "Here's the *Tanjug* bulletin," one would whisper to another, "but give it me back to-morrow—lots of others are asking for it."

The leaflets went from hand to hand. At that time this was not illegal. The S.E.D. had not yet "taken up its position" and many of us hoped for a kind of neutrality. However, we were soon to be disappointed.

On 4th July, 1948, all S.E.D. newspapers published on the front page a so-called "Declaration on the Yugoslav Question." Although the S.E.D. did not belong to the Cominform, it welcomed the Cominform Resolution without reservation.

The Campaign against Titoism

I went on conducting lectures and seminars at the Party Academy, but my heart was no longer in it. More and more my thoughts turned to the Yugoslavs, to the Party which was now realising something which I had often conjured up in my imagination: the creation of a Socialist society independent of Moscow. My thoughts, my sympathy, my hopes, my longings, were with the Yugoslav Communists as they were abused and reviled by the Cominform.

When I returned from the Party Academy to my room at Pankow one day a few weeks later, I found a pleasant surprise awaiting me. A parcel had arrived from Switzerland. Curiously, I opened it. It contained a number of thick pamphlets in German: the speeches of Tito and Kardelj and other documents from the Fifth Congress of the Yugoslav Communist Party, which had taken place in Belgrade a few weeks after the break with Moscow.

Nothing could have given me more pleasure at the time than this parcel. A few minutes later I was deep in the documents. Then I was suddenly brought to my senses again with a shock; there was a sharp knock on the door. It was the first time that I had been frightened by a knock on the door in East Berlin, but my shock was needless. At the door stood a casual visitor.

When I returned to my room at the Party Academy I carefully locked up the pamphlets and the *Tanjug* bulletins up to date. This was the first time that I had ever deliberately hidden anything from the Party. I had not the slightest sense of guilt, because I knew that the Yugoslav Communists were in the right and the Cominform in the wrong. This was a question in which there was no longer any room for even the most far-fetched justifications. I had reached my decision.

The Party authorities had made their declaration on 3rd July and had explicitly defined their position on 29th July, but this was by no means the end of the great campaign against the Yugoslav Communists and Titoism: it was no more than the beginning. In December, 1948, a special meeting of the Party leadership was summoned to deal with the question: it was the thirteenth Party meeting and the sole object of it was to condemn the Yugoslav Communists. The Cominform's decision was again, for the second time, welcomed in yet another obsequious exposition of the official attitude, and complete support of the Soviet Union was reaffirmed. After the meeting a lengthy Resolution was published under the verbose title: "The Theoretical and Practical Significance

of the Decision of the Information Bureau on the
Position of the Communist Party of Yugoslavia and
its Lessons for the S.E.D."

In sycophantic terms the leadership of the S.E.D.
thanked the *politburo* of the Communist (Bolshevik)
Party of the Soviet Union, and especially Comrade
Stalin, for having detected the errors of the Communist Party of Yugoslavia in good time. The Cominform Resolution, with all its crudity and lies, was
characterised as an outstanding contribution to the
theory of Marxism-Leninism. By way of self-criticism, they added that the S.E.D. had hitherto under-
rated the significance of the document published
by the Communist Parties' Information Bureau, and
that only a small proportion of the leaders of the
Party and the meetings of its members had taken
a correct attitude. The Resolution was directed
against indications of a concession to hostile ideologies (meaning the statements of the Yugoslav Communists) and it asserted that not enough had been
done to familiarise Party members with the experiences of the struggle for Socialism in the Soviet
Union, or with the lessons of the history of the Communist (Bolshevik) Party of the Soviet Union, or
with the leading role played by the Soviet Union in
the struggle for peace and against imperialism, or
with the liberating role of the Soviet Army.

Then the last link that still bound me to the Party
was snapped—the theory of a separate German road
to Socialism. The Marxist thesis of a separate German road to Socialism was condemned in the following words: "The Party leadership confirms that
false theories about a separate German road to Socialism are current even in the S.E.D. The attempt to

create such a separate German road to Socialism can only lead to a disregard of the great Soviet example."

Many prominent senior officials of the Party immediately expressed themselves in conformity with the new line. Ackermann, whose name was particularly linked with the theory of a separate German road to Socialism, was at first silent; but on 24th September he broke his silence, and published, no doubt against his better judgment, a detailed article under the title "On the Only Possible Road to Socialism." In it he recanted his former Marxist views on the separate German road to Socialism in the following terms: "This theory contains the seeds of a severance from the working class and the Bolshevik Party of the Soviet Union."

The condemnation of the Yugoslav Communists was the cause of my spiritual divorce from the S.E.D., through the denunciation of the theory of a separate road to Socialism. It cut the last threads that bound me to the Party which I had striven with such dedicated enthusiasm to re-establish and develop. The weeks and months that followed were hard to bear. The persecution of the Yugoslavs, and the rising tide of abuse against anyone who had been particularly active in propagating the theory of a separate road to Socialism, took on ever sharper forms. Meetings and conferences on the Cominform Resolution and the condemnation of the theory of a separate road to Socialism went on endlessly in the Party Academy. The decisive lectures were given by Fred Oelssner, who was now clearly coming to the fore as the chief exponent of S.E.D. Party ideology after Ackermann's self-criticism. A series of speakers took part in discussion after his lecture. Everything went very much according to plan—a little too much according to plan. I could see that these discussions had been planned and organised in advance. I knew this to be true of many meetings in the Soviet Union, but until now nothing like it had happened in the Party Academy. One could see the S.E.D. taking yet another step in the direction of assimilation to the Communist Party of the Soviet Union.

I found no difficulty now in imagining to myself what was to come next. The plan of events required that still wider publicity should shortly be given to the *History of the Communist Party of the Soviet Union;* then would follow criticism and self-criticism on the Stalinist pattern; and finally purges would begin within the Party in the Soviet zone. Then every honest official of independent mind would be removed, expelled from the Party, misrepresented as a spy, and finally arrested on fabricated charges.

Reunion with my Mother

In August, 1948, I spent my leave in a "reserved" Rest Home at Zinnowitz on the Baltic Sea. I was lying on the beach dozing one day when somebody yelled at me: "Telephone call from Berlin!"

At the other end was an official of the cadre section: "Your mother has arrived! Come back to Berlin at once!"

A few hours later I was in a car on my way back to Berlin, to see my mother again after twelve years of separation. I thought of all the things that had happened since that evening in October, 1936, when

I had seen her for the last time in Moscow. Since then I had passed out of the Soviet School, gone to college, joined the *Komsomol*, graduated from the Comintern School, and become an executive official of the S.E.D., while my mother had seen life in the Soviet Union from a very different point of view: she had spent twelve years in Soviet concentration camps.

Officially, my mother had been condemned to only five years—a punishment which was regarded as mild in the period of the purges from 1936 to 1938. Her period of imprisonment came to an end in October, 1941, but since the outbreak of war, with very few exceptions, no political prisoners had been released. At the end of the war the time of her release appeared to have come at last. I had often tried to get some action out of the cadre section, but I always received a negative answer. Finally I turned to Wilhelm Pieck, when I was at his house one evening. He had known my mother from the time of the *Spartakusbund* and the Kapp *Putsch* of 1920.

"There's nothing I can do for the time being," Pieck told me, "but we'll go on trying. I'll tell you as soon as it becomes possible."

At last, in February, 1947, Pieck sent for me. "There is a possibility now of your mother being released and coming here. The best thing would be for you to put in a request to that effect." The following day I presented a request at Wilhelm Pieck's secretariat. Now, at last, I hoped the day of our reunion had come! But I was to be put to a severe test, and my mother still more so.

"The matter has been referred to higher authority," was the only answer I received. I did not know at that time that my mother had been deported by then to a small state farm (*Sovkhoz*) in the Altai District. Nor did I know what an incredible battle she had, to get through the local authorities of the N.K.V.D. what had already been sanctioned in Moscow. One week followed another; one month followed another. It was not till July 1948 that my mother received from the N.K.V.D. in Barnaul her permit to travel. Six weeks later, on 29th August, 1948, she arrived in Berlin. She had spent thirteen years in the Soviet Union, twelve of them in prisons, concentration camps, and exile.

When I reached the Party building, I was greeted by an official who told me: "Your mother has been put up at the Central Secretariat guest house."

I had not seen her for twelve years, and I could hardly wait for the reunion. I rushed into the room. As I flung the door open, she started and looked at me with mingled joy and doubt. In her memory she still retained a picture of her son as he had been twelve years before.

But she too was changed. She had a haggard look, and it was easy to see the signs of years of deprivation that she had suffered. When someone passed by on the stairs and shouted something, she started. All through our first conversation I was more and more struck by her bewildered, intimidated air. "Is that all right? Can I do that? Where ought I to report?" she asked anxiously time and again. It was not till later that she told me what had happened since that night of 25th-26th October, 1936, when she was arrested in Moscow.

They put her first in the Lubyanka and afterwards in the notorious Butyrki Prison in Moscow. It was not until eight months later, in June, 1937, that she heard her sentence—five years. She was sent to the Komi Republic, and after spending a long time in various transit camps she finally arrived in January 1938 at Kochmes in the concentration camp area of Vorkuta. Partly here, and partly at the hospital camp at Adak, she spent more than eight years of her life. Finally, in April, 1946, nine and a half years after her arrest, she was released from the camp, but she continued to be detained with all the other Germans at Kozhva on the Pechora. There she was told of the N.K.V.D. order that no Germans were allowed to return to their previous place of residence: all of them were to be compulsorily deported to Siberia. The choice between two districts—Omsk and Altai—was offered them. She decided in favour of a small village called Kalmanka in the Altai mountains. She arrived there in May, 1946, but things were even worse there than in the camp at Vorkuta. Finally, more than two years later, she received her travel permit on 19th July, 1948, and she travelled back to Berlin via Moscow with two other women.

Both of us had spent a large part of our lives in the Soviet Union, though under completely different circumstances. For both of us, questions involving our whole attitude to life had always played a decisive role, so it was only natural that politics and related topics came up from the start, even in our first conversation.

At first we could hardly find a common language; so different had been the twelve years which we had passed, she in a concentration camp, and I in the *Komsomol* and Party. At first, I sharply rejected the expressions of opposition to the régime which she brought out in our earliest conversations. I was determined in no circumstances to allow my mother's fate to influence my political reasoning. It was not till a week later, when she had joined me in my house, that I decided to abandon my previous reticence and to tell her openly that in spite of being ostensibly a loyal Party official, in spite of my education in the Soviet Union, I too was secretly with the opposition and felt sympathy for the Yugoslavs. She looked at me in wide-eyed astonishment. At last she said with relief: "I always thought you had become a 100% loyalist."

I told her about the hopes we had had in 1944 in Moscow; about Ackermann's argument on a separate German road to Socialism; about my own "political collywobbles"; and above all, about Yugoslavia and its severance from Moscow to take its own independent way to Socialism. Both of us were now in opposition to Stalinism, but our opposition had different roots and turned on different questions. She had before her eyes the suffering and deprivations of her fellow prisoners, and her anger in those days was certainly more violent than mine. She spoke of the millions of slave labourers, of the tens and hundreds of thousands of deserving former revolutionaries who had been denounced by Stalin as counter-revolutionaries and put under arrest; of the unbelievable sacrifices and the ideals which had been distorted almost beyond recognition. "The Soviet Union is no Socialist country!"

This was going too far for me at the time. My opposition still turned only on the question of an independent road to Socialism and equality among the Socialist countries. In spite of everything, I was

still convinced that the Soviet Union *was* a Socialist country. Still, this conversation brought us nearer
together.

It did not take my mother long to adjust herself
to her new life, and she soon wanted to find work
again. "I and the two women who travelled with me
are in the hands of the cadre section," she said, "and
in the next few days we shall know their decision."
What my mother wanted was to find non-political
work of the most neutral possible kind. She was
finally appointed as a reader in a publishing house
called "Culture and Progress." Her two fellow travellers on the other hand immediately joined the
S.E.D., and one of them was given a responsible political post.

My mother took a room not far from where I lived
in Pankow. After that I spent every week-end with
her. She was astonishingly quick at making herself
at home in the new conditions. I was now able to
unburden my heart to her quite freely, and I told
her of my plan to escape to Yugoslavia.

"If you escape, I must leave here too," she said.
We did not need to waste many words discussing
that: she accepted my decision, and only asked
when. Life had accustomed her to anything.

"I shall stay as long as I can. I want first to en-
lighten as many of my comrades as possible about
the truth of the struggle with the Cominform."

"This week?—next week?" she asked me, whenever I visited her at the week-end.

"Wait a little longer. Get everything ready. I'll tell
you when the time comes."

"If it comes even at a moment's notice, call me
at once. Just tell me when you're going to send your

article to the editor, and that will tell me the date of your escape."

My mother had instinctively fallen into the tone of voice in which she used to talk in the days of her clandestine work.

"Agreed," I said, and the question was settled.

Titoist Propaganda at the Party Academy

On 22nd November, 1948, I had an unpleasant surprise. The latest issue of the wall newspaper was posted up in the entrance hall to the main building of the Party Academy. In it I noticed an article prominently displayed under the title "Yugoslavia and Comrade Leonhard." Approaching nearer, I read the following contribution signed by Rudolf Fritsche:

"With the participation of both instructors and students at our school, the errors of the Yugoslav Communist Party have been thoroughly discussed. The result was to achieve clarification of certain wrong and unsatisfactory attitudes, and thus to reach a unanimous point of view. The foundation of our discussion was the Resolution of the Information Bureau and the decision of the Central Secretariat of the S.E.D. The matter could now be regarded as closed were it not that not only I, but also other Party members, have noticed a failure cn the part of Comrade Leonhard to adopt a clear and frank attitude throughout the dispute. I still recall a lecture by Comrade Leonhard in which he used his wide experience and knowledge to depict the situation in Yugoslavia. In persuasive language he passed in review the achievements of Tito and the Yugoslav people and presented the work of the Yugoslav Com-

munist Party as virtually beyond criticism. Yugoslavia was advancing on the road to Socialism ahead
of all the other People's Democracies. So much for
that. I set it down not with the intention of digging
up again the ancient, long-forgotten past; but it
might nevertheless be profitable for all of us, even
including Comrade Leonhard, to hear from his own
lips a frank and unequivocal self-criticism such as
we have for so long looked for in vain from him."

It was clear to me at once that Rudolf Fritsche,
a student in the Economics Faculty, had not written this article on his own initiative. It was a warning
shot from on high. The intention was clear: I was to
be called upon to practise self-criticism. What
should I do? I thought it over again and again. For
days on end, I could not get the problem out of my
head. Finally, I composed a reply, consisting only
of a few lines, in which I suggested that the problem
of Yugoslavia was too complicated to be dealt with
simply in a brief article in a wall newspaper, but I
was quite ready to discuss it in the presence of any
comrades who might be interested. I took my article
to one of the editors of the wall newspaper. He read
it through quickly and looked me sceptically in the
face.

"Do you think they will be content with that,
Comrade Wolfgang?"

The peculiar accent and the little word "they"
took me aback. Soon I was deep in a lively conversation with the editor of the wall newspaper, and I
noticed that he too showed signs of "political collywobbles" over the Yugoslav question. This editor was
a young West German comrade who was known at
the Party Academy as Wunderlich. His real name

was Herman Weber. He also broke with Stalinism some years after me, and is now living in Western Germany. He has in his possession the original of the article against me in the wall newspaper.

The article was enough to show me that further measures would be taken against me if I did not soon declare myself unequivocally in favour of the Cominform Resolution; but this was a question on which there was no longer any possibility of compromise or justification for me. So I now completed my preparations for my escape to Yugoslavia.

The discussions on Yugoslavia continued. More and more often students on the course, or officials from Berlin, came to me to ask my opinion. It was impossible for me to acquiesce in the universal verdict against the Yugoslav Communists—I could not bring myself to do it. On the other hand, I could not give my opinion openly to everyone. So I was compelled to resort to those ambiguities which are the inevitable outcome of Stalinism. To faithful adherents of the Party line my answers were evasive; to those officials who were capable of thinking for themselves, I indicated that I regarded the assertions in the Cominform Resolution as false; to those who belonged to the opposition, I gave translations of the Yugoslav documents.

The results were inevitable. Almost all of them pointed to the one fact which had most impressed them: "In Yugoslavia they have published both the Cominform Resolution and the Yugoslav reply, so that everyone can judge for himself; but here we have only had the Cominform Resolution published."

Occasionally I came across officials in the opposition where I least expected them. On one occasion I was going for a walk with a Party official who was above any kind of suspicion. It was only with considerable hesitation that I gave him the Yugoslav material, carefully observing that it was only for information: "since you and I belong, after all, to circles where one can read this sort of thing without danger of misunderstanding."

Three days later I met him again in the grounds of the Party Academy. He looked round. There was nobody near. "I can't put up with it here any longer," he said with astonishing frankness. "This Yugoslav affair is a dirty business, but it's not only a matter of the political lying. There's something more behind it. What's behind it is Stalin—that half-educated savage who can't put up with seeing another Party, like the Yugoslavs, and another leader, like Tito, becoming more popular with the West European Communists than himself. If you only knew how I hate Stalin! Yes—I hate Stalin!"

He was quite white with anger, as I was with fear. I had never heard words like these before, least of all in the grounds of the S.E.D. Party Academy. Then he took control of himself and said: "Between ourselves?" He offered me his hand.

"Between ourselves," I confirmed.

That morning I went for a walk by myself in a thoughtful mood. I remembered having read somewhere that militant atheists often came out of Jesuit schools. Was history going to repeat itself? Was the S.E.D. Karl Marx Party Academy to produce the most dangerous of all heretics? (This speculation was to prove justified a few years later. When I arrived in Western Germany in November, 1950, I met many other graduates of the S.E.D. Party Academy who had broken with Stalinism after me, while remaining Socialists.)

The leading officials of the Party, on the other hand, remained true to the Party line. I had one more week-end—my last—in the wired-off colony of villas at Niederschönhausen, where the ten principal S.E.D. leaders lived. In the last few weeks and months I had had so many talks with members of the opposition that I found it difficult to restrain myself while I was in the villa belonging to one of the leading officials, whose picture one could see so often in *Neues Deutschland*.

The S.E.D. leader offered me brandy and cigarettes.

"You look very depressed," he said turning to me. "Collywobbles over Yugoslavia?"

"I have read a few of the latest Yugoslav pieces," I replied.

"You shouldn't read too many of them," he said with a smile, but I detected the seriousness behind his words.

"These latest pieces of theirs don't simply pose the question whether the Cominform Resolution is right or wrong—they also throw up one or two fundamental questions which one can't just brush aside."

My interlocutor looked at me calmly and coolly. "There are many situations in politics in which a good case is presented with bad arguments and a bad case with good arguments."

Once again I could not help noticing with astonishment and dismay the sort of meaningless jargon with which many officials tried to justify obvious contradictions to others, and probably in particular to themselves.

Cautiously I ventured a step farther. "In this case it doesn't seem to me to be just a question of good or bad arguments, but of certain fundamental Marxist principles. The Yugoslavs point out in their writings that the emergence of the People's Democracies has created a new situation. These countries are already on their way to Socialism, and this poses the question of what should be their relationship to the Soviet Union. The Yugoslavs demand what I consider to be right on Marxist principles—a relation of complete equality between the People's Democracies and the Soviet Union. They say there can't be leading Socialist states and dependent Socialist states, only equal countries."

My interlocutor was obviously irritated and brushed this aside. "But Wolfgang, let us get down to plain facts. What does equality mean in this context? Look—the world-wide struggle which is going on to-day is in the last analysis a vast game of chess." The gestures of his hands described a chess board. He continued: "On this chess board there are only black pieces and white pieces. Two parties oppose each other. Each of them has various pieces of different value which he can move forwards and backwards. But to determine the movements of these pieces, is something which can only be done from a single centre and that centre can only be Moscow —or," he added in an ironic tone, "would you like to substitute Belgrade for Moscow, perhaps?"

I remembered Marx and Engels, who had always set themselves against a leading party within the International; and Lenin who even after the victory of

the revolution in Russia had always rejected and
condemned the thoughts of leadership cherished by
the victorious Bolshevik Party. My silence was interpreted differently by my interlocutor. He presumably
took it that I had been impressed by his parable of the
game of chess.

"We must look at the facts quite frankly. You
didn't start working in the Party yesterday. Have you
never noticed a peculiar thing about the terms Soviet Union and U.S.S.R.?"

I didn't understand at once what he was getting
at.

"These terms contain no reference to the name
of Russia. That is not fortuitous. It makes it possible
for other Socialist states that come into being later
to join the Union. Do you really imagine that when
we in the People's Democracies, and later in the
Soviet Zone, have laid the foundations of Socialism
we shall be able to continue to exist as countries
on our own, independent of the Soviet Union? We
must look at these things in terms of political reali-
ties. Here, between ourselves, we can at least talk
openly about them."

Although we were alone in the room, he lowered
his voice automatically. "It is entirely possible—I
don't say it is inevitable—that at some later date the
People's Democracies will join the U.S.S.R. as new
Union Republics. Of course, we shall not say that
to-day, and you must never mention it to anyone, but
you should at least know it. These are facts, not just
vague talk about equal relations between Socialist
countries."

This conversation convinced me that I had nothing more to look for in the S.E.D. My goal was not

a new republic in the Soviet Union, but an independent, equal Socialist Germany.

It was February, 1949. The S.E.D. was growing closer and closer to the Soviet model. At the First Party Conference from 25th to 28th January, 1949, the status of equality between former members of the Socialist Party and members of the Communist Party was abolished—principally to the benefit of those Communist Party officials who had been in the emigration to Moscow. The Central Secretariat of the S.E.D. was dissolved. Its place was taken by a *politburo* consisting of nine members, of whom six were former leading functionaries of the Communist Party and three were former Social Democrats. A small secretariat was created under the chairmanship of Ulbricht for day-to-day work. Next came a Central Party Control Commission under the chairmanship of Hermann Matern. All this was carried out under the slogan of evolution into a new kind of Party, but in reality it was nothing but a closer assimilation of the S.E.D. to the Stalinist Party of the Soviet Union. The Communist Parties of Western Europe were spared nothing: at the end of February, 1949, their leaders were required to declare publicly that in the event of military conflict their Parties would support the troops of the Soviet Union. On 2nd March, 1949, the *politburo* of the S.E.D. also made an announcement to this effect. Thus the last pretence of independence was abandoned, and the Party openly declared itself to be an auxiliary of the Soviet Army. It was the last announcement of the S.E.D. to come out while I was in the Soviet Zone of Germany.

A few days later an official came to my room in

the Party Academy. He hummed and hawed a bit then said: "I should like to have a talk between ourselves."

"Political collywobbles?"

"Yes, and deadly serious."

"All right. Between ourselves—what's up?"

For about half an hour we spoke to each other in cautious hints. Then he suddenly said: "You know, I sometimes have the feeling that what we are told about Yugoslavia isn't all it should be."

Joyfully I offered him my hand. "Your feeling is not mistaken. I'm convinced that the Yugoslavs are in the right."

He looked at me in astonishment. He had never expected that. I opened my locker, which I always kept locked, and took out a whole bundle of Yugoslav pamphlets in German. I laid them on the table.

"Let me read them!" he said, in a fever of impatience. "I've never been able to get hold of anything before. This is just what I was waiting for."

"Gently, gently!" I had to check my new fellow-conspirator. "Here you have first the Yugoslav reply to the Cominform Resolution, and Tito's speech at the Fifth Party Congress. When you have read it bring it back and then you can have some more—but be careful!"

He gave me his promise and, stuffing the papers in his inside pocket, he went away. I looked after him anxiously. His political instinct was sound, but had he the experience to avoid giving himself away? He was a year younger than myself, although he held a relatively higher position, and he had not been through so severe a training.

Very early the following morning he came back. He was full of enthusiasm. "At last I have found a comrade to whom I can talk openly!"

Then he began to overwhelm me with the reasons for his opposition. My anxiety mounted. His honesty was disarming, but his exuberant manner could easily be catastrophic. Three days later, to my horror, I saw this young official in the dining-room at the Party Academy, eating lunch, surrounded by a whole group of interested colleagues. There were some 150% loyalists there, but he was doing the talking.

I went away. Later I learned that the catastrophe had begun during that lunch. He had in fact spoken openly in the dining-room of the Party Academy about Yugoslavia and the Cominform Resolution, and he had answered all the questions that were put to him, some of which were certainly provocative. He had all the facts, and right was on his side, but then over-enthusiasm led him to disregard all the rules of conspiracy and to name me as his principal witness.

"Wolfgang Leonhard has even said that . . ."

The next moment he tried to correct himself, but the words were already out of his mouth. It was too late.

My last Self-Criticism

The next day I was on my way to my usual seminar, well aware of what had happened. A message reached me to go and see Rudolf Lindau at once. Lindau, the Director of the Party Academy, was standing at the door of his room. His manner was grave and hostile. Without offering me his hand as usual he said curtly: "I should like to speak to you after the seminar."

Never had I enjoyed conducting a seminar less. I kept on looking at the clock. Finally the three hours were up. I went to Lindau. Without a word he led me into his room. Five officials were sitting there. Paper and pencils lay in front of them.

It was just like the scene in the Comintern School in the autumn of 1942. Six and a half years had since elapsed. Now in the spring of 1949 the same thing awaited me: examination by these cold-blooded *apparatchiks*, criticism and self-criticism.

I looked calmly at the officials sitting in front of me. Certainly there was nothing to encourage me, but I was no longer impressed by them. "These are no Communists," I thought to myself. "The real Communists are those who are fighting against subjection to the Soviet Union, against their inhuman methods of espionage."

The examination began. Apart from Rudolf Lindau, only one of the others present was known to me. I could hardly believe my eyes. There sat Herbert Henschke, who had been in the Comintern School with me in 1942. At that time he was one of the weakest students and Paul Wandel (Klassner) had often got me to help him in his preparation for examinations.

Then began a repetition of what I had been through six and a half years before in the Comintern School: the long nerve-racking pause; the political introduction, with its allusions to the general situation, loyalty to the Party and the Soviet Union, and to the need to combat deviations. But what had so deeply moved me in its time now left me completely cold. The first time I had still felt myself entirely one with the Party. Now it was quite different; at heart I had already broken with the Party, and the play-acting no longer impressed me.

Throughout the whole session I quietly pursued my own thoughts. "The thesis of the separate road to Socialism is based on the doctrines of Marx, Engels and Lenin. The Yugoslav Communists are right in taking a road appropriate to their own conditions. Those who condemn the Yugoslav Communists have abandoned the ground of Marxism-Leninism. The thesis of equality between Communist Parties within the Communist Workers' Movement is in accord with the doctrines of Marx, Engels and Lenin. Those who had substituted for it the thesis of a leading role for the Soviet Union are no longer taking their stand on the ground of Marxism."

By this time Rudolf Lindau had finished his introduction. In accordance with the usual pattern, two others spoke after him, but the spell was broken. The influence which had chained me for so many years was no more.

It was only when the third speaker had begun, which meant that the real examination must come next, that I really came to appreciate my situation. There was not the slightest point in arguing with these *apparatchiks*. They were no militants of the working class, however often they might so describe themselves. They were no Marxist-Leninists, although they continually claimed to be such. There was only one thing that mattered now—to gain time to get to Yugoslavia—so I had to adopt a tactical course. I had been taught these tactics;

now I was to use them against their authors. I decided to admit certain shortcomings and to put on a pose of being in doubt. This was the only way of making sure that measures were not taken against me at once, and that a second session would be convened.

Play for time! Perhaps my escape to Yugoslavia would still succeed!

"I think we can now go on to the specific questions." It was Lindau's voice, speaking at Klein-Machnow in Berlin in the spring of 1949, but it was the same voice and the same accent as in the autumn of 1942 at Kushnarenkovo in the distant Bashkir Republic. The voice of the Stalinist *apparatchik* is the same everywhere.

The questions rained down on me. "Is it true that you have given Party members Yugoslav material hostile to the Party to read?"

"Yes."

Heads were lowered. In the short pause after my answer all five had made notes.

"Is it true that in conversation with students on the course at the Party Academy, you have spoken of two types of officials—those who stayed in the country and worked clandestinely and others who were in the Soviet Union on instructions from the Party?"

"Yes, but . . ."

"You will have time later to explain yourself in detail. For the time being you have only to reply 'yes' or 'no'."

"Yes."

"Is it true that you held up those who were active in the country as models to your students and as-

serted that they had been fighting for a more independent policy? And in this connection, did you
mention the following names: Tito, Gomulka,
Markos, and Mao Tse-tung?"

"Mao Tse-tung too?" asked Herbert Henschke in
a shocked tone. He clearly still regarded me as a
political authority. He received a reproving look
from the senior *apparatchik* and went red.

"Is it true that you expressed doubts in the presence of another student about the justification for
the existence of Soviet joint stock companies in the
Soviet Zone and that you expressed disapproval of
Soviet advisers in the People's Democracies?"

"Yes," I replied, well knowing that I had no alternative in any case. However, I was much shaken by
the last questions. I had not spoken on these subjects
with my over-enthusiastic friend. I had spoken about
them to two other officials, who must have reported
on me.

"Is it true that you gave the students an extract
from one of Koestler's concoctions?"

"Yes, but I did not in any way identify myself with
Koestler."

"That is not what we asked. It is enough to know
that you passed on these concoctions." A pause.

"Did you, in conversation with students on the
course, express the view that the anti-party writings
of the Yugoslav Trotskyites and Nationalists ought
to be printed in the Party press and submitted for
discussion?"

"Yes."

Play for time, play for time! That was the only
thing I was thinking of now.

The direct examination was at an end. Next would come the evaluation and analysis. A representative of the cadre section took over.

"I need hardly tell you, Comrade Leonhard, that these matters are extremely serious." His tone was threatening. Nevertheless I felt a great weight lifted off my heart. He still addressed me as "Comrade." This meant that there would be no immediate consequences. Possibly I should only be put on probation.

"Matters are all the more serious in your case, because you are a Party member brought up in the Soviet Union. There will be more to be said on the question of your conduct and your expressions of hostility to the Party, but to-day the Party needs everyone. Despite the exceptional gravity of your situation, the Party will take into consideration your previous work and give you the opportunity to make good your grave shortcomings by intensified activity in the future. But this must not blind you to the fact that the opinions you have expressed constitute a grave abuse of the Party's confidence."

Then the *apparatchik* paused and looked gravely at me shaking his head. It was obviously difficult for him to understand my case. Hitherto the only people in his experience who had allowed themselves to be guilty of deviations were former Social Democrats or old Communists.

"Tell me, Comrade Leonhard, how was it possible for you to take the path you have taken? How could it have happened that you were so misled over the Yugoslav question?"

Take care, I thought to myself; take care!

All eyes were on me.

"Yes . . . well . . . it's like this. After all, it's

not every day it happens that a Communist Party comes into conflict with the Soviet Union and the Communist Parties' Information Bureau. These are serious questions, which one must reflect on. Is it surprising that one has ideas on the subject?"

An *apparatchik* who had been silent hitherto interrupted me. "Now tell us straight out: what is your position on the Resolution of the Communist and Workers' Parties' Information Bureau and the Resolution of our Party on Yugoslavia—or do you want to consult the traitors in control at Belgrade?"

How I would have liked to let myself go, to tell them what I had read in the months since 1948, what I had been thinking about, and what conclusions I had come to! But I restrained myself.

"One or two things are still not clear to me, and for that reason I would very much like to have the opportunity of discussing them. The matter seems to me so grave that I regard it as essential to examine the question more basically."

"What do you mean by a basic examination?" asked another of my examiners, who was not yet used to dealing with such a phenomenon as an official educated in the Soviet Union who had become a heretic.

"I can understand that in the present state of the Party it may not be justifiable to publish all the documents on both sides. Possibly even here at the Party Academy it is impossible to present the problem in this form for discussion by the students. But would it not be possible at least to read the Yugoslav documents at a general meeting of the teachers at the Party Academy, and to discuss the matter thoroughly and seriously? After all, what is at issue is an ideological and political, and even to some extent a theoretical question."

The first *apparatchik* interrupted me. "You are wrong, Comrade Leonhard. Yugoslavia is not a political question, but merely an administrative one," he said in an incisive tone.

"Administrative"—I knew that word. It had been applied to the arrests of 1936-38. The hint was clear. I had gone as far as was possible under present conditions. One more suggestion from me, and I should not be a free man at the end of the examination.

"The matter can now be brought to a close. As you know, Comrade Leonhard, all questions of policy and personnel among the body of instructors at the Party Academy are decided directly and immediately by the *politburo* of the Party. This applies more particularly to your own case. A report on your hostile statements about the Party and on to-day's discussion will be submitted to the *politburo*. In a few days' time the *politburo* will communicate to you its decision on your case."

My Escape to Belgrade

"In a few days," he had said. So I still had time. The examining commission disappeared into the Director's room. I was alone. Slowly I left the central teachers' building to go back to my room, which was in a villa immediately facing the permanently guarded exit. It was possible that I was under surveillance already, so I decided to do nothing that would look still more suspicious.

Once in my room, I collected the smallest briefcase I possessed, of the kind that was generally carried by every instructor when he went to a seminar. I looked round the room once more. There were a number of important things there, including a few relics of the time of the Ulbricht Group: a twenty-page report on a session with Marshal Chukov, and letters to and from Party officials; but none of them were of political importance. It was out of the question to take them with me. I might possibly be searched at the exit from the Party Academy, and if such things were found on me, I was lost. I could not burn them, so I left the papers as they were, put on my overcoat, and set out for the exit.

On the way I met one of our drivers who always used to drive me into town. He knew nothing yet—to him I was still *persona grata*.

"Comrade Leonhard, I have to go to the Central Party Building. Would you like to come too?"

"All right," I replied calmly. And so my escape began in a Party Academy car.

We had to stop at the gate. The porter saw me and at once signalled us to go on. Evidently no new instructions had reached him yet.

The car took me as far as Düppeln station, which was exactly on the border between the Western Sector of Berlin and the Soviet Zone.

"I'll get out here," I said.

"Good-bye, Comrade Leonhard."

"Good-bye."

It was not till several years after that I learned from another former student at the Party Academy who broke with Stalinism later than me that this car journey was thought to have been a particularly dirty trick. A statement was made at one of the gather· ·gs at the Party Academy after my escape that "for a spy to have the impudence to have himself driven away from here in a car belonging to the Party Academy is beyond everything."

The car disappeared. I took the train and went to my second room in Pankow, where I put on warm clothes and packed the minimum I needed in my little brief-case. I told the officials with whom I shared rooms that I was going on a special mission and would be away several weeks. Then began my long-prepared flight from Berlin-Pankow to Belgrade.

I went first to a telephone box and had three conversations. In the middle of a conversation with my mother, I said: "My article will be finished this evening." This was the code we had agreed for me to let her know the date of my escape. I said the same to my friend Ilse, who had also made all her own preparations to escape, so that she could follow me immediately to Yugoslavia by another route.

Then came the third conversation, which was a signal for the beginning of my escape. It was five o'clock in the evening. Fifteen minutes later a car stopped at a pre-arranged spot.

"Ready?"

"Ready!"

"Good."

It was now a quarter past five. Five and half hours later, at a quarter to eleven at night, I was only a few miles from the frontier between the Soviet Zone and Czechoslavakia.

"Here it is!" said my companion. We got out at a small inn. He led me to a table where two men were sitting. We greeted each other and exchanged a few innocent remarks.

"I think we could start now," said one of the men after we had settled our bill.

The last preparations were made in a little house. A bundle of bank notes disappeared into the pocket of the man who was to take me across the frontier. He had no idea who I was, and he was not interested. All he wanted was to get me safely over the frontier and to get back himself, when an even larger sum would be waiting for him. He looked at me curiously, but was relieved to see that I had heavy boots on and was well equipped for the adventure before us.

"Can you last out?"

"Yes, I'm quite used to it."

"Well, you're still young. Let's start, then."

The car disappeared with my previous companion. I was now entirely in the hands of the illegal frontier guide. It was seven hours since I had left the Party Academy. I reckoned that as soon as my disappearance was noticed the first people to be questioned would be the officials with whom I shared an apartment in Pankow—a married couple. They would report the message I had left behind: that I was on a special mission. Several more days would certainly have passed before they had inquired at all the Party offices. Luckily special missions were surrounded by great secrecy, so I had a good start.

"We must hurry up!" my companion whispered to me. It was only four kilometres farther to the frontier, so we had to be very careful.

An hour later, we were in the immediate neighbourhood of the frontier. We did not speak any more. My companion looked at his watch from time to time: it was one o'clock in the morning. We must be over before first light.

Suddenly my companion caught me by the arm. We flung ourselves flat. A little stream lay in front of us. This was the frontier.

"Czechoslovakia!" he whispered to me, pointing to the other side of the stream. The stream was very low and we crossed it on tiptoe . . . Suddenly, my companion raised his head and signalled to me. We flung ourselves into the snow.

By this time, I could hear voices too. They seemed to come nearer. One or two anxious minutes passed. They must surely be frontier police: they were talking in German. What now? One thought kept on going round and round in my head: what was I to say if they discovered me? Should I reveal myself as an instructor at the S.E.D. Party Academy? Then what was I to say after that? How should I explain what I was doing here?—on the frontier between the Soviet Zone and Czechoslovakia in the middle of a Saturday night, of all times?

Suddenly, to my horror I saw my companion stand up. This was the end, I thought to myself. But he signalled to me not to worry. "It's all right—they're frontier crossers like us. I know them."

With these words he went up to the group and I followed him. They held out their hands without a word. They were bringing contraband from Czechoslovakia. One of them offered us cigarettes. I tried in vain to get my companion away.

"Don't worry. Everything's very quiet on this sector at this time of night."

The others, who were also obviously experienced frontier crossers, nodded in agreement. But my anxieties were not in the least put at rest. If I were caught, a much worse fate awaited me than the smugglers.

At last the horrible minutes of delay were over. We wished each other a happy journey and parted.

"On!" This time it was my companion who spurred me on. "We must hurry for the next two hours, till we get to the house where my friend is waiting for us."

It was three o'clock in the morning. A cold head-wind rose, and we pressed on against it.

"It's not so dangerous from now on. We don't need to be so careful. The Czech frontier police don't take much trouble at this time of night," said my companion to put me at ease. So with the first of the dangers passed and our goal—his friend's house—in front of us, I felt better again.

An hour and a half later, we saw a small snowed-up village in the distance. It was half past four in the morning.

"There it is!" he whispered, pointing to a little wooden house on the edge of the village. We now became just as cautious again as on the Czecho-slovak frontier.

"No one to be seen. Now for it!" With rapid steps he went up to the house. I followed him at a short distance and heard the tap of a signal on the door. To my relief, I saw the door open.

That was that! My companion was warmly welcomed in German by the housewife and her daughter. Our wet clothes were hung up to dry and we were given hot tea at once.

My companion wanted to be on his way back a few hours later. "And you?" asked the woman.

I said nothing, but he replied for me: "We have to

take him to Podmokly (the Czech name for Boden-bach). There's a friend waiting there to take him on."

"When has he to be in Podmokly?"

"Between twelve and two."

"It can't be done. The bus service from here to Podmokly hasn't been working for the last few days."

That was a bitter blow for me. Up till now all my thoughts had been concentrated on getting safely to Podmokly.

"Isn't there any other possibility?"

The woman hesitated. "A man from the local committee of the National Front is going to Teplice to-day by sledge. It might be possible for him to take you with him. From there, you can take the train to Podmokly."

It was not a pleasant prospect and might be highly dangerous, but I had no alternative. The woman's daughter was already on her way to see what could be arranged.

She came back an hour later: "The man from the local committee of the National Front is willing to take my mother to Teplice, and also our cousin who's staying with us. That's you," she said, turning to me with a smile.

I looked forward to the journey with mixed feelings, all the more so since I knew not a word of Czech; but the woman told me not to worry. "It doesn't matter. He's a very silent man and he won't ask you anything. All you have to do is greet him and say good-bye when we get there."

I spent the next few hours learning the twenty commonest Czech words by heart. Within an hour I had made considerable progress.

"Is that right—*naskledano?*"

"Wonderful! You speak just like a Czech."

When the sledge arrived I greeted the local official in Czech. It worked. He showed no sign of suspicion.

An hour later we were in Teplice. "*Naskledano!*" I said as we parted, just as if this was how I had said good-bye all my life. A few minutes later, the train left for Podmokly. My luck seemed to be holding. Soon I should be meeting my friend; he was to meet me on the right of the exit from the station. After that everything would be easy.

"Podmokly" was written in large letters on the platform. I walked quickly out of the station, followed by the woman who was still with me. My friend was not there. I looked at the time: half past five. It was almost four hours after the latest appointed time.

"Perhaps he has just gone away for a moment and will come back again later," my companion tried to reassure me. We wandered about the little town for an hour and a half, coming back to the station from time to time. There was not a sign of my friend to be seen. What now?

"I'm going back," said my companion. She had carried out her mission of bringing me to Podmokly. I did not blame her for leaving me now. I got her to change some money for me, so that at least I had enough Czech crowns in my pocket to make me feel a little more secure. I walked up and down in front of the station for another half-hour, irresolute and perplexed. Finally, I decided to make my way to Prague on my own. As I was trying rather helplessly to decipher the notices in Czech on the station, a railway official came up and spoke to me in Czech.

"I don't understand Czech and I would be glad if you would help me," I said in fluent Russian, as calmly and confidently as I could. "I want to get a ticket to Prague."

The railway official made a short, obsequious bow and politely showed me the way to the booking office. There he ordered the ticket for me.

"The train leaves in three minutes."

Very helpful and polite, he led me to the platform. The train left almost immediately. A few minutes later, after the last exciting twenty-four hours, I was sleeping like a log.

"Prague!" One of my fellow-travellers had given me a nudge. I got out with all the others. It was ten-thirty p.m. Only one thing was now in my mind: the name of a street and the number of a house. It was the address in Prague to be used in the event of a failure to make contact at Podmokly. I knew Prague slightly from a visit in the summer of 1947, and it was not difficult to find the street.

The nearer I got to the house, the higher my hopes rose. Only a few minutes more and I should have made contact with the friends who were to help me on to Belgrade.

There it was!—the house that was to be my salvation.

I knocked on the door. There was no reply.

I knocked again. Again no reply.

Again and again, in vain.

My situation was now very serious. I was all alone in Prague, I had relatively little Czech money in my pocket and no one to whom I could turn. Worst of all, it was now after eleven o'clock at night. What was I to do?

Should I go to a hotel? Impossible. I knew no Czech, and besides I had no Czech documents of any sort. The sudden arrival of a foreigner would be reported immediately.

Should I spend the whole night walking about the streets? Very dangerous. One would be very conspicuous, particularly after midnight, and one might well be asked for papers.

Should I go out of town and perhaps spend the night in a peasant house? It was too late for that, too.

Desperately, I tried to recall all the instructions which we had had at the Comintern School in the periods on clandestine work, but no instructions had ever been given us which covered the situation of a man on the run at eleven o'clock at night, with little money and no documents, in the capital of a country whose langauge he could not speak.

Within a few minutes I had taken my decision. First of all, I must get away from this deserted quarter with its empty streets and go somewhere where there were plenty of people. There I must somehow, however great the risk, find a place to spend the night.

The best idea was to go back to the station. When I arrived there, it was already a quarter to twelve. I felt safer here at once. On the steps in front of the station I lit myself a cigarette. There was a middle-aged man standing near me. Without speaking I offered him a cigarette too. He took it and said something in Czech.

"I am afraid I can't speak Czech—only Russian and German." I said in both languages in turn.

He preferred to speak German. "Where are you from then?"

"From Berlin." I was simply unable to think up any other story at short notice.

Possibly he could give me a tip about where to spend the night. I began cautiously: "Actually, I was supposed to be going on to-night, but things have broken down. Now I can't go on till to-morrow, but I have no idea where I can spend the night."

"Where are you going to, then?"

I decided to risk everything on one card.

"To Belgrade."

"To Belgrade?" he whispered excitedly and looked rapidly round him. "Come with me! I was expecting somebody to-day, but he can't be coming anyway by now. You can spend the night with me."

We left the station hurriedly and I had some difficulty in keeping up with him. He said nothing on the way, and I began to have doubts. Wasn't it an act of extreme folly on my part to have told a complete stranger that I was going on Belgrade, of all places? Where was he going to take me? Would he really take me to his house? Ought I to run away again? But where could I go?

We had been walking for about a quarter of an hour when we found ourselves in a deserted street. "It's not much farther," he whispered to me.

Finally, he stopped in front of a house and pulled a key out of his pocket. Meanwhile I satisfied myself with a quick look that there were no plaques on the wall to indicate that it was an office building. No, it was a residential house—but did that make me any safer? Wasn't it true that the most dangerous offices

were those which had no names outside? But somehow or other I had the feeling that it would not be
dangerous to go in with him.

He stopped on the third floor and opened a door.
As we entered, I saw that we were in a simple two-
room apartment. Suddenly, a man came in out of one
of the rooms. I started.

"Don't worry. It's only my friend," I was told re-
assuringly.

"A German?" the newcomer asked.

"Yes, he's going to Yugoslavia."

Again I saw the astonished look of pleasure.

"Hope you get through all right!"

In the course of the conversation which ensued,
I observed that both my new acquaintances attached
no more credence to the official accusations against
Yugoslavia than I did myself. My acquaintance from
the station had to restrain his friend from beginning
a discussion on the spot.

"Let him have a rest——he's on the run. He must
certainly have been through a lot. We'll let him have
a sleep first."

They got ready a place for me to sleep, and wished
me good night. I was able to lie down with a feeling
of relief. To think of all that had happened in the
last twenty-four hours! My escape from the Party
Academy, crossing the frontier, the journey to Podmokly and Prague, the terrible night that I had been
so afraid of—all this was now over. I was so exhausted that I was soon asleep. I hardly even thought
of the coming day.

I was woken early with a shout of: "Hallo, there,
traveller to Yugoslavia! Get up! We've both got to
go off to work."

I dressed myself quickly.

"Will you be going on to-day?"

"Yes, I'm quite sure everything will be all right to-day. And many, many thanks! Without you I should never have known where to spend the night."

"There's nothing to thank us for. At times like these, one must always help people on the run. Good luck on your way to Yugoslavia! If you get there all right, tell them that there are still Czechs who haven't forgotten their friendship for Yugoslavia."

I promised.

I wandered slowly through the town. Walking about Prague was not so dangerous at this time of day. The streets were full of people and nobody noticed me. I felt refreshed and full of vigour, as at nine o'clock in the morning I knocked on the same door before which I had waited in vain the previous evening. This time the door opened. My friend offered me his hand with relief and joy.

"Splendid! You've arrived! I was beginning to think things had gone wrong."

I told him of my misfortunes. It now came out that he had waited at Podmokly till five o'clock and then driven back to Prague in the expectation of meeting me there. When he did not find me in Prague, he had driven back to Podmokly. That was how we had missed each other.

"But the chief thing is that you are here now. Now we will arrange everything and soon you will be in Belgrade."

It was the 14th March. I felt quite reassured. I was in touch with an official belonging to the opposition, who was very experienced in these matters and stood for the same point of view as myself.

Days followed in which my nerves were stretched almost to breaking point. I never knew what the next hour would bring, but gradually I drew nearer to my goal—Belgrade. I will never forget the people who helped me in my escape. They were Party members belonging to the opposition who stood by me as a matter of conviction. For obvious reasons I cannot give their names or mention the places where I stopped on the way.

At last I reached Belgrade at six o'clock on the evening of 25th March, 1949. I was there! My flight had lasted thirteen days. I was saved: in Yugoslavia at last!

I immediately rang up a good friend who was an official in the Yugoslav Party. Half an hour later he fetched me in his car and took me to his house.

"You can stay with me. Have a rest first and then we can talk it all over."

Two days later I was invited to the Central Committee of the Yugoslav Communist Party.

"Veljko Vlahovic is waiting for you now," his secretary told me.

Veljko Vlahovic I knew to be a leading member of the Central Committee, and head of the International Section of the Party leadership.

"I am so glad you've arrived safely, Comrade Leonhard," he said in fluent Russian. "Now, tell me, what had you thought of doing in Yugoslavia?"

"First of all I should like to draw up a complete account of the origins and course of the conflict between the Yugoslav Party and the Cominform for the benefit of my comrades in the opposition in Germany. What has reached them so far has dealt only with particular points of detail about which our comrades know little, so it is sometimes difficult for them to form a picture."

"Good. You shall write that. We'll have it printed here in German, in Yugoslavia."

He turned to my companion: "Is it possible for you to find him a German stenographer?" My companion nodded. The question was settled.

"Good! That will keep you occupied for the immediate future. But what had you in mind as a permanent occupation in Yugoslavia?"

"Would it perhaps be possible for me to join the German editorial staff on Belgrade Radio?"

He picked up the telephone and had a short conversation in Serb.

"You can report to the Director of Belgrade Radio in the next few days. You can work there as soon as your pamphlet is finished."

The conversation was at an end. These few moments had sufficed to settle everything. There had been no examination, only a friendly welcome for a comrade from abroad who had broken with Stalinism after a long inner conflict. The Yugoslavs already knew me and were aware from their own experience what it was like to make such a break.

The effects of Moscow's excommunication were already to be seen. The economic blockade by the Cominform countries had created shortages and many difficulties were in store for me. I had exchanged the comfort of a senior official entitled to *payoks* and accommodation and transport, a life full of lies and falsifications, for a life of great material difficulties and perhaps also of great danger; for at that time nobody knew what fate had in store for Yugoslavia. Nevertheless, I was full of happiness to have found refuge in the country which had adopted as its goal the creation of a socialist order without the hegemony of a hierarchical *apparat* or a centralised bureaucratic control of the economy; without any of the inhuman features of the Stalinist system; free from terror and Stalinist purges, from Party directives to artists and scientists; free from the cult of a leader and the dogmatism and superstition of authority.

I still felt dizzy as I left the Party building in Belgrade. On the walls of the houses opposite I saw pictures of Marx, Engels and Lenin. There was no picture of Stalin. My life under Stalinism was at an end.

Epilogue

IT IS NOW seven years since I broke with Stalinism
and found refuge in Yugoslavia. I lived there for almost two years (March, 1949 to November, 1950) in
the difficult conditions imposed by the blockade of
the East European countries; but I had the deep satisfaction of living with and under people who had,
most of them, been along the same road and through
the same experiences as I myself. Since 1950 I have
been living in the West and have been trying in a series of articles to analyse as objectively as possible the
trend of Soviet developments. This is in fact the subject of a book I am now preparing for publication
next year.

While I was still in Yugoslavia, I saw the hide-
bound dogmatism of Stalin progressively defeated,
both in theory and in practice. The cutting down of
the bureaucracy, the decentralisation of the State
and administration, the reduction of official privileges, the introduction of Workers' Councils in the
factories, the diminution of governmental influence
and its replacement by communal autonomy—these
were the nodal points in the process.

When we used to discuss these things in Belgrade
at the time, in the summer of 1950, we were firmly
convinced that these ideas were not something in-
herent in the case of Yugoslavia, but quite the contrary: the same questions were bound to be raised
sooner or later, though perhaps in different forms, in

all the countries of the Eastern *bloc*. They would
have to be faced, and appropriate measures and modifications were bound to ensue. Three years later,
after the death of Stalin, it was to be proved how
right our ideas were. And now the same questions are
demanding consideration even in the Soviet Union.

Even the leaders of the Soviet Government have
found themselves compelled to retreat from some of
the policies of Stalinism; to soft-pedal the anti-Yugo-
slav campaign and even to visit Belgrade; and
finally to admit at the Twentieth Party Congress
(particularly in Khrushchev's secret speech on 25th
February, 1956) that under Stalin thousands of innocent Party members, including many old Bolsheviks,
had been arrested and even shot. Welcome though
this partial break with Stalinism was, it seems so
far no more than a hesitant first step.

The campaign of criticism of the Stalinist era has
until now been conducted under the banner of a
"struggle against the cult of personality." There has
been no mention of the basic questions: how this cult
originated, how Stalin could achieve this personal
dictatorship, or what were the social and political
conditions which facilitated Stalin's autocracy. Criticism is thus confined to the results, disregarding
the fundamental questions about the Stalinist system.
The system itself is essentially still unchanged. Such
changes as there have been consist only in modernisation and rationalization . . . in freeing the system
of some of the "superfluous" points of friction characteristic of the Stalinist era.

The changes in the Eastern *bloc* since Stalin's
death, limited though they are for the present, seem
to me to owe their origin principally to the basic

contradiction between the centralised bureaucracy characteristic of Stalinism on the one hand, and on the other the new social forces that have emerged since the end of the nineteen-twenties in the train of the Soviet Union's process of industrialisation. The last twenty-five to thirty years have seen the creation in the U.S.S.R. of a modern industry, and with it a modern working class—a class of technicians with twentieth-century minds, demanding independence, and a modern officers' corps; that is to say, a group of social forces which finds itself continually in conflict with the centralised bureaucracy of the Stalinist system and its methods. This is what Marxist text-books call a contradiction between base and superstructure. The Soviet leaders have been taking belated and hesitant steps since Stalin's death to try gradually to adapt the superstructure to the new circumstances.

The closing years of the Stalinist era, the period of the new purges from 1948 to 1952 and the introduction of the "de-Stalinising" policy after his death, have all left their mark on many of the characters in this book. Anton Ackermann, the author of the thesis on a separate German road to Socialism, was removed from all posts of responsibility in the Party after the events of 17th June, 1953, and demoted to the post of controller of the East German Film Company, *DEFA*. Jakob Berman, who taught the Polish section of the Comintern School and later, in 1945 and after, scaled the highest rungs of the Party leadership, was removed from the *politburo* when the movement for Polish independence gained ground in the summer of 1956. At the historic Eighth Plenum in October, 1956, which inaugurated the

beginning of a new, independent road to Socialism
for the Poles, he made a pitiful attempt to depreciate
his own activities in the past and to adapt himself to
the new course of events. Erno Gerö, whom I had
got to know as the political adviser of the National
Committee for Free Germany, also tried to make his
peace with the new forces pressing for de-Stalinisation in 1956. He turned up in the Crimea at Tito's
conversations with Khrushchev, and subsequently
travelled to Belgrade as leader of the Hungarian Party.
But on his return to Budapest he was overthrown
soon after the outbreak of the revolution, and has
since passed into oblivion.

Other characters in this book have climbed to
new heights of power since Stalin's death. Marshal
Zhukov, whom I met twice in the summer of 1945,
was withdrawn from Germany in the autumn of
1946 and relegated to a subordinate post in the Soviet
Union, where he was hardly even mentioned in the
press for several years. Immediately after Stalin's
death, however, he became Deputy Minister for Defence, and after Malenkov's resignation in February,
1955, he moved up to the position of Minister for
Defence, since when his influence seems to have
steadily increased. General Serov, again, who was
responsible for questions of security in Germany in
the summer of 1945, was appointed Chairman of the
Committee of State Security in the U.S.S.R. in the
spring of 1954, presumably as a reward for his services in the removal and execution of Beria and the
subordination of the State Security Service to the
Party leadership.

Ulbricht, however, has remained to this day im-
pervious to the stormy events of the last few years.

Just as in the past, he has succeeded in adapting himself to the fluctuations of the Party line; and he is still First Secretary of the S.E.D. in the Soviet Zone. His fate may be supposed to hang, like that of all the Party officials depicted in this book, on the conflict now in progress within the system of the Eastern *bloc*. It becomes daily clearer that there are within the Eastern *bloc* and even to some extent within the international Communist movement two major tendencies, two major forces locked in combat.

The first is composed of the adherents of a thoroughgoing policy of de-Stalinisation. They claim the right to criticise the Stalinist period uninhibitedly, to put the whole system under the microscope, and on the basis of such an analysis to sponsor a complete and fundamental break with Stalinism. The autonomy which these forces are striving for is inextricably linked with their demands for a far-reaching political and economical decentralisation, the introduction of workers' councils in factories, the abolition of compulsory deliveries, the establishment of autonomy in agricultural co-operatives, the liberation of art and literature from the straightjacket of "Socialist realism" and Party control. Their aim is to bring about a change in the nature of the Communist parties from quasi-military brigades of yes-men into live revolutionary organisations, capable of developing further the ideas of Marx and Engels to deal with the problems of the present century, and by free discussion to outline a policy to fit the requirements of the country; thereby closing the monstrous rift at present existing between party functionaries and the mass of the population.

The second force, which still seems to have the upper hand at present, is composed of those who regard it as imperative to restrict criticism of Stalinism to specific periods of time and specific events. It is opposed to any basic change either in the Soviet system itself or in relations between the U.S.S.R. and the East European countries. But the only result that this policy can have is to make the breach wider, deeper and more complete.

The advocates of de-Stalinisation and the forces making for Socialist independence have been greatly strengthened since 1948. At that date Yugoslavia stood opposed to a seemingly united Eastern *bloc*. To-day the Polish Party has taken its stand essentially on the same ground, and the Chinese Party is approaching nearer to it. In 1948 the Yugoslavs had to propagate and reintroduce into practice ideas which had been taboo for twenty-five years; to-day the advocates of de-Stalinisation can base themselves on official statements by the Soviet leaders at the Twentieth Party Congress. In 1948 Moscow was the sole undisputed centre, and Mao Tse-tung's partisans were still in the hills of Shensi. To-day there is a Communist China as well as the Soviet Union.

Thus the balance of forces has basically changed. The attempt made after the Hungarian revolution by the Soviet leadership and their acolytes to put a brake on the process of de-Stalinisation, may well be crowned with partial success for a time in some of the East European countries. But in the long run all the evidence seems to suggest that the great process of modernisation and of possible future democratisation of the countries of the Eastern *bloc* can scarcely be brought to a halt.

Glossary

Agitprop: The Agitation and Propaganda section of the Central Committee Secretariat of the Communist Party.

Apparat/Apparatchik: lit.: "apparatus," "member of the aparatus," i.e., the controlling mechanism of the Communist Party.

Cominform: Communist Information Bureau (in full, "the Information Bureau of the Communist and Workers' Parties") located first at Belgrade, later at Bucharest: founded October, 1947, dissolved April, 1956.

Comintern: The Third or Communist International, with its headquarters in Moscow: founded March, 1919, dissolved May, 1943.

Gestapo: Geheime Staatspolizei (Secret State Police, under the Nazi régime in Germany).

Kolkhoz: Collective farm.

Komsomol: Kommunisticheskii Soyuz Molodezhi (Communist League of Youth): see also V.L.K.S.M.

Kulak: lit.: "fist," hence "tight-fisted person": a nickname for well-to-do peasants, applied especially to the opponents of the collectivisation of agriculture.

Nachalnik: Chief.

Payok: Allowance, ration; especially the privileged packets of food, cigarettes, etc., for Communist Party officials.

Politburo: Political bureau, an inner committee of leading Communist Party officials within the Central Committee, and the principal policy-making organ of the Party.

Schutzbund: Defence League, the para-military organisation of the Austrian Social Democratic Party, outlawed in February, 1934.

Spartakusbund: Spartacus League (called after the gladiator Spartacus, who led the rebellion against Rome of 73-71 B.C.), a left-wing revolutionary organisation which took part in the abortive German revolution of 1918, and helped to found the German Communist Party.

Wehrmacht: The German armed forces.

Abbreviations

D.D.R.	*Deutsche Demokratische Republik* (German Democratic Republic, official name of the Soviet Zone).
F.D.G.B.	*Freier Deutscher Gewerkschaftsbund* (Free German Trade Union Federation).
F.D.J.	*Freie Deutsche Jugend* (Free German Youth).
G.P.U.	*Gosudarstvennoe Politicheskoe Upravlenie* (State Political Administration, predecessor of the N.K.V.D.).
J.S.U.	*Juventud Socialista Unificada* (United Socialist Youth, a Spanish Communist-controlled organisation).
K.P.D.	*Kommunistische Partei Deutschlands* (Communist Party of Germany, merged in the S.E.D. in the Soviet Zone).
M.O.P.R.	*Mezhdunarodnaya Organizatsiya Pomoshchi Bortsam Revoliutsii* (International Organisation for Aid to Militants of the Revolution).
N.K.V.D	(later M.V.D.) *Narodny Komissariat (Ministerstvo) Vnutrennykh Del* (People's Commissariat (Ministry) for Internal Affairs).
N.S.D.A.P.	*Nationalsozialistische Deutsche Arbeiterpartei* (National Socialist German Workers' Party, the official name of the Nazis).
P.D.W.	*Partei der Werktätige* (Workers' Party).
R.F.B.	*Roter Frontkämpferbund* (League of Red Front Combatants).

R.I.A.S.   Radio in American Sector (of Berlin).

S.A.P.   *Sozialistische Arbeiterpartei* (Socialist
               Workers' Party).

S.E.D.   *Sozialistische Einheitspartei Deutschlands*
               (Socialist Unity Party of Germany, in
               the Soviet Zone only).

S.M.A   *Sowjetische Militär-Administration* (So-
               viet Military Administration).

V.L.K.S.M.   *Vsesoyuzny Leninskii Kommunisticheskii*
               Soyuz Molodezhi (All-Union Leninist
               Organisation of Communist Youth,
               Komsomol).

V.M.A.U.   *Voennoe Morskoe Aviatsionnoe Uchil-*
               ishche (Naval Air War College).

Index

Schmidt, Elli, 419

Schmidt, Waldemar, 453

Schmidt, Wilhelm, 143

Schroeder (Evangelical priest), 332

Schulze, Karl (Deputy Mayor, Berlin), 398

Schutzbund (Austrian Defence League), 12, 21, 22, 23

Schwenk, Paul (Deputy Mayor, Berlin), 398

Sectarianism, struggle against, 254-262

S.E.D. (Socialist Unity Party of Germany), 184, 217, 220, 342, 343, 361, 362, 363-364; flag of, 445; foundation of, 447-451; first elections, 452-456; attitude to "nominal Nazis," 452-454; Sovietisation of, 456-462, 474-475, 512, 513; Party Academy, 462-471, 489, 496, 497, 506-510, 513-524; officials "privileges, 475-480; and Cominform Resolution on Yugoslavia, 495-500, 506-511, 514, 515

Self-criticism, 17-18, 239-254, 515-522

Serebryakov, Leonid P., 29, 30

Sering, Paul, 487

Serov, General, 386, 541-542

Seydlitz, General Walter von, and League of German Officers, 318, 321, 325, 344, 353

Shanghai, 257-258

Shcherbakov, Colonel-General Alexander, 315, 316

Shlyapnikov (Bolshevik leader), 83, 225

Short History of the Communist Party of the Soviet Union, 66, 85, 123

Shvalek, Roman, 424, 425

Sickert, Irmgard, 156, 176, 184

Sobotta, Gustav, 419

Social Democrats (S.P.D.), 377, 379-380, 381-382, 384, 398, 404, 455, 464, 465, 479; re-establishment of, 409, 423, 442, 443; growth of, 443; campaign for unity with K.P.D., 442-447; merged in S.E.D., 447-451

Socialism: first established in Soviet Union, 54, 55, 251; not to be encouraged in Germany, 353-354; "to be established without Red Army," 416-418; Ackermann's thesis of separate road to, 438-442, 452, 459, 460, 498-500, 504, 517, 540, 541; Stalinism's betrayal of, 474-476. *See also* S.E.D.; Social Democrats

Socialist Unity Party—*see* S.E.D.

Socialist Workers' Party, 404

Society of Old Bolsheviks, 14-15

Sokolnikov, G. Y., 29, 30

Sokolovsky, Marshal, 457